Lecture Notes in Computer Science 4587

Commenced Publication in 1973
Founding and Former Series Editors:
Gerhard Goos, Juris Hartmanis, and Jan van Leeuwen

Richard Cooper   Jessie Kennedy (Eds.)

Data Management

Data, Data Everywhere

24th British National Conference on Databases,
BNCOD 24
Glasgow, UK, July 3-5, 2007
Proceedings

 Springer

Volume Editors

Richard Cooper
University of Glasgow
Dept. of Computing Science
17 Lilybank Gardens, Glasgow G12 8QQ, UK
E-mail: rich@dcs.gla.ac.uk

Jessie Kennedy
Napier University
School of Computing
10 Colinton Road, Edinburgh, EH10 5DT, UK
E-mail: j.kennedy@napier.ac.uk

Library of Congress Control Number: 2007929676

CR Subject Classification (1998): H.2, H.3, H.4

LNCS Sublibrary: SL 3 – Information Systems and Application, incl.
Internet/Web and HCI

ISSN   0302-9743
ISBN-10   3-540-73389-2 Springer Berlin Heidelberg New York
ISBN-13   978-3-540-73389-8 Springer Berlin Heidelberg New York

Springer is a part of Springer Science+Business Media

springer.com

© Springer-Verlag Berlin Heidelberg 2007
Printed in Germany

Typesetting: Camera-ready by author, data conversion by Scientific Publishing Services, Chennai, India
Printed on acid-free paper   SPIN: 12085071   06/3180   5 4 3 2 1 0

Preface

BNCOD has, for the past 27 years, provided a forum for researchers world-wide to gather to discuss the topical issues in database research. As the research challenges have evolved, so BNCOD has changed its topics of interest accordingly, now covering data management more widely. In doing so, it has evolved from a local conference mostly attended by British researchers to a truly international conference that happens to be held in Britain. This year, for instance, significantly less than half of the presentations are from UK or Irish authors, other contributions coming from continental Europe, Asia and the USA.

Currently, one of the most pressing challenges is to find ways of evolving database technology to cope with its new role in underpinning the massively distributed and heterogeneous applications built on top of the Internet. This has affected both the ways in which data has been accessed and the ways in which it is represented, with XML data management becoming an important issue and, as such, heavily represented at this conference. It has also brought back issues of performance that might have been considered largely solved by the improvements in hardware, since data now has to be managed on devices of low power and small memory as well as on standard client and powerful server machines.

We therefore invited papers on all aspects of data management, particularly related to how data is used in the ubiquitous environment of the modern Internet by complex distributed and scientific applications. Of the 56 submissions from 14 countries we selected 15 full papers, 3 short papers and 7 posters for presentation, all of which appear in this volume along with 2 invited papers.

In recent years, BNCOD has been expanded to include workshops held before the main conference. This year saw the fifth running of the workshop on Teaching Learning and Assessment of Databases (TLAD). This workshop has attracted authors interested in novel ways of teaching and assessing the subject. We also saw the first BNCOD workshop on the Web and Information Management (WEBIM). As this topic was in the same area as the main conference, it was interesting to see that the bulk of the papers also concentrated on XML retrieval and query processing, but also included papers on Web application design and Web site usage.

We were also very fortunate in attracting two internationally renowned researchers in the area of distributed data management. **Stefano Ceri** is a full professor of Database Systems at the Dipartimento di Elettronica e Informazione, Politecnico di Milano and was a visiting professor at the Computer Science Department of Stanford University between 1983 and 1990. He is chairman of LaureaOnLIne, a fully online curriculum in Computer Engineering, and is a member of the Executive board of Alta Scuola Politecnica.

He is responsible for several EU-funded projects at the Politecnico di Milano, including W3I3: "Web-Based Intelligent Information Infrastructures" (1998-2000), WebSI: "Data Centric Web Services Integrator" (2002-2004), Cooper: "Cooperative Open Environment for Project Centered Learning" (2005-2007) and ProLearn "Network of Excellence in Professional Learning" (2005-2008). In 2006 he won an IBM Faculty Award and led a joint team of scholars who won the Semantic Web Challenge.

He was Associate Editor of ACM-Transactions on Database Systems and IEEE-Transactions on Software Engineering, and he is currently an associated editor of several international journals. He is co-editor-in-chief of the book series "Data Centric Systems and Applications" (Springer-Verlag).

He began his research career in the area of distributed databases and his work not only resulted in a large number of influential research papers, but also in the standard textbook in the area. He then proceeded to carry out extensive research in deductive and active rule-based databases. In looking to enhance the programming interfaces to such systems, he incorporated object orientation in the way in which such databases could be designed and programmed against. He also evolved methods of designing databases and produced a standard textbook on Database Design co-authored with Carlo Battini and Shamkant Navathe. Work followed on data mining and querying systems for XML.

All of this led, seemingly inevitably, to work on design methodologies for Web applications, since such applications are distributed, involve object oriented programming and XML. His main research vehicle, Web ML (US Patent 6,591,271, July 2003), has become the *de facto* standard for disciplined conceptual Web application design. The commercialisation of WebML was achieved by the Politecnico di Milano start-up company, Web Models, of which he was co-founder. The product WebRatio is the outcome of the work. Stefano's talk described extensions of WebML.

Norman Paton is a professor in the School of Computer Science at the University of Manchester. Previously he was a lecturer at Heriot-Watt University and a research assistant at Aberdeen University, from which he graduated with a BSc in 1986 and a PhD in 1989. He is co-leader of the Information Management Group in Manchester and co-chair of the Global Grid Forum Database Access and Integration Services Working Group.

His research interests initially centred on styles of programmatic interface to databases, initially concerning a functional approach and then merging deductive and object-oriented mechanisms in the research prototype, ROCK & ROLL. He moved on to work on active databases and spatio-temporal databases, producing the research prototype Tripod. He also worked on attempts to bring discipline to the design of user interfaces to database systems.

Much of his work is based on managing biological and scientific information, a theme that has run through his work since his PhD. He has produced a considerable body of work in the area of Genome Data Management, including the projects: CADRE: Central Aspergillus Data Repository; COGEME: Consortium for the Functional Genomics of Microbial Eukaryotes; e-Fungi: Comparative

Functional Genomics in the fungi; GIMS: Genome Information Management System; and MCISB: Manchester Centre for Integrated Systems Biology.

He is heavily involved in the UK e-Science initiative to provide grid support to scientists and co-ordinates the E-Science North West Centre. His research projects in this area include: myGrid: Supporting the e-Scientist; vOGSA-DAI: Database Access and Integration Services for the Grid; OGSA-DQP: Service-Based Distributed Query Processing on the Grid; and DIAS-MC: Design, Implementation and Adaptation of Sensor Nets.

Much of the work described above was first presented at previous BNCOD conferences, and we were delighted to invite him back to give a keynote presentation this year. The talk concentrated on the need to manage data in a more efficient way since it may now be used by a wide variety of applications in a wide variety of contexts. Careful and costly design and redesign methodologies may not be sustainable across so many uses, and so a degree of automation in the processes of data management may be required. Norman described some of the autonomic processes available.

The rest of the conference was organised into six paper presentation sessions and a poster session. Three of the sessions centred around the use of XML, which is unsurprising considering the way in which the W3C has made XML the central mechanism for describing internet data making it virtually a layer in its own right. The other sessions concerned database applications, clustering and security, and data mining and extraction.

The first session concerned a variety of database applications. Ela Hunt presented a new facet of her work in using databases to accelerate searching biological data, in this case searching for short peptide strings in long protein sequences. Hao Fan's paper described techniques for finding derivations of integrated data from a collection of repositories. Loh et al. describe techniques for speeding up the recognition of Asian characters, while Jung and Cho describe a Web service for storing and analysing biochemical pathway data.

Session two, the first XML session, concentrated on searching XML documents. He, Figeras and Levine described a new technique for indexing and searching XML documents based on concise summaries of the structure and content by extending XPATH with full-text search. Kim, Kim and Park discussed an XML filtering mechanism to search streamed XML data, while Taha and Elmasri described OO programming techniques for answering loosely structured XML queries.

The third session followed with more papers on XML querying. Böttcher and Steinmetz discussed techniques for evaluating XPATH queries on XML data streams, while Archana et al. described how to use interval encoding and metadata to guide twig query evaluation. Boehme and Rahm presented a new approach for accelerating the execution of XPATH expressions using parameterised materialised views.

Session four, the final XML session, was more general and contained a paper by Roantree et al. describing an XML view mechanism, followed by Wang et al. discussing order semantics when translating XQuery expressions into SQL.

The poster session included posters on a transport network GIS by Lohfink et al.; a neural network agent for filtering Web pages (Adan-Coello et al.); a healthcare management system from Skilton et al.; and a mechanism for estimating XML query result size suitable for small bandwidth devices (Böttcher et al.). Other posters described: a partitioning technique to support efficient OLAP (Shin et al.); a mining technique to find substructures in a molecular database (Li and Wang); and a technique for querying XML streams (Lee, Kim and Kang).

The fifth paper session, entitled Clustering and Security, started with a paper describing the use of clustering for knowledge discovery from Zhang et al. This was followed by the paper of Loukides and Shao, which described a clustering algorithm used to group data as a precursor to using k-anonymisation to add security. The final paper in the session from Zhu and Lu presented a fine grained access control mechanism that extends SQL to describe security policies.

The final session centred on data mining and information extraction. It started with a paper by Cooper and Manson extending previous work on extracting data from syntactically unsound short messages to cover the extraction of temporal information. The second paper of this session discussed the mining of fault tolerant frequent patterns from databases (Bashir and Baig) and the final paper from Le-Khac et al. discussed data mining from a distributed data set using local clustering as a start point.

The contents of this volume indicate that there is no sign of research challenges to the database community running out. Rather new areas open up as we develop new ways in which we want to use computers to exploit the wealth of information around us. Next year's BNCOD will be the 25th and we look forward to yet more exciting work to help us celebrate our silver jubilee.

Acknowledgements

We would like to thank Robert Kukla for help with the conference submission system, and the Glasgow University Conference and Visitor Services for help with registration. The Programme Committee were very prompt with the reviews for which we are also thankful. We would also like to thank John Wilson for organising the workshops and Karen Renaud and Ann Nosseir for assistance and support of various kinds.

April 2007   Jessie Kennedy
                                                               Richard Cooper
                                                               BNCOD 24

Conference Committees

Steering Committee

Alex Gray (Chair)	University of Wales, Cardiff
Richard Cooper	University of Glasgow
Barry Eaglestone	University of Sheffield
Jun Hong	Queen's University Belfast
Anne James	Coventry University
Keith Jeffery	CLRC Rutherford Appleton
Lachlan McKinnon	University of Abertay Dundee
David Nelson	University of Sunderland
Alexandra Poulovassilis	Birkbeck College, University of London

Organising Committee

Conference Chair	Richard Cooper (University of Glasgow)
Programme Chair	Jessie Kennedy (Napier University)
Workshops	John Wilson (University of Strathclyde)
Committee	Karen Renaud (University of Glasgow)
	Ann Nosseir (University of Strathclyde)

Programme Committee

David Bell	Queen's University Belfast
Albert Berger	Heriot-Watt University
Richard Connor	University of Strathclyde
Richard Cooper	University of Glasgow
Barry Eaglestone	University of Sheffield
Suzanne Embury	University of Manchester
Alvaro Fernandes	University of Manchester
Mary Garvey	Wolverhampton University
Alex Gray	University of Wales, Cardiff
Jun Hong	Queen's University Belfast
Mike Jackson	University of Central England
Anne James	Coventry University
Keith Jeffery	CLRC Rutherford Appleton
Kevin Lu	Brunel University
Sally McClean	University of Ulster
Lachlan McKinnon	University of Abertay Dundee
Nigel Martin	Birkbeck College, University of London
Ken Moody	University of Cambridge

Fionn Murtagh   Royal Holloway, University of London
David Nelson   University of Sunderland
Werner Nutt   Free University of Bozen-Bolzano
Norman Paton   University of Manchester
Alexandra Poulovassilis Birkbeck College, University of London
Karen Renaud   University of Glasgow
Mark Roantree   Dublin City University
Alan Sexton   University of Birmingham
Paul Watson   Newcastle University
John Wilson   University of Strathclyde

Table of Contents

XML Transformation

Poster Papers

Clustering and Security

Data Mining and Extraction

Design Abstractions for Innovative Web Applications

Stefano Ceri

Dipartimento di Elettronica e Informazione, Politecnico di Milano
Piazza L. Da Vinci, 32. I20133 Milano, Italy
Stefano.ceri@polimi.it

Extended Abstract

Web Modelling Language (WebML) [1-2] was defined, about 8 years ago, as a conceptual model for data-intensive Web applications. Early deployment technologies were very unstable and immature; as a reaction, WebML was thought as a high level, implementation-independent conceptual model, and the associated design support environment, called WebRatio [7], has always been platform-independent, so as to adapt to frequent technological changes. WebML is based upon orthogonal separation of concerns: content, interface logics, and presentation logics are defined as separate components. The main innovation in WebML comes from the interface logics, that enables the computation of Web pages made up of logical components (units) interconnected by logical links (i.e., not only the units but also the links have a formal semantics); the computation is associated with powerful defaults so as to associate to simple diagrams all the required semantics for a full deployment, through code generators.

While the Web has gone through waves of innovation, new application sectors have developed, and revolutionary concepts – such as enabling the interaction of software artefacts rather than only humans – are opening up. While the foundations of the WebML model and method are still the same, the pragmatics of its interpretation and use has dramatically changed through the last years [3-6]. A retrospective consideration of our work shows that we have addressed every new challenge by using a common approach, which indeed has become evident to us during the course of time, and now is well understood and consolidated. For every new research directions, we had to address four different kinds of extensions, respectively addressing the development process, the content model, the hypertext meta-model, and the tool framework.

- *Extensions of the development process* capture the new steps of the design that are needed to address the new functionalities, providing as well the methodological guidelines and best practices for helping designers.
- *Extensions of the content model* capture state information associated with providing the new functionalities, in the format of standard model, e.g. a collection of entities and relationship that is common to all applications; this standard model is intertwined with the application model, so as to enable a unified use of all available content.
- *Extension of the hypertext meta-model* capture the new abstractions that are required for addressing the new functionalities within the design of WebML

R. Cooper and J. Kennedy (Eds.): BNCOD 2007, LNCS 4587, pp. 1–2, 2007.
© Springer-Verlag Berlin Heidelberg 2007

specifications, through new kinds of units and links which constitute a functionality-specific "library", which adds to the "previous" ones.

- *Extensions of the tool framework* introduce new tools in order to extend those modelling capability falling outside of standard WebRatio components (content, interface logics, presentation logics), or to empower users with new interfaces and wizards to express the semantics of new units and links in terms of existing ones, or to provide direct execution support for new units and links (e.g. invoking a web service).

In this talk, I first illustrate the common approach to innovation, and then show such approach at work in two contexts. One of them, dealing with "Service-Oriented Architectures" (SOA), has reached a mature state; the other one, "Semantic Web Services" (SWS), is at its infancy, but promises to deliver very interesting results in the forthcoming years.

Acknowledgement

I wish to recall and thank all the people who work in the WebML framework: the WebML group at Politecnico di Milano (and particularly Piero Fraternali), the WebRatio staff (and particularly Aldo Bongio), the CEFRIEL Semantic Web Activities group (and particularly Emanuele della Valle). Work on SOA was performed together with Piero Fraternali, Ioana Manolescu, Marco Brambilla, and Sara Comai; work on SWS was performed together with Marco Brambilla, Emanuele della Valle, Federico Facca, Christina Tziviskou, Dario Cerizza, Irene Celino and Andrea Turati.

References

[1] Ceri, S., Fraternali, P., Bongio, A.: Web Modeling Language (WebML): a modeling language for designing Web sites. WWW9 / Computer Networks 33 (2000)

[2] Ceri, S., Fraternali, P., Bongio, A., Brambilla, M., Comai, S., Matera, M.: Designing Data-Intensive Web Applications. Morgan Kaufmann, San Francisco (2002)

[3] Manolescu, I., Brambilla, M., Ceri, S., Comai, S., Fraternali, P.: Model-Driven Design and Deployment of Service-Enabled Web Applications. ACM TOIT, 5(3) (2005)

[4] Brambilla, M., Ceri, S., Fraternali, P., Manolescu, I.: Process Modeling in Web Applications. ACM TOSEM, 15(4) (2006)

[5] Ceri, S., Daniel, F., Matera, M., Facca, F.: Model-driven Development of Context-Aware Web Applications, ACM TOIT, 7(1) (2007)

[6] Brambilla, M., Celino, I., Ceri, S., Cerizza, D., Della Valle, E., Facca, F.: A Software Engineering Approach to Design and Development of Semantic Web Service Applications. In: Cruz, I., Decker, S., Allemang, D., Preist, C., Schwabe, D., Mika, P., Uschold, M., Aroyo, L. (eds.) ISWC 2006. LNCS, vol. 4273, Springer, Heidelberg (2006)

[7] WebRatio: http://www.webratio.com/

Automation Everywhere: Autonomics and Data Management

Norman W. Paton

School of Computer Science, University of Manchester
Oxford Road, Manchester M13 9PL, UK
npaton@manchester.ac.uk

Abstract. Traditionally, database management systems (DBMSs) have been associated with high-cost, high-quality functionalities. That is, powerful capabilities are provided, but only in response to careful design, procurement, deployment and administration. This has been very successful in many contexts, but in an environment in which data is available in increasing quantities under the management of a growing collection of applications, and where effective use of available data often provides a competitive edge, there is a requirement for various of the benefits of a comprehensive data management infrastructure to be made available with rather fewer of the costs. If this requirement is to be met, automation will need to be deployed much more widely and systematically in data management platforms. This paper reviews recent results on autonomic data management, makes a case that current practice presents significant opportunities for further development, and argues that comprehensive support for automation should be central to future data management infrastructures.

1 Introduction

Database management systems provide an impressive list of capabilities; they can answer complex declarative questions over large data sets, exhibit well defined behaviours over mixed workloads of queries and updates, present a consistent interface in the context of many changes to how or where data is being stored, etc. However, the development, deployment and maintenance of database applications remains a lengthy and complicated process. As a result, there are ongoing activities, in particular within the database vendors, to improve support for, or even to automate, tasks that have traditionally been carried out by skilled database administrators (e.g. [1,10,36]). In addition, as query processors are increasingly used in less controlled environments, there has been a growing interest in adaptive query processing, whereby queries can be revised during their evaluation to compensate for inappropriate assumptions about the data (e.g. [3,26]) or to react to changes in the environment (e.g. [28]).

Several of these activities can be related to a broader activity in *autonomic computing*, which seeks to reduce the total cost of ownership of complex computing systems. Autonomic systems are often characterised by whether or not

R. Cooper and J. Kennedy (Eds.): BNCOD 2007, LNCS 4587, pp. 3–12, 2007.

they support *self-configuration*, *self-optimization*, *self-healing* or *self-protection* [20]. However, although several techniques recur in autonomic computing (e.g. [16,34]), and there are even preliminary proposals for toolkits that can be applied to multiple problems (e.g. [17]), it cannot yet be said that there are well established methodologies for the development of autonomic systems. Relating this work to the state-of-the-art in databases, several basic techniques have been adopted in both areas, such as the use of control theory where it is applicable [35], but many proposals for autonomic behaviours seem to be developed largely in isolation, and to address specific problems rather than to make automation a central design goal in the development of complex infrastructures.

This is somewhat in contrast with the software architectures that underpin high-profile internet applications, such as Google or Yahoo. In such contexts, highly scaleable architectures have been designed that are less often associated with challenging systems management issues. Such scaleability is often achieved through the provision of judiciously selected functionalities, but raises the question as to whether there are interesting middle grounds between current data management and information retrieval systems that provide some of the benefits of both without incurring the design and management costs of classical database applications. This paper reviews current work on autonomic data management in Section 2, where it will be shown that there are a wide range of proposals, but that these can rarely be felt to integrate seamlessly to provide intrinsically adaptive data management infrastructures. Section 3 highlights several recurring limitations of current activities in autonomic data management, and makes some suggestions as to how they might be addressed. More speculatively, Section 4 suggests that automation should be a central tenant in the design of data management infrastructures, and that where this is the case, new areas may open up for the application of database technologies.

2 Examples: Automation in Data Management

Autonomic computing is motivated by the observation that computing systems are increasingly capable, pervasive and distributed, and that the cost of managing systems cannot be allowed to grow in line with their number and complexity. The same motivation underlies the desire to increase the role of automation in data intensive infrastructures, both to reduce management costs and to make performance more dependable in uncertain environments.

Much work in autonomic computing involves a control loop, in which feedback obtained by monitoring a system or the environment in which it is deployed leads to focused changes in the behaviour of the system. Such a model can be applied in general terms to a wide range of data management activities, and many aspects of data management are associated with some measure of autonomic behaviour. The following are examples of work to date:

Database Administration: The responsibilities of a database administrator include the classical self-management goals of autonomic computing mentioned in Section 1, namely configuration, optimization, healing and protection [11]. For self-configuration, a system may determine dynamically where to construct indexes, how to allocate memory to different functions, or which views to materialize (e.g. [36]). For self-optimization, a system may dynamically update the parameters used by cost functions, or automatically reorganise indexes to reduce fragmentation (e.g. [23,25]). For self-protection, a system may dynamically limit the resources provided to a long-running query to reduce the impact of any one request on others. Overall, there is a substantial body of work on automating administrative tasks in database systems, and the major commercial products all provide tools to support and to automate various aspects of database administration.

Query Evaluation: Classically, query processing involves two distinct phases, namely optimization and evaluation. In optimization, alternative query plans are explored using a range of equivalence rules, and ranked on the basis of a cost model so that a preferred plan can be identified. In evaluation, the preferred plan is executed to yield the results of the query. However, this two-phase approach may yield significantly sub-optimal plans, for example if the cost model is based on partial or out-of-date statistics, or if the data is skewed in a way that is not taken into account by the optimizer. In adaptive query processing, decisions made by the query optimizer at compile time may be revised in the light of feedback obtained at query runtime [2,13]. For example, specific proposals have been made that reoptimize queries, reusing at least some of the results produced to date, when selectivity estimates are shown to be inaccurate (e.g. [18,33,3]), or to rebalance load in parallel query evaluation (e.g. [14,30,31]). Overall, there is a substantial body of work on adaptive query processing, but at present few of the techniques have been incorporated into commercial database systems.

Data Integration: Most emphasis within the database community on data integration has sought to support the description of precise mappings between independently developed databases. Such mappings may be represented in many different ways (e.g. [8,27,32]), but are typically constructed and maintained manually. Both activities have proved challenging in practice, and at least partly as a result, database centred data integration products are not as ubiquitous as might have been anticipated. Various researchers have sought to develop schemes that automate the identification of mappings between models (e.g. [29]) or for change detection (e.g. [22]), in part accepting that the resulting mappings may be associated with different levels of confidence, in turn opening up the possibility that database integration technologies are used to provide lower cost and lower quality data integration, as in the vision for dataspaces [15]. However, there is wider interest in and benefit to be gained from inferring metadata in a distributed setting – for example, service descriptions are inferred from workflows in [5] – and higher-level data services such as discovery and integration often lean heavily on metadata, for which some measure of automatic creation and maintenance could significantly increase uptake. However, while there is now a growing body of work on automatic metadata capture, there has been less emphasis on incremental maintenance and refinement, as required by truly autonomic infrastructures.

3 Limitations

Although, as argued in the previous section, work on automation in data management is widespread, for the most part this work is quite fragmented. As a result, automation *per se* is not a major theme in the database community (the call for papers for VLDB in 2007 contains no mention of autonomic topics, although both SIGMOD and ICDE mention database tuning as an area of interest). A consequence is that there is little emphasis within the community on recurring pitfalls or potentially generic solutions. This section identifies some limitations in the state-of-the-art in the use of autonomic techniques in the database community.

Predictability: Autonomic behaviours involve intervention in the progress of an activity. As such interventions commonly incur some cost, may block ongoing activities while changes are made, and may discard partially completed tasks when changing the state of a system, there is certainly the potential for more harm to be done than good. For example, [3] describes circumstances in which an adaptive query processor may thrash by repeatedly identifying alternative strategies during the evaluation of a query, sometimes resorting to a previously discarded plan. An earlier proposal contains a threshold on the number of adaptations it may carry out with a view to limiting the consequences of repeated adaptations in an uncertain setting [26]. Both [3] and [26] make particularly well motivated decisions as to when to adapt, and thus may be felt to be less prone to unproductive adaptations than many proposals. A comparison of several adaptive load balancing strategies [28] revealed circumstances in which all of the adaptive strategies did more harm

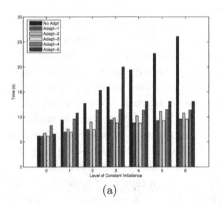
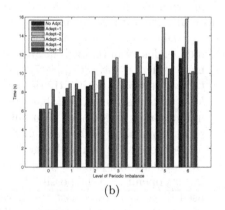

(a)   (b)

Fig. 1. Comparisons of the response times of several adaptive load balancing strategies for the same query in environments with different characteristics. (a) The query is running on three nodes, one of which has a high load for the duration of the run of the query, the level of which is varied in the experiment. (b) The query is running on three nodes, one of is subject to load spikes of duration 1s every 2s, the level of which is varied in the experiment. Most of the adaptive strategies improve significantly on the static strategy (*No Adapt*) in (a), but struggle to respond successfully to the much less stable environment in (b).

than good, as illustrated in Figure 1, although all the techniques compared sometimes improved on static oprimization. Overall, however, the design, control and evaluation of adaptive techniques often seems to be as much an art as a science; we note, for example, that the developers of several of the proposals compared in [28] did not have a good understanding of the circumstances in which their techniques would perform better or worse than others or the non-adaptive case.

Methodology: Mature development activities tend to apply well defined methodologies that deliver predictable results. In autonomic systems development, a range of generic techniques have been explored, although their application in data management has been patchy; it is not always obvious which kinds of problem are most readily addressed by which techniques. Autonomic problems can often be characterised by a functional decomposition in which *monitoring, analysis, planning* and *execution* steps are identified, and proposals exist for toolkits that implement such components [17]. Such a framework, however, leaves open how the different components may be implemented, and in particular how decisions are made as to *what* changes are made and *when*. Applications of control theory to software systems are increasingly widespread [16], in which a model is developed of the behaviour of a system in response to changes in specific parameters. The resulting feedback control loops have been widely deployed for database tuning [35], but the changes made to an executing query in adaptive query processing are typically more radical than can be represented by changes to parameter values (e.g. many adaptive query processing strategies reoptimize queries at runtime, and thus the relationship between the state of the system before and after an adaptation is complex). Competitive algorithms [19], in contrast with control loops, focus principally on *when* to adapt, by trading off the risks of premature adaptation with the consequences of maintaining the status quo. However, although analyses have been developed that guarantee worst case performance of some adaptive algorithms relative to their static counterparts (this is where the word "competitive" comes from in "competitive algorithm"), it is not yet clear that they can be applied to typical adaptations proposed in data management. As such, significant work remains to be done to understand how best techniques developed in other domains can be applied to support adaptive data management systems.

Composability: Proposals for adaptive techniques in databases tend to address individual problems. For example, when automating database administration, techniques have been developed that determine which indexes to create or which views to materialise. However, such decisions tend to be made in isolation, even though the overall performance of a system depends on complex interplays between these individual decisions. For the examples described, the need for views to be materialised may be affected by the presence of indexes, and vice versa. However, as such decisions tend to be made on the basis of mathematical models of system behaviour, and the design of the associated utility functions is problematic when multiple criteria must be taken into account [21], it remains an unsolved problem how to combine multiple autonomous components in a way that yields the desired overall behaviour [35]. Similarly, in adaptive query processing there may be ordering dependencies between adaptations. For example, in a parallel database that supports both partitioned and pipelined parallelism there may be adaptive techniques that remove imbalance in partitioned parallelism and bottlenecks in pipelined parallelism. However, a bottleneck may be able to be fixed by removing imbalance, and there may be no point removing an imbalance if there is a bottleneck elsewhere in the plan. As a result, the decision as to which adaptation should be applied in a specific context is not one that can always be made locally, even where specific problems with an evaluating query have been identified. Much of the state-of-the-art in adaptive databases involves the use of individual techniques in isolation, and few proposals have explored decision making for multiple strategies.

Semantics: Adaptive techniques change the behaviour of executing systems. As the executing systems are complex, and the changes made to their behaviour may be non-trivial, it may be desirable to have certain guarantees as to the behaviour of a technique. Such guarantees could, for example, place bounds on the worst case performance that adaptation could lead to [19], or demonstrate that the outcome of a request is sure to be unchanged by an adaptation [12]. However, rather few proposals for adaptive techniques are accompanied by formal characterisations of their semantics or behavioural guarantees, and generic techniques for specifying and reasoning about such systems seem not to be well established [4].

4   Opportunities

The limitations of adaptivity in database systems identified in Section 3 present certain challenges to the research community. In terms of *predictability*, a better understanding of benchmarking for adaptive systems and more comprehensive comparative studies may identify requirements that can inform the development of more effective development methods. In terms of *methodology*, the more systematic application of generic techniques, such as control loops or utility functions, may lead to a clearer understanding as to which kinds of problems can be supported by established and well founded techniques, and which stand to benefit from novel adaptive infrastructures. In terms of *composability*, foundational work is required to understand how to plan effectively in the context of multiple adaptive strategies, which in turn might hope to benefit from more systematic description of the *semantics* of adaptive behaviours. Such activities may in turn may be able to be applied to improve existing database systems or to support the development of new kinds of data management infrastructure:

Increasing the Manageability of Database Technologies: It is widely accepted that database technologies are labour intensive to administer, and that a significant portion of the cost of ownership of a database system is spent on administrators [23]. As discussed in Section 2, various aspects of database administration are now able to be automated, or at least supported by tools that monitor the use being made of a database installation. Some researchers have argued, however, that current commercial database systems are too complex, and that there is merit in developing data management platforms from collections of components, which themselves may be self-tuning [9]. Such components could include trimmed-down query processing capabilities, or storage managers specialised for specific kinds of data (e.g. video streaming). This proposal seems unlikely to be retrofitted to existing large-scale database platforms, but seems consistent with the recognised need for light-weight database systems, such as Apache Derby (http://db.apache.org/derby/), particularly for embedded use, or in support of distributed applications. To date, there has been little work on ensuring that lighter-weight database platforms are self-tuning; identifying the key features for which self-tuning is of benefit for such platforms, along with the provision of tools to support integration of self-tuning techniques across those features, seems like an important but viable activity.

Extending the Reach of Database Technologies: Although   database technologies are dominant in many business sectors, web platforms that support data with different levels of structure largely ignore database models for description or languages for querying. Examples of structured data in the web include data behind web pages in the *deep web*, annotations in resources such as Flickr (http://www.flickr.com/), and online storage platforms such as Google Base (http://base.google.com/). The vision of dataspaces [15] seeks to bring database style querying to diverse data resources, whether or not they are managed using database management systems. Subsequent early proposals vary significantly in their context and emphasis, from integrating structured and unstructured data on a web scale [24], through the provision of enterprise level data access [6], to the management of an individual's data [7]. However, all such proposals share the need for automation in all the areas identified in Section 2, to enable low-cost data resource administration, efficient querying in unpredictable settings, and integration of data from potentially numerous sources. Typically, dataspaces are proposed for use in settings where certain sacrifices can be accommodated in the quality of query answers, as long as the cost of maintaining the data management infrastructure that provides those answers remains low.

5   Conclusions

Database management systems provide comprehensive facilities for creating, using and evolving potentially huge collections of structured data. As new requirements have been reflected in database systems over many years, the principal database management systems have become increasingly complex, and thus expensive to manage effectively. As a result, the requirement for greater use of automation to support data management tasks has become increasingly evident. In the main, automation has been seen as something of an afterthought in most database systems, but the need to reduce the cost of deploying and maintaining data management infrastructures for data that is everywhere will necessitate a more central role for automation in future.

This paper has reviewed current practice in autonomic data management; the situation is that there has been widespread but largely uncoordinated exploration of the use of adaptive techniques for database administration, query evaluation, and data integration. Although individual proposals have been shown to be effective in specific contexts, the development of many adaptive techniques seems somewhat *ad hoc*; few proposals provide guarantees as to their worst case behaviour, and composition of different techniques into a comprehensively adaptive infrastructure remains largely unexplored. These characteristics reflect the fact that autonomic data management is rarely seen as a discipline in its own right, and to date much less attention has been given to the development of effective methodologies or to the understanding of good practice than to the development of solutions to specific problems. However, future data management platforms are likely to need to provide ever more robust behaviour in increasingly unpredictable settings, and thus automation is likely to be more central to their design than in current platforms. If database technologies are to be able to contribute effectively to the management and querying of ubiquitous data, automation will need to be ubiquitous too.

Acknowledgement. Research on autonomic data management at Manchester is supported by the Engineering and Physical Sciences Research Council, whose support we are pleased to acknowledge.

References

1. Agrawal, S., Bruno, N., Chaudhuri, S., Narasayya, V.R.: Autoadmin: Self-tuning database systems technology. IEEE Data Eng. Bull. 29(3), 7–15 (2006)
2. Babu, S., Bizarro, P.: Adaptive query processing in the looking glass. In: CIDR, pp. 38–249 (2005)
3. Babu, S., Bizarro, P., DeWitt, D.: Proactive Re-Optimization. In: Proc. ACM SIGMOD, pp. 107–118 (2005)
4. Barringer, H., Rydeheard, D.E.: Modelling evolvable systems: A temporal logic view. In: We Will Show Them (1), pp. 195–228. College Publications (2005)
5. Belhajjame, K., Embury, S.M., Paton, N.W., Stevens, R., Goble, C.A.: Automatic annotation of web services based on workflow definitions. In: International Semantic Web Conference, pp. 116–129 (2006)
6. Bhattacharjee, B., Glider, J.S., Golding, R.A., Lohman, G.M., Markl, V., Pirahesh, H., Rao, J., Rees, R., Swart, G.: Impliance: A next generation information management appliance. In: CIDR, pp. 351–362 (2007)
7. Blunschi, L., Dittrich, J.-P., Girard, O.R., Karakashian, S.K., Vaz Salles, M.A.: A dataspace odyssey: The imemex personal dataspace management system. In: CIDR, pp. 114–119 (2007)
8. Calvanese, D., De Giacomo, G., Lenzerini, M., Nardi, D., Rosati, R.: Information integration: Conceptual modeling and reasoning support. In: Proc. of the 6th Int. Conf. on Cooperative Information Systems (CoopIS'98), pp. 280–291 (1998)

9. Chaudhuri, S., Weikum, G.: Rethinking database system architecture: Towards a self-tuning risc-style database system. In: VLDB, pp. 1–10 (2000)

10. Dageville, B., Dias, K.: Oracle's self-tuning architecture and solutions. IEEE Data Eng. Bull. 29(3) (2006)

11. Elnaffar, S., Powley, W., Benoit, D., Martin, P.: Today's dbmss: Dow autonomic are they? In: Proc. 14th DEXA Workshop, pp. 651–655. IEEE Press, New York (2003)

12. Eurviriyanukul, K., Fernandes, A.A.A., Paton, N.W.: A foundation for the replacement of pipelined physical join operators in adaptive query processing. In: EDBT Workshops, pp. 589–600 (2006)

13. Gounaris, A., Paton, N.W., Fernandes, A.A.A., Sakellariou, R.: Adaptive query processing: A survey. In: Eaglestone, B., North, S.C., Poulovassilis, A. (eds.) Advances in Databases. LNCS, vol. 2405, pp. 11–25. Springer, Heidelberg (2002)

14. Gounaris, A., Smith, J., Paton, N.W., Sakellariou, R., Fernandes, A.A.A.: Adapting to Changing Resources in Grid Query Processing. In: Pierson, J.-M. (ed.) Data Management in Grids. LNCS, vol. 3836, pp. 30–44. Springer, Heidelberg (2006)

15. Halevy, A.Y., Franklin, M.J., Maier, D.: Principles of dataspace systems. In: PODS, pp. 1–9 (2006)

16. Hellerstein, J.L., Tilbury, D.M., Diao, Y., Parekh, S.: Feedback Control of Computing Systems. Wiley, Chichester (2004)

17. Jacob, B., Lanyon-Hogg, R., Nadgir, D.K., Yassin, A.F.: A Practical Guide to the IBM Autonomic Computing Toolkit. IBM Redbooks (2004)

18. Kabra, N., DeWitt, D.J.: Efficient mid-query re-optimization of sub-optimal query execution plans. In: SIGMOD Conference, pp. 106–117 (1998)

19. Karlin, A.R.: On the performance of competitive algorithms in practice. In: Fiat, A. (ed.) Online Algorithms. LNCS, vol. 1442, pp. 373–384. Springer, Heidelberg (1998)

20. Kephart, J.O., Chess, D.M.: The Vision of Autonomic Computing. IEEE Computer 36(1), 41–50 (2003)

21. Kephart, J.O., Das, R.: Achieving self-management via utility functions. IEEE Internet Computing 11(1), 40–48 (2007)

22. Leonardi, E., Bhowmick, S.S.: Xandy: A scalable change detection technique for ordered xml documents using relational databases. Data Knowl. Eng. 59(2), 476–507 (2006)

23. Lightstone, S., Lohman, G.M., Zilio, D.C.: Toward autonomic computing with db2 universal database. SIGMOD Record 31(3), 55–61 (2002)

24. Madhavan, J., Cohen, S., Dong, X.L., Halevy, A.Y., Jeffery, S.R., Ko, D., Yu, C.: Web-scale data integration: You can afford to pay as you go. In: CIDR, pp. 342–350 (2007)

25. Markl, V., Lohman, G.M., Raman, V.: Leo: An autonomic query optimizer for db2. IBM Systems Journal, 42(1) (2003)

26. Markl, V., Raman, V., Simmen, D.E., Lohman, G.M., Pirahesh, H.: Robust query processing through progressive optimization. In: Proc. ACM SIGMOD, pp. 659–670 (2004)

27. McBrien, P., Poulovassilis, A.: Data integration by bi-directional schema transformation rules. In: Proc. ICDE, pp. 227–238 (2003)

28. Paton, N.W, Raman, V., Swart, G., Narang, I.: Autonomic Query Parallelization using Non-dedicated Computers: An Evaluation of Adaptivity Options. In: Proc. 3rd Intl. Conference on Autonomic Computing, pp. 221–230. IEEE Press, New York (2006)

29. Rahm, E., Bernstein, P.A.: A survey of approaches to automatic schema matching. VLDB J. 10(4), 334–350 (2001)
30. Raman, V., Han, W., Narang, I.: Parallel querying with non-dedicated computers. In: Proc. VLDB, pp. 61–72 (2005)
31. Shah, M.A., Hellerstein, J.M., Chandrasekaran, S., Franklin, M.J.: Flux: An adaptive partitioning operator for continuous query systems. In: Proc. ICDE, pp. 353–364. IEEE Press, New York (2003)
32. Ullman, J.D.: Information integration using logical views. In: Afrati, F.N., Kolaitis, P.G. (eds.) ICDT 1997. LNCS, vol. 1186, pp. 19–40. Springer, Heidelberg (1996)
33. Urhan, T., Franklin, M.J., Amsaleg, L.: Cost based query scrambling for initial delays. In: SIGMOD Conference, pp. 130–141 (1998)
34. Walsh, W.E., Tesauro, G., Kephart, J.O., Das, R.: Utility functions in autonomic systems. In: Proc. ICAC, pp. 70–77. IEEE Press, New York (2004)
35. Weikum, G., Mönkeberg, A., Hasse, C., Zabback, P.: Self-tuning database technology and information services: from wishful thinking to viable engineering. In: Proc. VLDB, pp. 20–31 (2002)
36. Zilio, D.C., Rao, J., Lightstone, S., Lohman, G.M., Storm, A., Garcia-Arellano, C., Fadden, S.: Db2 design advisor: Integrated automatic physical database design. In: Proc. VLDB, pp. 1087–1097 (2004)

Exhaustive Peptide Searching Using Relations

Ela Hunt

Department of Computer Science, ETH Zurich, 8092 Zurich, Switzerland
hunt@inf.ethz.ch

Abstract. We present a new robust solution to short peptide searching, tested on a relational platform, with a set of biological queries. Our
algorithm is appropriate for large scale scientific data analysis, and has
been tested with 1.4 GB of amino-acids. Protein sequences are indexed
as short overlapping string windows, and stored in a relation. To find
approximate matches, we use a neighbourhood generation algorithm.
The words in the neighbourhood are then fetched and stored in a relation. We measure execution time and compare the matches found to
those delivered by BLAST. We report some performance gains in exact
matching and searching within edit distance 1, and very significant quality improvements over heuristics, as we guarantee to deliver all relevant
matches.

1 Introduction

Biological sequence comparison involves searching large repositories of string
data for approximate matches to a string of interest. Strings use alphabets such
as DNA={A,C,G,T} or the protein alphabet of over 20 letters. Such searches are
now supported by database technologies [5,32] and are based on BLAST [1,2]
and not on indexing. These solutions use the heuristic method, BLAST, and
traverse the entire data set while searching for a string of interest. In relational
terms this might be seen as equivalent of a full table scan, and is slow, as the
complexity of searching is dominated by the size of the data set one searches
against. For a database of size n, it will be $O(n)$ at least. An exhaustive search
using dynamic programming (DP) which builds a comparison matrix aligning
each query letter with each database letter, for a query of length m, has the
complexity of $O(mn)$ [27,31], and is often impractical for that reason.

Since 1995 [7] we have experienced a dramatic increase in the amount of
available biological sequence data, and a simultaneous desire to perform new
forms of searching. This forces us to rethink the assumptions of such work. One
of the new directions is persistent sequence indexing [25,23,13,14]. Another comes
from new sequence analysis requirements involving micro array probe mapping
[8], miRNA mapping[29], and motif searches [6,30,35], which all involve short
query strings and very large databases, often larger than 1 GB. Indexing can
reduce search times from linear in n, to, ideally, logarithmic, as an index tree
depth is a logarithm of data size.

This work explores three issues we encountered in the execution of searches
for short peptide strings (length 7) against the background of 1.4 GB of protein

R. Cooper and J. Kennedy (Eds.): BNCOD 2007, LNCS 4587, pp. 13–24, 2007.

sequences. The first issue of interest is search complexity reduction from linear in n to logarithmic, achieved using indexing. The second issue is the need to deliver all matches fulfilling a given definition, as BLAST only offers statistical guarantees of quality, and is not exhaustive. The third is a simplification of the search algorithms described by Myers [25] and Baeza-Yates and Navarro [3] who partition a long query into short fragments and then assemble the result from fragments. Here, short queries directly use the index, with no post-processing.

The contributions of this paper are as follows. We build a protein sequence index in a commercial database. To our knowledge, this is the first report of index-based large-scale sequence comparison using a relational platform. We study the performance of approximate matching on a large repository of protein sequences and a set of experimentally derived short peptides, and we report on both time and quality comparison with BLAST.

Our findings are presented as follows. Section 2 motivates the need for exhaustive searches on short strings. Section 3 introduces the algorithms. Section 4 describes the implementation and Section 5 presents an experimental evaluation. A discussion is offered in Section 6, along with the context of other research, and conclusions are presented in Section 7.

2   Motivation

We briefly outline why short queries are of interest. The focus here is on an experiment called *phage display* [30,35]. This experiment can be used to understand which proteins have the capacity to interact, and what peptide sequences mediate their interaction. A phage is a small microorganism, that can be made to carry attached sequences on its outer surface, and therefore bind to tissues, using that extra sequence. In this work the sequences added to phages are 7-letter peptides, representing all the possible 7-letter combinations over the protein alphabet. After the experiments, the 7-letter peptides bound to the tissue are sequenced, and serve as queries. In this work we query for 26 peptides, each in two directions, so for peptide 'ABCDEFG' we also query in 'GFEDCBA'. We are looking for exact matches, matches with one mismatch, and with two mismatches. At a later stage all the matches will be clustered with regard to the sequences and organisms they match. They may also be visualised with regard to their position in a 3D protein structure.

The second scenario is approximate matching of short DNA or RNA sequences. RNA alphabet is {A, C, G, U}. Queries may be around 20 to 30 characters in length, and a small number of mismatches are allowed [29]. Such searches are performed on a genome scale (around 3 billion letters), and about 1 million queries may be sent to model a complete experiment [8].

BLAST is not a perfect choice for such queries, as it does not allow one to define the required match length or stringency, and is not exhaustive. In Section 5 we will come back to this point and show the types of matches returned by BLAST and by exhaustive matching. In the following we describe the technology that satisfactorily performs these approximate matching tasks. Our solution allows us to both define the match quality, and to return all results with a guarantee of completeness, as defined by a particular biological scenario.

3   Algorithms

The edit distance Ed [20] is the minimum number of character insertions, deletions or replacements needed to transform string a into b. Ed for a and b is calculated recursively. Here j and i are the positions of the current characters: a_j is the jth character in a. The following formula is used.

$$Ed[j,0] = j, \quad Ed[0,i] = i, \quad Ed[j,i] = \quad if \ (a_j = b_i) \ then \ Ed[j-1,i-1],$$
$$else \ 1 + min\{Ed[j-1,i-1], Ed[j-1,i], Ed[j,i-1]\}.$$

The task of finding all words of length m with up to k mismatches involves a search for all possible matching words for $Ed \leq k$. This can be accomplished in at least four different ways. (1) Traverse the entire target sequence of n letters and carry out dynamic programming, to compare query and target exhaustively, creating an edit distance matrix, and returning positions where $E[m,i] \leq k$, for $i \leq n$. This has complexity $O(mn)$. (2) Alternatively, create a data structure (index) on all possible words over a given alphabet Σ of length m for which $Ed \leq k$. All the words which satisfy the given definition, for instance $Ed \leq k$, are called a neighbourhood and can be indexed in an automaton or a hash table [25,10] in memory. Use this index while traversing the n characters. This enables faster execution of the comparison, but is still linearly dependent on n [10,26]. (3) Create a neighbourhood, as in (2), and probe pre-indexed text. This reduces the dependence on n down to $\log n$. (4) Lastly, perform DP directly on an index to the text, such as a suffix array or suffix tree [33,10,3].

Methods (1) and (2) are not suitable for large data sets, as all n characters of the target have to be traversed. However, (2) is used by BLAST, and we use this program as a benchmark. Currently, database research focuses on variants of (3) and (4), and the question which method is better is open. (4) was recently examined for protein sequences [21] and shown to work well in practice. However, (4) requires the construction of a suffix tree index, which is not part of the commercial database toolkit. It also will work better on a machine with RAM large enough to hold n characters, as those characters are looked up during the neighbourhood calculation. Our work examines (3), in a relational setting, in order to minimise memory requirements, and produce a solution easy to implement and use in any relational system.

We create an index to all protein sequences by traversing all target data once, and recording all the windows of length m. The data structure is a relation PROTEIN, listing all (overlapping) text windows of length 7. Each window is a string over the protein alphabet. Each window, such as AAAAAAA or GRYKADA is called *code* and stored in a tuple

PROTEIN(code char(7), sequenceID number(7), position number(5)).

The relation PROTEIN is stored as one table, range-partitioned on *code*, according to the first letter of the corresponding text window, and indexed on *code, sequenceID*, and *position*.

Neighbourhood generation for edit distance k can be performed by generating all the variants of each query with up to k mismatches, instead of carrying out the full DP calculation. The alphabet $\Sigma = \{A, B, C, D, E, F, G, H, I, K, L, M, N, P, Q, R, S, T, V, W, X, Y, Z\}$ has 23 letters.

EXAMPLE 1. Query RRRRRRR. For $Ed = 0$ the neighbourhood U contains just the query itself. For $Ed \leq 1$, it includes 155 words such as RRRRRRR, ARRRRRR, BRRRRRR, ..., RARRRR, etc., while for $Ed \leq 2$, $|U| = 10,319$, and for $Ed \leq 3$, $|U| = 382,999$.

The number of different words with $Ed = k$ is $C_m^k \times (|\Sigma| - 1)^k = \binom{m}{k}(|\Sigma| - 1)^k$. This is because k letters can be selected for replacement out of m in $\binom{m}{k}$ ways and each of those k letters can be replaced with $|\Sigma| - 1$ letters.

A neighbourhood is generated recursively [25], as shown in Fig. 1. Array *protChars* is initialised to Σ. The neighbourhood is saved in a HashSet *neighbours*. The class *Neighbourhood* accepts a query and an edit distance value. Then it traverses the query and mutates recursively up to *ed* letters, using the protein alphabet array *protChars*.

```
Neighbourhood(query, ed) { // ed, edit distance
    neighbours.add(query); // add query to neighbourhood
    mutate (query, 0, ed);
}

mutate(q, pos, ed) { // pos is position in query q
    word = q
    if (pos <word.length) {
      if (ed>0) {
        mutate(word, pos+1, ed);
        for (int i=0; i<protChars.length; i++) {
            word[pos]=protChars[i]; // mutate the letter
            neighbours.add(word);
            mutate(word,pos+1, ed-1);
        }
      }
    }
}
```

Fig. 1. Neighbourhood generation

Alternative spellings of the query, generated by the algorithm, are saved in a relation, and this relation is joined with the relation PROTEIN on *code* (7-gram), to produce the results. The results are written to a table and kept for subsequent biological and statistical data analysis.

4   BLAST Algorithm

In protein BLAST the query is split into short windows. Each window is exhaustively mutated, and at the same time the calculation of similarity between a query window and all possible mutated windows, which uses DP, is carried out. Similarity uses a formula similar to Ed, and a cost matrix encoding a similarity value for every pair of amino-acid (AA) letters. Windows scoring above a threshold constitute a neighbourhood, and are saved in a pattern matching automaton. Those indexed windows are matched exactly to all the strings one queries against. Then any two exactly matching windows which score highly and are close together in a target sequence trigger the calculation of DP for the string between the two exactly matching windows, and extension towards the outside of the area. Scores are then interpreted statistically, with regard to the size of the database and target sequence length, and can be output as a table, listing query, target protein, alignment length, sequence identity, score, and e-value.

5   Implementation

We constructed an index to 1.4 GB of amino-acid strings. Window size was 7. We map each sequenceID to its name, in relation

SEQUENCE (sequenceID number(7), name varchar),

so that results can be compared to those produced by BLAST. The query data set contained 26 peptides of length 7, and queries and their reverses were placed in a relation. The matching task was set to search for all strings with up to two mismatches. We also carried out a search for $Ed = 3$ but this produced too much data, and could not be used by our biological collaborators.

Neighbourhood was implemented in Java. This generates all the neighbours which are passed via JDBC for insertion into a temporary relation. This relation is joined on *code* with the relation PROTEIN, and the results are written to an existing table, specifying the query and every resulting match, with sequenceID, edit distance and position.

We used an INTEL PENTIUM(R)4 PC, 3 GHz, 1 GB RAM, with three disks. Seagate ST3160021A held the database installation and tmp tables, and two Western Digital 250GB SATA-300 NCQ, Caviar SE16, 7200 RPM, 16 MB Cache held the PROTEIN relation. OS was Windows XP. Oracle version 10.2.0.2 was used. BLAST and Java executions were submitted using Perl [34], with the query and its reverse submitted separately and time measured in seconds.

AA sequences were taken from www.expasy.org (SWISSPROT and TREMBL) and www.ensembl.org (human, mouse and rat peptides). Data were processed in Java, to generate database load files. The total was over 2 mln sequences, containing 1.4 GB of letters, at 1 B/letter.

BLAST was sourced from ftp.ncbi.nih.gov/blast/executables/release/2.2.15, version 2.2.15. We followed the advice at www.ncbi.nlm.nih.gov/BLAST for short nearly exact matches and used PAM30, word size 2, and high e-value of 1000 to 500,000.

6   Results

We first report on the time of matching for BLAST, with various e-value settings, and database matching with varying edit distance values. Figure 2 shows time in seconds for BLAST with three expectation values e, 1000, 10,000 and 20,000, for 52 queries. The times registered for $e = 50,000$ were similar to those obtained for $e = 20,000$. As e-value grows, BLAST requires slightly more time, and the fastest execution is for $e = 1000$. BLAST requires around 28 to 46 seconds per query (average 39.42 s). In Fig. 3 we show time in seconds, on a log scale, for the database approximate matching, with $Ed \leq 3$. For $Ed = 0$, the results are returned within 1 second and this series does not show on the graph for that reason. For $Ed \leq 1$ the execution time is 2-19 s (avg 5.33 s), for $Ed \leq 2$

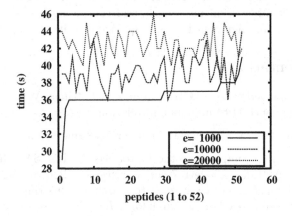

Fig. 2. BLAST times for 52 queries and e-values of 1000, 10,000 and 20,000

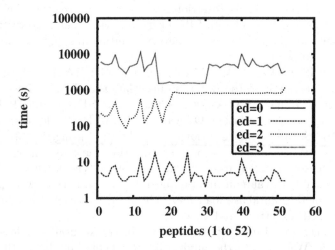

Fig. 3. DB times for 52 queries and edit distances between 0 and 3

between 84 s and 1208 s (avg 614.25 s), and for $Ed \leq 3$, 4342 s on average. Exact queries and queries with one mismatch are delivered much faster than BLAST. Queries with $Ed \leq 2$ take significantly longer than BLAST, at least twice as long, and maximum 26 times as long. However, considering the fact that exhaustive matching is needed, the execution time of 1208 s (20 minutes) is acceptable, as searching is an important step in data analysis.

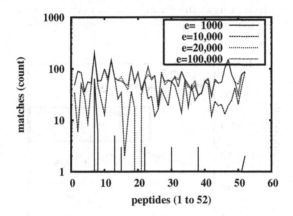

Fig. 4. Count of BLAST matches for 52 queries and four e-value settings

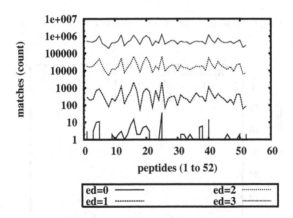

Fig. 5. Count of DB matches for ED values 0 to 3

We now compare the counts of matches found by both methods. Figure 4 shows the number of matches found by BLAST, for e up to 100,000. With the increase in e-value, for some queries more matches are found, and for some fewer. The maximum numbers of matches found by BLAST for the five settings of $e = \{1000, 10000, 20000, 100000, 500000\}$ are $\{64,202,199,198,197\}$, and the minimum are $\{0,0,16,19,19\}$. The difference in the number of matches between $e = 20,000$ and $e = 100,000$ for the same query lies between -18 and 33, which means that by increasing e to $100,000$, maximally 33 matches are gained, and 18 lost. When e value is increased from $100,000$ to $500,000$, one gains maximum 18 matches and loses maximum 27 matches.

Figure 5 summarises the count of matches for the database method, and $Ed \leq 3$, using log scale on the y-axis. At $Ed = 0$ we observe up to 36 matches per query. For $Ed \leq \{1, 2, 3\}$ the maxima are 2181, 65,802, and 1,202,545. The last count represents 1% of the relation PROTEIN and it is common knowledge that retrieving that much data from the database is bound to be slow, and a sequential scan of the table, instead of indexed access might be preferable in this case.

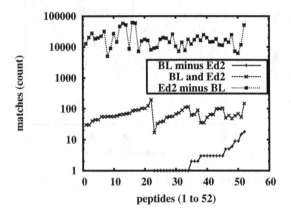

Fig. 6. Matches for BLAST e=50,000 and $Ed \leq 2$

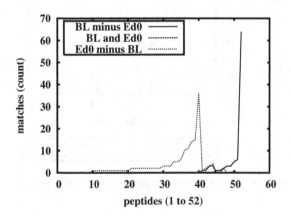

Fig. 7. Matches for BLAST e=1000 and $Ed = 0$

We now consider the differences in match quality in BLAST with $e = 50,000$ and in the database implementation of approximate matching using $Ed \leq 2$. Since we were looking for matches of length 7, all longer matches delivered by BLAST are excluded. We count target protein sequences matching the query, divided into three subsets: shared matches, matches found by BLAST and not by the DB method, and matches found by the DB method but not by BLAST. Figure 6 shows the number of matches found by BLAST but not found with $Ed \leq 2$ (as BL minus Ed2), matches found by both methods (BL and Ed2) and matches found with $Ed \leq 2$ but not by BLAST (Ed2 minus BL), using log scale on the y-axis. For 22 queries $Ed \leq 2$ misses no BLAST matches, for 12 it misses one BLAST match, and for one query 18 BLAST matches are not found using $Ed \leq 2$. This is due to the fact that BLAST uses statistics which are not relevant in our search scenario. BLAST delivers only a small fraction of results which are of interest. Database searching with $Ed \leq 2$ delivers thousands of matches not found by BLAST.

In Fig. 7 we summarise a comparison of quality for BLAST with $e = 1000$ and exact matching, $Ed = 0$. BLAST misses out a significant number of exact matches of length 7, with 40 matches missed in one case. On the other hand, for one of the queries BLAST returns 64 approximate matches, in a situation where there is no exact match. Very few hits are shared by those two settings: for 2 queries 3 hits are found by both methods, and for another 2 queries 1 match is common. It is possible that using BLAST with word size set to 7 would replicate exact matching, but we decided not to pursue this strategy, as the database method is much faster in this case.

7 Discussion

The comparison of BLAST and edit distance based matching is quite an eye-opener, especially to our biological colleagues who treat BLAST as a gold standard. It appears that the two methodologies are currently complementary. Since it is now possible to run BLAST with indexing support [19], running BLAST faster is possible, but is not the required solution. Where exhaustivity is needed, a database implementation of matching based on the edit distance model is superior to BLAST, and performs acceptably. Even with the setting of $e = 50,000$ BLAST cannot satisfy the requirements we set out. On the other hand, the edit model does not model BLAST, and the way to guarantee that all BLAST hits are returned would be to simply use the PAM30 matrix within the neighbourhood calculation [25,21].

The method we presented is slower than BLAST for edit distance 2. This is due to the uneconomical space usage in the database engine. The load files containing the relation PROTEIN are very large, 26.2 GB in total, and this has an impact on query performance, as the relation will be of that size, and additional space will be needed to hold the indexes. We would prefer to store the index more efficiently. Using techniques presented by Myers [25] or Hunt [12] would require significantly less storage, possibly less than 4 GB, as it would not suffer from the overheads incurred by current database technologies. However, such a solution would not be easily usable for data interpretation, as it does not support efficient joins needed in data analysis. The solution presented by Hyyrö [11] is not very competitive in terms of storage, as it keeps all the text, as well as additional data needed by the suffix array data structure. We think a different data layout would be more appropriate, with storage in vertical relations a distinct option. Also, compression could be used.

An index based solution to sequence searching has to perform well in a server context. Our solution is disk-limited only during results generation and independent of the disk at neighbourhood generation time. It should therefore be easy to use disk and CPU parallelism to improve performance.

Sequence indexes have been used in a variety of settings in the past, including scenarios very similar to ours [23,4,22] but none of these tools have been as popular as BLAST. SSAHA [28] is a DNA search tool based on an in-memory index, and BLAT [18] uses a memory-resident index for proteins (indexing non-overlapping windows) and for DNA, but it finds fewer matches than BLAST. A recent issue of the IEEE Data Engineering Bulletin (vol 27(3), 2004) provides a number of recent papers in the area. Approaches to indexing represent a wide range of techniques. Kahveci and Singh introduced "wavelets" which summarise the statistics of sequence data and filter out unpromising sequence regions [15,16]. Karakoç and co-authors [17] demonstrate that sequence similarity can be approximated by a metric supported with metric space indexing, while Miranker and others focus on sequence management issues, and joins performed on a data structure similar to the one we present [24]. Improving the performance of dynamic programming can also be made via the use of FPGA technology [9,36] which might potentially support a DBMS.

In the future work we will focus on the design and analysis of the algorithms used to combine partial results into longer alignments, in the database context, and on the performance of approximate matching. We will also test DP with biological cost matrices. Another area of research is an extension to DNA and RNA in genomic context, as outlined in Section 2, and an investigation into possible combination of search and visualisation technologies in this area. A further extension still would be to adapt this methodology to searches in protein structures.

8   Conclusions

This paper presented approximate matching in a relational setting. An index to over 1.4 GB of protein was produced, and we demonstrated that exhaustive searching is feasible, and produces results within reasonable time frames. Our solution satisfies the biological data analysis requirement, and falls under the heading of relational data mining. Our prototype shows that further work in this direction may hold some promise. Our technique satisfies a scientific requirement, and indicates that it will be possible in the near future to use relational technology for approximate string searching. We believe that performance can be improved by careful programming, and the use of more efficient storage and data access schemes.

Acknowledgements. We gratefully acknowledge the following funding: an EU Marie Curie Fellowship to E.H., a previous MRC fellowship to E.H., and the Wellcome Trust Cardiovascular Functional Genomics Initiative (066780) to A.F. Dominiczak.

References

1. Altschul, S.F., Gish, W., Miller, W., Myers, E.W., Lipman, D.J.: Basic local alignment search tool. J. Mol. Biol. 215, 403–410 (1990)
2. Altschul, S.F., Madden, T.L., Schaeffer, A.A., Zhang, J., Zhang, Z., Miller, W., Lipman, D.J.: Gapped BLAST and PSI-BLAST: a new generation of protein database search programs. Nucleic Acids Research 25, 3389–3402 (1997)
3. Baeza-Yates, R., Navarro, G.: A Hybrid Indexing Method for Approximate String Matching. JDA 1, 205–239 (2001)
4. Burkhardt, S., et al.: q-gram Based Database Searching Using a Suffix Array. In: RECOMB, pp. 77–83. ACM Press, New York (1999)
5. Eckman, B.A., Kaufmann, A.: Querying BLAST within a Data Federation. IEEE Data Eng. Bull. 27(3), 12–19 (2004)
6. Eidhammer, I., Jonassen, I., Taylor, W.R.: Protein Bioinformatics. Wiley, Chichester (2003)
7. Fleischmann, R.D., Adams, M.D., White, O., Clayton, R.A., Kirkness, E.F., Kerlavage, A.R., Bult, C.J., Tomb, J.F., Dougherty, B.A., Merrick, J.M., McKenney, K., Sutton, G., FitzHugh, W., Fields, C., Gocayne, J.D., Scott, J., Shirley, R., Liu, L.-I., Glodek, A., Kelley, J.M., Weidman, J.F., Phillips, C.A., Spriggs, T., Hedblom, E., Cotton, M.D., Utterback, T.R., Hanna, M.C., Nguyen, D.T., Saudek, D.M., Brandon, R.C., Fine, L.D., Fritchman, J.L., Fuhrmann, J.L., Geoghagen, N.S.M., Gnehm, C.L., McDonald, L.A., Small, K.V., Fraser, C.M., Smith, H.O., Venter, J.C.: Whole-genome random sequencing and assembly of Haemophilus influenzae Rd. Science 269(5223), 496–512 (1995)
8. Gautier, L., et al.: Alternative mapping of probes to genes for Affymetrix chips. BMC Bioninformatics, p. 111 (2004)
9. Guccione, S.A., Keller, E.: Gene Matching using JBits. In: Glesner, M., Zipf, P., Renovell, M. (eds.) FPL 2002. LNCS, vol. 2438, pp. 1168–1171. Springer, Heidelberg (2002)
10. Gusfield, D.: Algorithms on strings, trees and sequences: computer science and computational biology. Cambridge University Press, Cambridge (1997)
11. Hyyrö, H., Navarro, G.: A Practical Index for genome Searching. In: Nascimento, M.A., de Moura, E.S., Oliveira, A.L. (eds.) SPIRE 2003. LNCS, vol. 2857, pp. 341–349. Springer, Heidelberg (2003)
12. Hunt, E.: Indexed Searching on Proteins Using a Suffix Sequoia. IEEE Data Eng. Bulletin 27(3), 24–31 (2004)
13. Hunt, E., Atkinson, M.P., Irving, R.W.: A database index to large biological sequences. In: VLDB, pp. 139–148. Morgan Kaufmann, San Francisco (2001)
14. Hunt, E., Atkinson, M.P., Irving, R.W.: Database Indexing for Large DNA and Protein Sequence Collections. The. VLDB Journal 11, 256–271 (2002)
15. Kahveci, T., Singh, A.K.: An Efficient Index Structure for String Databases. In: VLDB, pp. 351–360. Morgan and Kaufmann, Washington (2001)
16. Kahveci, T., Singh, A.K.: Progressive searching of biological sequences. IEEE Data Eng. Bull. 27(3), 32–39 (2004)

17. Karakoç, E., Özsoyoglu, Z.M., Sahinalp, S.C., Tasan, M., Zhang, X.: Novel approaches to biomolecular sequence indexing. IEEE Data Eng. Bull. 27(3), 40–47 (2004)
18. Kent, W.J.: BLAT: The BLAST-like Alignment Tool. Genome Res. 12(4), 656–664 (2002)
19. Kim, Y.J., Boyd, A., Athey, B.D., Patel, J.M.: miBLAST: Scalable Evaluation of a Batch of Nucleotide Sequence Queries with BLAST. Nucleic Acids Research 33, 4335–4344 (2005)
20. Levenstein, V.I.: Binary codes capable of correcting insertions and reversals. Sov. Phys. Dokl. 10, 707–710 (1966)
21. Meek, C., Patel, J.M., Kasetty, S.: OASIS: An Online and Accurate Technique for Local-alignment Searches on Biological Sequences. In: VLDB 2003, pp. 910–921 (2003)
22. Mewes, H.W., Hani, J., Pfeiffer, F., Frishman, D.: MIPS: a database for protein sequences and complete genomes. Nucleic Acids Research 26, 33–37 (1998)
23. Miller, C., Gurd, J., Brass, A.: A RAPID algorithm for sequence database comparisons: application to the identification of vector contamination in the EMBL databases. Bioinformatics 15, 111–121 (1999)
24. Miranker, D.P., Briggs, W.J., Mao, R., Ni, S., Xu, W.: Biosequence Use Cases in MoBIoS SQL. IEEE Data Eng. Bull. 27(3), 3–11 (2004)
25. Myers, E.W.: A sublinear algorithm for approximate key word searching. Algorithmica 12(4/5), 345–374 (1994)
26. Navarro. G.: NR-grep: A Fast and Flexible Pattern Matching Tool. Technical report (2000). TR/DCC-2000-3. University of Chile, Departmento de Ciencias de la Computacion, www.dcc.uchile.cl/~gnavarro
27. Needleman, S.B., Wunsch, C.D.: A General Method Applicable to the Search for Similarities in the Amino Acid Sequence of two Proteins. J. Mol. Biol. 48, 443–453 (1970)
28. Ning, Z., Cox, A.J., Mullikin, J.C.: SSAHA: A Fast Search Method for Large DNA Databases. Genome Res. 11(10), 1725–1729 (2001)
29. Sethupathy, P., et al.: A guide through present computational approaches for the identification of mammalian microRNA targets. Nat Methods 3(11), 881–886 (2006)
30. Sidhu, S.S. (ed.): Phage Display In Biotechnology and Drug Discovery. Taylor and Francis (2005)
31. Smith, T.A., Waterman, M.S.: Identification of common molecular subsequences. J. Mol. Biol. 147, 195–197 (1981)
32. Stephens, S., Chen, J.Y., Thomas, S.: ODM BLAST: Sequence Homology Search in the RDBMS. IEEE Data Eng. Bull. 27(3), 20–23 (2004)
33. Ukkonen, E.: Approximate string matching over suffix trees. In: Apostolico, A., Crochemore, M., Galil, Z., Manber, U. (eds.) Combinatorial Pattern Matching. LNCS, vol. 684, pp. 228–242. Springer, Heidelberg (1993)
34. Wall, L., Schwartz, R.L., Christiansen, T., Potter, S.: Programming Perl. Nutshell Handbook. O'Reilly & Associates, 2nd edn. (1996)
35. Work, L.M., Bining, H., Hunt, E., et al.: Vascular Bed-Targeted *in vivo* Gene Delivery Using Tropism-Modified Adeno-associated Viruses. Molecular Therapy 13(4), 683–693 (2006)
36. Yamaguchi, Y., Miyajima, Y., Maruyama, T., Konagaya, A.: High Speed Homology Search Using Run-Time Reconfiguration. In: Glesner, M., Zipf, P., Renovell, M. (eds.) FPL 2002. LNCS, vol. 2438, pp. 281–291. Springer, Heidelberg (2002)

Data Lineage Tracing in Data Warehousing Environments

Hao Fan

International School of Software, WuHan University, China, 430072
hfan@iss.whu.edu.cn

Abstract. Data lineage tracing (DLT) is to find derivations of integrated data in integrated database systems, where the data sources might be autonomous, distributed and heterogeneous. In previous work, we present a DLT approach using partial schema transformation pathways. In this paper, we extend our DLT approach to using full schema transformation pathways and discuss the problem of lineage data ambiguities. Our DLT approach is not limited in one specific data model and query language, and would be useful in general data warehousing environments.

1 Introduction

Data from distributed, autonomous and heterogeneous data sources is collected into a central repository in a data warehouse system, in order to enable analysis and mining of the integrated information. However, in addition to analyzing the data in the integrated database, we sometimes also need to investigate how certain integrated information was derived from the data sources, which is the problem of *data lineage tracing* (DLT).

AutoMed[1] is a heterogeneous data transformation and integration system which offers the capability to handle data integration across multiple data models. In the AutoMed approach, the integration of schemas is specified as a sequence of primitive schema transformation steps, which incrementally add, delete, extend, contract or rename schema constructs, thereby transforming each source schema into the target schema. AutoMed uses a functional programming language based on comprehensions as its intermediate query language (IQL).

In previous work [8], we discussed how AutoMed metadata can be used to express the schemas and the cleansing, transformation and integration processes in heterogeneous data warehousing environments. In [7] and [9], we give the definitions of lineage data in terms of bag algebra, and present a DLT approach using partial schema transformation pathways, *i.e.* only considering IQL queries and add and rename transformations. In this paper, we extend our DLT approach to considering full schema transformation pathways, which include queries beyond IQL, and delete, extend and contract transformations, and discuss the problem of lineage data ambiguities, namely the fact that equivalent queries may have different lineage data for identical tracing data. The tracing data is the data which lineage should be computed.

---

[1] See http://www.doc.ic.ac.uk/automed/

R. Cooper and J. Kennedy (Eds.): BNCOD 2007, LNCS 4587, pp. 25–36, 2007.

The outline of this paper is as follows. Section 2 gives a review of related work. Section 3 gives an overview of AutoMed and our DLT approach using partial schema transformation pathways. Section 4 extends our DLT approach by considering queries beyond IQL, and delete, extend and contract transformations, and Section 5 discusses the ambiguity of lineage data. Finally, Section 6 gives our concluding remarks.

2   Related Work

The problem of data lineage tracing in data warehousing environments has been formally studied by Cui *et al.* in [6,5]. In particular, the fundamental definitions regarding data lineage, including *tuple derivation for an operator* and *tuple derivation for a view*, are developed in [6], and [5] introduces a way to trace data lineage for complex views in data warehouses. However, the approach is limited to the relational data model.

Another fundamental concept of data lineage is discussed by Buneman *et al.* in [2], namely the difference between "why" provenance and "where" provenance. Why-provenance refers to the source data that had some influence on the existence of the integrated data. Where-provenance refers to the actual data in the sources from which the integrated data was extracted.

In our approach, both why- and where-provenance are considered, using bag semantics. In [7], we define the notions of *affect-pool* and *origin-pool* for data lineage tracing in AutoMed — the former derives all of the source data that had some influence on the tracing data, while the latter derives the specific data in the sources from which the tracing data is extracted. In [9], we develop DLT formulae and algorithms for deriving the affect-pool and origin-pool of a data item along a virtual or partially materialised transformation pathway, where intermediate schema constructs may or may not be materialised.

Cui and Buneman in [4] and [2] also discuss the problem of ambiguity of lineage data. This problem is known as *derivation inequivalence* and arises when equivalent queries have different data lineages for identical tracing data. Cui and Buneman discuss this problem in two scenarios: (a) when aggregation functions are used and (b) when where-provenance is traced. In this paper, we investigate when ambiguity of lineage data may happen in our context and we describe how our DLT approach for tracing why-provenance can also be used for tracing where-provenance, so as to reduce the chance of derivation inequivalence occurring.

3   Data Lineage Tracing in AutoMed

3.1   Overview of AutoMed

AutoMed supports a low-level hypergraph-based data model (HDM). Higher-level modelling languages, such as relational, ER, OO, XML, flat-file and multidimensional data models, are defined in terms of this HDM. An HDM schema consists of a set of nodes, edges and constraints, and each modelling construct of a higher-level modelling language is specified as some combination of HDM nodes, edges and constraints. For any modelling language $\mathcal{M}$ specified in this way, via the API of AutoMed's Model

Definitions Repository [1], AutoMed provides a set of primitive schema transformations that can be applied to schema constructs expressed in $\mathcal{M}$. In particular, for every construct of $\mathcal{M}$ there is an **add** and a **delete** primitive transformation which add to and delete from a schema an instance of that construct. For those constructs of $\mathcal{M}$ which have textual names, there is also a **rename** primitive transformation.

In AutoMed, schemas are incrementally transformed by applying to them a sequence of primitive transformations $t_1, \ldots, t_r$. Each primitive transformation adds, deletes, or renames just one schema construct, expressed in some modelling language. Thus, the intermediate (and indeed the target) schemas may contain constructs of more than one modelling language.

Each **add** or **delete** transformation is accompanied by a query specifying the extent of the new or deleted construct in terms of the rest of the constructs in the schema. This query is expressed in a functional query language IQL[2]. Also available are **extend** and **contract** transformations which behave in the same way as **add** and **delete** except that they state that the extent of the new/removed construct cannot be precisely derived from the other constructs present in the schema. More specifically, each **extend/contract** transformation takes a pair of queries that specify a lower and an upper bound on the extent of the new construct. The lower bound may be Void and the upper bound may be Any, which respectively indicate no known information about the lower or upper bound of the extent of the new construct.

An Example of Data Integration. In this example, we use schemas expressed in a simple relational data model to illustrate the process of data integration in AutoMed. However, we stress that these techniques are applicable to schemas defined in *any* data modelling language that has been specified within AutoMed's Model Definitions Repository, including modelling languages for semi-structured data [1,12].

In the simple relational model, there are two kinds of schema construct: **Rel** and **Att**. The extent of a **Rel** construct $\langle\!\langle R \rangle\!\rangle$ is the projection of relation R onto its primary key attributes $k_1, ..., k_n$. The extent of each **Att** construct $\langle\!\langle R, a \rangle\!\rangle$ where a is a non-key attribute of R is the projection of R onto $k_1, ..., k_n, a$. We refer the reader to [10] for an encoding of a richer relational data model, including the modelling of constraints.

Suppose that MAtab(CID, SID, Mark) and IStab(CID, SID, Mark) are two source relations for a data warehouse respectively storing students' marks for two departments MA and IS, in which CID and SID are the course and student IDs. Suppose also that a relation CourseSum(Dept, CID, Total, Avg) is in the data warehouse which gives the total and average mark for each course of each department.

The following transformation pathway expresses the schema transformation and integration processes in this example. Due to space limitations, we have not given the steps for removing the source relation constructs (note that this 'growing' and 'shrinking' of schemas is characteristic of AutoMed schema transformation pathways). Schema constructs $\langle\!\langle \text{Details} \rangle\!\rangle$ and $\langle\!\langle \text{Details}, \text{Mark} \rangle\!\rangle$ are temporary ones which are created for integrating the source data and then deleted after the global relation is created.

Note that the queries appearing in the transformation steps are IQL queries. The IQL function gc is a higher-order function that takes as its first argument an aggregation

---

[2] IQL is a comprehensions-based functional query language. Such languages subsume query languages such as SQL and OQL in expressiveness [3].

function and as its second argument a bag of pairs; it groups the pairs on their first component, and then applies the aggregation function to each bag of values formed from the second components.

addRel ⟨⟨Details⟩⟩   [{'MA',k1,k2}|{k1,k2} ← ⟨⟨MAtab⟩⟩]
                           ++[{'IS',k1,k2}|{k1,k2} ← ⟨⟨IStab⟩⟩];
addAtt ⟨⟨Details, Mark⟩⟩   [{'MA',k1,k2,x}|{k1,k2,x} ← ⟨⟨MAtab, Mark⟩⟩]
                           ++[{'IS',k1,k2,x}|{k1,k2,x} ← ⟨⟨IStab, Mark⟩⟩];
addRel ⟨⟨CourseSum⟩⟩   distinct [{k,k1}|{k,k1,k2} ← ⟨⟨Details⟩⟩]
addAtt ⟨⟨CourseSum, Total⟩⟩ [{x,y,z}|{{x,y},z} ← (gc sum
                             [{{k,k1},x}|{k,k1,k2,x} ← ⟨⟨Details, Mark⟩⟩])];
addAtt ⟨⟨CourseSum, Avg⟩⟩   [{x,y,z}|{{x,y},z} ← (gc avg
                             [{{k,k1},x}|{k,k1,k2,x} ← ⟨⟨Details, Mark⟩⟩])];
delAtt ⟨⟨Details, Mark⟩⟩   [{'MA',k1,k2,x}|{k1,k2,x} ← ⟨⟨MAtab, Mark⟩⟩]
                           ++[{'IS',k1,k2,x}|{k1,k2,x} ← ⟨⟨IStab, Mark⟩⟩];
delRel ⟨⟨Details⟩⟩   [{'MA',k1,k2}|{k1,k2} ← ⟨⟨MAtab⟩⟩]
                           ++[{'IS',k1,k2}|{k1,k2} ← ⟨⟨IStab⟩⟩];
...

3.2   The DLT Approach

In heterogenous data integration environments, the data transformation and integration processes can be described using AutoMed schema transformation pathways (see [8]). Our DLT approach is to use the individual steps of these pathways to compute the lineage data of the tracing data by traversing the pathways in reverse order one step at a time. In particular, suppose a data source LD with schema LS is transformed into a global database GD with schema GS, and the transformation pathway LS $\rightarrow$ GS is $ts_1, ..., ts_n$. Given tracing data td belonging to the extent of some schema construct in GD, we firstly find the transformation step ts_i which creates that construct and obtain td's lineage, dl_i, from ts_i. We then continue by tracing the lineage of dl_i from the remaining transformation pathway $ts_1, \ldots, ts_{i-1}$. We continue in this fashion, until we obtain the final lineage data from the data source LD.

Tracing data lineage with respect to a transformation rename(O, O') is simple — the lineage data in O is the same as the tracing data in O'. Considering add transformations, a single add transformation step can be expressed as v=q, in which v is the new schema construct created by the transformation and q is an IQL query over the current schema constructs. In our DLT approach, we use a subset of IQL, *Simple IQL* (SIQL), as the query language. More complex IQL queries can be encoded as a series of transformations with SIQL queries on intermediate schema constructs. As we have developed a method to decompose an IQL query into a sequence of SIQL queries (see [9]), we assume q in an add transformation is a SIQL query.

In [7], we have developed a DLT formula for each type of SIQL query which, given tracing data in v, evaluates the lineage of this data from the extents of the schema constructs referenced in v=q. If these extents and the tracing data are both materialised, Table 1 gives the DLT formulae for tracing the affect-pool of a tuple t, $DL(t)$, in which $D|t$ denotes all instances of the tuple t in the bag D (i.e. the result of the query $[x|x \leftarrow D; x = t]$). Since the results of queries of the form group D and gc aggFun D

Table 1. DLT Formulae

v	$DL(t)$
group D	$[\{x, y\} \mid \{x, y\} \leftarrow D; x = \overline{a}]$
sort D	$D \mid t$
distinct D	$D \mid t$
aggFun D	D
gc aggFun D	$[\{x, y\} \mid \{x, y\} \leftarrow D; x = \overline{a}]$
$D_1 \,{+}{+}\, D_2 \,{+}{+}\, \ldots \,{+}{+}\, D_n$	$\forall i.D_i \mid t$
$D_1 \,{-}{-}\, D_2$	$D_1 \mid t, D_2$
$[\overline{x} \mid \overline{x_1} \leftarrow D_1; \ldots; \overline{x_n} \leftarrow D_n; C]$	$\forall i.[\overline{x_i} \mid \overline{x_i} \leftarrow D_i; \overline{x_i} = ((\texttt{lambda } \overline{x}.\overline{x_i})\, t)]$
$[\overline{x} \mid \overline{x} \leftarrow D_1; \texttt{member } D_2\ \overline{y}]$	$D_1 \mid t, [\overline{y} \mid \overline{y} \leftarrow D_2; \overline{y} = ((\lambda \overline{x}.\overline{y})\, t)]$
$[\overline{x} \mid \overline{x} \leftarrow D_1; \texttt{not(member } D_2\ \overline{y})]$	$D_1 \mid t, D_2$
map (lambda $\overline{x}.$e) D	$[\overline{x} \mid \overline{x} \leftarrow D, e = t]$

are a collection of pairs, in the DLT formulae for these two queries we assume that the tracing tuple t is of the form $\{\overline{a}, \overline{b}\}$.

If all schema constructs created by add transformations are materialised, a simple way to trace the lineage of data in the global database GD is to apply the above DLT formulae on each transformation step in the transformation LS $\rightarrow$ GS in reverse from GS, finally ending up with the lineage data in the original data source LD. However, in general transformation pathways not all schema constructs created by add transformations will be materialised, and the above simple DLT approach is no longer applicable because it does not obtain lineage data from a virtual schema construct.

In [9], we have developed a set of DLT formulae using virtual arguments expressing virtual intermediate schema constructs and virtual lineage data, so that to extend the DLT formulae to handle the cases of both the tracing data and the source data could be virtual or materialised. Based on the formulae, our algorithms perform data lineage tracing along a general schema transformation pathway, in which each add transformation step may create either a virtual or a materialised schema construct.

Since delete and contract transformations do not create schema constructs, in previous work, they are ignored in the DLT process, and only partial schema transformation pathways are used in our DLT approach. In this paper, we will discuss how these transformations can also be used for DLT, as well as extend transformations, so that full schema transformation pathways are used in DLT processes.

4 Extending the DLT Approach

In Section 3.2, only IQL queries, add and rename transformations are considered for DLT. In practice, queries beyond IQL, delete, contract, and extend transformations are also used for integrating warehouse data. How these queries and transformations can be used for DLT should also be considered.

4.1 Using Queries Beyond IQL

In a typical data warehouse, add transformations for warehousing activities, such as single-source cleansing [8], may contain built-in functions which cannot be handled by our DLT formulae. In order to go back all the steps to the data source schemas, the DLT process may therefore need to handle queries beyond IQL. In particular, suppose the construct c is created by the following transformation step, in which f is a function defined by means of an arbitrary IQL query and $s_1, ..., s_n$ are the schemes appearing in the query: $addT(c, f(s_1, ..., s_n))$. There are three cases for tracing the lineage of a tracing tuple $t \in c$:

1. f is an IQL query, in which case the DLT approach described above can be used to obtain t's lineage;
2. $n = 1$ and f is of the form $f(s_1) = [h\ x | x \leftarrow s_1; C]$ for some h and C, in which case the lineage of t in s_1 is given by: $[x | x \leftarrow s_1; C; (h\ x) = t]$
3. For all other cases, we assume that the data lineage of t in the data source s_i is all data in s_i, for all $1 \leq i \leq n$.

4.2   Using **Delete** Transformations

The query in a **delete** transformation specifies how the extent of the deleted construct can be computed from the remaining schema constructs.

delete transformations are useful for DLT when the construct is unavailable. In particular, if a virtual intermediate construct with virtual data sources must be computed during the DLT process, normally we have to use the AutoMed Global Query Processor to derive this construct from the original data sources. However, if the virtual intermediate construct is deleted by a **delete** transformation and all constructs appearing in the **delete** transformation are materialised, then we can use the query in the **delete** transformation to compute the virtual construct. Since we only need to access materialised constructs in the data warehouse, the time of the evaluation procedure is reduced.

This feature can make a view *self-traceable*. That is, for the data in an integrated view, we can identify the names of the source constructs containing the lineage data, and obtain the lineage data from the view itself, rather than access the source constructs.

4.3   Using **Extend** Transformations

An **extend** transformation is applied if the extent of a new construct cannot be precisely derived from the source schema. The transformation $extend(c, ql, qu)$ adds a new construct c to a schema, where the query ql determines from the schema what is the minimum extent of c (and may be Void) and qu determines what is the maximal extent of c (and may be Any) [11].

If the transformation is $extend(c, Void, Any)$, this means that the extent of c is not derived from the source schema. We simply terminate the DLT process for tracing the lineage of c's data at that step.

If the transformation is $extend(c, ql, Any)$, this means the extent of c can be partially computed by the query ql. Using ql, a part of the lineage of c's data is obtained.

However, we cannot simply treat the DLT process via such an **extend** transformation as the same as via an **add** transformation by using the DLT formulae described in Section 3. Since in an **add** transformation, the whole extent of the added construct is exactly specified, while in an **extend** transformation it is not. The problem that arises is that extra lineage data may be derived because the tracing data contains more data than the result of the query, ql, in the **extend** transformation.

For example, transformation **extend**$(c, D_1 -- D_2, \text{Any})$, where $D_1 = [1, 2, 3]$, $D_2 = [2, 3, 4]$. Although the query result is list $[1]$, the extent of c may be $[1, 2]$, in which $''2''$ is derived from other transformation pathways. If we directly use the DLT algorithm described above, the obtained lineage data of $2 \in c$ are $D_1|[2]$ and $D_2|[2, 3, 4]$. While in fact, the data $''2''$ has no data lineage along this **extend** transformation.

Therefore, in practice, in order to trace data lineage along an **extend** transformation with the lower-bound query, ql, the result of the query must be recomputed and be used to filter the tracing data during the DLT process.

If the transformation is **extend**(c, Void, qu), this means that the extent of c must be fully computed in the result of the query qu. Although extra data may appear in qu's result, it cannot appear in the extent of c. We use the same approach as described for **add** transformations to trace lineage of c's data based on qu. However, we have to indicate that, extra lineage data may be created.

Finally, if the transformation is **extend**(c, ql, qu), we firstly obtain the lineage of c's data based on these two queries, and then return their intersection as the final lineage data, which would be much more accurate but still may not be the exact lineage data.

4.4   Using **Contract** Transformations

A **contract** transformation removes a construct whose extent cannot be precisely computed by the remaining constructs in the schema. The transformation **contract**(c, ql, qu) removes a construct c from a schema, where ql determines what is the minimum extent of c, and qu determines what is the maximal extent of c. As with **extend**, ql may be Void and qu may be Any.

If the transformation is **contract**$(c, \text{Void}, \text{Any})$, we simply ignore the **contract** transformation in our DLT process. Otherwise, we use the **contract** transformation similarly to the way we use **delete** transformations described above. However, we also have to indicate that if using ql, only partial lineage data can be obtained; if using qu, extra lineage data may be obtained; and if using the intersection of the results of both ql and qu, we can also only obtain an approximate lineage data.

5   Ambiguity of Lineage Data

The ambiguity of lineage data, also called *derivation inequivalence* [6], relates to the fact that for queries which are equivalent but different syntactically DLT processes may obtain different lineage data for identical tracing data. This section investigates how this problem may happen in our context.

Two queries are *equivalent* if they give identical results for all possible values of their base collections. That is, given two queries q_1 and q_2 both referring to base collections $b_1, ..., b_n$, q_1 and q_2 are equivalent if $q_1[b_1/I_1, ..., b_n/I_n] = q_2[b_1/I_1, ..., b_n/I_n]$ is true for all instances $I_1, ..., I_n$ of $b_1, ..., b_n$ respectively. In this section, we use $v1 \equiv v2$ to denote that views $v1$ and $v2$ are defined by equivalent queries, use $AP_v(t)$ to denote the affect-pool of tracing data t in the data source v, and use $OP_v(t)$ to denote the origin-pool of t in v. We refer the reader to [7] for the definitions of the affect-pool and the origin-pool, and the difference between them.

5.1 Derivation for Difference and Not Member Operations

Ambiguity of lineage data may happen when difference (*i.e.* $--$ in IQL) and not member operations are involved in the view definitions.

For example, consider two bags $R = [0, 1, 1, 2, 3]$, $S = [-1, 1, 2, 3, 3]$. Two pairs of equivalent views, $v1 \equiv v2$ and $v3 \equiv v4$, are defined as follows.

$v1 = R -- (R -- S) = [1, 2, 3]$
$v2 = S -- (S -- R) = [1, 2, 3]$
$v3 = [x|x \leftarrow R; member\ S\ x] = [1, 1, 2, 3]$
$v4 = [x|x \leftarrow R; not\ (member\ [y|y \leftarrow R; not\ (member\ S\ y)]\ x)] = [1, 1, 2, 3]$

The lineage of data in an IQL view can be traced by decomposing the view into a sequence of intermediate SIQL views. In order to trace the lineage of data in the above four views, intermediate views are required: for $v1$, $v1' = (R--S) = [0, 1]$; for $v2$, $v2' = (S -- R) = [-1, 3]$; for $v3$, no intermediate view needed; and for $v4$, $v4' = [y|y \leftarrow R; not\ (member\ S\ y)] = [0]$.

With the above intermediate views, we can now trace the lineage of the views' data. For example, the affect-pool of the data item $t = 1 \in v1$ and $t = 1 \in v2$ are as follows. Here, we denote by $D\,|\,d1$ the lineage data $d1$ in the collection D, *i.e.* all instances of the tuple $d1$ in the bag D (the result of the query $[x|x \leftarrow D; x = d1]$).

$AP_{v1}(t) = \langle R|[x\,|\,x \leftarrow R; x = 1], R -- S \rangle = \langle R|[1, 1], v1' \rangle$
$\qquad = \langle R|[1, 1], R|[x\,|\,x \leftarrow R; member\ v1'\ x], S \rangle$
$\qquad = \langle R|[1, 1], R|[0, 1, 1], S|[-1, 1, 2, 3, 3] \rangle = \langle R|[0, 1, 1], S|[-1, 1, 2, 3, 3] \rangle$
$AP_{v2}(t) = \langle S|[x\,|\,x \leftarrow S; x = 1], S -- R \rangle = \langle S|[1], v2' \rangle$
$\qquad = \langle S|[1], S|[x\,|\,x \leftarrow S; member\ v2'\ x], R \rangle$
$\qquad = \langle S|[1], S|[-1, 3, 3], R|[0, 1, 1, 2, 3] \rangle = \langle R|[0, 1, 1, 2, 3], S|[-1, 1, 3, 3] \rangle$

We can see that the affect-pool of identical tracing data in $v1$ and $v2$ are inequivalent. The affect-pool of tuple $t = 1 \in v3$ and $t = 1 \in v4$ are:

$AP_{v3}(t) = \langle R|[x\,|\,x \leftarrow R; x = 1], S|[x\,|\,x \leftarrow S; x = 1] \rangle = \langle R|[1, 1], S|[1] \rangle$
$AP_{v4}(t) = \langle R|[x\,|\,x \leftarrow R; x = 1], v4' \rangle = \langle R|[1, 1], R|[y\,|\,y \leftarrow R; member\ v4'\ y], S \rangle$
$\qquad = \langle R|[1, 1], R|[0], S|[-1, 1, 2, 3, 3] \rangle = \langle R|[1, 1], S|[-1, 1, 2, 3, 3] \rangle$

We can see that the affect-pool of above identical tracing data in $v3$ and $v4$ are also inequivalent.

The reason for the inequivalent affect-pool of the data in views defined by equivalent queries involving the $--$ and not member operators is the definition of affect-pool. The affect-pool in a data source $D2$ in queries of the form $D1 -- D2$ or $[x|x \leftarrow D1; not\ (member\ D2\ x)]$, includes all data in $D2$. So the computed affect-pool in $D2$ may contain some "irrelevant" data which does not affect the existence of the tracing data in the view. For example, if the tracing data is $t = 1$ in the view $R -- S$, the irrelevant data in S are $[-1, 2, 3, 3]$, which are also included in t's affect-pool.

Although origin-pool is defined to contain the minimal essential lineage data in a data source, ambiguity of lineage data may also occur for tracing origin-pool. For example, in the case of the above four views, the origin-pool of the tracing data item $t = 1$ are also inequivalent (we use $D|\emptyset$ to denote no lineage data in D):

$$\text{OP}_{v1}(t) = \langle R|[x\,|\,x \leftarrow R; x = 1], (R -- S)|[x\,|\,x \leftarrow (R -- S); x = 1]\rangle$$
$$= \langle R|[1,1], v1\,'\,|[x\,|\,x \leftarrow [0,1]; x = 1]\rangle = \langle R|[1,1], v1\,'\,|[1]\rangle$$
$$= \langle R|[1,1], R|[x\,|\,x \leftarrow R; x = 1], S|[x\,|\,x \leftarrow S; x = 1]\rangle$$
$$= \langle R|[1,1], R|[1,1], S|[1]\rangle = \langle R|[1,1], S|[1]\rangle$$
$$\text{OP}_{v2}(t) = \langle S|[x\,|\,x \leftarrow S; x = 1], (R -- S)|[x\,|\,x \leftarrow (S -- R); x = 1]\rangle$$
$$= \langle S|[1], v2\,'\,|[x\,|\,x \leftarrow [-1,3]; x = 1]\rangle = \langle S|[1], v2\,'\,|\varnothing\rangle = \langle S|[1]\rangle$$

and

$$\text{OP}_{v3}(t) = \langle R|[x\,|\,x \leftarrow R; x = 1], S|[x\,|\,x \leftarrow S; x = 1]\rangle = \langle R|[1,1], S|[1]\rangle$$
$$\text{OP}_{v4}(t) = \langle R|[x\,|\,x \leftarrow R; x = 1], v4\,'\,|\varnothing\rangle = \langle R|[1,1]\rangle$$

5.2 Derivation for Aggregate Functions

Ambiguity of lineage data may also happen when queries involve aggregate functions. Suppose that bags R and S are the same as in Section 5.1. Consider DLT processes over the following two pairs of equivalent views, $v5 \equiv v6$ and $v7 \equiv v8$:

$$v5 = \text{sum } R = 7$$
$$v6 = \text{sum } [x\,|\,x \leftarrow R; x \neq 0] = 7$$
$$v7 = \max S = [3,3]$$
$$v8 = \max [x\,|\,x \leftarrow S; x > (\min S)] = [3,3]$$

The affect-pool of $t = 7 \in v5$ and $t = 7 \in v6$ are:

$$\text{AP}_{v5}(t) = \langle R\rangle = \langle R|[0,1,1,2,3]\rangle$$
$$\text{AP}_{v6}(t) = \langle R|[x\,|\,x \leftarrow R; x \neq 0]\rangle = \langle R|[1,1,2,3]\rangle$$

and the affect-pool of $t = 3 \in v7$ and $t = 3 \in v8$ are:

$$\text{AP}_{v7}(t) = \langle S\rangle = \langle S|[-1,1,2,3,3]\rangle$$
$$\text{AP}_{v8}(t) = \langle S|[x\,|\,x \leftarrow S; x > (\min S)]\rangle = \langle S|[1,2,3,3]\rangle$$

The affect-pool of identical tracing data for these equivalent views are inequivalent.

The reason for this ambiguity of affect-pool is that, according to the DLT formulae of affect-pool in Table 1, the affect-pool of data in an aggregate view includes all the data in the data source, which can bring irrelevant data into the derivation. In above example, views $v6$ and $v8$ filter off some irrelevant data by using predicate expressions, so that the computed affect-pool over the two views does not contain this irrelevant data.

Such problems may be avoided in tracing the origin-pool, since the origin-pool is defined to contain the minimal essential lineage data in the data sources, and any data item and its duplicates in the origin-pool are non-redundant.

For example, the origin-pool of $t = 7 \in v5$ and $t = 7 \in v6$ are identical:

$$\text{OP}_{v5}(t) = \langle R|[x\,|\,x \leftarrow R; x \neq 0]\rangle = \langle R|[1,1,2,3]\rangle$$
$$\text{OP}_{v6}(t) = \langle R|[x\,|\,x \leftarrow [y\,|\,y \leftarrow R; y \neq 0]; x \neq 0]\rangle = \langle R|[1,1,2,3]\rangle$$

and the origin-pool of $t = 3 \in v7$ and $t = 3 \in v8$ are also identical:

$$\text{OP}_{v7}(t) = \langle S|[x\,|\,x \leftarrow S; x = 3]\rangle = \langle S|[3,3]\rangle$$
$$\text{OP}_{v8}(t) = \langle S|[x\,|\,x \leftarrow [y\,|\,y \leftarrow S; y > (\min S)]; x = 3]\rangle = \langle S|[3,3]\rangle$$

However, the derivation inequivalence problem cannot always be avoided in tracing the origin-pool. For example, suppose $v9 \equiv v10$ are defined as follows:

$$v9\ \ = \text{sum } S = 8$$
$$v10 = \text{sum } [x\,|\,x \leftarrow S; \text{not } (\text{member } [x1\,|\,x1 \leftarrow S; x2 \leftarrow S; x1 = (-x2)]\ x)] = 8$$

In order to trace the origin-pool of $v10$'s data, the intermediate views for $v10$ are defined as follows:

$$v10\,'\ \ = [x1\,|\,x1 \leftarrow S; x2 \leftarrow S; x1 = (-x2)] = [-1,1]$$
$$v10\,''\, = [x\,|\,x \leftarrow S; \text{not } (\text{member } v10\,'\ x)] = [2,3,3]$$
$$v10\ \ \ = \text{sum } v10\,''\, = 8$$

Then, the origin-pool of $t = 8 \in$ v9 and $t = 8 \in$ v10 are:

$\text{OP}_{\text{v9}}(t) = \langle \text{S}|[x\,|\,x \leftarrow \text{S}; x \neq 0]\rangle = \langle \text{S}|[-1,1,2,3,3]\rangle$

$\text{OP}_{\text{v10}}(t) = \langle \text{v10}''|[x\,|\,x \leftarrow \text{v10}''; x \neq 0]\rangle = \langle \text{v10}''|[2,3,3]\rangle$

$\qquad\qquad = \langle [x\,|\,x \leftarrow \text{S}; \text{not (member v10}'\ x)]|[2,3,3]\rangle$

$\qquad\qquad = \langle \text{S}|[2,3,3], \text{v10}'|\varnothing\rangle = \langle \text{S}|[2,3,3]\rangle$

We can see that $\text{OP}_{\text{v9}}(t) \neq \text{OP}_{\text{v10}}(t)$. This is because the view v10 is firstly applying a select operation over the data source S, to eliminate data item d in S and its inverse d^{-1}, i.e. $d + d^{-1} = 0$.

5.3   Derivation for Where-Provenance

The problem of where-provenance is introduced in Buneman *et al.*'s work [2]. In that paper, tracing the where-provenance of a tracing tuple consists of finding the lineage of one component of the tuple, rather than the whole tuple. Also, the where-provenance is not exact data, but rather a path for describing where the lineage is. That paper describes that derivation inequivalence may happen when tracing where-provenance.

Examples of where-provenance inequivalence [3]
Suppose that w1 is a view over a relational table $\langle\!\langle\text{Staff}\rangle\!\rangle$, where the extent of $\langle\!\langle\text{Staff}\rangle\!\rangle$ table is a list of 3-item tuples containing name, pay and tax information of employees. The definition of w1 is as following:

w1 $= [\{\text{name},\text{pay}\}|\{\text{name},\text{pay},\text{tax}\} \leftarrow \langle\!\langle\text{Staff}\rangle\!\rangle; \text{pay} = 1200]$

If $\{'\text{Tom}', 1200\}$ is a tuple in w1 and the data 1200 in the tuple only comes from the tuple $\{'\text{Tom}', 1200, 100\}$ in the extent of $\langle\!\langle\text{Staff}\rangle\!\rangle$, then the where-provenance of 1200 is the path $''\langle\!\langle\text{Staff}\rangle\!\rangle.\{\text{name} : '\text{Tom}'\}.\text{pay}''$, which means that 1200 comes from the attribute pay in the relation $\langle\!\langle\text{Staff}\rangle\!\rangle$ where the value of the attribute name is $'\text{Tom}'$.

However, if we consider the view w2 as following over construct $\langle\!\langle\text{Staff}\rangle\!\rangle$, which is an equivalent view to w1,

w2 $= [\{\text{name}, 1200\}|\{\text{name},\text{pay},\text{tax}\} \leftarrow \langle\!\langle\text{Staff}\rangle\!\rangle; \text{pay} = 1200]$

the where-provenance of 1200 in $\{'\text{Tom}', 1200\}$ is the query (view definition) itself, since the value is directly appearing in the query expression.

Another example illustrating inequivalent where-provenance is as follows. Suppose that w3 $\equiv$ w4 where

w3 $= [\{\text{id},\text{ns}\}|\{\text{id},\text{s},\text{b},\text{ns}\} \leftarrow \langle\!\langle\text{D}\rangle\!\rangle; \text{s} = \text{b}; \text{s} = \text{ns}]$

w4 $= [\{\text{id},\text{ns}\}|\{\text{id},\text{s},\text{b},\text{ns}\} \leftarrow \langle\!\langle\text{D}\rangle\!\rangle; \text{member } [\{\text{id1},\text{ns1}\}|$
$\qquad\qquad\qquad \{\text{id1},\text{s1},\text{b1},\text{ns1}\} \leftarrow \langle\!\langle\text{D}\rangle\!\rangle; \text{s1} = \text{b1}]\ \{\text{id},\text{ns}\}; \text{s} = \text{ns}]$

In the case of w3, the attribute ns in the result view depends on attributes: s, b and ns, in relational table $\langle\!\langle\text{D}\rangle\!\rangle$. While in the case of w4, the attribute ns in the result view depends on attributes: id, s, b and ns, in $\langle\!\langle\text{D}\rangle\!\rangle$.

In our DLT approach, we only consider tracing the lineage data of an entire tuple, which is termed why-provenance in [2]. However, in AutoMed, each extensional modelling construct of a high-level modelling language is specified as an HDM node or edge and cannot be broken down further. For example, each attribute in a relational table is a construct in the AutoMed relational schema.

In other words, in our DLT approach, not only the why-provenance but also the where-provenance has been considered, when the AutoMed data modelling technique

---

[3] The examples illustrated in this section are derived from [2].

is used for modelling data, *e.g.*, using the simple relational data model. In this sense, we deal with the problem of tracing where-provenance and why-provenance simultaneously, so that the problem of inequivalent where-provenance is avoided.

For example, by using the simple relational data model and SIQL queries, the above four view definitions can be rewritten (denoted as $\rightsquigarrow$) as follows. In the simple relational data model, constructs of the relational table $\langle\!\langle \mathsf{Staff} \rangle\!\rangle$ include: $\langle\!\langle \mathsf{Staff} \rangle\!\rangle$, $\langle\!\langle \mathsf{Staff}, \mathsf{name} \rangle\!\rangle$, $\langle\!\langle \mathsf{Staff}, \mathsf{pay} \rangle\!\rangle$ and $\langle\!\langle \mathsf{Staff}, \mathsf{tax} \rangle\!\rangle$; constructs of the table $\langle\!\langle \mathsf{D} \rangle\!\rangle$ include: $\langle\!\langle \mathsf{D} \rangle\!\rangle$, $\langle\!\langle \mathsf{D}, \mathsf{id} \rangle\!\rangle$, $\langle\!\langle \mathsf{D}, \mathsf{s}, \rangle\!\rangle$, $\langle\!\langle \mathsf{D}, \mathsf{b} \rangle\!\rangle$ and $\langle\!\langle \mathsf{D}, \mathsf{ns} \rangle\!\rangle$.

w1 $\rightsquigarrow$ w1' = [{name,pay} | {name,pay} $\leftarrow$ $\langle\!\langle \mathsf{Staff}, \mathsf{pay} \rangle\!\rangle$; pay = 1200]
w2 $\rightsquigarrow$ w2' = [{name,pay} | {name,pay} $\leftarrow$ $\langle\!\langle \mathsf{Staff}, \mathsf{pay} \rangle\!\rangle$; pay = 1200]
    w2'' = map (lambda {name,pay}.{name,1200}) w2'

Obviously, w1' and w2' are identical, and w2'' uses a lambda expression replacing by the constant 1200 the pay values in the result of w2'. Here, we cannot trace the lineage data of 1200 separately. If it is required to do that, definitions of w1 and w2 can be rewritten as:

w1 $\rightsquigarrow$ w1a' = [{name,pay} | {name,pay} $\leftarrow$ $\langle\!\langle \mathsf{Staff}, \mathsf{pay} \rangle\!\rangle$; pay = 1200]
    w1a'' = map (lambda {name,pay}.{pay}) w1a'
w2 $\rightsquigarrow$ w2a' = [{name,pay} | {name,pay} $\leftarrow$ $\langle\!\langle \mathsf{Staff}, \mathsf{pay} \rangle\!\rangle$; pay = 1200]
    w2a'' = map (lambda {name,pay}.{1200}) w2a'

We can see that, although intermediate views w1a'' and w2a'' have the same result in the current specific situation, they have different definitions. In this sense, views w1 and w2 can be regarded as inequivalent and the problem of derivation inequivalence does not arise for these two views. However, even we admit that these two views are equivalent in the current situation, according to the DLT formula in Table 1, the lineage data of 1200 in w1a'' and w2a'' are obtained as follows:

    w1a'|[{name,pay} | {name,pay} $\leftarrow$ w1a'; pay = 1200]
    w2a'|[{name,pay} | {name,pay} $\leftarrow$ w2a'; 1200 = 1200]

Since views w1a' and w2a' are identical, 1200 over the two views have the same lineage. As to views w3 and w4, their definitions can be rewritten as follows:

w3 $\rightsquigarrow$ w3' = [{id,s} | {id,s} $\leftarrow$ $\langle\!\langle \mathsf{D}, \mathsf{s} \rangle\!\rangle$; member $\langle\!\langle \mathsf{D}, \mathsf{b} \rangle\!\rangle$ {id,s}]
    w3'' = [{id,ns} | {id,ns} $\leftarrow$ $\langle\!\langle \mathsf{D}, \mathsf{ns} \rangle\!\rangle$; member w3' {id,ns}]
w4 $\rightsquigarrow$ w4' = [{id,ns} | {id,ns} $\leftarrow$ $\langle\!\langle \mathsf{D}, \mathsf{ns} \rangle\!\rangle$; member $\langle\!\langle \mathsf{D}, \mathsf{s} \rangle\!\rangle$ {id,ns}]
    w4'' = [{id,s} | {id,s} $\leftarrow$ $\langle\!\langle \mathsf{D}, \mathsf{s} \rangle\!\rangle$; member $\langle\!\langle \mathsf{D}, \mathsf{b} \rangle\!\rangle$ {id,s}]
    w4''' = [{id,ns} | {id,ns} $\leftarrow$ w4'; member w4'' {id,ns}]

We can see that tuple {id,ns} in the two views have the same lineage coming from $\langle\!\langle \mathsf{D}, \mathsf{ns} \rangle\!\rangle$, $\langle\!\langle \mathsf{D}, \mathsf{s} \rangle\!\rangle$ and $\langle\!\langle \mathsf{D}, \mathsf{b} \rangle\!\rangle$ constructs.

6 Concluding Remarks

This paper have discussed how queries beyond IQL, and delete, extend and contract transformations can be used for tracing data lineage. With our previous work of tracing data lineage using add and rename transformations, our DLT approach would be implemented in a general data warehousing environment.

We also investigated when ambiguity of lineage data may happen in our context — the problem may happen when tracing the lineage of the data in views defined by IQL queries involving $--$, not member filters and aggregation operations. In Cui *et al*'s work [6], the definition of data lineage results in the same problem of derivation in-equivalence. Ambiguity of lineage may also happen when tracing where-provenance. We observed that the process of tracing where-provenance can be handled by the process of tracing why-provenance when AutoMed is used for modelling data, so that the problem of inequivalent where-provenance can be reduced.

In addition, since our algorithms consider in turn each transformation step in a trans-formation pathway in order to evaluate lineage data in a stepwise fashion, they are useful not only in data warehousing environments, but also in any data transformation and integration framework based on sequences of primitive schema transformations. For example, [12] present an approach for integrating heterogeneous XML documents using the AutoMed toolkit. A schema is automatically extracted for each XML docu-ment and transformation pathways are applied to these schemas. Reference [11] also discusses how AutoMed can be applied in peer-to-peer data integration settings. Thus, with the extension in this paper, our DLT approach is readily applicable in peer-to-peer and semi-structured data integration environments.

References

1. Boyd, M., Kittivoravitkul, S., Lazanitis, C., et al.: AutoMed: A BAV data integration sys-tem for heterogeneous data sources. In: Persson, A., Stirna, J. (eds.) CAiSE 2004. LNCS, vol. 3084, pp. 82–97. Springer, Heidelberg (2004)
2. Buneman, P., Khanna, S., Tan, W.C.: Why and Where: A characterization of data prove-nance. In: Van den Bussche, J., Vianu, V. (eds.) ICDT 2001. LNCS, vol. 1973, pp. 316–330. Springer, Heidelberg (2000)
3. Buneman, P., et al.: Comprehension syntax. SIGMOD Record 23(1), 87–96 (1994)
4. Cui, Y.: Lineage tracing in data warehouses. PhD thesis, Computer Science Department, Stanford University (2001)
5. Cui, Y., Widom, J.: Lineage tracing for general data warehouse transformations. In: Proc. VLDB'01, pp. 471–480. Morgan Kaufmann, San Francisco (2001)
6. Cui, Y., Widom, J., Wiener, J.L.: Tracing the lineage of view data in a warehousing environ-ment. ACM Transactions on Database Systems (TODS) 25(2), 179–227 (2000)
7. Fan, H., Poulovassilis, A.: Tracing data lineage using schema transformation pathways. In: Knowledge Transformation for the Semantic Web, vol. 95, pp. 64–79. IOS Press, Amsterdam (2003)
8. Fan, H., Poulovassilis, A.: Using AutoMed metadata in data warehousing environments. In: Proc. DOLAP'03, pp. 86–93. ACM Press, New York (2003)
9. Fan, H., Poulovassilis, A.: Using schema transformation pathways for data lineage tracing. In: Jackson, M., Nelson, D., Stirk, S. (eds.) Database: Enterprise, Skills and Innovation. LNCS, vol. 3567, pp. 133–144. Springer, Heidelberg (2005)
10. McBrien, P., Poulovassilis, A.: A uniform approach to inter-model transformations. In: Jarke, M., Oberweis, A. (eds.) CAiSE 1999. LNCS, vol. 1626, pp. 333–348. Springer, Heidelberg (1999)
11. McBrien, P., Poulovassilis, A.: Defining peer-to-peer data integration using both as view rules. In: Aberer, K., Koubarakis, M., Kalogeraki, V. (eds.) Databases, Information Systems, and Peer-to-Peer Computing. LNCS, vol. 2944, pp. 91–107. Springer, Heidelberg (2004)
12. Zamboulis, L.: XML data integration by graph restructuring. In: Williams, H., MacKinnon, L.M. (eds.) Key Technologies for Data Management. LNCS, vol. 3112, Springer, Heidelberg (2004)

Fast Recognition of Asian Characters Based on Database Methodologies

Woong-Kee Loh[1], Young-Ho Park[2], and Yong-Ik Yoon[2]

[1] Department of Computer Science & Engineering, University of Minnesota
200 Union Street SE, Minneapolis, MN 55455, USA
lohw@cs.umn.edu
[2] Department of Multimedia Science, Sookmyung Women's University
53-12 Chungpa-Dong, Yongsan-gu, Seoul 140-742, Korea
{yhpark,yiyoon}@sm.ac.kr

Abstract. Character recognition has been an active research area in the field of pattern recognition. The existing character recognition algorithms are focused mainly on increasing the recognition rate. However, as in the recent Google Library Project, the requirement for speeding up recognition of enormous amount of documents is growing. Moreover, the existing algorithms do not pay enough attention to Asian characters. In this paper, we propose an algorithm for fast recognition of Asian characters based on the database methodologies. Since the number of Asian characters is very large and their shapes are complicated, Asian characters require much more recognition time than numeric and Roman characters. The proposed algorithm extracts the feature from each of Asian characters through the Discrete Fourier Transform (DFT) and optimizes the recognition speed by storing and retrieving the features using a multidimensional index. We improve the recognition speed of the proposed algorithm using the association rule technique, which is a widely adopted data mining technique. The proposed algorithm has the advantage that it can be applied regardless of the language, size, and font of the characters to be recognized.

Keywords: character recognition, Discrete Fourier Transform, multidimensional index, association rule.

1 Introduction

Character recognition has been an active research area since 1980s in the field of pattern recognition. Many character recognition algorithms have been implemented for various applications including postal services, and many commercial software packages have been released until recently.

The characters to be recognized can be categorized into two groups: printed and handwritten characters [7,13]. The printed characters are those in printed materials such as textbooks, magazines, and newspapers. A lot of research on recognition of printed characters has been performed historically, and the recognition rate on printed numbers and Roman characters reaches almost up to 100%.

R. Cooper and J. Kennedy (Eds.): BNCOD 2007, LNCS 4587, pp. 37–48, 2007.

The handwritten characters are those written by human hands. Since the variation in handwritten characters is more salient than the printed characters, the recognition rate on the former is generally much lower than the latter. Although the recognition rate on correctly handwritten characters reaches up to 90%, the recognition on cursive and unsegmented characters is still a tough research issue. The recognition process of printed characters consists of two phases [13]. In the first phase, a template is generated for each of characters to be recognized by extracting abstract feature from the shape of the character, and in the second phase, given a scanned character as an input, a template with the closest feature to the character is returned.

The existing character recognition algorithms in the pattern recognition field are focused mainly on the correctness of recognition, but not on recognition speed. The requirement on recognition speed was originated by the applications that recognize enormous amount of documents. An example is Google Library Project, which digitizes and recognizes the contents of books stocked in big libraries and provides the service of searching on the book contents [9]. Moreover, the existing algorithms do not pay enough attention to Asian characters. In general, different character recognition algorithms should be used depending on the character set and the number, size, and font of the characters to be recognized. Especially, the number of Asian characters is much more than Roman characters and their shapes are much more complicated. For example, the number of all Korean characters is as many as 11,172, and even the number of frequently used ones goes up to 2,350 [12].

In this paper, we propose an algorithm for fast recognition of printed Asian characters based on the database methodologies. The proposed algorithm extracts the feature from each Asian character through the Discrete Fourier Transform (DFT) [1,15], and optimizes recognition speed by storing and retrieving the features in a multidimensional index [3,5]. We improve the recognition speed of the proposed algorithm using the association rule technique [2], which is a widely adopted data mining technique. In the proposed algorithm, an association rule is a pattern of character sequence that frequently appears in a document, and is used to improve the recognition speed by reducing the number of unnecessary feature comparisons. The proposed algorithm has the advantage that it can be applied regardless of the language, size, and font of the characters to be recognized.

This paper is organized as follows. In Section 2, we briefly describe previous related work. In Section 3, we explain in detail about the proposed algorithm. In Section 4, we perform experiments to evaluate the performance of the proposed algorithm. Finally, we conclude this paper in Section 5.

2   Related Work

The algorithms for printed character recognition generate a template for each character to be recognized by extracting abstract feature from the shape of the character [13]. Since the performance of the algorithms is highly dependent on

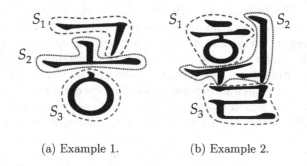

(a) Example 1.   (b) Example 2.

Fig. 1. Component Segmentation of Korean Characters

the feature, a lot of research on the features such as moment invariants [4] has been performed. However, the features were focused on improving the correctness of recognition, but not on the speed. The algorithm proposed in this paper uses the feature based on the DFT for fast character recognition.

The number of Asian characters such as Korean, Chinese, and Japanese characters is much larger and their shapes are much more complicated than Roman characters. Hence, the algorithms for recognizing Roman characters are far from sufficient for recognizing Asian characters. Due to the complicated shapes of Asian characters, many algorithms for recognizing them first segment a character into a few components and then integrate the recognition result for each of the components [7,16]. For example, a Korean character can be segmented into three components: initial, medial, and final sounds. The segmentation approach does make sense since the total number of components is much smaller than the number of all characters and the shapes of components are much simpler than the characters. For example, while the number of all Korean characters is 11,172, the total number of initial, medial, and final sounds is as small as 67 ($= 19 + 21 + 27$).

However, the approach has a few severe problems as follows. First, it is very hard to segment an Asian character into components. Figure 1 shows two Korean character examples segmented into three components, which are represented as S_1, S_2, and S_3. As shown in the figure, since the sizes and positions of components vary with characters, the segmentation itself is prone to error and can be a reason for degrading recognition speed and correctness. Second, even a recognition error on a component can lead to a recognition error of a whole character. Supposing the recognition rate for a component is 95%, then the recognition rate for a Korean character is about 86% ($= .95 \times .95 \times .95$). For Chinese characters consisting of more components, the recognition rate would be even worse. Third, it is almost impossible that a segmentation algorithm for a language is applied to other languages. For example, the segmentation algorithm for Korean characters cannot be used for Chinese characters. The proposed algorithm processes a character as a whole without segmentation, and thus can be used regardless of languages.

In [1], a one-dimensional time-series of length n was mapped to an n-dimensional vector and transformed into an f-dimensional ($f \ll n$) vector through the DFT for efficient indexing and retrieval. While only one-dimensional time-series were handled in [1], the proposed algorithm handles two-dimensional characters. In [14], an algorithm using Harr Discrete Wavelet Transform (DWT) was proposed for similarity search in two-dimensional image databases. Since the DFT can be used for any length that is not a power of two, the proposed algorithm chooses the DFT rather than the DWT for extracting features for character recognition.

They might consider the algorithms based on neural networks [6] or Hidden Markov Models (HMM) [8] for recognizing printed Asian characters. Since the number of Asian characters is very large and their shapes are complicated, the neural network-based algorithms have the following problems. First, the learning step of the algorithms requires very long time, and thus it is very hard to optimize the network. Second, the network for recognizing Asian characters should be much more complicated than Roman characters, and thus it can cause degradation of recognition speed and/or correctness. Third, even though the recognition rate is not satisfactory, it is very hard to find the precise reasons and to fix them. Actually, there is no guarantee that the recognition rate of neural network-based algorithms is higher than feature extraction-based algorithms. The HMM is used mostly in the applications with temporal aspects such as speech recognition and natural language processing, and is good for recognizing handwritten characters. However, the number of states of the HMM for recognizing Asian characters should be much larger than Roman characters, and thus it can also cause degradation of recognition speed and/or correctness.

3   The Proposed Algorithm

In this section, we explain in detail about the proposed algorithm for fast recognition of Asian characters. First, we define the similarity between characters, and explain the method for extracting features from the characters. Next, we describe the method to store and retrieve the extracted features in an index. Finally, we improve the recognition speed of the algorithm more based on association rules.

In this paper, a character is represented by a two-dimensional bitmap function $c(x, y)$. The ranges of x and y are the horizontal and vertical lengths of the rectangle containing the character, respectively ($0 \leq x < w, 0 \leq y < h$). For any two characters $c_1(x, y)$ and $c_2(x, y)$, the similarity between them is defined as the two-dimensional Euclidean distance between two bitmaps as the following:

Definition 1. The similarity $D(c_1, c_2)$ between any two characters $c_1(x, y)$ and $c_2(x, y)$ is defined as follows:

$$D(c_1, c_2) = \sqrt{\sum_{0 \leq x < w} \sum_{0 \leq y < h} (c_1(x, y) - c_2(x, y))^2} \ . \tag{1}$$

The smaller $D(c_1, c_2)$ value indicates the higher similarity between two characters c_1 and c_2.   □

The character recognition algorithm proposed in this paper can be summarized as follows. The proposed algorithm generates a template bitmap function $t(x, y)$ for each of characters to be recognized and stores the template with the character's unique code. Given a scanned character $c(x, y)$ as an input, the proposed algorithm returns the most similar template t ($\in \mathcal{T}$), which satisfies the following equation:

$$t = \{t \mid \forall t' \in \mathcal{T}, \ D(t, c) \le D(t', c)\} ,\tag{2}$$

where $\mathcal{T}$ is the set of all templates. Every template t in the template set $\mathcal{T}$ and the given character c have the same horizontal and vertical lengths.

A naive approach of the sequential scan compares all the templates one by one with the given character, which would take too much time. For example, for recognizing Korean characters, whose number is 2,350 $\sim$ 11,172, it might take almost a second to recognize two or three characters. To tackle the problem, we use a multidimensional index such as the R*-tree [3]. A character can be mapped to a wh-dimensional vector and then stored in the index. However, this approach also has a problem that the performance of retrieving a multidimensional index would be significantly degraded by managing high dimensional data. The performance could be even worse than the sequential scan[1].

For solving the problem, we transform the templates into f-dimensional vectors through the DFT and store them in an f-dimensional index. In [1], a one-dimensional time-series of length n was transformed to an f-dimensional ($f \ll n$) feature vector through the DFT. The DFT has the following property[2]:

$$D(v_1, v_2) = D(V_1, V_2) ,\tag{3}$$

where v_1 and v_2 are one-dimensional vectors of length n, and V_1 and V_2 are the DFT-transformed vectors for v_1 and v_2, respectively. While V_1 and V_2 have lengths n as well as v_1 and v_2, most of elements in V_1 and V_2 are very close to 0. Let V_1' and V_2' be f-dimensional vectors consisting of f elements that are not close to 0 in V_1 and V_2, respectively. Then we get the following equation [1]:

$$D(v_1, v_2) \ge D(V_1', V_2') ,\tag{4}$$

We show that the properties in Eq. (3) and (4) also hold for two-dimensional DFT in Lemmas 1 and 2. Before showing that, we briefly summarize the process of two-dimensional DFT on a two-dimensional function $c(x, y)$. First, for each row $c(., y)$ ($0 \le y < h$) in $c(x, y)$, the one-dimensional DFT is performed. Let $c'(x, y)$ be the two-dimensional function obtained through the process. Next, for each column $c'(x, .)$ ($0 \le x < w$) in $c'(x, y)$, the one-dimensional DFT is performed. The final two-dimensional function $C(x, y)$ is the result of two-dimensional DFT on $c(x, y)$.

---

[1] In general, the cost for retrieving a multidimensional index increases exponentially as the data dimension increases. This phenomenon is called *high dimensionality problem* or *high dimensionality curse* [5].

[2] The property is called *Parceval's Theorem*.

Lemma 1. Any two-dimensional functions $c_1(x, y)$ and $c_2(x, y)$, and their two-dimensional DFT-transformed results $C_1(x, y)$ and $C_2(x, y)$ satisfy the following:

$$D(c_1, c_2) = D(C_1, C_2) , \qquad (5)$$

where $D()$ is the distance between two-dimensional functions given in Eq. (1).

Proof: Let $c_1'(x, y)$ be the result of one-dimensional DFT on each of rows $c_1(., y)$ $(0 \leq y < h)$ in a two-dimensional function $c_1(x, y)$, and let $c_2'(x, y)$ be the result obtained with the same transform on $c_2(x, y)$. By Eq. (3), we get the following:

$$\forall y (0 \leq y < h), \ D(c_1(., y), c_2(., y)) = D(c_1'(., y), c_2'(., y)) .$$

Since the distance between the corresponding rows is unchanged before and after the DFT, the following holds for two-dimensional functions c_1 and c_2:

$$D(c_1, c_2) = D(c_1', c_2') . \qquad (6)$$

Let $C_1(x, y)$ be the result of one-dimensional DFT on each of columns $c_1'(x, .)$ $(0 \leq x < w)$ in a two-dimensional function $c_1'(x, y)$, and let $C_2(x, y)$ be the result obtained with the same transform on $c_2'(x, y)$. C_1 and C_2 are the result of two-dimensional DFT on c_1 and c_2, respectively. By Eq. (3), we get the following:

$$\forall x (0 \leq x < w), \ D(c_1'(x, .), c_2'(x, .)) = D(C_1(x, .), C_2(x, .)) .$$

Since the distance between the corresponding columns is unchanged before and after the DFT, the following holds for two-dimensional functions c_1' and c_2':

$$D(c_1', c_2') = D(C_1, C_2) . \qquad (7)$$

By combining Eq. (6) and (7), we get Eq. (5) shown above. □

Lemma 2. Let $C_1(x, y)$ and $C_2(x, y)$ be the result of two-dimensional DFT on two-dimensional functions $c_1(x, y)$ and $c_2(x, y)$, respectively. Let $C_1'(x, y)$ and $C_2'(x, y)$ be two-dimensional functions obtained by substituting all the elements in $C_1(x, y)$ and $C_2(x, y)$ with 0 except f elements whose absolute values are the largest among the entire elements. Then, we get the following equation:

$$D(c_1, c_2) \geq D(C_1', C_2') , \qquad (8)$$

where $D()$ is the distance between two-dimensional functions given in Eq. (1).

Proof: $D(C_1, C_2)$ can be expressed as the following according to Eq. (1):

$$D(C_1, C_2) = \sqrt{\sum_{0 \leq x < w} \sum_{0 \leq y < h} (C_1(x, y) - C_2(x, y))^2} .$$

Since $D(C_1', C_2')$ is the result of substituting $(wh - f)$ terms in square root above with 0 and every remaining term is positive, we get the following:

$$D(C_1, C_2) \geq D(C_1', C_2') . \qquad (9)$$

By combining Lemma 1 and Eq. (9), we get Eq. (8) shown above. □

The proposed algorithm performs the two-dimensional DFT on the template function $t(x, y)$ for each of characters to be recognized, and obtains $T'(x, y)$ by keeping only f elements that have the largest absolute values. The f element values are called *feature values* in this paper. The algorithm extracts f feature values from the same (x, y) positions in every template function. An f-dimensional feature vector is generated using the feature values and is stored in an f-dimensional index. The index storing the f-dimensional feature vectors is called the *template index* in this paper. Given a scanned character $c(x, y)$ as an input, the proposed algorithm performs the same transform with the templates on the character c. The algorithm transforms $c(x, y)$ into an f-dimensional feature vector C' and retrieves the template index using the feature vector C'. Although $D(c_1, c_2)$ is always larger than $D(C'_1, C'_2)$ according to Lemma 2, the ratio between them is not proportional. Hence, we perform the range search [11] on the template index. The threshold ϵ for the range search is obtained as follows:

$$\epsilon = \max\{D(C', T')\} , \tag{10}$$

where C' is the f-dimensional feature vector transformed from a character c, and T' from the template t of the same character c. Let T_C be the set of candidate templates returned by the range search on the template index. The proposed algorithm compares each of candidate templates one by one with the scanned character, and returns the template t ($\in T_C$) with the smallest distance from the scanned character, which satisfies the following equation:

$$t = \{t \mid \forall t_C \in T_C, \ D(t, c) \leq D(t_C, c)\} . \tag{11}$$

Since the proposed algorithm does not use any information on a specific language, it can be widely applied for any languages. For example, several Asian characters such as Korean, Chinese, and Japanese characters can be managed at the same time using only one template index. In such an application, since the number of characters managed by the algorithm can increase considerably, the distance between the closest template t and the second closest template t_2 might be very small and thus recognition result could be incorrect. For solving the problem, a template index of higher dimension should be constructed so that the inter-template distances should be enlarged. The proposed algorithm also supports multi-fonts of a language. For different fonts of the same character, the algorithm manages a separate template for each of the fonts, and stores all the templates for the same character in the same template index along with font information. If the documents to be recognized contain characters of only one font, a separate template index can be constructed for each of different fonts.

Since the algorithm proposed in this paper defines the similarity between a scanned character and a template as the Euclidean distance between two-dimensional bitmap functions as in Definition 1, the correctness of the algorithm is sensitive to displacement of the scanned character. Even when the scanned character is shifted from the template by a few pixels either horizontally or vertically, the distance between them can be largely increased, since the shapes of

Asian characters are complicated. The displacement can be caused by the noise generated while scanning, and may severely harm the correctness of character recognition. For solving the displacement problem, the proposed algorithm measures the distance between a scanned character and a template after aligning their *centers of mass* (or *centers of gravity*) [10]. The center of mass (x_C, y_C) of a character $c(x, y)$ can be computed using the following equation:

$$x_C = \frac{\sum_{0 \leq x < w} \left(x \cdot \sum_{0 \leq y < h} c(x, y) \right)}{\sum_{0 \leq x < w} \sum_{0 \leq y < h} c(x, y)} ,$$

$$y_C = \frac{\sum_{0 \leq y < h} \left(y \cdot \sum_{0 \leq x < w} c(x, y) \right)}{\sum_{0 \leq x < w} \sum_{0 \leq y < h} c(x, y)} . \tag{12}$$

In the rest of this section, we explain the method to improve the recognition speed of the proposed algorithm based on association rule technique [2]. In general, an association rule is represented in the form of '$A \Rightarrow B$,' where A and B are the sets of one or more objects or items. The meaning of an association rule $A \Rightarrow B$ is that, if the items in A appear in a transaction, the items in B are also likely to appear in the same transaction. In Market Basket Analysis, which is a representative application of association rule technique, if a customer purchases the items in A in a market such as Wal-Mart, it is highly probable that the customer also purchases the items in B at the same time. By adopting the technique in character recognition, if the character sequence in A is recognized, we can predict that the next character sequence would be B. Although association rule technique has no limitation on the number and order of items in A and B, we assume in this paper that there exists an order among n (≥ 1) characters in A, and that there is only one character in B. Hence, an association rule in this paper is represented as '$A \Rightarrow b$,' where b is a character.

There are two measures of interestingness for finding association rules $A \Rightarrow B$: *support* and *confidence*. The support is the percentage of the number of transactions containing $A \cup B$ divided by the number of the entire transactions; the confidence is the percentage of the number of transactions containing B divided by the number of the transactions containing A. In this paper, support and confidence are defined as follows. The support is defined as the percentage of the number of character sequences $A \cup b$ divided by the number of the entire character sequences of length $(n + 1)$ in a document. Any space and punctuations are ignored between characters. The confidence is the percentage of the number of character sequences that end with b divided by the number of character sequences that start with A. We deal with only the character sequences of length $(n + 1)$. In many cases, the confidence is set as $60 \sim 80\%$. The support and confidence in this paper can be represented as follows:

$$support(A \Rightarrow b) = P(A \cup b) ,$$
$$confidence(A \Rightarrow b) = P(b|A) . \tag{13}$$

The character recognition algorithm based on association rules consists of two phases as follows. In the first phase, after recognizing a scanned character b given as an input, if there exist association rules $A \Rightarrow b$ containing the character b in right hand side, the distance $d = D(t_b, b)$ computed using Eq. (1) is stored in the template index along with the template t_b for b. If a distance d' is already stored in the template index along with t_b, the larger one between d and d' replaces the existing distance in the template index. The first phase is performed on part of the documents to be recognized and the second phase is performed on the rest of the documents. In the second phase, if there exists an association rule $A \Rightarrow b$ where the character sequence A consists of n characters recognized most recently, we can predict the next character to recognize should be b. If there exists the template t_b for the character b in the set $\mathcal{T}_C$ of candidate templates t_C obtained by performing the range search on the template index, the template t_b becomes the first template to be compared with the scanned character c. If the distance $D(t_b, c)$ is less than or equal to the distance d stored in the template index along with the template t_b, we recognize the scanned character c as b. If there exists no such template t_b in $\mathcal{T}_C$ or the distance $D(t_b, c)$ is larger than d, the proposed algorithm compares c with every candidate template t_C in $\mathcal{T}_C$, and returns a template t satisfying Eq. (11). Since the proposed algorithm reduces the number of bitmap comparisons by skipping comparisons between the scanned character c and every candidate template t_C other than t_b in $\mathcal{T}_C$ based on association rules, it improves the speed of character recognition.

4   Performance Evaluation

In this section, we measure the execution time and recognition rate of the proposed algorithm while changing parameters such as search threshold ϵ and feature dimension f. The hardware platform for the experiments is a PC equipped with Intel Pentium 4 2.0GHz CPU, 1GB RAM, and 80GB hard disk, and the software platform is Microsoft Windows XP Service Pack 2. We used the R*-tree [3] as a multidimensional index for storing templates. We scanned Chapter One of 'The Lord of the Rings' Korean version, which contains more than 20,000 characters, as a document to be recognized.

In the first experiment, we executed the proposed algorithm for parameter combinations of thresholds $\epsilon = 10000, 20000, \dots, 80000$ and feature dimensions $f = 2, 4, 6,$ and 8, and measured execution time and recognition rate. Figure 2 shows the result of the first experiment. In Figures 2(a) and 2(b), the horizontal axis represents threshold ϵ, and the vertical axis execution time (in seconds) and recognition rate (%), respectively. As shown in Figure 2(a), since the size of the set $\mathcal{T}_C$ of candidate templates increases as ϵ increases, the execution time also increases. Since the distance between templates in the template index increases as f increases, the size of $\mathcal{T}_C$ is reduced for a fixed ϵ, and thus the execution time decreases. As shown in Figure 2(b), the recognition rate also increases as ϵ increases. The reason is that, when ϵ gets larger, it is more probable that the template corresponding to the scanned character is contained in $\mathcal{T}_C$. In the experiment, we obtained recognition rate of more than 90% with the threshold of higher than 50,000.

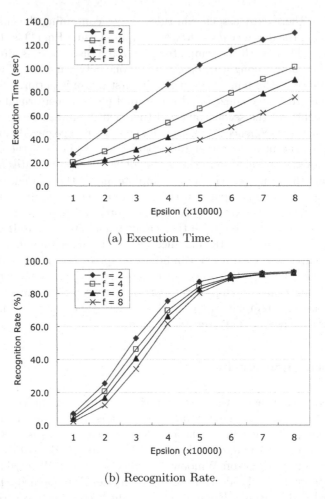

(a) Execution Time.

(b) Recognition Rate.

Fig. 2. Result of First Experiment: Comparison of Execution Time and Recognition Rate While Changing the Combination of Thresholds and Feature Dimensions

In the second experiment, we measured the ratio of improvement in recognition speed of the proposed algorithm based on association rules. As in the first experiment, we used the same parameter combinations of thresholds $\epsilon = 10000$, 20000, ... , 80000 and feature dimensions $f = 2, 4, 6$, and 8. The support and confidence for finding association rules were set as 0.1% and 60%, respectively. Figure 3 shows the result of the second experiment. In the figure, the horizontal axis represents threshold ϵ, and the vertical axis the improvement ratio (%). As shown in Figure 3, the improvement ratio increases as ϵ increases. The reason is that, since the size of the set $\mathcal{T}_C$ of candidate templates increases as ϵ increases, the number of candidate templates not to be checked based on association rules also increases. The improvement ratio based on association rules is closely related with recognition rate. If the character sequence A in an association rule

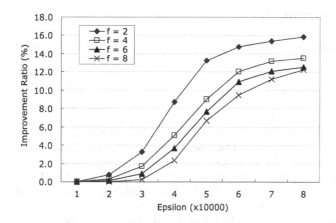

Fig. 3. Result of Second Experiment: Comparison of Execution Improvement Ratio While Changing the Combination of Thresholds and Feature Dimensions

$A \Rightarrow b$ cannot be correctly found due to low recognition rate, the association rule cannot be applied for improving the recognition speed. The reason that the improvement ratio goes higher than 10% even with much smaller support value 0.1% is that there are a large number of association rules satisfying the support. There was almost no change in recognition rate after applying association rules.

As the result of our experiments, the proposed algorithm recognized about 500 characters per second with recognition rate of more than 90%. We tried to compare the performance of the proposed algorithm with the commercial software for Asian character recognition such as Readiris Pro for Windows[3]. However, the recognition rate for Korean characters of the software was far below expectation. In the worst case, the recognition rate was less than even 10%. Thus, we concluded it was meaningless to compare the proposed algorithm with the commercial software.

5   Conclusions

In this paper, we proposed an algorithm for fast recognition of printed Asian characters based on the database methodologies. Since the number of Asian characters is very large and their shapes are complicated, Asian characters require much more recognition time than numeric and Roman characters. The proposed algorithm extracts feature from each of Asian characters through the DFT, and optimizes recognition speed by storing and retrieving the features in a multidimensional index. The recognition speed of the proposed algorithm is improved more based on association rule technique. The proposed algorithm has the advantage that it can be applied regardless of the language, size, and font of the characters to be recognized.

---

[3] http://www.irislink.com/

Acknowledgement

This Research was supported by the Sookmyung Women's University Research Grants 2006.

References

1. Agrawal, R., Faloutsos, C., Swami, A.N.: Efficient Similarity Search in Sequence Databases. In: Proc. Int'l Conf. on Foundations of Data Organization and Algorithms (FODO), Chicago, Illinois, pp. 69–84 (October 1993)
2. Agrawal, R., Imielinski, T., Swami, A.N.: Mining Association Rules between Sets of Items in Large Databases. In: Proc. Int'l Conf. on Management of Data, ACM SIGMOD, Washington, D.C. pp. 207–216 (May 1993)
3. Beckmann, N., Kriegel, H.-P., Schneider, R., Seeger, B.: The R*-Tree: An Efficient and Robust Access Method for Points and Rectangles. In: Proc. Int'l Conf. on Management of Data, ACM SIGMOD, pp. 322–331. Atlantic City, New Jersey (May 1990)
4. Belkasim, S.O., Shridhar, M., Ahmadi, M.: Pattern Recognition with Moment Invariants: a Comparative Study and New Results. Pattern Recognition 24(12), 1117–1138 (1991)
5. Berchtold, S., Keim, D.A., Kriegel, H.-P.: The X-tree: An Index Structure for High-Dimensional Data. In: Proc. Int'l Conf. on Very Large Data Bases (VLDB), Mumbai, India, pp. 28–39 (September 1996)
6. Bishop, C.M.: Neural Networks for Pattern Recognition. Oxford University Press, Oxford (1996)
7. Bunke, H., Wang, P.S.P.: Handbook of Character Recognition and Document Image Analysis, World Scientific Publishing Company (1997)
8. Cho, W., Lee, S.-W., Kim, J.H.: Modeling and Recognition of Cursive Words with Hidden Markov Models. Pattern Recognition 28(12), 1941–1953 (1995)
9. Google Book Search Library Project (2006) http://books.google.com/googleprint/library. html
10. Halliday, D., Resnick, R., Walker, J.: Fundamentals of Physics, 7th edn. Wiley, Chichester (2004)
11. Kamel, I., Faloutsos, C.: On Packing R-trees. In: Proc. Int'l Conf. on Information and Knowledge Management (CIKM), Washington, D.C. pp. 490–499 (November 1993)
12. KS C 5601-1992, Code for Information Interchange (in Korean) (1992)
13. Mori, S., Nishida, H., Yamada, H.: Optical Character Recognition. Wiley, Chichester (1999)
14. Natsev, A., Rastogi, R., Shim, K.: WALRUS: A Similarity Retrieval Algorithm for Image Databases. IEEE Trans. Knowledge & Data Engineering (TKDE) 16(3), 301–316 (2004)
15. Press, W.H., Flannery, B.P., Teukolsky, S.A., Vetterling, W.T.: Numerical Recipes in C: The Art of Scientific Computing, 2nd edn. Cambridge University Press, Cambridge (1992)
16. Sim, D.-G., Ham, Y.-K., Park, R.-H.: On-Line Recognition of Cursive Korean Characters Using DP Matching and Fuzzy Concept. Pattern Recognition 27(12), 1605–1620 (1994)

SPDBSW: A Service Prototype of SPDBS on the Web*

Tae-Sung Jung[1] and Wan-Sup Cho[2]

[1] Dept. of Information Industrial Engineering, Chungbuk National University, 361763
Cheongju, Chungbuk, Korea
mispro@chungbuk.ac.kr
[2] Dept. of Management Information Systems, Chungbuk National University, 361763
Cheongju, Chungbuk, Korea
wscho@chungbuk.ac.kr

Abstract. As the amount of pathway information for various organisms is
increasing very rapidly, performing various analyses on the full network of
pathways for even multiple organisms can be possible and therefore developing
an integrated database for storing and analyzing pathway information is
becoming a critical issue. Until now analyzing these networks is not easy
because of the nature of the existing pathway databases, which are often
heterogeneous, incomplete, and/or inconsistent. We presented a database
system called SPDBS to solve this problem. However, application-oriented
systems like SPDBS have some limitations on the extension and integration of
the heterogeneous databases.

In this paper, we extend previous SPDBS into a web service prototype
(SPDBSW) where all functions can be serviced on the web environment. The
web services include pathway database integration/search, import/export of
SBML documents, pathway reconstruction/visualization. SPDBSW has been
implemented by the combination SPDBS and external web services such as
OLS, KEGG and NCBI. And user can get more confidential and delicate
information from KEGG or NCBI through their web services. The system can
be extended or modified immediately by replacing its component web services.
We provide SPDBSW at the website *http://database.chungbuk.ac.kr/SPDBSW*.

1 Introduction

Biochemical pathways can be viewed as interconnected processes including an
intricate network of interactions between molecular compounds in the cell[1]. There
are three kinds of biochemical pathways: metabolic, regulatory, or signal transduction
pathways[1]. Metabolic pathways are responsible for carrying out the chemical
reactions that provide basic biological functions (DNA, RNA, protein synthesis and
degradation, energy metabolism, fatty acid synthesis, and many others). Regulatory
pathways are responsible for converting genetic information into proteins (gene
products). Signal transaction pathways are concerned with coordinating metabolic

* "This work was supported by the Korea Research Foundation Grant funded by the Korean
Government(MOEHRD)" (The Regional Research Universities Program/Chungbuk BIT
Research-Oriented University Consortium).

R. Cooper and J. Kennedy (Eds.): BNCOD 2007, LNCS 4587, pp. 49–57, 2007.
© Springer-Verlag Berlin Heidelberg 2007

processes with transcription and protein synthesis. Each of these pathways has been kept in a separate (independent) database with distinct attributes even though they are related each other.

Pathway databases contain data of biochemical pathways which consist of two kinds of information: biochemical components (e.g., substrates, enzymes, products) and their interactions [1]. Most existing pathway databases focus on specific types of pathways rather than an integrated one: e.g., Transpath[2] for protein-DNA interactions, KEGG for metabolic pathways, EcoCyc and MetaCyc[6] for E. coli and other organisms' metabolic pathways, BIND[2] for signal transduction pathways, PathFinder[3], WIT[8], PathMAPA[9], BioJAKE[11], and MPW[12] for metabolic pathways. Pathway databases raise many important and challenging computational and bioinformatics issues, such as querying, navigation, and visualization of the pathways; seamless integration/analysis of the heterogeneous pathway data distributed in diverse sources.

We proposed the SPDBS [14] (SBML-based Biochemical Pathway Database System: *http://database.chungbuk.ac.kr/SPDBS/*) for the integration and management of heterogeneous biochemical pathways. *Systems Biology Markup Language (SBML)* is an XML-based language for describing simulations in systems biology. The language is oriented towards representing biochemical networks common in research on a number of topics, including: cell signaling pathways, metabolic pathways, biochemical reactions, gene regulation, and many others[4]. We developed an object database for implementing SBML data model[4]. SPDBS provides dynamic pathway reconstruction or estimation by using an orthologous database[7] for a genome sequence data. However, it is impossible to integrate all of databases in the internet and there are some limitations in the maintainability and extensibility.

Web services provide a standard means of interoperating between different software applications, running on a variety of platforms and/or frameworks [18]. Web services are characterized by their great interoperability and extensibility, as well as their machine-processable descriptions thanks to the use of XML [18]. They can be combined in a loosely coupled way in order to achieve complex operations [18]. Programs providing simple services can interact with each other in order to deliver sophisticated added-value services [18]. For example, Google, a popular Internet search engine, provides the web service called the Google Web API. The service enables users to develop software that accesses and manipulates a massive amount of web documents that are constantly refreshed. In the field of genome research, a similar kind of web service called DAS [17] (distributed annotation system) has been used on several web sites, including Ensembl, Wormbase, Flybase, SGD and TIGR [17]. And some of the conventional systems such as KEGG, NCBI and GeneCruiser are providing the web service already.

In this paper, we propose a service prototype (SPDBSW) which integrates the functions of SPDBS and external systems such as KEGG and NCBI by using web services. Many well-known bioinformatics databases, such as OLS (Ontology Lookup Service) [10], KEGG, NCBI, EMBL, and DDBJ, provide web services to the users. SPDBSW provides the functions of SPDBS on the web and other functions of external web services. At the result, it allows to integrate data from external database such as KEGG, MetaCyc using SBML with semantic lookup service of OLS, reconstruction of metabolic pathway for protein sequences and visualization of the result pathway on the web. In addition, it provides the retrieval service from KEGG and NCBI on the same environment. The proposed system is more flexible in the extensibility. In other words, SPDBSW can be integrated with another web services. Also, SPDBSW provides more interactive and refreshness user interface which was involved Ajax development method.

The paper is organized as follows. In Section 2, we present related work. In Section 3, we describe the service architecture of the SPDBSW. In Section 4, we present the special features of SPDBSW in detail. In Section 5, we conclude our paper.

2 Related Work

In this section, we discuss technical environments in developing SPDBSW. We first describe Ajax, web service, and SPDBS in detail. We then introduce external web services such as KEGG, NCBI, and GeneCruiser which are invoked in the SPDBSW.

2.1 Ajax and Web Service [5,16]

The traditional web application works as follows [5]: Most user actions in the interface trigger an HTTP request back to a web server. The web server does some processing such as retrieving data, talking to various legacy systems and then returns an HTML page to the user-side. This approach makes a lot of technical sense, but it doesn't make for a great user experience [5]. While the server is doing some things, users have to wait. And the users have to wait some more at every step in a task. Figure 1 show the difference of the traditional web application mode and the Ajax model[5].

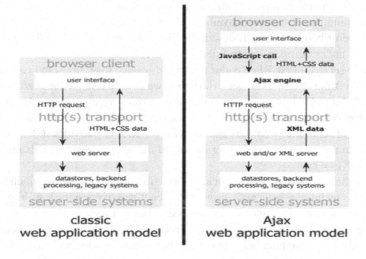

Fig. 1. Comparison of classic web application model and the Ajax model [5]

But with Ajax, instead of loading a webpage the browser loads an Ajax engine at the start of the session. This Ajax engine is responsible for both rendering the user interface and communicating with the web server. The Ajax engine allows the user's interaction with the application asynchronously; communicate with the web server independently. So the user is never waiting around for the server to do something.

And web service technique is a base technique for SOA(Service-Oriented Architecture)[16]. SOA is an integrated software infrastructure and design approach to the development and integration of service-oriented applications. The concept of service orientation has been around for some time, based on the use of earlier forms of technology, such as message-oriented middleware (MOM), CORBA, and more recently, integration platform solutions. The most significant new enabler of SOA is the maturation of Web services standards that provide another, more flexible and open way of implementing service-oriented applications [16].

2.2 SPDBS (SBML-Based Biochemical Pathway Database System)[14]

SPDBS is an integrated biochemical pathway analysis system developed by Chungbuk National University. SPDBS consists of several databases and tools. The databases include a sequence database for 88 species, an orthologos database extracted from KO[7], a biochemical pathway database (which contains about 13,000 pathways information from KEGG), and the ontology database from GO (Gene Ontology). In addition, SPDBS includes a pathway reconstruction system (PRS), an SBML management system(SMS)[13], and a visualization system.

2.3 External Web Services: OLS, KEGG, NCBI and GeneCruiser

The OLS (Ontology Lookup Service: http://www.ebi.ac.uk/ontology-lookup/) was developed for the integration of available biomedical ontologies into a single database and a programmatic interface is available to query the webservice using SOAP. The service is described by a WSDL descriptor file available online. All OLS source code is available under the open source Apache Licence.

The web service of NCBI provides a retrieval service for Entrez, and can download information from NCBI web site (http://www.ncbi.nlm.nih.gov/entrez/query/static/esoap_help.htm). E-Utilities is one of the web services which provides 15 methods to search from many databases. And user can get some data from all of KEGG's databases through the web service of KEGG. KEGG provides 60 web service methods to the users. Figure 2 shows a part of the web service methods provided by NCBI and KEGG.

One of the representative biological information analysis systems which based on web service technique is GeneCruiser [15]. GeneCruiser provides a web application and a web service for microarray analysis. GeneCruiser is freely available in http://genecruiser.org. GeneCruiser is a system allowing users to annotate their genomic data by mapping microarray feature identifiers to gene identifiers from databases, such as UniGene, while providing links to web resources [15].

ⓘ KEGGPortType		
❋ list_databases		
▷] Input		
◁] Output	☞ return	🖭 ArrayOfDefinition
❋ list_organisms		
▷] Input		
◁] Output	☞ return	🖭 ArrayOfDefinition
❋ list_pathways		
▷] Input	☞ org	▣ string
◁] Output	☞ return	🖭 ArrayOfDefinition
❋ list_ko_classes		
▷] Input	☞ class_id	▣ string
◁] Output	☞ return	🖭 ArrayOfDefinition

ⓘ eUtilsServiceSoap		
❋ run_eGquery		
▷] Input	☞ parameters	⒠ eGqueryRequest
◁] Output	☞ parameters	⒠ Result
❋ run_eGquery_MS		
▷] Input	☞ parameters	⒠ eGqueryRequestMS
◁] Output	☞ parameters	⒠ ResultMS
❋ run_eInfo		
▷] Input	☞ parameters	⒠ eInfoRequest
◁] Output	☞ parameters	⒠ eInfoResult
❋ run_eInfo_MS		
▷] Input	☞ parameters	⒠ eInfoRequestMS
◁] Output	☞ parameters	⒠ eInfoResultMS

(a) Methods of KEGG web service   (b) Methods of NCBI web service

Fig. 2. A part of the web service methods from NCBI and KEGG

3   SPDBSW: SPDBS on the Web

In this section, we will describe the service architecture and prototype of SPDBSW. Figure 3 show the service architecture of SPDBSW. As shown in the figure, SPDBS is the core module for the web service. Several functions of SPDBS have been

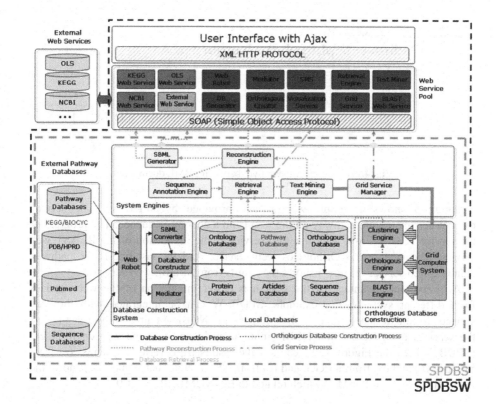

Fig. 3. Architecture of SPDBSW

published as web service. The web service pool contains the external web service such as KEGG and NCBI. In SPDBSW, various biological information analysis processes can be done by the combination of the internal or external web services.

We constructed a local pathway database from KEGG database [5] and the MetaCyc [6] database. But these databases may use different terminology (i.e., synonym) for the same information. Figure 4 shows two terminologies in the different SBML documents. These synonym terminologies should be converted into the standardized ones according to the gene ontology before the database construction and querying to database. Without this process, the result database may have severe duplication, which brings data inconsistency. To solve this problem, we use the gene ontology database from GO consortium. An important problem in using GO database is refreshment problem. Since all modified ontologies of GO are updated weekly, we should update our gene ontology database synchronously. Web service of OLS solves this refreshment problem. In SPDBSW, OLS web service has been adopted for the ontology refreshment.

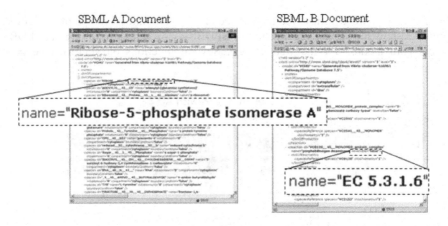

Fig. 4. An example of synonym between SBML documents

Figure 5 shows a sample web service provided by SPDBSW. The service reconstructs metabolic pathway on the web from a genome sequence. The progress of the service is as follows. The first web service is the invocation of the BLAST web service. The next one is Orthologos web service. And the last one is the pathway database web service. Figure 5 shows the results from SPDBS web service.

An important advantage of the system is easier integration of the web services from different systems. For example, SPDBSW can be integrated with the web services from external systems such as KEGG and NCBI. As a result, user can utilize the services from KEGG and NCBI simultaneously on the same web environment (SPDBSW). In the Figure 3, we can see the results from various systems: (a) from SPDBS, (b) and (d) from KEGG, and (c) from NCBI. Note that Figure 3(c) shows the list of article's ID of PubMed which related to EC-NUMBER '5.3.1.9'.

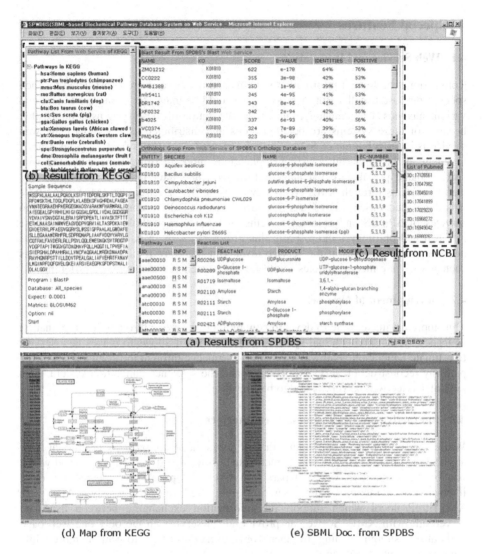

(d) Map from KEGG   (e) SBML Doc. from SPDBS

Fig. 5. A integrated service prototype using Web services

However, a fundamental problem of web based user interfaces is the slow response time when some item on a page has to be updated. Usually, the whole page needs to be reloaded. To solve this problem we involved the Ajax which recently developed web development method [8]. Ajax allows transferring data between the client side and server side asynchronously in the background using XMLHttpProtocol. For example, the service of pathway reconstruction needs several processes. These processes take about 5~10 seconds in usually. In worst case, it may take about 1 minute. In this condition, SPDBSW users can enjoy other services such as retrieval service, SBML service, and visualization service while progressing pathway reconstruction.

4 Special Features

4.1 Web Service and Integration

Conventional biological information systems and databases were constructed by each specific purpose usually. But these systems should be integrate for more efficient and various analysis. Unfortunately, physically integration of these systems is impossible because of these systems are heterogeneous and distributed as we know. The web service is base technique of SOA (Service Oriented Architecture). It provides a basis to integrate the numerous existing applications more flexibly. Especially, the web service make possible to exchange information and data integration between the variety systems through XML (Web service using SOAP based on XML). SPDBSW was developed based on web service technique. SPDBSW consists of several web services of SPDBS and external systems such as blast, orthologs search, database retrieval and ontology lookup. From this prototype, we can integrate heterogeneous and distributed systems at the service level. But there are reminded some problems such as semantic inconsistencies, syntactic inconsistencies and language differences.

4.2 Development of New Service

This approach makes able to develop new biological service through the combination of legacy system and external systems. For example, it allows to makes new service to estimate a metabolic pathway for FASTA sequence through the combination of the pathway reconstruction service in SPDBS and the sequence annotation system. This kind of service will be very useful to biologists.

4.3 Interactive and Refreshness User Interface

While the server is doing some things, users have to wait in traditional web applications. But, SPDBSW was implemented using Ajax development method which one of the method in web 2.0 paradigm. Web 2.0 paradigm appeared for more interactive interaction with user on the web asynchronously. Ajax use XMLHttpProtocol which support the information exchanging between user and server-side with XML. So we can provide all of service on the only one web page without refreshing/reloading. In other words, users don't have to wait anymore while the server doing something.

5 Conclusions and Future Work

Web services describes a standardized way of integrating Web-based applications using the XML, SOAP, WSDL and UDDI open standards over an Internet protocol backbone. Web services allow organizations to communicate data without intimate knowledge of each other's IT systems behind the firewall. Because of this level of application integration (service level integration), Web services have grown in popularity and are beginning to improve business processes.

SPDBSW has been devised for the integration of numerous biological information systems at the service level. The system integrates not only the service functions of

SPDBS but also those of external systems such as KEGG and NCBI. Of course, the system adds or replaces new services without modification of the current system. SPDBWS shows service results from several systems on a web page by using Ajax and web services. We ensure that SPDBSW will become a basis to develop a new biological information analysis service.

In the future, we will develop complex biological business processes using the web services provided by the local or global systems. BPM and SOA will be the core technology for the development of the biological business process management.

References

[1] Deville, Y., et al.: An overview of data models for the analysis of biochemical pathways. Briefings in Bioinformatics 4(3), 246–259 (2003)
[2] Schacherer, F., et al.: The TRANSPATH signal transduction database: a knowledge base on signal transduction networks. Bioinformatics 17(11), 1053–1057 (2001)
[3] Goesmann, A., et al.: PathFinder: reconstruction and dynamic visualization of metabolic pathways. Bioinformatics 18, 124–129 (2002)
[4] Hucka, M., et al.: The Systems Biology Markup Language (SBML): A Medium for Representation and Exchange of Biochemical Network Models. Bioinformatics 19(4), 524–531 (2003)
[5] Garrett, J. J.: AJAX: A new approach to web applications (February 18, 2005) http://www.adaptivepath.com/publications/essays/archives/000385.php
[6] Karp, P.D., et al.: The MetaCyc database. Nucleic Acids Res. 30, 59–61 (2000)
[7] Oh, J.S., et al.: Othologous Group Clustering System based on the Grid Computing. In: Proc. of the International Joint Conference on InCoB, AASBi, and KSBI (BioInfo 2005), pp. 72–77 (2005)
[8] Overbeek, R., et al.: WIT: integrated system for high throughput genome sequence analysis and metabolic reconstruction. Nucleic Acids Res. 28, 123–125 (2000)
[9] Pan, D., et al.: PathMAPA: a tool for displaying gene expression and performing statistical tests on metabolic pathways at multiple levels for Arabidopsis. BMC Bioinformatics 4, 56 (2003)
[10] Cote, R.G., et al.: The Ontology Lookup Service, a lightweight cross-platform tool for controlled vocabulary queries. BMC Bioinformatics, 7(97) (2006)
[11] Salamonsen, W., et al.: BioJAKE: a tool for the creation, visualization and manipulation of metabolic pathways. In: Proc. Pac. Symp. Biocomput. pp. 392–400 (1999)
[12] Selkov, E., et al.: MPW: the Metabolic Pathways Database. Nucleic Acids Res. 43–45
[13] Jung, S.-H., Jung, T.-S., et al.: An Efficient Storage Model for the SBML Documents Using Object Databases. In: Dalkilic, M.M., Kim, S., Yang, J. (eds.) VDMB 2006. LNCS (LNBI), vol. 4316, pp. 94–105. Springer, Heidelberg (2006)
[14] Jung, T.-S., et al.: SPDBS: An SBML based Biochemical Pathway Database Systems. In: Huang, D.-S., Li, K., Irwin, G.W. (eds.) ICIC 2006. LNCS (LNBI), vol. 4115, pp. 543–550. Springer, Heidelberg (2006)
[15] Liefeld, T., et al.: GeneCruiser: a web service for the annotation of microarray data. Bioinformatics 21(18), 3681–3682 (2005)
[16] Vollmer, K., et al.: Integratio. In: A Service-Oriented World. Forrester Research (2004)
[17] DAS: The Distributed Annotation System, http://biodas.org/
[18] Web service. http://www.w3.org/2002/ws/Activity

Indexing and Searching XML Documents Based on Content and Structure Synopses

Weimin He, Leonidas Fegaras, and David Levine

University of Texas at Arlington, CSE
Arlington, TX 76019-0015
{weiminhe,fegaras,levine}@cse.uta.edu

Abstract. We present a novel framework for indexing and searching schema-less XML documents based on concise summaries of their structural and textual content. Our search query language is XPath extended with full-text search. We introduce two novel data synopsis structures that correlate textual with positional information in an XML document and improves query precision. In addition, we present a two-phase containment filtering algorithm based on these synopses that improves the searching process. Our experimental evaluation shows that our data synopses indexing scheme outperforms the standard XML indexing scheme based on inverted lists; the query evaluation based on our data synopses is more accurate than related approximate approaches that do not consider positional information; our two-phase containment filtering algorithm is more efficient than a single-phase brute force algorithm.

1 Introduction

As XML has become the *de facto* form for representing and exchanging data, there is an increasing interest in indexing and searching text-centric XML documents. Recently, XML query languages, such as XPath and XQuery, have been extended with full-text search capabilities. These queries are potentially more precise than simple IR-style keyword-based queries, not only because each search keyword can be associated with a structural context, which is typically the path to reach the keyword in a document, but structural constraints can also be used to specify the structural relationship between multiple search keywords.

Consider, for example, the running query Q used throughout the paper:

```
//auction//item[location ~ "Dallas"]
   [description ~ "mountain" and "bicycle"]/price
```

against a pool of indexed XML documents. It searches for the prices of all auction items located in Dallas that contain the words "mountain" and "bicycle" in their description. When searching for documents that satisfy this query, we do not want to waste any time by considering those that do not match the structural constraints of the query or those that do not contain the search keywords at relative positions as specified by the structural relationships in the query. For

R. Cooper and J. Kennedy (Eds.): BNCOD 2007, LNCS 4587, pp. 58–69, 2007.
© Springer-Verlag Berlin Heidelberg 2007

example, we do not want to consider a document that, although has items located in Dallas, none of these items has both "mountain" and "bicycle" in their descriptions, even though there may be other items in this document, which are not located in Dallas but have both "mountain" and "bicycle" in their titles.

Current XML indexing techniques, such as [6], combine structure indexes and inverted lists extracted from XML documents to fully evaluate a full-text query against these indexes and return the actual XML fragments that answer the query. This is accomplished by performing containment joins over the sorted inverted lists derived from the element and keyword indexes. Since all elements and keywords have to be indexed, such indexing schemes may consume a considerable amount of disk space and may be time-consuming to build. More importantly, the query evaluation based on these indexes may involve many joins against very long inverted lists that may consider many irrelevant documents at the early stages. Although many sophisticated techniques have been proposed to improve these joins by skipping the irrelevant parts of these lists, it is still an open research problem to make them effective for a large document pool.

In this paper, we present a new framework for indexing and searching schemaless XML documents based on condensed summaries extracted from the structural and textual content of the documents. Instead of indexing each single element or term in a document, we extract a structural summary and a small number of data synopses from the document, which are indexed in a way suitable for query evaluation. The result of a query evaluation is a list of document locations that best match the query. A document location includes meta information about the document, such as the document URL, structural summary, and description. Based on the retrieved meta information, the client can choose some of the returned document locations and request a full evaluation of the query over the chosen documents using any existing XML query engine and return the XML fragments as query answers. To find all indexed documents that match the structural relationships in a query, the *query footprint* is extracted from the query and is converted into a pipelined plan to be evaluated against the indexed structural summaries. The resulting document locations that match the query footprint are further filtered out using the data synopses associated with the search predicates in the query and returned to the client.

2   Related Work

There is an increasing interest in recent years for full-text search over XML documents. Khalifa *et al* [1] propose a bulk algebra called TIX, which integrates simple IR scoring schemes into a traditional pipelined query evaluator for an XML database. TeXQuery [2] supports a powerful set of fully composable full-text search primitives, which can be seamlessly integrated into the XQuery language. In [3], the authors present a framework that relaxes a full-text XPath query by dropping some predicates from its closure and scoring the approximate answers using predicate penalties. XRank [5] extends Google-like keyword search to XML. The authors propose an algorithm for scoring XML elements that takes into account both hyperlink and containment edges. A recent work, XK-Search [7], introduces the concept of *smallest lowest common ancestors* (SLCAs) and proposes two efficient algorithms, Indexed Lookup Eager and Scan Eager, for keyword search in XML documents according to the SLCA semantics. However, all these proposals consider fully indexing and querying XML documents, which may involve costly containment joins among long inverted lists to evaluate a full-text XML query.

3   Query Language and Meta-data Indexing

Our query language is XPath extended with a full-text search predicate $e \sim S$, where e is an XPath expression. This predicate returns true if at least one element from the sequence returned by e matches the *search specification*, S. A search specification is a simple IR-style boolean keyword search that takes the form

$$\text{"term"} \mid S_1 \underline{\text{ and }} S_2 \mid S_1 \underline{\text{ or }} S_2 \mid (S)$$

where S, S_1, and S_2 are search specifications. A term is an indexed term that must be present in the text of an element returned by the expression e.

As an XML document is indexed, all essential meta-data are extracted from the document. In particular, three kinds of meta-data are indexed: *Structural Summary (SS)*, *Content Synopses (CS)*, and *Positional Filters (PF)*.

3.1   Structural Summary

A structural summary is a tree that describes the structural make-up of the XML data in a document. It concisely captures all unique paths in an XML document. For example, the structural summary of an XML document related to auctions is shown in Figure 1(a). Each node in an SS has a tagname and Id and one SS node may be associated with many elements in the actual document.

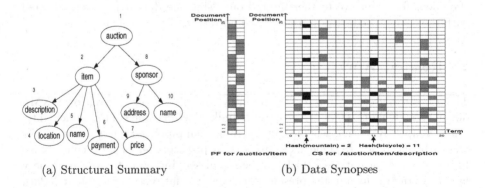

(a) Structural Summary   (b) Data Synopses

Fig. 1. Structural Summary & Data Synopses Examples

3.2 Content Synopses

A node in a structural summary is called a text node if the node contains text in the document. To capture the textual content of a document, for each text node k in the structural summary S of the document D, we construct a *content synopsis* (CS) H_p^D to summarize the textual data associated with k, where the path p is the unique simple path from the root of S to the node k in S. H_p^D is a bit matrix of size $L \times W$, where W is the number of term buckets and L is the document positional ranges of the elements that directly contain terms associated with node k. The positional information is represented by the document order of the begin/end tags of the elements. More specifically, for each term t contained directly in an element associated with k, whose begin/end position is b/e, we set all matrix values $H_p^D[i, \text{hash}(t) \bmod W]$ to one, for all $\lfloor b \times L/|D| \rfloor \le i \le \lfloor e \times L/|D| \rfloor$, where 'hash' is a string hashing function and $|D|$ is the document size. That is, the $[0, |D|]$ range of tag positions in the document is compressed into the range $[0, L]$. H_p^D is implemented as a B-tree index with index key p because during the query processing, we need to retrieve the content synopses of all documents for a given path p. For example, the content synopsis for SS node **description** is illustrated on the right in Figure 1(b). Each dark cell represents a bit set to one. As we can see, after the term "bicycle" is hashed to the term bucket 11, we obtain a bit vector that has 4 one-bit ranges (displayed with black color). Each one-bit range represents a **description** element that directly contains "bicycle" in the document. The start/end of a range corresponds to the document order of begin/end tag of a **description** element. Since a node in a structural summary may correspond to many elements in a document, the positional dimension is very useful information when evaluating search predicates in a query. In our running query example, both "mountain" and "bicycle" have to be in the same description element in a document to satisfy the query Q. If we had used one-dimensional Bloom filters [4], to check whether the bits for both terms are on, we may have gotten a prohibitive number of false positives. For instance, Q may have returned an unqualified document that has an item whose description contains "mountain", and another item whose description contains "bicycle". As such, term positional information is crucial in increasing the search precision. With our content synopses, we can evaluate the search predicate description $\sim$ "mountain" and "bicycle" by bitwise *anding* the vectors $H_3[\text{"mountain"}]$ and $H_3[\text{"bicycle"}]$, which are the two black-bit vectors extracted from the content synopsis in Figure 1(b). If all bits in the resulting bit vector are zeros, the corresponding document does not have both terms in the same **description** element and thus does not satisfy the search predicate.

3.3 Positional Filters

Although the positional information in CS enforces the constraint that the terms in a single search predicate must be in the same element associated with the predicate, it can not ensure that different elements associated with different search predicates are contained in the same element in a document. For example, given the relevant bit vectors $H_3[\text{"mountain"}]$, $H_3[\text{"bicycle"}]$, and $H_4[\text{"Dallas"}]$ only, we can not enforce the containment constraint in Q that the item whose location contains "Dallas" must be the same item whose description contains "mountain" and "bicycle". To address this problem, for each non-text node n in the structural summary of a document, we construct another type of data synopsis, called *Positional Filter* (PF), denoted by F_p^D. As we did for H_p^D, F_p^D is also implemented as a B-tree with index key p. F_p^D is a bit matrix of size $L \times M$, where L is the document positional ranges of the elements associated with node n that is reachable by the label path p, and M is the number of bit vectors in F_p^D. Here, the value of M should be no less than 2 because we want to map consecutive elements in a document to different bit vectors, thus reducing the bit overlaps of consecutive elements when their mapped begin/end ranges intersect. The positional filter for SS node **item** is demonstrated on the left in Figure 1(b). The 7 one-bit ranges indicate there are 7 **item** elements in the document.

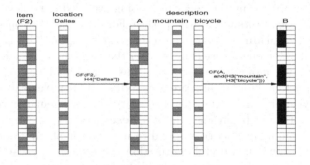

Fig. 2. Testing query Q Using Data Synopses

3.4   Containment Filtering

With positional filters, we can enforce the element containment constraints in the query using an operation called *Containment Filtering*. Let F be a positional filter of size $L \times M$ and V be a bit vector extracted from a content synopsis whose size is $L \times W$. The *Containment Filtering* $CF(F, V)$ returns a new positional filter F'. The bit $F'[i, m]$ is on iff:

$$\exists k \in [0, L] : V[k] = 1 \ \land \ \forall j \in [i, k] : F[j, m] = 1$$

Basically, the *Containment Filtering* copies a continuous range of one-bits from F to F' if there is at least one position within this range in which the corresponding bit in V is one. Figure 2 shows how the data synopses are used to determine whether a document is likely to satisfy the query Q (here $M = 2$). First, we do a containment filtering between the initial positional filter F_2 and the bit vector $H_4[\text{"Dallas"}]$. In the resulting positional filter A, only 5 one-bit ranges out of 7 in $F2$ are left. Counting from bottom to top, the $2nd$ and $4th$ one-bit ranges in $F2$ are discarded in A because there is no any one-bit range in H_4["Dallas"] that intersects with the $2nd$ or $4th$ range, which means that neither the $2nd$ nor $4th$ **item** element contains a **location** element that contains the term "Dallas". Similarly, we can do containment filtering between A and the resulting bit vector derived from the bitwise *anding* between H_3["mountain"] and H_3["bicycle"]. The 3 one-bit ranges in B indicate that 3 **items** out of 7 in F_2 satisfy all element containment constraints in the query. Thus, the document is considered to satisfy the query.

4   Query Processing

In this section, we briefly present the query processing in our framework. The first step in evaluating a full-text XPath query is deriving a query footprint from the query. A query footprint captures the essential structural components and all the *entry points* associated with the search predicates. In our running example, the query footprint of Q is:

```
//auction//item:1[location:2][description:3]/price
```

The numbers 1, 2, and 3 are the numbers of the entry points in the query footprint that indicate the places where data synopses are needed for query evaluation (one positional filter for the label path associated with entry point 1 and two content synopses for the label paths associated with the entry points 2 and 3). We have developed a general footprint derivation algorithm but, due to the space limitation, the algorithm is not presented in the paper.

Our numbering scheme, which is similar to that in [8], encodes each node k in a structural summary S by the triple (b, e, l), where b/e is the begin/end numbering of k and l is the level of k in S. Structural summaries are indexed as the mapping: $\mathcal{M}_{ss} : tag \to \{(S, k, b, e, l)\}$, where tag is the tagname of the node k in S, and b,e,l are as defined above. Thus, the key operation in the structural summary matching is a structural join between two tuple streams corresponding to two consecutive location steps in the query footprint. We leverage the iterator model in relational databases to form a pipeline of iterators derived from the query footprint to retrieve all matching structural summaries.

Let QF be the structural footprint of a query. The structural summary matching is accomplished by the function $\mathcal{SP}[\![QF]\!]$ that returns a set of tuples (ρ, S, k, b, e, l), where (S, k, b, e, l) is similar to that of $\mathcal{M}_{ss}$ and ρ is a vector of node numbers, such that $\rho[i]$ gives the node number in S corresponding to the ith entry point in QF. The function $\mathcal{SP}[\![QF]\!]$ is defined recursively based on the syntax of QF, generating structural joins for each XPath step. From the node numbers in ρ, we can derive the label paths from the structural summary that match the entry points in QF. In our running example, the label paths are `/auction/item`, `/auction/item/location`, and `/auction/item/description`. Based on the retrieved label paths, documents that have data synopses associated with these label paths are retrieved and filtered using the containment filtering, and qualified documents are filtered out and returned to the client.

5   Hash-Based Query Optimization

Using paths only as keys for data synopses indexing is not efficient because a popular path may be contained in a large number of documents and thus is associated with a large number of data synopses in the indexes. These retrieved long data synopsis lists may lead to an expensive join operation between two large lists at each step of the containment filtering. Based on the above observations, we refine our indexing scheme for data synopses and propose a hash-based two-phase containment filtering algorithm to improve query processing.

In order to reduce the number of content synopses and positional filters retrieved from the local indexes for a full label path during the containment filtering, as a document D is indexed, instead of using a full label path p as the key, we employ (p, hc) as the key to store a content synopsis H_p^D or a positional filter F_p^D, where p is the full label path associated with H_p^D or F_p^D, and hc is an integer value, which is the hash code of the document ID when mapped to a bit vector, called the *Document Mapping Vector (DMV)*. Basically, a *DMV* groups all the documents containing path p by the hash value of their document ID. Combined with another data structure called *Document Synopsis*, the above indexing scheme can reduce the number of data synopses retrieved for the path p during the containment filtering.

5.1   Document Synopses

In the first phase of the containment filtering, the goal is to quickly identify the documents that may contain all the path-term pairs derived from the structural summary matching and prune unqualified documents that contain only partial path-term pairs. This information derived from the first phase will guide the actual containment filtering in the second phase. To summarize, for all the documents that contain a path-term pair in the corpus, we construct a data structure called *Document Synopsis*, denoted by DS_p. Basically, for each text label path p, a document synopsis is a bit matrix of size $DL \times DW$, where DW is the number of term buckets and DL is the size of the hash table(DMV) for the document ID mapping. As a document containing the path-term pair (p, t) is indexed, p is first used as the key to find the corresponding DS_p in the indexes. Then, the term t is mapped to some bucket along the **Term** axis of DS_p to obtain the bit vector V along the **Document ID** axis, that summarizes all the documents containing (p, t). Finally, the ID of the document is mapped to some bit in V and the bit is set to one if it is zero.

The structure of a document synopsis is shown in Figure 3. The dark cells represent the one-bits. Suppose that the document synopsis is associated with the path /biblio/book/paragraph, since document 12 contains the path-term pair (/biblio/book/paragraph, "XML"), the corresponding bit is set to one, which is emphasized by a black cell in the figure. Note that different documents may be mapped to the same document ID slot and different terms may be hashed to the same term bucket.

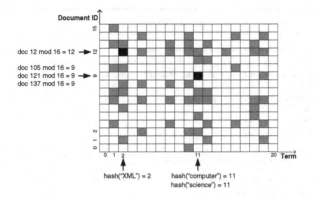

Fig. 3. A Document Synopsis Example

5.2 Two-Phase Containment Filtering

Based on the new indexing scheme and document synopses, we propose a two-phase containment filtering strategy to optimize our query processing, which is given in Algorithm 1. The first phase is a pre-processing stage that prunes unqualified documents that do not contain all the path-term pairs. The resulting bit vector V_f is a filter that carries information about all the documents that may contain all the path-term pairs $(p_1, t_1), (p_2, t_2), ..., (p_n, t_n)$, which is indicated by the one-bits in V_f. In the second phase, the real containment filtering is carried out with the guide of V_f. Basically, at each step of the containment filtering, (p_i, hc_i) is used as the key to retrieve all content synopsis hits or positional filter hits, where p_i is the corresponding path derived from SS matching, and hc_i is the index number of the one-bit in V_f. The goal is using V_f to avoid accessing unqualified data synopses and retrieve only the data synopses of the documents that contain all the path-term pairs, thus effectively reducing the number of data synopses retrieved from the indexes before the join operation.

6 Experimental Evaluation

We have implemented our framework using Java (J2SE 5.0) and Berkeley DB Java Edition 1.7.1 was employed as the storage manager. Our experiments were conducted on a WindowsXP machine with 2.8GHz CPU and 512M memory. The two datasets we used were synthetically generated from the XBench [10] and XMark benchmarks. The main characteristics of our datasets and data synopses size are summarized in Table 1. The query workload over each dataset is shown in Table 2. For the indexing scheme comparison experiment, we chose XBench as the dataset because the dataset size is the key factor for this experiment. To measure the query precision and our optimization algorithm, we chose XMark as the dataset because the number of documents is the key factor for these two experiments.

Algorithm 1: Two-phase Containment Filtering

Input: p_0 /* the path associated with positional filter */
$\quad\quad\quad$ (p_1,t_1), (p_2,t_2), ... , (p_n,t_n) /* n path-term pairs associated with content synopses */
Output: L_{PF} /* the list of positional filter hits of qualified documents */
1: $L_{PF} := emptyList$;
2: /* Obtain the filtering vector V_f in phase one */
3: **for** i = 1 to n **do**
4: $\quad$ Use p_i as the key to retrieve DS_{p_i} in local indexes;
5: $\quad$ Map t_i along the Term axis in DS_{p_i} to obtain the bit vector $V_{p_i}^{t_i}$;
6: **end for;**
7: $V_f := \bigcap_{i=1}^{n} V_{p_i}^{t_i}$;   /* bitwise anding all bit vectors */
8: /* Do actual containment filtering with the guide of V_f in phase two */
9: **for** each one-bit b_j in V_f **do**
10: $\quad$ k : = the index number of b_j in V_f;
11: $\quad$ $L_0^{b_j} :=$ the positional filter list retrieved using (p_0,k) as the key;
12: $\quad$ **for** i = 1 to n **do**
13: $\quad\quad$ $L_i^{b_j} :=$ the positional filter list retrieved using (p_i,k) as the key;
14: $\quad\quad$ $L_0^{b_j} := CF(L_0^{b_j},L_i^{b_j})$;
15: $\quad$ **end for;**
16: $\quad$ $L_{PF} := L_{PF} \cup L_0^{b_j}$;
17: **end for;**
18: **return** L_{PF};

Table 1. Data Set Characteristics and Data Synopses Size

Data Set	Data Size (MB)	Files	Avg. File Size (KB)	Avg. SS Size (Byte)	Avg. CS Size (Byte)	Avg. PF Size (Byte)
XBench	1050	2666	394	432	20564	178
XMark	55.8	11500	5	417	306	16

6.1   Indexing Scheme Comparison

To demonstrate the efficiency of our Data Synopses Indexing (DSI) scheme, we implemented the standard inverted list-based XML indexing scheme(ILI) [8] using Berkeley DB and compared DSI with ILI in terms of space and time cost. Figure 4 shows that, since DSI avoids indexing each single element and keyword in the database, DSI consumes less than 8% index build time than ILI and the index size of DSI is only about 3% of that of ILI. The query response time of DSI is over 40 times faster than that of ILI because the query evaluation is over concise data synopses instead of over full inverted lists.

6.2   Query Precision Measurement

Since our data synopsis correlates content with positional information, we call it Two-Dimensional Bloom Filter (TDBF). We implemented the traditional One-Dimensional Bloom Filter (ODBF) [4] in our framework and compared the query precision of our TDBF with that of ODBF. The result is shown in Figure 5. The false positive rate of a query is defined as (1 - the relevant set size/the answer set size). We exploited XQuery engine Qizx/open [9] to evaluate each XMark

Table 2. Query Workload over Each Dataset

Dataset	Query	Query Expression
XMark	Q1	/site//item[location ~ "United"][payment ~ "Creditcard" and "Check"]/description
XMark	Q2	//regions//item[location ~ "States"][payment ~ "Creditcard" or "Cash"]/name
XMark	Q3	/site//item[location ~ "United"][payment ~ "Creditcard"]/description
XMark	Q4	//regions//item[location ~ "States"][payment ~ "Check"]/quantity
XMark	Q5	/site//item[description//text ~ "gold"]/name
XMark	Q6	/regions//item[description//text ~ "character "]/payment
XMark	Q7	//closed_auction[type ~ "Regular"][annotation//text~ "heat"]/date
XMark	Q8	//closed_auction[annotation//text~ "heat" or "country"]/seller
XMark	Q9	//closed_auction[annotation//text~ "heat" and "country"]/buyer
XMark	Q10	//closed_auction[annotation//text~ "country"]/type
XBench	Q11	/article//body[abstract/p ~ "hockey"][section/p ~ "hockey" and "patterns"]/section
XBench	Q12	//article//body[section/p ~ "regular"][abstract/p ~ "hockey" or "patterns"]/abstract
XBench	Q13	/article//body[section/subsec/p ~ "hockey"][abstract/p ~ "hockey"]/abstract
XBench	Q14	/article//body[section/subsec/p ~ "regular"][abstract/p ~ "patterns"]/section
XBench	Q15	/article//body[section/p ~ "patterns"][abstract/p ~ "patterns"]/abstract
XBench	Q16	/article//body[section/p ~ "hockey"][abstract/p ~ "patterns"]/abstract
XBench	Q17	//prolog[keywords/keyword ~ "bold" or "regular"][title~ "regular"]/authors
XBench	Q18	//prolog[keywords/keyword ~ "bold"][title~ "bold"]/title
XBench	Q19	//prolog[genre ~ "Travel"] [keywords/keyword ~ "bold" or "stealth"]//author/name
XBench	Q20	//prolog[genre ~ "Travel"] [keywords/keyword ~ "bold"]/title

query over the dataset to obtain the accurate relevant set for the query. From Figure 5, we can see that for queries Q_1, Q_2, Q_3, Q_4 and Q_7, the false positive rate of ODBF is over two times higher than that of TDBF because each of these queries contains multiple search predicates and the positional dimension in TDBF can effectively remove false positives during the containment filtering. For queries Q_5, Q_6, Q_8 and Q_{10}, two approaches produce the same false positive rate because each query contains only a single search predicate and the search predicate contains only one term or the boolean operator is "or". In that case, TDBF performs only a bitwise *oring* operation and the positional information is not helpful to reduce the false positives. For query Q_9, TDBF is better than ODBF because although it contains a singe search predicate, the boolean

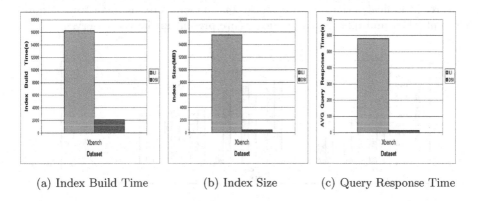

(a) Index Build Time   (b) Index Size   (c) Query Response Time

Fig. 4. Comparison between ILI and DSI

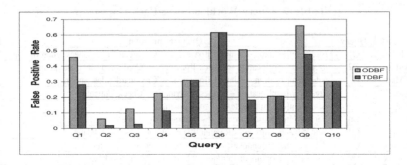

Fig. 5. Query Precision Comparison with One Dimensional Bloom Filter

operator is "and", in which case the positional information can reduce the false positives during the containment filtering. The above result shows that TDBF is superior to ODBF when multiple predicates are presented in the query or a single predicate contains multiple disjunctive terms.

6.3   Efficiency of Optimization Algorithm

To examine the efficiency of our Two-Phase Containment Filtering(TPCF) algorithm, we implemented One-Phase Containment Filtering(OPCF) algorithm in our framework. Then we evaluated all the XMark queries in Table 2 and compared the query response times between TPCF and OPCF. As we can see from Figure 6, for queries Q_1, Q_2, Q_3, Q_4 and Q_7, TPCF is one time faster than OPCF because these queries contain more search predicates, which may involve more containment filtering steps and more joins between long data synopsis lists during the query evaluation. In that case, TPCF can effectively prune the unqualified document locations in the first phase, thus reduce the overall query response time. For the remaining queries, since each query only contains one search predicate and only one containment filtering step is needed in the query evaluation, the query efficiency improvement from TPCF is not very significant. This result indicates that our two-phase containment filtering algorithm is more efficient when multiple search predicates are present in the user query.

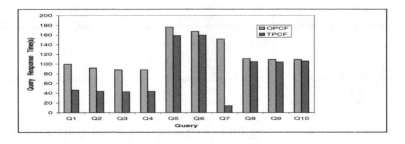

Fig. 6. Efficiency of Two Phase Containment Filtering Algorithm

7   Conclusion

We have presented a framework for indexing and searching XML documents based on condensed summaries extracted from the structural and textual content of the documents. Our indexing scheme is more efficient than traditional indexing schemes based on full inverted lists. Our data synopses correlate content with positional information and result in a more accurate evaluation of textual and containment constraints in a query. Our two-phase containment filtering algorithm can accelerate the searching process.

Acknowledgments. This work is supported in part by the National Science Foundation under the grant IIS-0307460.

References

1. Al-Khalifa, S., Yu, C., Jagadish, H.V.: Querying Structured Text in an XML Database. In: Proc. of ACM SIGMOD, San Diego, USA, pp. 4–15 (2003)
2. Amer-Yahia, S., Botev, C., Shanmugasundaram, S.: TeXQuery: A Full-Text Search Extension to XQuery. In: Proc. of the 13th Int. Conference on World Wide Web(WWW), New York, USA, pp. 583–594 (2004)
3. Amer-Yahia, S., Lakshmanan, L.V.S., Pandit, S.: FleXPath: Flexible Structure and Full-Text Querying for XML. In: Proc. of ACM SIGMOD, Paris, France, pp. 83–94 (2004)
4. Bloom, B.: Space/Time Trade-offs in Hash Coding with Allowable Errors. Communications of the ACM 13, 422–426 (1970)
5. Guo, L., Shao, F., Botev, C., Shanmusundaram, J.: XRANK: Ranked Keyword Search over XML Documents. In: Proc. of ACM SIGMOD, San Diego, USA, pp. 16–27 (2003)
6. Kaushik, R., Krishnamurthy, R., Naughton, J.F., Ramakrishnan, R.: On the Integration of Structure Indexes and Inverted Lists. In: Proc. of ACM SIGMOD, Paris, France, pp. 779–790 (2004)
7. Xu, Y., Papakonstantinou, Y.: Efficient Keyword Search for Smallest LCAs in XML Databases. In: Proc. of ACM SIGMOD, Maryland, USA, pp. 537–538 (2005)
8. Zhang, C.: On Supporting Containment Queries in Relational Database Management Systems. In: Proc. of ACM SIGMOD, Santa Barbara, USA, pp. 425–436 (2001)
9. Qizx/open. http://www.axyana.com/qizxopen/
10. XBench. http://se.uwaterloo.ca/~ddbms/projects/xbench/

PosFilter: An Efficient Filtering Technique of XML Documents Based on Postfix Sharing

Jaehoon Kim[1], Youngsoo Kim[2], and Seog Park[1]

[1] Department of Computer Science, Sogang University
1-1 Shinsu-Dong Mapo-Gu Seoul Korea 121-742
jhkimygk@gmail.com, spark@dblab.sogang.ac.kr
[2] Samsung Electronics CO. LTD.,
Maetan-3-Dong Yeongtong-gu Suwon Kyungki-do Korea 443-742
Youngsoo.kim@samsung.com

Abstract. XML message filtering is to evaluate the path matching of a large number of registered path queries over a continuous stream of XML messages in real time. For this purpose, YFilter system has been suggested to exploit the prefix commonalities that exist among path expressions. Sharing such commonality gives the benefit of improving filtering performance through the tremendous reduction in filtering machine size. However, postfix sharing also can be useful for an XML filtering situation. For example, if a stream of XML messages does not have any defined DTD (or XML schema), the XPath queries beginning with the ancestor-descendant axis ('//') can be used often, e.g., '//buyer/name', '//seller/name', and '//name', and such query type is most likely to have the postfix sharing. Therefore, in this paper, we propose a bottom up filtering approach exploiting postfix sharing against the top down approach of YFilter exploiting prefix sharing. Some experimental results show that our method has better performance in the postfix-shared scenario.

1 Introduction

RSS (Really Simple Syndication) is defined as a service for a web content syndication [3]. The current architecture of RSS dissemination is based on a pulling scheme, where the RSS reader of each user periodically pulls RSS files from a contents server and checks the renewal status. However, this architecture tends to lose scalability when the publication of RSS files suddenly explodes. In addition, the renewal status cannot be immediately alerted and unnecessary pulling operation makes the RSS feeder and reader waste resources [2, 9]. In order to resolve this problem, efforts to apply a publish/subscribe scheme to RSS system have been made [7]. In the publish/subscribe scheme, users subscribe their profile to the system and data, generated by a publisher, which matches the registered profile, are delivered to the interested users [8].

Recently, XML message filtering systems have been studied to support the publish/subscribe scheme: XFilter [6], YFilter [11], XMLTK [10], AFilter [5], etc. In such systems, a user profile is represented as XPath query language [12] and a given

R. Cooper and J. Kennedy (Eds.): BNCOD 2007, LNCS 4587, pp. 70–81, 2007.

set of registered XPath queries is continuously evaluated over XML message streams in real time. Among researches above, YFilter has been especially proposed to exploit commonality that exists among path expressions. The commonality is for prefixes sharing. For example, for the registered queries '/a/b', '/a/b/c', and '/a/b/d', the partial path expression '/a/b' is shared. YFilter combines all XPath queries into a single *Nondeterministic Finite Automaton* (NFA) to exploit such prefix commonality. This approach brings about the tremendous reduction in filtering machine size and as a result, it gives the benefits of higher filtering performance and scalability. However, YFilter does not consider postfix sharing, e.g., the path expressions '//b/c' and '//c' are shared for the queries '/a/b/c', '//b/c', and '//c'. Our experimental results showed that if the postfix-shared query pattern appears more often in the total query set, the throughput of YFilter degrades. Thus, in this paper, we introduce a novel bottom-up filtering approach exploiting the common postfixes in the NFA-based scheme, opposed to the top-down approach of YFilter. We name the new method as PosFilter. The key idea of our method is that the state transition in the NFA execution is performed at the end-of-element event to exploit the common postfixes of XPath queries. However, the execution of YFilter is performed at the start-of-element event.

Similar to our concept, AFilter [5] has been recently proposed for the postfix sharing. Moreover, the approach was intended to benefit from prefix commonalities, while simultaneously leveraging postfix commonalities. However, in conclusion, we think that they fail to suggest the adaptable filtering. Because in the reference [5], they do not show how it can be defined the concrete threshold for the unfolding condition (i.e., the switch from postfix sharing to prefix sharing) and how deep is the overhead of calculating the threshold, which is able to significantly affect the overall filtering performance. In addition, AFilter is not an automata-based scheme. It uses its own specific memory organization and a path matching algorithm. Hence, although the scheme of AFilter can give further improvement of path matching speed, we think that the substantial benefits of expressiveness and incremental maintenance provided by the NFA model outweigh the speed improvement as mentioned in the reference [11].

This paper is organized as follows. In Section 2, we review other researches related to our method. Section 3 presents the basic idea of this paper, and Section 4 describes the proposed PosFilter technique. Section 5 presents some experimental results for the throughput comparison of PosFilter, YFilter and AFilter. Section 6 finally concludes this paper.

2   Related Work

XFilter system [6] may be an early study on an automata-based XML filtering. The research point of the system is to use Finite State Machine (FSM) and an inverted index on all the subscribed XPath queries. XFilter converts each XPath query to a FSM and an inverted index (called Query Index) is built over the states of all FSMs. When a start-of-element event is triggered, the related SAX event handler looks up the element name in the Query Index and it is checked whether there are matched queries. Using the Query Index gives the benefit of achieving high performance filtering. The features of XFilter system are the simple construction and maintenance of the filtering machine and the assurance of high performance filtering and scalability.

However, XFilter does not consider exploiting the commonality that exists among path expressions. Exploiting the commonality can bring about the reduction of redundant processing. Thus, to eliminate such redundancy, YFilter system [11] has been proposed. YFilter combine all queries into a single Nondeterministic Finite Automaton (NFA). As such, the common prefixes of queries are represented only once in the NFA. For example, for the registered XPath queries '/a/b/c' and '/a/b/d', the state transitions labeled by 'a' and 'b' are represented only once. However, there can be a situation where postfix sharing is useful (e.g., the labels 'b' and 'c' are shared for the queries '//a/b/c', '//b/c', and '//c'). YFilter does not consider the postfix sharing and in this paper, we investigate an NFA approach based on postfix sharing. Although using an NFA can lead to performance degradation due to the multiple transitions from each state, the research result showed that applying the NFA to XML filtering system is reasonable. The reason is that the cost of path evaluation using the NFA is not the dominant cost of filtering and rather, other costs such as document parsing are more expensive. Therefore, YFilter is valuable in that it provides the substantial benefits of expressiveness and incremental maintenance provided by the NFA model along with assuring the reasonable speed of path matching.

In fact, in order to avoid the performance degradation by the multiple transition of the NFA, a technique changing the NFA to Deterministic Finite Automata (DFA) such as XMLTK [10] was studied. However, the XML filtering technique basically using the NFA-to-DFA conversion has the following problems. If XPath queries are often inserted, deleted, and updated, the maintenance cost of changing NFA to DFA becomes significant. In addition, if a large number of XPath queries include the ancestor-descendant axis ("//"), it has the shortcoming that memory usage increases rapidly due to the explosion in the number of states.

Recently, AFilter system [5] has been suggested to leverage both prefix and postfix commonalities for reducing overall filtering time. Their basic idea is to exploit the postfix sharing as well as the prefix sharing similar to our research work and furthermore, they introduce a novel technique for the adaptive processing of prefixes and postfixes sharing. However, the scheme is not an automata-based approach. They contrived their own specific memory organization (AxisView, PRLabel-tree, SFLabel-tree, and StackBranch) and a path matching algorithm. Although they suggested the late unfolding approach of postfix clusters for the adaptive processing of prefixes and postfixes sharing, they did not show how it can be defined the concrete threshold for the unfolding condition (i.e., the switch from postfix sharing to prefix sharing) and how deep is the overhead of calculating the threshold, which is able to significantly affect the overall filtering performance. They only mentioned that the unfolding condition is in the following cases: (1) the postfix clusters are small or (2) the prefix cache hit rate is low.

3 Motivation

YFilter shares the common prefixes of registered XPath queries to efficiently handle similar, but not exactly identical queries. However, postfixes sharing also can be useful for an XML filtering situation. For example, let us consider a situation where although any Document Type Definition (DTD) (or XML Schema) is not

defined, streaming XML documents have similar tag names and tag structure like
Figure 1(a)(b). In this situation, the primary query type of the registered XPath queries may be a partial matching path query of Figure 4(a), because users are most
likely to subscribe XPath queries based on their own experience and knowledge, that
is, remembering the previously familiar tag names and structure.

```
<auctions>
  <auction>
    <seller>
      <person>
        <name>Youngsoo</name>
        <email>Youngsoo@samsung.com</email>      <closed_transactions>
      </person>                                     <seller>
    </seller>                                          <name>Youngsoo</name>
    <buyer>                                            <email>Youngsoo@samsung.com</email>
      <person>                                       </seller>
        <name>Jaehoon</name>                         <bidder>
        <email>Jaehoon@sogang.ac.kr</email>            <name>Jaehoon</name>
        <phone>02-333-4444</phone>                     <email>Jaehoon@sogang.ac.kr</email>
      </person>                                         <tel>02-333-4444</tel>
    </buyer>                                          </bidder>
    <item>                                           <items>
      <name>toy</name>                                 <item>
      <link>http://www.toy.com</link>                    <name>toy</name>
    </item>                                               <price>10000</price>
    <price>10000</price>                                  <homepage>http://www.toy.com</homepage>
    <payment>                                           </item>
      <date>2004/10/22</date>                         </items>
      <money>10000</money>                           ::     ::     ::
    </payment>                                      </closed_transactions>
  </auction>
  ::     ::     ::
</auctions>
```

(a) A document published from site A   (b) A document published from site B

Fig. 1. A stream of similar XML documents not having any shared schema

Definition 1 (Partial matching path query). *This query type begins with the ancestor-descendant axis ('//'). For example, the query Q4 of Figure 4(a) has the same
query result as full path queries, which begin with the root element ('/'),
'/auctions/auction/seller/person/name' and '/auctions/auction/buyer/person/name'.*

If the partial matching path queries occur often, there can be a situation where the
postfix sharing can be more advantageous than the prefix sharing. Figure 2 shows the
NFA of YFilter exploiting the prefix sharing, which corresponds to our postfix sharing scheme of Figure 4(d). First, we can observe that the XPath queries in Figure 4(a)
tend toward the postfix sharing. Next, the machine size of our PosFilter is smaller
than that of YFilter, because Q1, Q2, Q3, and Q4 queries share the path '//name' and
'//person/name'. Therefore, it can be expected that the number of automata states in a
runtime stack should be smaller in our PosFilter method and the throughput should
increase. In the next section, we will introduce this bottom up filtering approach based
on the postfix sharing in detail.

In order to assure the *semantic interoperability* of the given queries against the XML document of Figure 1(b), we can consider a translation technique such as OBSERVER [14] and OntoMorph [4]. That is, the statement of a given query can be translated into another statement using the vocabularies of Figure 1(b). However, since the investigation is beyond the scope of this paper, we will not deal with the problem.

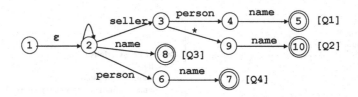

Fig. 2. YFilter exploiting the prefix sharing

4   PosFilter: An NFA-Based Approach Exploiting Postfix Sharing

4.1   Incremental Construction of a Combined NFA

Prior to introducing the PosFilter construction, let us consider representing each XPath query as a non-deterministic finite automaton. Figure 3 shows the four basic location steps in our subset of XPath: "/a", "//a", "/*", and "//*". The symbol "*" (or called wildcard operator) matches any one XML element. The symbol "ε" (or called empty string) is used to mark a transition that requires no input, and it has the following properties: $u\varepsilon = u = \varepsilon u$ and $u\varepsilon v = uv$ for arbitrary XML elements u and v. Note that the automata of Figure 3 are represented bottom up so that the common postfixes of subscribed queries can be shared.

When a path expression begins with the ancestor-descendant axis ("//"), the ε-transition and the state with a self-loop in Figure 3 can be omitted. The reason is that when the path matching is evaluated bottom up, the last evaluation of the ancestor-descendant axis does not affect the query result. For example, the automaton of the query Q1 of Figure 4(a) is represented as Figure 4(b). In fact, such benefit by our bottom up approach is important in that it can reduce the state explosion in the run-time stack of an NFA machine.

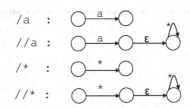

Fig. 3. NFA representation for basic location steps

We now describe the incremental construction of our PosFilter. Let NFA_p denote the non-deterministic finite automaton for a path expression and $combined\text{-}NFA_p$ denote a single NFA which all NFA_ps are combined into.

(step 1) Create a single initial state (*state* 1) shared by all NFA_ps.

(step 2) If an XPath query is first inputted, create the initial $combined\text{-}NFA_p$ starting from the state 1.

(step 3) Whenever a new XPath query is subscribed, add the NFA_p for the query into the $combined\text{-}NFA_p$.
  – Match up the NFA_p to the $combined\text{-}NFA_p$ starting from each initial state.
  – If the final state of the NFA_p is reached or a state is reached for which there is no transition matched, make the final state an accepting state in the $combined\text{-}NFA_p$, add the query ID to the matching query set associated with the accepting state, or create a new branch from the last state reached in the $combined\text{-}NFA_p$.

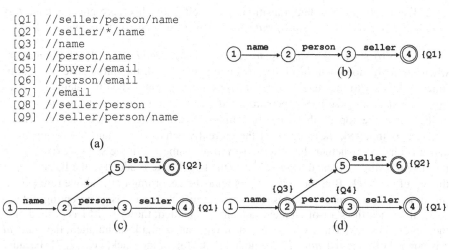

```
[Q1] //seller/person/name
[Q2] //seller/*/name
[Q3] //name
[Q4] //person/name
[Q5] //buyer//email
[Q6] //person/email
[Q7] //email
[Q8] //seller/person
[Q9] //seller/person/name
```

Fig. 4. Sample XPath queries and combining the NFA of each query

For the illustration, let us see the example of Figure 4. When the XPath query Q1 of Figure 4(a) is subscribed first, the initial $combined\text{-}NFA_p$ is constructed like Figure 4(b). Next, when the query Q2 is subscribed, a new transition (wildcard operator) from the last matched state (state 2) is added like Figure 4(c). When the queries Q3 and Q4 are subscribed, the final states (state 2 and 3) are marked as an accepting state (denoted by two concentric circles) like Figure 4(d). For the duplicate query Q9, the query ID Q9 will only be added into the matching query set {Q1}.

4.2 Executing the PosFilter

PosFilter is executed in an event-driven fashion using SAX parser. When an arriving XML document is parsed, events raised by the parser callback the event handlers and drive the transitions in the $combined\text{-}NFA_p$. The following three events are defined.

startDocument. This event is raised when an XML document is arrived. At this time, the execution of the *combined-NFA$_p$* begins at the initial state. That is, the *state_id* of the common initial state (state 1) is pushed to a runtime stack as the active state.

startElement. This event is raised when a new element name is read from the document. At this time, the *state_id* 1 is pushed onto the top of the runtime stack as the active state.

endElement. This event is raised when an end-of-element name is read from the document. PosFilter uses the end-of-element for the state transition from currently active states. The following NFA execution is performed at this time.

(1) The *state_id*s of all active states at the top of the runtime stack are popped off and the *state_id*s of target states of all matching transitions from the active states are added to the top of the runtime stack as new active states. At this time, if any *state_id* at the top of the stack corresponds to the state 1 or a final state in the *combined-NFA$_p$*, it is removed.

(2) Especially, for the state transition with a self-loop (this represents *the ancestor-descendant axis ('//')*), its own *state_id* is always added to the top of the stack.

Figure 5(b) shows the stack state change in the *combined-NFA$_p$* of Figure 5(a) when the XML document of Figure 1(a) is inputted. First, the initial state of the runtime stack is set to the state 1 at the *startDocument* event. When the elements <auctions>, <auction>, <seller>, <person>, and <name> are inputted, the *state_id* 1 is pushed onto the top of the stack five times. Next, when the first end-of-element </name> is inputted, the *state_id* of the currently active state (state 1) is popped off and it is checked whether the state transition of 'name' from the state 1 exists. Since the state transition exists, the *state_id* 2 of the target state is added to the ID set {1} at the top of the stack. But, the *state_id* 1 is removed according to the above rule (1). At this time, the query result of Q3 is returned, because the state 2 is an accepting state.

Again, when the start-of-element <email> is inputted, the *state_id* 1 is pushed onto the top of the stack. Then, when the end-of-element </email> is inputted, the *state_id* 1 is popped off, and the *state_id* 7 is added to the top of the stack, i.e., {2, 7}, because the state transition of 'email' from the state 1 exists. At this time, the query result of Q7 is returned. When the end-of-element </person> is inputted, it is checked whether the state transition of 'person' from the state 2 or 7 exists. Since the transitions to the target states 3, 5, 8, and 10 are matched, the *state_id*s are added to the top of the stack. The query Q4 and Q6 are matched. For the end-of-element of </seller>, the *state_id* 4, 6, and 8 are added to the top of the stack and the query Q1, Q2 and Q9 are matched. In the stack, the *state_id* 4 and 6 will be removed, because the states are a final state in the *combined-NFA$_p$*. The *state_id* 8 is added again according to the above rule (2). The processing for the remaining elements follows the same procedure.

It is important to understand that our PosFilter execution follows the state transition at the *endElement* event to share the common postfixes of XPath queries. This bottom up filtering approach restricts the streaming XML document to being bounded and not huge size, because surely the endless stream of XML data cannot be buffered

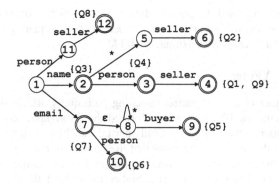

(a) The *combined- NFA_p* for the sample queries

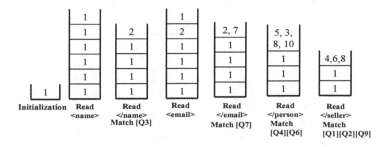

(b) The runtime stack operation

Fig. 5. PosFilter execution

until an end-of-element is reached. Although this restriction makes the PosFilter not applicable to an environment having unbounded XML data stream, we believe our method to be reasonable. Because we can also consider many application domains having the bounded XML data stream such as online news, online auction, and online stock sites.

5 Performance Evaluation

In this section, we will present the results of some experiments to analyze the performance of our PosFilter system. We have compared PosFilter with YFilter and partially AFilter with respect to the postfix sharing.

5.1 Experimental Setup

We have implemented PosFilter in Java (JDK 1.4). For the comparison of YFilter, we used the implementation provided at the website [13] and we could measure the filtering time of both methods. All experiments were performed on a Windows XP computer with 512MB of memory and 1.7 GHz Pentium IV CPU.

For the test data, we used the auction data generated by the xmlgen of XMark [1] and for the test queries, we used the queries generated by the query generator of YFilter [13]. The test data size is approximately 100 MB.

5.2 PosFilter *vs.* YFilter

First, to see whether or not the partial matching path query affects the filtering performance of PosFilter and YFilter, we performed the throughput comparison of both methods for the query sets consisting of only partial matching path queries. The graph of Figure 6 shows the results in the cases that the number of queries is each 100, 500, and 1,000. Here, the throughput is defined as the number of filtered elements per one second. We can see that PosFilter has a higher throughput than YFilter in all the cases. As indicated in Section 3, this result reflects that our PosFilter approach is advantageous to the partial matching path query with postfix sharing.

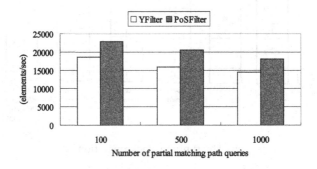

Fig. 6. Throughput comparison according to the number of partial matching path queries

Next, to analyze how deep is the impact of the partial matching path query, we performed the throughput comparison of PosFilter and YFilter according to the occupying proportion of partial matching path queries to the total query set. The number

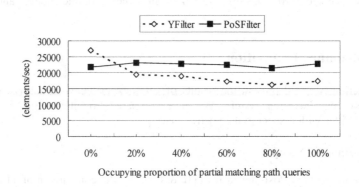

Fig. 7. Throughput comparison according to the occupying proportion of partial matching path queries

of total queries is 100 and the proportion is varied from 0% to 100%. The graph of Figure 7 shows that the throughput of YFilter gets worse according to the increase of the proportion. Even at the proportion of 20%, the throughput of YFilter is lower than PosFilter.

Particularly, we can see that the decrease of YFilter is slow and that of PosFilter is even horizontal. This is because we allowed duplicate path queries in our experiments. That is, if a subscribed XPath query is duplicated, the query ID is only added to the matching query set of an accepting state (as mentioned at the end of Subsection 4.1) and the automaton does not need to be changed. Hence, the throughput is steady.

5.3 PosFilter *vs.* AFilter

AFilter as introduced in the related work of Section 2 exploits the postfix sharing similar to our method. However, unlike state machine-based schemes (such as PosFilter and YFilter), it uses its own specific memory organization and path matching algorithm. In this experiment, we compare our PosFilter with especially the suffix-clustering method of AFilter.

Since we could not obtain the optimized implementation of AFilter, we performed the performance analysis through measuring the number of states pushed into the runtime stack of each filtering method. The number of states pushed into a stack should be associated closely with the throughput. The reason is that newly inputting one state into a stack means that there are many related operations such as the stack operation of *push* and *pop*, the automata operation of state transition, and memory-related operations. Therefore, we can roughly compare the filtering performance of each method by counting the number of the pushed states.

Especially, in AFilter [5], it is separately required the *traversal of pointers* from a stack object to a root object in order to identify the corresponding matching of given queries. Such traversal cost is no less significant than the cost of state transition. Therefore, for the measurement of AFilter, we counted the number of the pointer traversal in addition to the number of pushed states. The number of pushed states for AFilter in Figure 8 represents the sum of both measurements.

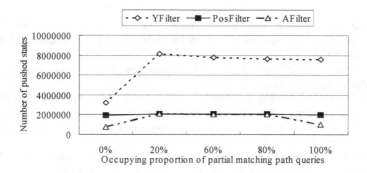

Fig. 8. The number of pushed states according to the occupying proportion of partial matching path queries

The graph of Figure 8 shows that PosFilter and AFilter exploiting the postfix sharing have a higher throughput than YFilter; note that the larger the number of pushed states, the longer the filtering time. In addition, we can see that the throughput of PosFilter is similar to that of AFilter. However, as mentioned in the introduction of Section 1, although the scheme of AFilter can give further improvement of path matching speed, our NFA-based scheme should have more substantial benefits in terms of the expressiveness and the incremental maintenance.

6 Conclusions

In this paper, we have introduced a bottom up filtering approach of continuous XML messages. The suggested PosFilter exploits the postfix commonalities across registered XPath queries. Some experimental results showed that our PosFilter approach is more efficient than YFilter under the circumstance that the primary query type of subscribed queries is the partial matching path query and the postfix-shared query. As considered in Section 3, if streaming XML messages do not have any shared DTD (or an XML schema) or there is semantic heterogeneity from multiple data sources, the partial matching path queries with the postfix sharing are most likely to be subscribed often. Therefore, our PosFilter approach is useful in such XML filtering situation. As compared to AFilter which is a recent study on the postfix sharing, our experiment shows that there is no significant difference between two methods. Furthermore, since our PosFilter basically follows the NFA model, we believe that it should provide the benefits of better scalability and simpler maintenance along with assuring the high performance filtering.

Acknowledgements. This study is supported in part by the Second Stage of BK21. In addition, this work was supported by the Korea Science and Engineering Foundation(KOSEF) grant funded by the Korea government(MOST) (No. R01-2006-000-10609-0).

References

1. Schmidt, A.R., Waas, F., Kersten, M.L., Carey, M.J., Manolescu, I., Busse, R.: XMark: a benchmark for XML data management. In: Proceedings of VLDB, Hong Kong, China, pp. 974–985 (2002)
2. Dickerson, C.: RSS Growing Pains (2004). available at http://www.infoworld.com/article /04/07/16/29OPconnection_1.html
3. Winer, D.: RSS 2.0 Specification (2005). available at http://blogs.law.harvard.edu/tech/rss
4. Chalupsky, H.: OntoMorph: a translation system for symbolic knowledge. In: Proceedings of 7th international conference on knowledge representation and reasoning (KR), Breckenridge (CO US), pp. 471–482 (2000)
5. Candan, K.S., Hsiung, W., Chen, S., Tatemura, J., Agrawal, D.: AFilter: Adaptable XML Filtering with Prefix-Caching and Suffix-Clustering. In: Proc. of VLDB, Seoul, Korea, pp. 559–570 (2006)
6. Altinel, M., Franklin, M.J.: Efficient Filtering of XML Documents for Selective Dissemination of Information. In: Proc. of VLDB, Cairo, Egypt, pp. 53–64 (2000)

7. Petrovic, M., Liu, H., Jacobsen, H.: G-ToPSS: Fast Filtering of Graph-based Metadata. In: Proc. of the International Conference on World Wide Web, pp. 539–547 (2005)
8. Eugster, P.Th., Felber, P.A., Guerraoui, R., Kermarrec, A.: The Many Faces of Publish/Subscribe. ACM Computing Surveys 35(2), 114–131 (2003)
9. Miller, R.: RSS Traffic Burdens Publisher's Servers (2004). available at http://news.netcraft.com/archives/2004/07/19/rss_traffic_burdens_publishers_servers.html
10. Green, T.J., Miklau, G., Onizuka, M., Suciu, D.: Processing XML Streams with Deterministic Automata. In: Calvanese, D., Lenzerini, M., Motwani, R. (eds.) ICDT 2003. LNCS, vol. 2572, pp. 173–189. Springer, Heidelberg (2002)
11. Diao, Y., Altinel, M., Franklin, M.J., Zhang, H., Fischer, P.: Path Sharing and Predicate Evaluation for High-Performance XML Filtering. ACM Transactions on Database Systems 28(4), 467–516 (2003)
12. XML Path Language (XPath) Version 1.0, http://www.w3.org/TR/xpath
13. YFilter 1.0 release, http://yfilter.cs.umass.edu/code_release.htm
14. Mena, E., Kashyap, V., Illarramendi, A., Sheth, A.: Domain Specific Ontologies for Semantic Information Brokering on the Global Information Infrastructure. In: Proc. of the International Conference on Formal Ontology in Information Systems, pp. 269–283 (1998)

OOXSearch: A Search Engine for Answering Loosely Structured XML Queries Using OO Programming

Kamal Taha and Ramez Elmasri

Department of Computer Science and Engineering
The University of Texas at Arlington, USA
kamal.taha@cse.uta.edu, elmasri@cse.uta.edu

Abstract. There has been extensive research in XML keyword-based and loosely structured querying. Some frameworks work well for certain types of XML data models and fail in others. The reason is that the proposed techniques are based on finding relationships between solely individual nodes while overlooking the context of these nodes. The context of a leaf node is determined by its parent node, because it specifies one of the characteristics of its parent node. Building relationships between individual leaf nodes without consideration of their parents may result in relationships that are semantically disconnected. Since leaf nodes are nothing but characteristics of their parents, we observe that we could treat each parent-children set of nodes as one unified entity. We then find semantic relationships between the different unified entities. Based on those observations, we propose an XML semantic search engine called OOXSearch, which answers loosely structured queries. The recall and precision of the engine were evaluated experimentally and compared with two recent proposed systems [1, 2] and the results showed marked improvement.

Keywords: Canonical Tree, Ontology Label, Relevant Canonical Tree, Search Term Context.

1 Introduction

The spectrum of users who interact with XML and their levels of skill have significantly widened due to the popularity and widespread use of XML. Since that spectrum includes naïve users, extensive research in XML keyword-based querying has been done. Even sophisticated users who are not aware of the XML document's schema may find keyword-based and loosely structured querying helpful. The studies that have been done could be categorized into four groups. The first expands structured query languages [15, 16]. The second uses keyword-based search techniques for ranking results based on importance and relevance [9,10, 24]. The key drawback of those ranking techniques is that they do not consider search semantics. The third employs search techniques based on semantic relationships between individual nodes [1, 2, 3]. The fourth proposes modeling the XML document as a graph and processing the graph based on driven schema

R. Cooper and J. Kennedy (Eds.): BNCOD 2007, LNCS 4587, pp. 82–100, 2007.

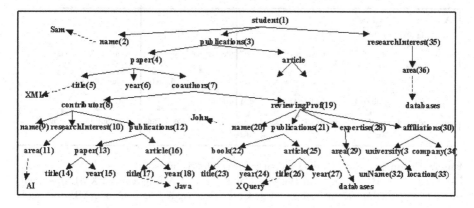

Fig. 1. A graduate school's authors and coauthors bibliography XML tree with sample data instances (student.xml doc)

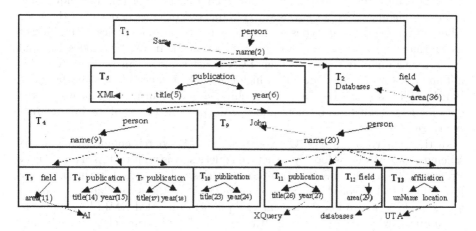

Fig. 2. Canonical Trees graph of the XML tree presented in Figure 1

[22, 23, 26]. While each of these proposed techniques has advantages, it also has drawbacks, such as returning redundant and/or wrong answers. The reason is that they propose frameworks based on finding relationships between individual nodes while overlooking the "context" of those nodes. The context of a leaf node is determined by its parent node because a leaf node is a characteristic of its parent. If for example a node is labeled "title", we cannot determine whether the node refers to a book title or a job title without referring to the parent of the node. The techniques proposed by [1] and [2] for example may return wrong answers as a result of not considering leaf nodes contexts. In [1], the authors propose that if the relationship tree that connects nodes a and b does not include two or more nodes that have the same label, then nodes a and b are related. In Figure 1, for example, the relationship tree of nodes 2 and 4 contains nodes 2,

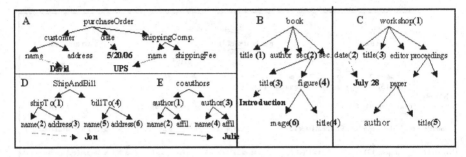

Fig. 3. Fragments of XML docs taken from the following sources: A) Taken from the Use Cases [11]. B) Taken from the Use Cases [11]. C) A fragment of XML document taken from [10]. D) Taken from the Use Cases [11]. E) A fragment of XML doc taken from the web.

1, 3, and 4. Since the relationship tree doesn't contain two or more nodes with the same label, then nodes 2 and 4 are related. Applying this technique may return wrong answers if a data model contains two or more nodes with the same label but having different types or if it contains two or more nodes with different labels that belong to the same type (see section 2). In [2], two nodes "a" and "b" are meaningfully related if their LCA (least common ancestor), node 'c' is not an ancestor of some node "d", which is a LCA of node "b" and another node that has the same label as "a". This technique may return wrong answers if the data model contains two or more nodes with the same label but having different types (see sec. 2).

In this paper, we propose OOXSearch, an XML search engine that answers schema-aware as well as loosely structured queries. It is built on top of an XQuery Processor. It accepts loosely structured queries, whose search terms have the form "label = keyword" and returns elements have the form "label". If a user for example wants to know the year of a publication titled XML, he could submit a query, whose search term is "title = XML" and return element is "year". Thus, the user does not have to be aware of the schema.

Our proposed framework employed by OOXSearch is inspired by the following observations. If we fragment an XML data model to the simplest semantically meaningful fragments, we will find that each fragment will consist of a parent node and its leaf children nodes. We call each such fragment a Canonical Tree. Thus, a Canonical Tree is a union of a parent node and its leaf children nodes (see Figure 2). Leaf children nodes represent the characteristics of their parent node. For instance the leaf children nodes "title" and "year" of publication represent some of the characteristics of their parent node "book". Therefore, the "book", "title", and "year" nodes represent a meaningful union. We can treat each Canonical Tree as one entity. A data model is a metaphor of real-word entities. Two real-word entities may have different names but belong to the same type (e.g. a book and an article belong to the same publication type), or may have the same names but refer to two different types (e.g. a "name" of a student and a "name" of a school). To overcome that labeling ambiguity, we observe that if we cluster Canonical Trees based on the reduced essential characteristics and cognitive qualities of their parent nodes, we will identify a number of clusters. Each cluster contains Canonical Trees whose parent nodes belong to the same ontological concept. For example, we can have a cluster that contains a Canonical Tree whose parent node is "book" and also a Canonical Tree whose parent node is "article", since both "book" and "article" fall under the same "publication" ontology concept. Thus, though "book" and "article" have different labels, they belong to the same type. On the other hand, a Canonical Tree, whose parent node is "student" falls under the "person" cluster (ontology concept), and the Canonical Tree whose parent node is "school" falls under the "institution" cluster; therefore, the "name" node in the "student" Canonical Tree and the "name" node in the "school" Canonical Tree are not semantically identical; rather, they are two distinct nodes referring to two different types of entities. If we consider the ontology label of each cluster as a supertype and the label of each Canonical Tree that falls under the cluster as a subtype, then any characteristic that describes the supertype can also describe all its subtypes (a form of inheritance). For instance, the "publication" supertype could be characterized by "title" and "year" of publication, and likewise its subtypes "book" and "article". This behavior is analogous to the concept of a subclass that inherits attributes from its superclass in Object Oriented models (see sec 6).

Our work is motivated by the following conclusions, which are based on the above observations:

(1) Fragmenting a data model to Canonical Trees enables us to compute speedily and efficiently off-line for each Canonical Tree T_i, the Canonical Trees that are related and relevant to T_i.

(2) If Canonical Tree T_j is related and relevant to C. Tree T_i, all leaf children nodes of T_j are also related to all the leaf children nodes of T_i. Thus, the same computational overhead used for determining a relationship between two individual nodes can be used for determining relationships between groups of nodes.

(3) Constructing a framework for determining the semantic relationships between nodes based on their ontology works well in all types of data models; unlike determining the relationships based on solely the labels of the nodes.

(4) The structure of Canonical Trees is analogous to the modular fashion of Object Oriented models, which enables us to use Object-Oriented techniques to locate the answer return element nodes and to extract instance values contained in those nodes. If we incorporate behaviors (methods) into a Canonical Tree entity, this entity would have all the characteristics and behaviors of an OO object. Thus, each Canonical Tree could be viewed as an object and its nodes as the object's attributes. We can associate every Canonical Tree object with a class. The attributes of the class are the Canonical Tree's leaf nodes and its methods operate on those attributes. If we construct a class for an ontological label of a cluster, this class could be considered a superclass, and if we construct a class for each Canonical Tree that falls under this cluster, each of these classes could be considered a subclass. Subclasses inherit the attributes and methods of their

superclass e.g. "article" and "book" subclasses inherit the "title" attribute from their superclass "publication".

This paper is organized as follows. In section 2 we present Related Work. In section 3 we present the preliminary notation used in the paper. In section 4, we show how related Canonical Trees are determined. In section 5, we show how related Canonical Trees are determined for complex queries that have more than one search term. In section 6 we present the prototype system implementation. Section 7 presents the experimental results and section 8 presents our conclusion.

2   Related Work

Keyword querying in Relational Databases has been studied extensively [6, 8, 7]. These approaches model the database as a graph, where tuples are regarded as the graph's nodes and the relationships between tuples are regarded as the graph's edges. Then, a keyword query is answered by returning a subgraph that satisfies the search keyword. A number of studies have been done in keyword search in XML docs [9,10, 24]. Those studies employ techniques for ranking results based on importance and relevance. Their key drawback is that they do not consider search semantics. They may return answers that are semantically unrelated.

Some studies [22, 23, 26] propose modeling the XML document as a graph and processing the graph based on driven schema. The problem with the proposed techniques is that they are rather complex and don't guarantee correct results.

There have been a number of recent studies employing semantic search over XML documents [1, 2, 3]. The common underlying technique for these studies is the computation of Least Common Ancestor (LCA) node of the search terms and returning element nodes. While [1] is based on the computation of pure LCA, [2] and [3] refines the selection of LCA. Even though those techniques employ semantic search, they suffer significant drawbacks. We are going to take [1] as a representative for the systems that employ pure LCA semantic search and [2] as a representative for the systems that employ refined LCA semantic search. In [1] if the relationship tree of two nodes doesn't include two or more nodes with the same label, then those nodes are related. The subtree rooted at the Least Common Ancestor (LCA) node of those two nodes is returned as the context of the query evaluation. In [2], nodes "a" and "b" are NOT meaningfully related if their LCA, node 'c' is an ancestor of some node "d", which is a LCA of node "b" and another node that has the same label as "a". Consider for example nodes 5, 23, and 24 in Figure 1. Node 24 (year) and node 5 (title) are not related, because their LCA (node 4) is an ancestor of node 22, which is the LCA of nodes 24 and 23, and node 23 has the same label as node 5. Therefore, node 24 is related to node 23 and not to node 5. Node 22 is considered the Meaningful Least Common Ancestor (MLCA) of nodes 23 and 24.

In [28] we present example scenarios that cause [1] and [2] to return faulty recall (the ratio of the number of relevant records retrieved to the total number of relevant records in the database) and precision (the ratio of the number of relevant records retrieved to the total number of irrelevant and relevant records retrieved). Each example scenario represents a sample of the types of data models and queries that cause each of them to return faulty answers.

3   Preliminaries

In this section we present definitions of key notations and basic concepts used in this paper. We model XML docs as rooted and labeled trees. A node in a tree represents an element in an XML document. The nodes are numbered for easy reference. Leaf nodes contain keywords. OOXSearch accepts loosely structured queries that have the following XQuery[15] format:

for δd in doc("XML document name") where δd//node's label = "keyword" return δd//node's label

We call each label-keyword pair in the where clause a search term and we call each label in the return clause a return element. The where clause may contain more than one search term and the return clause may contain more than one answer return element. As we can see, a loosely structured query doesn't require a user to be aware of the schema. The user needs to know only the label(s) of the search term element(s) and the label(s) of the return element(s). We call a node in a data model that matches a query's return element and satisfies its search term an answer return element node.

Definition 3.1 Ontology Label: If we cluster parent nodes in a data model based on their reduced characteristics and cognitive qualities, the label of each of these clusters is an Ontology Label. Table 1 shows the Ontology Labels and their clusters of parent nodes in the XML tree shown in Figure 1.

Definition 3.2 Canonical Tree: If we fragment an XML tree to the simplest semantically meaningful fragments (subtrees), each fragment is called a Canonical Tree and it consists of a parent node and its leaf children nodes. That is, if a parent node has a leaf child/children, the leaf children along with their parent node constitute a Canonical Tree. The leaf children nodes represent the characteristics of their parent. Each parent node in a Canonical Tree is labeled with the Ontology Label of the cluster that the parent node belongs to, and this Ontology Label represents the label of the Canonical Tree. Figure 2 shows the Canonical Trees of the XML tree presented in Figure 1.

Definition 3.3 T_i: T_i is an identifier and denotes Canonical Tree number i, where $1 \geq i \geq |T|$. The upper Canonical Tree in Figure 2, for example, whose Ontology Label is "person", is identified by the unique identifier "T_1".

Definition 3.4 OLT_i: OLT_i denotes the Ontology Label of Canonical Tree T_i. In Figure 2 for example OLT_1 is person.

Definition 3.5 Relevant Canonical Trees (RCT): Each Canonical Tree T_i has few other Canonical Trees that are relevant and closely related to it. Those relevant Canonical Trees are most likely to contain the answer return element node(s) of ANY query, whose search term(s) is contained in T_i. We call those Canonical Trees the Relevant Canonical Trees (RCT) of T_i.

Definition 3.6 RCT_{Ti}: RCT_{Ti} denotes the set of Canonical Trees that are relevant and related to Canonical Tree T_i.

Definition 3.7 Search Term Context (STC): A Search Term Context (STC) is a Canonical Tree(s) that contains a query's search term(s). If there is only one search term or there are several search terms but they are all contained in one Canonical Tree T_i, then T_i is the STC. If for example the search term is "title = XML", then T_3 is the STC (see Figure 2). If however, there is more than one search term and they are contained in different Canonical Trees, the STC consists of all the Canonical Trees located in the Canonical relationship tree, which connects the Canonical Trees that contain the search terms (see section 5).

Table 1. Ontology Labels of parent nodes in Figure 1

Ontology Label	Parent nodes and their numbers
publication	paper (4, 13), article (16, 25), book (22), publications (3, 12, 21)
person	student (1), contributor (8), reviewingProf(19)
field	researchInterest (10, 35), expertise (28)
affiliation	university (31), company (34)

4   Computing the RCT of Each Canonical Tree

The process of computing the RCT of Canonical Tree T_i is done by eliminating all Canonical Trees that are unlikely to contain a query's return element node(s) if T_i is the STC. The remaining Canonical Trees are the RCT of T_i, which contain the answer return element nodes of ANY query, whose search term(s) is/are contained in T_i (T_i is the STC). In section 5 we present the mechanism of determining the RCT of a STC that consists of more than one Canonical Tree, which is used when a query has more than one search term and the nodes that satisfy those search terms are contained in more than one Canonical Tree.

We have to distinguish between two types of queries, query type A and query type B. In query type A, the search term element's label is different than the return element's label (e.g. the search term element is "name" and the return element is "title"). In query type B, both the search term element and the return element have the same label (e.g. the search term element is "name" and the return element is "name").

4.1   Computing RCT of a Canonical Tree for Query Type A

We are going to present properties, which are rules for eliminating (removing) Canonical Trees that are unlikely to contain query type A answer return element node(s). Thus, these properties are used to construct RCTs that answer query type A exclusively (see section 4.2 for queries of type B). For each Canonical Tree T_i, these properties compute the RCT of T_i when T_i is an STC. The properties are defined based on lemmas, for which we are going to sketch the proofs.

Lemma 1: Let S_{p_i} denote a set of Canonical Trees located in the same path from a STC (path P_i). Each Canonical Tree in set S_{p_i} is denoted by $T_{p_i}^j$, where j is its distance from the STC and p_i is the path number where the Canonical Tree is located. The distance of a Canonical Tree is defined as the number of Canonical Trees located between it and the STC.

If $\exists T_{p_i}^x \in S_{p_i} : \forall T_{p_i}^y \in S_{p_i} : |S_{p_i}| \geq x, y \geq 0 : x \neq y$, then only $T_{p_i}^x$ in path p_i may contain an answer return element node for a query, $T_{p_i}^y$ will not, and $1 \geq |T_{p_i}^x| \geq 0$. That is, in each path from a STC, there is at most one Canonical Tree that contains a valid answer return element node for a query type A.

Proof: See [28].

Lemma 2: Consider the same notations used in lemma 1. Let $RCT_{STC}^{P_i}$ denote a set that contains the RCT of the STC in path p_i. Thus, $RCT_{STC}^{P_i} \subseteq S_{p_i}$. If $\exists T_{p_i}^x \in RCT_{STC}^{P_i} : \forall T_{p_i}^y \in RCT_{STC}^{P_i} : |RCT_{STC}^{P_i}| \geq x, y \geq 0 : x \neq y$, then $OL_{T_{p_i}^x} \neq OL_{T_{p_i}^y}$ (the Ontology Label of $T_{p_i}^x$ is different than the Ontology Label of $T_{p_i}^y$). That is, in each path from a STC, all Canonical Trees located in this path, which are part of the RCT of the STC should have distinct Ontology Labels.

Proof: See [28].

Property 1: This property is based on lemma 2. When computing the RCT of T for query type A, a Canonical Tree $T^\sim$ should be eliminated (pruned) if there is another Canonical Tree $T^\sim$ located between $T^\sim$ and T whose Ontology Label is the same as $T^\sim$.

Lemma 3: Let Canonical Tree T be a STC. $T^\sim$ can be one of the Canonical Trees that comprise the RCT of T in a meaningful and intuitive query type A if and only if $OL_T \neq OL_{T^\sim}$. That is, a Canonical Tree $T^\sim$ can be one of the Canonical Trees that comprise the RCT of a STC in a meaningful and intuitive query type A if and only if its Ontology Label is different than the Ontology Label of the STC.

Proof: See [28].

Property 2: This property is based on lemma 3. When computing the RCT of a Canonical Tree T for query type A, any Canonical Tree, whose Ontology Label is the same as the Ontology Label of T should be eliminated (pruned).

Lemma 4: Let T_{rem} denote: Canonical Tree T has been pruned by either property 1 or property 2. Let $A_{T_{rem}}^{T_i}$ denote: Canonical Tree T_i is an ancestor of Canonical Tree T_{rem}. Let $D_{T_{rem}}^{T_i}$ denote: Canonical Tree T_i is a descendant of Canonical Tree T_{rem}. Let $\neg A_{STC}^{T_i}$ denote the negation of: Canonical Tree T_i is an ancestor of the STC. Let $\neg D_{STC}^{T_i}$ denote the negation of: Canonical Tree T_i is a descendant of the STC. T_i should be eliminated (pruned) if ($A_{T_{rem}}^{T_i}$ and $\neg D_{STC}^{T_i}$) or if ($D_{T_{rem}}^{T_i}$ and $\neg A_{STC}^{T_i}$). That is, when computing the RCT, a Canonical Tree should be pruned if it is an ancestor of a Canonical Tree that has been pruned by either property 1 or property 2 and is also not a descendant of the STC. It should also be pruned if it is a descendant of a Canonical Tree that has been pruned by either property 1 or property 2 and is also not an ancestor of the STC.

Proof: See [28].

Property 3: This property is based on lemma 4. When computing RCT, if there is any ancestor Canonical Tree of a Canonical Tree that has been pruned by either property 1 or 2, it should be pruned, if it is not a descendant of the STC. Also, if there is any descendant Canonical Tree of a Canonical Tree that has been pruned by either property 1 or 2 it should be pruned, if it is not an ancestor of the STC.

The following examples show how RCTs for query type A are determined: (Note: recall Definition 3.6 and Figure 2 for these examples)

Example 1: Determination of RCT_{T_1}: By applying property 2, T_9 and T_4 are pruned. By applying property 3, T_{10}, T_{11}, T_{12}, and T_{13} are pruned, because they satisfy ($D_{T_9}^{T_i}$ and $\neg A_{T_1}^{T_i}$). Also, T_5, T_6, and T_7 are pruned, because they satisfy ($D_{T_4}^{T_i}$ and $\neg A_{T_1}^{T_i}$). See Figure 4.

Example 2: Determination of $RCT_{T_{11}}$: By applying property 1, T_1 is pruned, because it is located in path T_1, T_3, T_9, T_{11} and its Ontology Label is the same as T_9, which is closer to T_{11} than T_1. By applying property 2, T_{10}, T_3, T_6, and T_7 are pruned. By applying property 3, T_2, T_4, and T_5 are pruned, because they satisfy ($D_{T_{rem}}^{T_i}$ and $\neg A_{T_{11}}^{T_i}$). See Figure 5.

Example 3: Determination of RCT_{T_5}: By applying property 1, T_1 is pruned, because it is located in path T_1, T_3, T_4, T_5 and its Ontology Label is the same as T_4, which is closer to T_5 than T_1. By applying property 1, T_9 is pruned, because it is located in path T_5, T_4, T_3, T_9 and its Ontology Label is the same as T_4, which is closer to T_5 than T_9. By applying property 3, T_{10}, T_{11}, T_{12}, T_{13}, and T_2 are pruned. So, RCT_{T_5} consists of T_3, T_4, T_6, and T_7.

Example 4: Determination of RCT_{T_9}: Property 2: T_1 and T_4 are pruned. Property 3, T_2, T_5, T_6, and T_7 are pruned. So, RCT_{T_9} consists of T_3, T_{10}, T_{11}, T_{12}, and T_{13}.

Example 5: Determination of RCT_{T_3} : By applying property 2, T_6, T_7, T_{10}, and T_{11} are pruned. So, RCT_{T_3} consists of T_1, T_2, T_4, T_5, T_9, T_{12}, and T_{13}.

Example 6: Determination of $RCT_{T_{12}}$: After applying properties 1 and 3, we find that $RCT_{T_{12}}$ consists of T_3, T_9, T_{10}, T_{11}, and T_{13}.

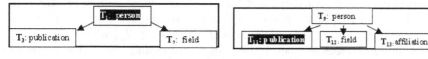

Fig. 4. RCT_{T1} **Fig. 5.** RCT_{T11}

The following examples show how answer return element nodes are extracted from RCTs (Note: recall Figures 1 and 2 for these examples):

Example 7: for δd in doc("student.xml") where δd//title = "XQuery" return δd//name, δd//area. The query asks for the name of the author who authored an article titled "XQuery", and also asks for his areas of expertise. Since the keyword "XQuery" is contained in Canonical Tree T_{11}, we use $RCT_{T_{11}}$ (see Figure 7). The answer return element nodes "name" and "area" are contained in T_9 and T_{12} respectively. The answer is nodes 20 and 29.

Example 8: for δd in doc("student.xml") where δd//name = "John" return δd//title. The query asks for all title of publications, which are either authored or coauthored by an author, whose name is "John". Since the keyword "John" is contained in T_9 , we use RCT_{T_9} (see example 4). The answer return element "title" is contained in C. Trees T_{10} , T_{11} , and T_3 . The answer is nodes 5, 23, and 26.

Example 9: for δd in doc("student.xml") where δd//title = "XML" return δd//name. The query asks for the names of the author and coauthors of a publication titled "XML". Since the keyword "XML" is contained in T_3 , we use RCT_{T_3} (see example 5). The return element node "name" is contained in T_1, T_4, and T_9. So, the answer is nodes 2, 9, and 20.

Example 10: Consider that the label of node 32 in Figure 1 is changed from "unName" to "name". The Canonical Trees in RCT_{T_3}, that contain a node labeled "name" will be (T_1, T_4, and T_9) whose Ontology Labels are "person" and also T_{13} whose Ontology Label is "affiliation". Now, consider the query presented in Example 9. The query could be interpreted as either "find the name of authors" or "find the name of the affiliation". The user expects only one of the two sets of answers, but not both. In this case the system should return to the user the two sets of answers with description of each set and have the user selects one of them. But, the system should not combine the nodes of the two sets as a collective answer and return them to the user. We note that most proposed schema unaware-based systems, such as [1, 2] can't determine whether or not two nodes belong to the same type if these nodes have the same label. Consequently, they may provide the user with answer consisting of a mixture of correct and incorrect data. This problem is shown in sections 2 and 7 with regard to [1] and [2]. We now introduce property 4 based on this notion.

Property 4: Let N denote the set of nodes in an XML document. Let R denote the set of nodes that satisfy a query's search term and their labels are the same as the query's return element label: $R \subseteq N$. Let Ans denote the set of nodes that are valid answer return element nodes for the query: $Ans \subseteq R$. Let $\exists n_i$, $\forall n_i \in Ans$, where i and j are indexes that indicate the position of node n in set Ans: $1 \leq i,j \leq |Ans|$. Let $n_i \in T_x$ and $n_j \in T_y$, where T_x and T_y denote Canonical Trees number x and y respectively and $x \neq y$. Then, the set of answer return element nodes may be correct if and only if $OL_{T_x} = OL_{T_y}$ .That is, all answer return element nodes should have the same Ontology Label. If for example there are m nodes that have the same label as a query's return element and they all satisfy its search term, and if each of these nodes belongs to a different type (Ontology Label), then m different sets of answers should be provided to the user with description of each set and have him select the set he wants (see example 10).

4.2   Computing RCT of Canonical Trees for Query Type B

Query type B concerns the types of queries where the user knows some information about something and wants additional information. In this type of query, the search term element and return element have the same labels. For example a user who knows that "XML" is a title of one of the books authored by "John" and wants to know the titles of the other books and articles authored by him could submit a loosely structured query consisting of the search term "title = XML" and return element "title". When answering this query, we ONLY look for Canonical Trees, whose Ontology Labels are "publication". So, when answering query type B, we look only for Canonical Trees, whose Ontology Labels are the same as the Ontology Label of the Canonical Tree that contains the search term.

Property 5: When a query's search term and return elements have the same label, we get the answer return element node(s) as follows. We look at the Canonical Trees graph (e.g. Figure 2) and the set of RCTs (e.g. computed from section 4). In the C. Trees graph and starting from the C. Tree Ti that contains the search term node we search ascending and descending Ti for the closest C. Tree, whose RCT contains Ti and also contains at least one more C. Tree, whose Ontology Label is the same as Ti. We call this Canonical Tree the pivoting entity and its RCT contains the query's answer return element node.

Example 11: for δd in doc("student.xml") where δd//name = "John " return δd//name.

The query asks for the names of the other authors of the "publication" authored by John. The keyword "John" is contained in T_9. The closest C. Tree to T_9, whose RCT contains T_9 and also contains another C. Tree(s), whose Ontology Label(s) is/are the same as T_9, is C. Tree T_3. So, the pivoting entity is T_3. Therefore, we use RCT_{T_3} (see example 5). The answer is nodes 2 and 9 contained in T_1 and T_4.

Example 12: for δd in doc("student.xml") where δd//title = "XQuery" return δd//title.

The query asks for the other publication titles of the "author", whose one of his publication's titles is XQuery. The keyword "XQuery" is contained in T_{11}. The closest Canonical Tree to T_{11}, whose RCT contains T_{11} and also contains another Canonical Tree(s), whose Ontology Label(s) is/are the same as T_{11}, is Canonical Tree T_9. So, the pivoting entity is T_9 "person". Therefore, we use RCT_{T_9} (see example 4). So, the answer would be nodes 23 and 5 contained in T_{10} and T_3 respectively.

Canonical Trees whose Ontology Labels are the same behave as rivals. They either cooperatively did something to the pivoting entity or something was done to them collectively by the pivoting entity. In Example 11, Canonical Trees T_1 , T_9, and T_4 cooperatively authored the pivoting entity T_3. In example 12, T_3, T_{10} , and T_{11} are collectively authored by the pivoting entity T_9.

The algorithm that computes the RCT of each Canonical Tree (algorithm ComputeRCTs) is found in [28].

5   Computing RCT for STC Consisting of More Than One Canonical Tree

Let $T_i...T_j$ denote the Canonical Trees that satisfy the search terms of a query, when the query has more than one search term. Let $S_{T_i...T_j}$ denote a set that contains the Canonical Trees located in the canonical relationship tree that connects $T_i...T_j$. If there are no two or more Canonical Trees in set $S_{T_i...T_j}$ whose Ontology Labels are the same, then the Canonical Trees in set $S_{T_i...T_j}$ collectively constitutes the STC of the query. Consider for example that the search terms of a query are "area = databases" and "name = Sam" (See figure 2). The keyword databases is contained in two Canonical Trees (T_2 and T_{12}), and the keyword Sam is contained in T_1. There are two sets of canonical relationship trees. The first connects T_1 with T_{12} and the second connects T_1 with T_2 as follows: $S_{T_1,T_{12}}$ = T_1, T_3, T_9, T_{12} and $S_{T_1,T_2} = T_1, T_2$. Set $S_{T_1,T_{12}}$ contains Canonical Trees T_9 and T_1, whose Ontology Labels are the same; therefore, the set is not a valid STC. Since set S_{T_1,T_2} doesn't contain Canonical Trees, whose Ontology Labels are the same, it is a valid STC. Thus, T_2 and T_1 collectively constitute the STC of the query. The rationale behind that is as follows. Consider Canonical Tree T_b is located in the canonical relationship tree that connects Canonical Trees T_a and T_c. T_b is related to both T_a and T_c and it semantically relates T_a to T_c. Thus, without T_b, the relationship between T_a and T_c is semantically disconnected. Therefore, if T_a and T_c satisfy the search terms of a query, the STC of the query should also include T_b. So, the STC will consist of T_a, T_b, and T_c.

To compute the RCT, we first merge the RCTs of all Canonical Trees located in a relationship tree. That is, we get the RCT of each Canonical Tree located in the relationship tree from the set of RCTs computed in section 4 and then merge them. Then, we apply properties 1, 2 and/or 3 on the merged Canonical Trees. When applying these properties, we have to consider that the STC consists of all Canonical Trees contained in the relationship tree. For example, when applying property 2, we prune any Canonical Tree, whose Ontology Label is the same as ANY of the Canonical Trees comprising the STC.

Example 13: for δd in doc("student.xml") where δd//name ="Sam" and δd// title = "XML" return δd//area. The query asks for the research interest area of the author whose name is "Sam" and who authored a paper titled "XML". The keywords "Sam" and "XML" are contained in T_1 and T_3 respectively. So, T_1 and T_3 collectively represent the STC. Therefore, we merge RCT_{T_1} and RCT_{T_3} (see Fig 6 and example 5). The merged RCTs look the same as RCT_{T_1}. We then apply property 2 and prune T_9 and T_4, since their Ontology Labels are the same as T_1. When applying property 3, we prune T_{12}, T_{13}, T_5. See Figure 6. The answer return element node is node 36 (see Figure 1).

Example 14: for δd in doc("student.xml") where δd//area = "databases" and δd//title = "XML" return δd//uNname. The query is interpreted as "in what university did the author, whose area of expertise is "databases" and who coauthored a paper titled "XML" use to work". The keywords "databases" and "XML" are contained in T12 and T3 respectively. The relationship tree that connects T_{12} and T_3 contains T_9. So, T_9 is also part of the STC. Therefore, we combine RCT_{T_3}, RCT_{T_9}, and $RCT_{T_{12}}$. All Canonical Trees contained in RCT_{T_9} are contained in RCT_{T_3} except for $RCT_{T_{10}}$ and $RCT_{T_{11}}$; therefore, we only attach $RCT_{T_{10}}$ and $RCT_{T_{11}}$ to RCT_{T_3}. All Canonical Trees contained in $RCT_{T_{12}}$ are contained in $RCT_{T_3} + RCT_{T_9}$ We then apply property 2 and prune T_1 and T_4, since their Ontology Labels are the same as the Ontology Label of T_9. We prune T_5, since its Ontology Label is the same as T_{12}. When applying property 3, we prune T_{10} and T_{11}, since their Ontology Labels are the same as T_3. We apply property 3 and prune T_2. The answer is node 32. See Figure 7.

6 System Implementation

6.1 Locating RCTs

For each Canonical Tree, we compute its RCT off line. We create a hash table called RCT-TBL. For each Canonical Tree, we store in table RCT-TBL its ID and the IDs of the Canonical Trees that constitute its RCT. The table entries are the IDs of the Canonical Trees. We then cache the RCT-TBL.

We also construct a Keyword Index Table. For each keyword, we save in this table the Canonical Tree(s) that contains that keyword. The Keyword Index Table helps in locating STCs efficiently. We populate part of this table offline with keywords that are most likely to be used, since on-line population is expensive [1]. If a query's keyword is not found in the table, we search the XML doc on-line to locate the Canonical Tree that contains it, and we then save this information in the Keyword Index Table for future references. So, we locate a STC from the Keyword Index Table and then locate its RCT from the RCT-TBL.

6.2 Getting Answers Using OO Programming

Due to the nature and construct resemblance of an object in OO programming and a Canonical Tree, OO programming is the most efficient mechanism to extract answer return element nodes from RCTs and to also extract instance values contained in those nodes. As stated previously, if we incorporate behavior (methods) to a Canonical Tree entity, this entity will have all the characteristics of an object in OO programming. The relationship between a STC and its RCT is similar to the relationships between objects in OO. A class in OO programming is the general template we use to define and create specific instances or objects. Every Canonical Tree object is associated with a class. Figure 8 shows the Entity Relationship Diagram of the Canonical Trees comprising RCT_{T_1}. Each of the 3 Canonical Trees in the Figure has a class. Class T_3 for instance contains attributes title and year (see Figure 8). As the Figure shows, class T_1 (the STC) contains methods to extract answer return element nodes from the objects of T_2 and T_3 .

Classes of Canonical Trees, whose Ontology Labels are the same behave as subclasses. Those subclasses inherit common attributes and methods from the superclass, which is a class that has the name of the Ontology Labels of the subclasses.

We can use the methods of a STC class (e.g. class T_1 in Figure 8), to extract both the answer return element nodes and the instance values contained in those nodes. To do that we can construct a hash table object for each attribute (leaf node) and populate it with the instance values contained in this node. Each attribute will contain a pointer to its hash table e.g. attribute "title" in Figure 8 contains a pointer to the hash table that contains the instance values of node 5 "title" (see Figures 1 and 2). Since populating a hash table for each attribute is very expensive especially when the XML document is large, we only populate hash tables for attributes that appear in Frequently Used Queries (FUQ). There are a number of studies that propose mechanisms to efficiently determining FUQ, such as [12], where efficient mechanisms to dynamically construct a list of FUQs were investigated. If a query is a FUQ, the system will first determine the query's answer return element nodes and then extract the result values from the hash table. This process is done using OO programming. For example, if the STC is T_1 and the query's return element is title (see Fig 8), class T_1 will use its method getTitle() to extract the "title" instance values contained in the hash table pointed to by attribute "title". If, however, the query is not a FUQ, the system will first extract the return element nodes and then get the data from the XML doc using XQuery processor. The system architecture in Figure 9 shows these processes. The arrows show the flow of information.

7 Experimental Results

We implemented OOXSearch and all its techniques described in this paper using Java. The experiments were carried out on a AMD Athlon XP 1800+ processor, with a CPU of 1.53 GHz and 736 MB of RAM, running the Windows XP operating system. To fully evaluate the system, we used data models from four different sources. We note that there are no XML benchmarks designed for testing loosely

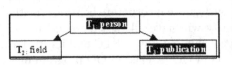

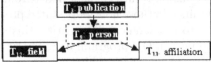

Fig. 6. RCT_{T1+T3}

Fig. 7. $RCT_{T3+T9+T12}$

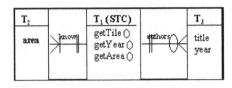

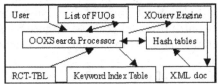

Fig. 8. Entity Relationship Diagram for Canonical Trees of RCT_{T1}

Fig. 9. System Architecture

structured query-based systems. We examined and compared the recall, precision, and search performance of OOXSearch with Schema-Free XQuery [2] and XSEarch [1]. The implementation of [2] has been released as part of the TIMBER project [21]. So, we used TIMBER for the evaluation of [2]. We note that we contacted one of the authors of [2], who helped us in the evaluation process. As for [1], we implemented the entire proposed system, since its demo hasn't been released to the public domain. Since we were aware of the types of data models and queries that cause [1] and [2] to yield low recall and precision, we gave the test data models to four computer science PhD students, who were not aware of the functionalities and techniques of neither OOXSearch nor [1] and [2] and we asked them to construct loosely structured queries based on those data models. The following are the four sources of our test data models:

XML Query Use Cases provided by W3C [11]: Each use case query is accompanied by a DTD and sample data. Some of these queries and data models emphasize textual content rather than node selection, because they are not designed for testing loosely structured query-based systems. The four students selected 11 data models from the use cases along with their accompanying queries that they thought are suitable for testing loosely structured query-based systems. They also constructed 9 additional queries based on those data models. We then generated 11 XML documents based on the 11 data models using [14]. The sizes of the docs ranged from 100 to 300 MB.

XMark Benchmark [19]: There are 20 queries written in schema aware XQuery accompanied by a 100 MB XML document.

XML Validation Benchmark from Sarvega [20]: The four students selected 14 out of the 25 provided XML docs that are suitable for testing loosely structured query-based systems. The sizes of the docs are small, but some of them are deeply nested.

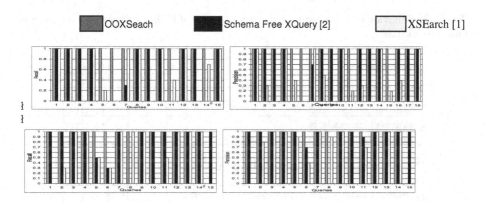

Fig. 10. The top tow Figures show the Recall/ Precision on W3C Use Cases queries and the bottom tow Figures show the Recall/ Precision on XML Validation Benchmark

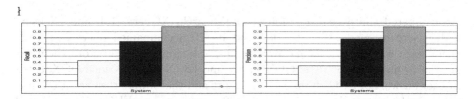

Fig. 11. Average Recall/ Precision on ALL the test data

Heterogeneous data models collected from the web: We collected 20 different data models from the web.

7.1 Recall and Precision Evaluation

Figures 10 shows the recall and precision of the three systems on the W3C Use Cases [11] and XML Validation Benchmark [20] respectively. In all the Figures, OOXSearch achieved 100 percent recall and precision in all the queries, except for query number 15 of the XML Validation Benchmark, where it achieved 0 percent recall and precision. [2] Achieved 0 percent recall and precision in four of the W3C Use Cases and in one of the XML Validation Benchmark queries, as the Figures show. As for [1], it achieved poor results. OOXSearch outperformed [2] and [1] while [2] Outperformed [1]. The recall and precision results of [1] and [2] on XMark are shown in the paper [2] (Figure 9). OOXSearch and [2] achieved 100 percent recall and precision on all XMark's 20 queries, while [1] achieved poor results (Figure is not shown due to space limitation). Figure 11 shows the average recall and precision of the three systems using ALL the test data and queries from the four sources of data stated previously. Based on the different experimentation results, we constructed a table to summarize the criteria of data models and queries that caused each of the three systems to achieve good or bad results (see Table 2).

Table 2. Behavior of OOXSearch, [1], and [2] under different criteria of data models and query types

Criteria of a data model/query	[1]		[2]		OOXSearch	
	R	P	R	P	R	P
All nodes in a data model have distinct labels and types	+	+	+	+	+	+
Two or more nodes have the same label but different types	+	-	+	-	+	+
Two or more nodes have the same label and type	-	+	-	+	+	+
Two or more nodes in a data model have different labels but belong to the same type	-	-	+	+	+	+
Query type B	-	+	-	+	+	+
The labels of one or more nodes match a query's return element but the nodes don't satisfy its search term	-	-	-	-	+	+
A parent node and its child node belong to the same type and both have leaf children nodes with the same label	+	+	-	+	-	-

7.2   Search Performance Evaluation

We compared the execution time of OOXSearch, XQuery [13], and [2] using XMark's ready-made 100 MB doc and its 20 accompanied queries. The 20 queries are written in schema aware XQuery language. We rewrote them using the formats accepted by OOXSearch and [2]. Note that since OOXSearch can get answers of FUQs from cached results and that lowers the execution time significantly, we considered each of the 20 queries as non-FUQ, and computed the execution times based on that. The results showed that the execution times of OOXSearch ranged from 121 percent to 232 percent of the execution times of [13], while the execution times of [2] ranged from 147 percent to 387 percent of the execution times of [13] (see [28]).

To evaluate the execution times of OOXSearch under different document sizes, we ran queries using different doc sizes (150, 200, 250, and 300 MB) of XMark, XQuery Use Cases, and XML Validation Benchmark. For each of the four doc sizes, we ran 60 random queries and computed the average execution time. We repeated the same process using XSEarch and Schema-Free XQuery. The results showed that OOXSearch outperformed [1] and [2] in ALL the tests (see [28]).

8   Conclusion

Using two recent works [1, 2] as samples we demonstrated how systems that employ semantic relationships between individual nodes are likely to return wrong and/or redundant answers. The reason is that a label of a node by itself isn't sufficient to convey the semantics of the node. We proposed an alternative framework solution, which takes into consideration the context of a node (its parent). The main contribution of this paper is the employing of semantic relationships between nodes based on their contexts and also the use of OO programming to extract data from those nodes. The proposed framework is efficient, robust, and works in heterogeneous data models. As shown in our experimental results, there is only 1 out of 7 data model criteria that causes our framework to return faulty recall and precision. In our future work we will expand OOXSearch and investigate a way to correct this single faulty criterion.

References

1. Cohen, S., Mamou, J., Kanza, Y., Sagiv, Y.: XSEarch: A Semantic Search Engine for XML. In: Aberer, K., Koubarakis, M., Kalogeraki, V. (eds.) Databases, Information Systems, and Peer-to-Peer Computing. LNCS, vol. 2944, Springer, Heidelberg (2004)
2. Li., Y., Jagadish, H.: Schema-Free XQuery. In: VLDB 2004 (2004)
3. Xu, Y., Papakonstantinou, Y.: Efficient Keyword Search for Smallest LCAs in XML Databases. In: SIGMOD 2005 (2005)
4. Amer-Yahia, S., Deutsch, A.: Flexible and Efficient XML Search with Complex Full-Text Predicates. In: SIGMOD 2006 (2006)
5. Al-Khalifa, S., Yu, C., Jagadish, H.: Querying Structured Text in an XML Database. In: SIGMOD 2003 (2003)
6. Hristidis, V., Papakonstantinou, Y.: DISCOVER: Keyword search in Relational Databases. In: Bressan, S., Chaudhri, A.B., Lee, M.L., Yu, J.X., Lacroix, Z. (eds.) CAiSE 2002 and VLDB 2002. LNCS, vol. 2590, Springer, Heidelberg (2003)
7. Chaudhuri, S., Das, G., Agrawal, S.: DBXplorer: a System for Keyword-Based Search Over Relational Databases. In: ICDE 2002 (2002)
8. Aditya, B., Sudarshan, S.: BANKS: Browsing and Keyword Searching in Relational Databases. In: Bressan, S., Chaudhri, A.B., Lee, M.L., Yu, J.X., Lacroix, Z. (eds.) CAiSE 2002 and VLDB 2002. LNCS, vol. 2590, Springer, Heidelberg (2003)
9. Balmin, A., Hristidis, V., Koudas, N.: A System for Keyword Proximity Search on XML Databases. In: Aberer, K., Koubarakis, M., Kalogeraki, V. (eds.) Databases, Information Systems, and Peer-to-Peer Computing. LNCS, vol. 2944, Springer, Heidelberg (2004)
10. Shao, F., Guo, L., Botev, C., XRANK,: Ranked Keyword Search over XML Documents. In: SIGMOD 2003 (2003)
11. XML Query Use Cases, W3C Working Draft 8 (June 2006). Available at http://www.w3.org/TR/xquery-use-cases/
12. Elmasri, R., Taha, K.: Caching: An Efficient XML Query Mechanism in Client-Server Architecture. SWDIM'06 (2006)
13. XQEngine version 0.69, downloaded from http://sourceforge.net/projects/xqengine
14. ToXgene, a template-based generator for large XML documents. Available at: http://www.cs.toronto.edu/tox/toxgene/
15. Boag, S.: XQuery 1.0: An XML Query Language. W3C Recommendation 2006. http://www.w3.org/TR/2006/CR-xquery-20060608/
16. Florescu, D., et al.: Integrating keyword search into XML query processing. Computer Networks 33, 119–135 (2000)
17. Bray, T.: Extensible Markup Language (XML). W3C. At: http://www.w3.org/TR/2004/REC-xml11-20040204/
18. Berglund, A.: XML Path Language (XPath) 2.0. W3C Working Draft 15 (September 2005)
19. XMark - An XML Benchmark Project. Available at http://monetdb.cwi.nl/xml/downloads.html

20. XML Validation Benchmark, Sarvega (an Intel company),
    http://www.sarvega.com/xml-validation-benchmark.html
21. TIMBER: http://www.eecs.umich.edu/db/timber/
22. Hristidis, V., Balmin, A.: Keyword Proximity Search on XML Graphs. In: ICDE
    2003 (2003)
23. Sara Cohen, B.: Kimelfeld. Interconnection Semantics for Keyword Search in XML.
    In: CIKM 2005 (2005)
24. Amer-Yahia, S., Deutsch, A.: Flexible and Efficient XML Search with Complex
    Full-Text Predicates. In: VLDB 2006 (2006)
25. Pradhan, S.: An Algebraic Query Model for Effective and Efficient Retrieval of
    XML Fragments. In: VLDB'06 (2006)
26. Balmin, A.: Authority Based Keyword Search in Databases. In: VLDB'04
27. Castor is an Open Source data-binding framework for Java. Available at
    http://www.castor.org/
28. The complete version of this paper is available at:
    //students.uta.edu/ks/kst0035/

Evaluating XPath Queries on XML Data Streams

Stefan Böttcher and Rita Steinmetz

University of Paderborn (Germany)
Computer Science
Fürstenallee 11 D-33102 Paderborn
stb@uni-paderborn.de, rst@uni-paderborn.de

Abstract. Whenever queries have to be evaluated on XML data streams - or when the memory that is available to evaluate the XML data is relatively small compared to the document - DOM based approaches that have to load and store large parts of the document in main memory will fail. In comparison, we present an approach to evaluate XPath queries on SAX streams that supports all axes of core XPath, including the sibling axes. Starting from the XPath query, our approach generates a stack of automata that uses the SAX stream as input and generates the result of the query as an output SAX stream. An evaluation of our implementation shows that in general our approach needs less main memory, but at the same time is faster than both, Saxon and YFilter.

1 Introduction

1.1 Motivation and Paper Organization

XML is becoming the de facto standard for information exchange and, as the amount of XML data is steadily growing, a key challenge is to process XML documents fast within the available main memory.

Our contribution focuses on scenarios, in which a system has to evaluate queries fast on documents that are multiple times larger than the main memory available to the system. One typical scenario is an XML news stream provided by a news agency using one of the typical XML formats NewsML [16] or NITF [17] to broadcast their news, and users who want to receive only parts of the news based on queries that represent their interests. Another typical scenario is that devices with a small amount of main memory (as e.g., mobile phones) shall work on large XML documents.

Whenever a scenario requires that the main memory available to evaluate queries on XML data is relatively small compared to the XML data size, approaches that are based on DOM will fail. These approaches have to load the complete XML document as a DOM tree into main memory, and as they need at least 4 pointers for each XML element (name, parent, first child, and next sibling) they yield a memory consumption that covers multiple times the size of the XML data.

Therefore, we propose a SAX based approach to the evaluation of XPath queries. Each input query is translated into an automaton that consists of only four different types of transitions, the treatment of which is described in Section 2. The small size of

R. Cooper and J. Kennedy (Eds.): BNCOD 2007, LNCS 4587, pp. 101–113, 2007.

the generated automata allows for a fast evaluation of the input XML data stream within a small amount of memory.

This paper is organized as follows: The remainder of the first section outlines the query language, summarizes the underlying assumptions, and outlines the problem definition. Section 2 summarizes the fundamental concepts used to describe our approach to evaluate XPath queries. The third section outlines some of the experiments that show the space efficiency and time efficiency of our prototype. Section 4 gives an overview on related work and is followed by the Summary and Conclusions.

1.2   Query Language

The subset of XPath expressions supported by our approach conforms to the set of *core XPath* as defined in [11]. This set is defined by the following EBNF grammar:

```
cxp          ::= `/' locationpath
locationpath    ::= locationstep ('/' locationstep)*
locationstep    ::= x `::' t | x `::' t `[' pred `]'
pred         ::= pred `and' pred | pred `or' pred
             | `not' `(' pred `)' | locationpath
             | locationpath '=' const |`(' pred `)'
```

"cxp" is the start production, "x" represents an axis (attribute, self, child, parent, descendant-or-self, descendant, ancestor-or-self, ancestor, following, preceding, following-sibling, preceding-sibling), "const" represents a constant, and "t" represents a "node test" (either an XML node name test or "*", meaning "any node name").

Note that our system supports the sibling axes, whereas other approaches like XMLTK[1], $\chi\alpha o\zeta$[4], AFilter[6], YFilter[9], XScan[14], SPEX[18], and XSQ[20] are limited to the parent-child and ancestor-descendant axes.

1.3   General Assumptions and Problem Definition

As our system is designed to efficiently evaluate XPath queries on a possibly infinite XML data stream, one requirement that our system has to meet is that each SAX event can be read only once, i.e., the stream has to be parsed in a single pass in document order. As we cannot jump backwards within the data stream, we have to rewrite user queries that use backward axes (i.e., ancestor-or-self, ancestor, preceding-sibling, and preceding) into equivalent queries containing only forward axes as described in [19]. The rewriting might lead to equivalent rewritten queries that are exponentially longer than the original queries, but as usually queries are rather short compared to the XML data, the growth of query length will usually not extend the runtime too badly.

Problem description: After rewriting queries, the remaining problem examined in this paper is the following. The input consists of a core XPath query containing only the forward axes and of an XML data stream in form of a SAX input event stream. The desired output is a SAX event stream of query results in document order. The main requirements of our system are to use as little main memory as possible in order to reach data throughput rates comparable to those of data streams.

2 Our Solution

In this section, we first explain how to transform the SAX input stream into a binary SAX event stream, containing firstchild::*, nextsibling::*, and parent::* events, and supporting self::a node tests. We then discuss how XPath queries are normalized, such that they contain only firstchild::*, nextsibling:*, and self::a location steps plus filters, and how normalized queries are transformed into XPath automata. Afterwards, we show how to evaluate the binary SAX event stream on an evaluation stack of an XPath automaton, which represents core XPath queries without any predicate filters. Finally, we extend the approach to queries with predicate filters.

2.1 Binary SAX Event Streams

We transform the SAX event stream of the input XML document into a stream of binary SAX events firstchild::*, nextsibling::*, parent::*, and self::a. Here, 'a' can be an element name, @ followed by an attribute name, or = followed by a constant. Transforming the SAX stream is done in two phases.

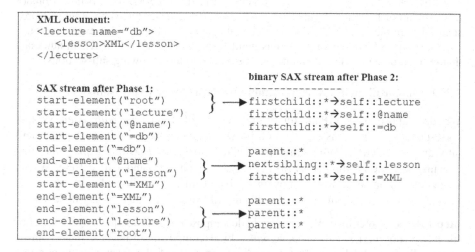

```
XML document:
<lecture name="db">
    <lesson>XML</lesson>
</lecture>


                                          binary SAX stream after Phase 2:
                                          ----------------
SAX stream after Phase 1:
start-element("root")          }  ──▶ firstchild::*→self::lecture
start-element("lecture")       ʃ      firstchild::*→self::@name
start-element("@name")                firstchild::*→self::=db
start-element("=db")
end-element("=db")                    parent::*
end-element("@name")           }  ──▶ nextsibling::*→self::lesson
start-element("lesson")        ʃ      firstchild::*→self::=XML
start-element("=XML")
end-element("=XML")                   parent::*
end-element("lesson")          }  ──▶ parent::*
end-element("lecture")         ʃ      parent::*
end-element("root")
```

Fig. 1. Example XML document with the resulting SAX and binary SAX streams

Phase 1: The SAX event character(T) generated for a text value T found in the XML document is transformed into a binary SAX event sequence start-element(=T), end-element(=T). Similar, each attribute/value pair A=AV found in the XML document is transformed into a binary SAX event sequence

start-element(@A), start-element(=AV), end-element(=AV), end-element(@A) .

As the symbols '@' and '=' have to be chosen to uniquely identify attributes and text nodes respectively, they are not allowed as an initial character for element-names.

Finally, we replace the SAX event start-document with an event start-element("root"), and we replace the SAX event end-document with an event end-element("root"). At the end of Phase 1, the transformed SAX event stream contains only two kinds of events: start-element(…) and end-element(…).

Phase 2: For the replacement of all the start-element and end-element events with first-child::*, next-sibling::* or parent::* events, we regard the four different kinds of consecutive pairs of start-element and end-element events:

1. A start-element(x) followed by a second start-element(a) corresponds to the firstchild axis, i.e., 'a' is the first child of 'x'. Therefore, the event sequence firstchild::*→self::a is created.

2. An end-element(x) followed by a start-element(a) corresponds to the nextsibling axis, i.e., 'a' is the next sibling of 'x'. Therefore, the event sequence nextsibling::*→self::a is created.

3. Furthermore, an end-element(x) followed by a second end-element(y) corresponds to the parent axis. Therefore, the event parent::* is created.

4. When a start-element(x) is followed by an end-element(x), no binary SAX event is created.

Altogether, Phase 1 and Phase 2 together transform a SAX stream into a binary SAX stream of firstchild::*, nextsibling::*, parent::*, and self::a events. Figure 1 presents an example of an XML document and the generated binary SAX event stream.

The binary SAX events are used as input 'symbols' for a stack of XPath automata that is constructed for an XPath query as described in the following sub-sections.

2.2 Decomposition and Normalization of XPath Query Expressions

We decompose each XPath query into a set of filter-free *path queries*, and, corresponding to the transformation of the SAX input stream, rewrite each path query into an equivalent XPath expression, called *normalized XPath expression*, that contains only the location steps firstchild::*, nextsibling::*, and self::a. Here, 'a' can be an element name, @ followed by an attribute name, or = followed by a constant as in binary SAX events, but 'a' can also be the wildcard '*' for an arbitrary node name.

Step 1 (Decomposition): We recursively decompose each XPath query Q into a set of filter-free sub-queries, called *query paths*, by decomposing Q into the main path M and predicate paths P1,…, Pn. A predicate path Pi of the form path = const is rewritten to path/text::const.

For example, an XPath query

```
Q=/descendant::a[child::b=xyz]/child::c[child::d/child::e]/f
```
is decomposed into 3 query paths: the *main path*

```
M=/descendant::a/child::c/child::f
```
and   the   *predicate   paths*   P1=child::b/text::xyz   and P2=child::d/child::e.

Step 2 (Normalization): After decomposing Q, each of its query paths M, P1,…, Pn is normalized separately as follows. We replace the axes following, descendant-or-self, attribute, and text according to the following rewrite rules:

```
(1) following::a      →  ancestor-or-self::*/following-sibling::*
                                            /descendant-or-self::a
(2) descendant-or-self::a  →    descendant::a | self::a
(3) attribute::a       →    child::@a
(4) text::v            →    child::=v
```

Note, that the disjunction (|) in rule (2) does not lead to an exponential growth of the query size, but only to one additional edge in the XPath automaton (c.f. Figure 2).

As the rewrite rule (1) which replaces the following axis leads to an ancestor-or-self axis, we eliminate the backward axis ancestor-or-self according to the rewrite rules (13)-(22) provided in [19]. As the result of Step 2, we get an equivalent XPath query that contains only the axes self, child, descendant, and following-sibling.

2.3 Transforming a Filter-Free XPath Query into an XPath Automaton

In order to evaluate a query path, we first build an XPath automaton and then start the XPath evaluation stack using this automaton and the binary SAX stream as input.

Definition 1 (XPath automaton): An XPath automaton of a query path is a NFA
$$XP = (Q, \Sigma, q0, \delta, f), \text{ where}$$

- Q is the finite set of states
- Σ={firstchild::*, nextsibling::*} $\cup$ {self::a | a is an element name, @ followed by an attribute name, = followed by a constant or '*' } is the set of input symbols
- $q0 \in Q$ is the start state
- $\delta : Q \times \Sigma \times Q$ is a relation of *transitions* (q1,e,q2) where q2 is a successor state of q1 if the event e is sent to the NFA,
- $f \in Q$ is the final state

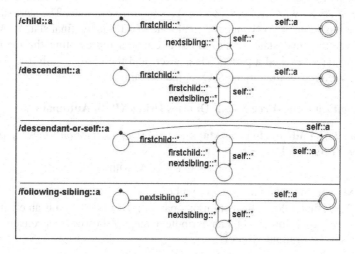

Fig. 2. Atomic XPath Automata

In order to build the XPath automaton for a given query path, we normalize each location step as described in Step 2 of Section 2.2. After normalization, we compute the so-called *atomic XPath automaton* for each location step. The atomic XPath automata for the location steps '/child::a', '/descendant::a', '/descendant-or-self::a', and '/following-sibling::a' are shown in Figure 2.

An atomic XPath automaton of the child axis, the descendant axis or the following-sibling axis location step (c.f. Figure 2) is an automaton that is equivalent to the regular expression that forms the right-hand-side of the following rewrite rules (which were inspired by [11]) for the corresponding location step.

```
(5) child::a➜  firstchild::*/
              (self::*/nextsibling::*)ⁱ/ self::a           0≤i<∞
(6) descendant::a  ➜  firstchild::*/ (self::*/(firstchild::* |
                          nextsibling::*)) ⁱ/self::a   0≤i<∞
(7) following-sibling::a➜  nextsibling::*/
                          (self::*/nextsibling::*)ⁱ/self::a   0≤i<∞
```

The right hand sides of the rules (5)-(7) correspond to regular expressions over the alphabet Σ of input symbols given in Definition 1, and the exponent 'i' corresponds to the kleene star operator in regular expressions. We have used the exponent i to avoid disambiguities between the kleene star operator for regular expressions and the (wildcard) *-operator in XPath expressions.

Note that the location step 'self::*' is inserted into the right hand sides of the rules (5)-(7), such that both the 'firstchild::*' and the 'nextsibling::*' location steps are followed by a self axis location step, which corresponds to the sequence of events of a binary SAX event stream as described in Section 2.1.

The complete XPath automaton of a query path is built by concatenating the atomic XPath automata of all the query path's locations steps in the order given by the location steps. To concatenate the atomic XPath automata ALS1 and ALS2 of two location steps LS1 and LS2 into a new XPath automaton XLS means to combine the final state of ALS1 with the start state of ALS2 to a single state. The start state of the XLS is the start state of ALS1 and the final state of XLS is the final state of ALS2.

Whenever the final state of the XPath automaton representing the main path is reached, we have reached a part of the answer, and the current "sub-tree" of the binary SAX stream is written to the SAX output stream.

2.4 Evaluating Filter-Free XPath Queries Using XPath Automata

Definition 2 (XPath evaluation stack): An *XPath evaluation stack of an XPath automaton XP* is a triple

$$XPE = (XP, \Sigma, \Delta) \text{ with}$$

- XP is used as the initial stack symbol
- Σ = {firstchild::*, nextsibling::*, parent::*} ∪ {self::a | a is an element name, @ followed by an attribute name, = followed by a constant or '*'} is the set of input symbols

- $\Delta(\Sigma)$ is an evaluation function that performs for a given input symbol a sequence of operations

Δ(firstchild::*) = {push(top()); top().event(firstchild::*);}

Δ(nextsibling::*) = {top().event(nextsibling::*);}

Δ(parent::*) = {pop();}

Δ(self::a) = { closure(top().event(self::a)); }

The operation 'XP Stack. top()' returns the XPath automaton on top of the stack, and the operation 'void XP.event(InputSymbol)' fires the event InputSymbol on the XPath automaton XP. The operation 'void Stack.push(XP)' puts the XPath automaton XP on top of the stack, such that Δ(firstchild::*) pushes a copy of the XP automaton that is the top stack element on top of the stack and passes the event firstchild::* to this copy. The operation 'void Stack.pop()' deletes the XPath automaton on top of the stack. Finally, the closure-operator in Δ(self::a) sends an event self::a to the automaton stored at top of stack as often as the state of this automaton changes.

Evaluation of filter-free XPath queries: Each filter-free XPath query X is evaluated on a stream of binary SAX events S as follows. We compute the XPath automaton XP of X and start the XPath evaluation stack with XP as initial stack symbol and with S as input. Each binary SAX event is passed as input symbol to the stack, and the $\Delta(\Sigma)$ function is performed for this input symbol which eventually causes stack operations and events on an automaton stored in the stack.

Whenever a final state of an XPath automaton that is stored on top of stack is reached, the XML sub-tree with the root element that corresponds to the SAX event last parsed is written to the SAX output stream.

Optimized implementation: As all XPath automata stored on the stack share the same structure, i.e., Q, Σ, q0, δ, and f are identical for all automata of the stack, in our implementation, we do not store and copy automata. Instead, there exists one global XPath automaton, and the stack stores only the set of active states on each level.

2.5 Evaluation of Automata for XPath Expressions with Predicate Filters

Whenever a location step LS contains a predicate filter, after query decomposition, a filter automaton F is created for the predicate path P corresponding to the filter, and F is attached to the final state fls of the atomic automaton of LS. A *filter automaton F* is an XPath automaton, but F's final state does not cause any output.

Whenever the state fls is reached by firing a transition, a so-called *reservation* is created and attached to fls and the start state of the attached filter automaton becomes active too, i.e., all binary SAX events are regarded as input for both the main automaton and the filter automaton. Each *reservation* is a Boolean variable, which will evaluate to either true as soon as the filter automaton has reached its final state or to false as soon as the automaton in which this filter automaton became active is popped from the stack.

More precisely, reservations are computed as follows. Let R, R1, R2 be sets of reservations, and let res: Q x $\wp$(R) be a mapping of XPath automaton states to sets of reservations. Each XPath automaton XP used in the XPath evaluation stack is initialized without any reservations, i.e., $\forall$ q$\in$XP.Q: res(q, {}). Whenever a state q is reached in XP, and a filter automaton F is attached to q, the mapping is changed from res(q,R) to res(q,R∪{r}), where r is a new reservation generated for F. Furthermore, when a transition of the form δ(q1,inputSymbol,q2) is fired, all reservations R1 for a state q1 become also reservations of the state q2 of XP. To summarize, the set of reservations R2 of q2 is R2=R1∪{r1,...,rf}, where r1,...,rf are the newly created reservations for the filter automata attached to q2.

If the final state f of an XPath automaton of the main path of the given XPath query is reached, and there exists a reservation r that is attached to f that is not yet evaluated, the output of the current sub-tree is queued and delayed until the reservation r is evaluated; the current sub-tree becomes an output *candidate*. Finally, when r is evaluated to true, the sub-tree is written to the output and deleted from the queue. If on the other hand r is evaluated to false, the sub-tree is deleted from the queue without writing it to the output.

A reservation r evaluates to true, if the corresponding filter automaton F reaches a final state. In this case, r is set to true, possibly queued sub-trees can be written to the output. If the automaton in which F became active is popped from the stack and no final state of F has been reached in the meantime, the reservation r for F evaluates to false, and possibly queued sub-trees that carry the reservation r are deleted without being written to the output and all active states s with res(s,R), r∈R, become inactive.

As a predicate filter can not only contain a single comparison path=value, but can be a composition of comparisons involving nested negations, disjunctions or conjunctions of comparisons, reservations can be logical compositions of sub-reservations, too. For example, a predicate filter [(comp1 or comp2) and not comp3], where comp1, comp2 and comp3 are comparisons or path expressions, results in a composed reservation r = ((r1 or r2) and not r3) and a filter automaton being created for each sub-reservation r1, r2, and r3.

Simple and composed reservations are administrated in a *lemma table*. Whenever a reservation is evaluated, the result is reported to the lemma table. The lemma table is used for checking whether a composed reservation can be evaluated completely, i.e., whether the lemma table knows enough results of sub-reservations to decide, whether the value of the composed reservation is true or false. The lemma table reports the value of the evaluated reservation back to the XPath automaton XP waiting for the reservation, such that XP can continue processing, and finally the main automaton can check the output queue, and output candidates might be written to the output.

3   Evaluation of Our Prototype Implementation

We have implemented a prototype of our solution (XPA) in Java 1.5 and have evaluated and compared it with two other systems on a Pentium 4 with 2.4 GHz Windows XP system with 1 GB of RAM running Java 1.5. On the one hand, we have compared XPA with the static XPath evaluator Saxon[21] that is DOM based, and therefore is not capable to evaluate data streams. On the other hand, we have compared XPA with YFilter[9], a system for information dissemination that is designed to evaluate a set of queries on large XML data streams.

Our test data set was generated by the XML generator of the XML Benchmark XMark[22]. The sizes of the documents of our data set can be seen in Table 1. A document Dn was created by the XMark generator providing the factor n/1000, i.e., D32 was generated by the XMark generator with the factor 0.032. This leads to a dataset with documents starting from the size of 116 kB to the size of more than 650 MB.

Table 1. Document sizes of the test collection (generated by XMark)

Document name	D1	D2	D4	D8	D16	D32	D64	D128	D256	D512	D1024	D2048	D4096	D6000
Document size (kB)	116	211	458	901	1,881	3,728	7,259	14,949	29,693	59,114	118,767	238,164	477,018	697,657

On our dataset, we have evaluated queries that were inspired by the queries Q1,...,Q5 of the XPath benchmark XPathMark[10] (we have omitted all backward axes in advance). The test queries can be seen in Table 2.

Table 2. XPathMark queries used for the evaluation of the XPath evaluation system XPA

Name	Query
Q1	/child::site/child::regions/child::*/child::item
Q2	/child::site/child::closed_auctions/child::closed_auction/child::annotation/ child::description/child::parlist/child::listitem/child::text/child::keyword
Q3	/descendant::keyword
Q4	/descendant-or-self::listitem/descendant-or-self::keyword
Q5	/child::site/child::regions/child::*[self::namerica]/child::item

Our tests have shown that our system outperforms the other two systems. Especially for large documents, our system is more than 2 times faster than Saxon and 20 times faster than YFilter. Table 3 shows the concrete figures for the query Q5. A visualization of the figures for the query Q5 can be seen in Figure 3(a), whereas Figure 3(b) and 3(c) show the evaluation times for all queries for document D1 or D1024 respectively.

Our tests have as well shown that our system consumes far less main memory than Saxon and than YFilter. Saxon consumes 4 times the document size on average, which is typical for DOM based systems, YFilter needs only 2 times the document size. In comparison, XPA consumes from 20% of the document size on average for simples XPath queries without predicate filters (Q1-Q4) up to 50 % of the document size on average for paths with predicate filters (Q5). In our experiments, an OutOfMemory-Exception for YFilter occured from D2048 on and for Saxon from D4096 on with 1 GB of heap space assigned to Java.

On average, we have measured a data throughput rate of more than 40MBit/s for our system. In comparison, ADSL2+, the fastest ADSL standard currently available, reaches a data download throughput rate of at most 24 MBit/s.

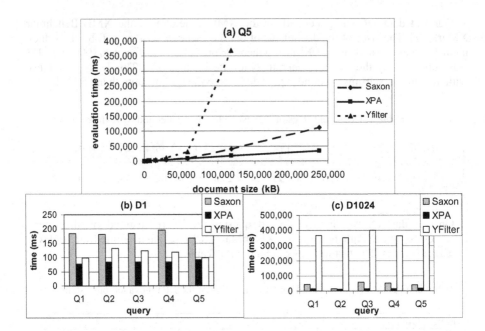

Fig. 3. (a) Evaluation time for different document sizes (query: Q5). (b) Evaluation time for document D1 for all queries. (c) Evaluation time for D1024 for all queries.

Table 3. Evaluation time for different document sizes (query Q5) (□ = OutOfMemory)

	D1	D2	D4	D8	D16	D32	D64	D128	D256	D512	D1024	D2048	D4096	D6000
XPA	92	123	136	219	383	688	1,204	2,288	4,194	8,623	16,983	32,945	109,471	186,282
Saxon	168	171	257	366	651	898	1,511	2,482	4,500	9,515	40,403	111,862	∅	∅
YFilter	99	159	256	422	778	1,387	2,640	5,102	10,115	30,914	367,790	∅	∅	∅

4 Relation to Other Works

There exist several different approaches to the evaluation of XPath queries on XML data streams. They can be divided into categories by the subset of XPath they support. Nearly all of them are based on automatons (X-scan[14], XMLTK[1], YFilter[9], [12], [13], AFilter[6], XSQ[20], SPEX[18]) or parse trees ([3], [4], [7], [8]). All of them support the axes child and descendant-or-self and most of them support predicate filters and wildcards, but none of them support the sibling-axes as our solution does.

X-scan[14], XMLTK[1], and YFilter[9] support XPath queries containing the child and descendant-or-self axes and wildcards using finite state automata. [12] (for the main path) and [13] (for the predicates) propose to construct deterministic finite automata (DFA) in a lazy way, i.e., the DFA is not generated completely at the beginning, but additional states are added only when needed.

AFilter[6] is an adaptable XPath query evaluation approach that needs a base memory requirement that is linear in query and data size. If more memory is provided to AFilter, AFilter uses the remaining main memory for a caching approach to evaluate queries faster than with only the base memory. AFilter is mainly based on a lazy DFA and it supports wildcard, but does not support predicate filters. Similar to YFilter[9], AFilter is designed to evaluate a large set of queries.

XSQ[20] and SPEX[18] use a hierarchical arrangement or network of transducers, i.e., automata extended by actions attached to the states, extended by a buffer to evaluate XPath queries. The XPath queries supported by XSQ contain predicates with the restriction that each query node can contain at most one predicate and each predicate can contain path-to-value comparisons with paths of size 1 containing only the axes child, text or attribute. The main idea is that a nondeterministic push-down transducer (PDT) is generated for each location step in an XPath query, and these PDTs are combined into a hierarchical pushdown transducer in the form of a binary tree.

The approach presented in [15] discusses how to handle the child and descendant-or-self axes, predicates (including functions and arithmetics) and wildcards in XQuery using TurboXPath. The input query is translated into a set of parse trees. Whenever a matching of a parse tree is found within the data stream, the relevant data is stored in form of a tuple that is afterwards evaluated to check whether predicate- and join conditions are fulfilled. The output is constructed out of those tuples the conditions of which have been evaluated to true.

$\chi\alpha o\zeta$[4] and [3] build a parse tree as well (plus a parse-dag in [4], as they support the parent and the ancestor axis in addition). These parse tree is used to 'predict' the next matching nodes and the level in which they have to occur. For example, consider the query //a/b and a matching of 'a' in level 3. Then the next interesting matching would be a node 'b' in level 4.

The approach discussed in [7] is mainly based on parse trees, but it collapses the parse tree into a prefix trie as follows. Common prefix sequences of child-axis location steps of different queries are combined into a leaner single path of the prefix trie.

The approach presented in [8] uses a structure which resembles a parse tree with stacks attached to each node. These stacks are used to store XML nodes that are solutions to the parse tree nodes subquery (or to store XML nodes that are candidates for a solution in case of predicate filters).

In comparison to all these approaches, we additionally support the 'sibling'-axes following and following-sibling. Furthermore, beyond [15] and [20], our approach is capable to parse streams of recursive XML, i.e., data in which the same element names do occur repeatedly along a root-to-leaf path.

5 Summary and Conclusions

Query processing on massive XML data streams and query processing of XML data on small mobile devices require a query processor to meet two conditions at the same time: the query processor shall consume a small amount of main memory and shall reach data throughput rates that are not smaller than the arrival rate of the XML data using today's broadband communication technologies.

In this paper, we have presented an XPath query processor that reaches data throughput rates that are higher than the download rates of ADSL2+ while at the same time consuming only 20%-50% of the document size in main memory. Furthermore, in comparison to most of the other query processors, our query processor supports all the axes of core XPath including the sibling axes.

Our query processor decomposes and normalizes each XPath query, such that the resulting path queries contain only three different types of axes, and then converts them into lean XPath automata for which a stack of active states is stored. The input SAX event stream is converted into a binary SAX event stream that serves as input of the XPath automata.

As XPath is used as data access standard in XSLT and XQuery, we are optimistic that the technology proposed in this paper can be used within XSLT processors or XQuery processors too.

References

[1] Avila-Campillo, I., Green, T.J., Gupta, A., Onizuka, M., Raven, D., Suciu, D., XMLTK,: An XML Toolkit for Scalable XML Stream Processin. In: Proceedings of PLANX (October 2002)

[2] Bar-Yossef, Z., Fontoura, M., Josifovski, V.: Buffering in query evaluation over XML streams. PODS 2005, pp. 216–227 (2005)

[3] Bar-Yossef, Z., Fontoura, M., Josifovski, V.: On the Memory Requirements of XPath Evaluation over XML Streams. PODS 2004, pp. 177–188 (2004)

[4] Barton, C., Charles, P., Goyal, D., Raghavachari, M., Fontoura, M., Josifovski, V.: Streaming XPath Processing with Forward and Backward Axes. ICDE 2003, pp. 455–466 (2003)

[5] Bry, F., Coskun, F., Durmaz, S., Furche, T., Olteanu, D., Spannagel, M.: The XML Stream Query Processor SPEX. ICDE 2005, pp. 1120–1121 (2005)

[6] Candan, K.S., Hsiung, W.-P., Chen, S., Tatemura, J., Agrawal, D.: AFilter: Adaptable XML Filtering with Prefix-Caching and Suffix-Clustering. VLDB 2006, pp. 559–570 (2006)

[7] Chan, C.Y., Felber, P., Garofalakis, M.N., Rastogi, R.: Efficient Filtering of XML Documents with XPath Expressions. ICDE 2002, pp. 235–244 (2002)

[8] Chen, Y., Davidson, S.B., Zheng, Y.: An Efficient XPath Query Processor for XML Streams. In: Proceedings of 22nd International Conference on Data Engineering (ICDE) (to appear, 2006)

[9] Diao, Y., Rizvi, S., Franklin, M.J.: Towards an Internet-Scale XML Dissemination Service. In: Proceedings of VLDB 2004 (August 2004)

[10] Franceschet, M.: XPathMark: An XPath Benchmark for the XMark Generated Data. In: Bressan, S., Ceri, S., Hunt, E., Ives, Z.G., Bellahsène, Z., Rys, M., Unland, R. (eds.) XSym 2005. LNCS, vol. 3671, pp. 129–143. Springer, Heidelberg (2005)

[11] Gottlob, G., Koch, C., Pichler, R.: Efficient Algorithms for Processing XPath Queries. VLDB 2002 (2002)

[12] Green, T.J., Gupta, A., Miklau, G., Onizuka, M., Suciu, D.: Processing XML Streams with Deterministic Automata and Stream Indexes Published in ACM TODS, vol. 29(4), pp. 752–788 (December 2004)

[13] Gupta, A., Suciu, D.: Stream Processing of XPath Queries with Predicate. In: Proceeding of ACM SIGMOD Conference on Management of Data (2003)

[14] Ives, Z.G., Halevy, A.Y., Weld, D.S.: An XML query engine for network-bound data. VLDB J. 11(4), 380–402 (2002)
[15] Josifovski, V., Fontoura, M., Barta, A.: Querying XML streams. VLDB J. 14(2), 197–210 (2005)
[16] NewsML 1.2: News Markup Language (October 2003) http://www.newsml.org/
[17] NITF 3.3: News Industry Text Format, http://www.nitf.org/
[18] Olteanu, D., Kiesling, T., Bry, F.: An Evaluation of Regular Path Expressions with Qualifiers against XML Streams. ICDE 2003, pp. 702–704 (2003)
[19] Olteanu, D., Meuss, H., Furche, T., Bry, F.: XPath: Looking Forward. EDBT Workshops 2002, pp. 109–127 (2002)
[20] Peng, F., Chawathe, S.S.: XPath Queries on Streaming Data. In: Proceedings of the ACM SIGMOD International Conference on Management of Data. June 9-12 2003, San Diego, California (2003)
[21] SAXON - XSLT and XQUERY Prozessor Version 8.8.0.4. 2006 http://saxon.sourceforge.net/
[22] Schmidt, A., Waas, F., Kersten, M.L., Carey, M.J., Manolescu, I., Busse, R.: XMark: A Benchmark for XML Data Management. VLDB 2002, pp. 974–985 (2002)

PSMQ: Path Based Storage and Metadata Guided Twig Query Evaluation

M. Archana, M. Lakshmi Narayana, and P. Sreenivasa Kumar

IIT Madras, Chennai,
India - 600036
archana.maram@gmail.com, lokesh512@gmail.com, psk@cs.iitm.ernet.in

Abstract. Efficient evaluation of queries on XML data is a major research issue. Structural join based techniques are well known for XPath evaluation. For the long path expressions, join techniques are not efficient as they increase the number of joins and disk I/O cost. Path based techniques try to reduce the number of joins. In this paper, we propose a metadata guided query evaluation technique which uses path based storage. We use interval encoding for the nodes. In addition, we use Strong DataGuide to assign integer path labels to distinct root-to-node label paths in the data tree. An *element list* is maintained for each distinct path consisting of nodes that can be reached by that path. The `Element-Map` gives the one-to-many mapping between element names (or tag names) to element lists with nodes having that tag-name. The `Path-Map` gives the root-to-leaf path for a given path label. Using these structures, we can combine top-down path matching and bottom-up path selections to efficiently evaluate linear path expressions. For twig queries, we perform structural joins at branch points. Through experimental evaluation on standard datasets, we show that our approach outperforms the existing path-index based approaches which in turn outperform structural join methods.

Keywords: DataGuide, XPath, structural summary, structural join.

1 Introduction

Many query languages such as XPath [4] and XQuery [9] have been proposed to query XML data. In this paper, we consider only the tree structured XML data i.e. data which does not include IDs and IDREFs and XPath queries are considered. We consider the queries that can be represented in the form of trees, called the *twig* queries.

Efficient processing of XPath expressions is one of the major recent research issues. Many techniques have been proposed to process path expressions efficiently. Some of the well known query evaluation techniques include join based algorithms [8,14], structural summary techniques [12] and path-ID based algorithms [17,5,10].

The structural join approaches [8,14] split the query into a set of binary structural join operations. The intermediate results of these joins are merged to get

R. Cooper and J. Kennedy (Eds.): BNCOD 2007, LNCS 4587, pp. 114–124, 2007.
© Springer-Verlag Berlin Heidelberg 2007

the final result of the query. All the above mentioned structural join algorithms use interval encoding as the node identification scheme. To evaluate all the XPath axes, Staircase Join Algorithm [15] which uses pre-post node encoding scheme is proposed. In join approaches computation cost due to the style of one-join-per-location-step becomes unacceptably huge, especially when the path expression is long.

Unlike join approaches, structural summary based approaches restrict the search to only relevant portion of XML data. Examples of such approaches include DataGuide [12] and Index Fabric [6]. These techniques can efficiently process the absolute paths.

To reduce the number of joins and disk accesses, path based techniques such as BLAS [17] and MQEB [5] are proposed. These algorithms assign *pid*(path id also called P-Label) to each element and also to all the possible paths in the document. The *pid* of a node encodes the root-to-node path(also called as source path of the node) for that node. When compared to structural join techniques, these approaches reduce the number of joins and disk I/O cost. BLAS needs joins at each ancestor-descendant step and branching points but MQEB needs joins only at branching points. For non-branching path expressions, MQEB does not need any joins. But both of these approaches fail to assign *pid* values to elements in case of XML documents that are deep and have large number of distinct elements. As the P-Label calculation depends on the number of distinct tags information they need to reassign the P-Labels if a new tag-name is added.

The other path based technique XRel [10] is a relational system. XRel converts the given XML document into four tables: `Element`, `Attribute`, `Text` and `Path`. The schema of the tables is as follows:

```
Element(docID, pathID, start, end, index, reindex)
Attribute(docID, pathID, start, end, value)
Text(docID, pathID, start, end, value)
Path(pathID, pathexp)
```

This system also uses interval encoding to assign *start* and *end* values to all the elements, attributes and text in the document. Given XPath queries are converted to SQL and executed on relational tables.

BLAS and MQEB perform better than join approaches but have difficulties in assigning P-Labels. The XRel system has the additional overhead of query conversion. To overcome the problems with existing path based approaches, we propose a system called as PSMQ(**P**ath Based **S**torage and **M**etadata Guided **Q**uery Evaluation). We use interval encoding for node identification and strong DataGuide to assign P-Labels (or path labels) efficiently. We keep path summaries in the form of metadata to reduce the search effort while evaluating queries. Unlike BLAS and MQEB, we do not need to reassign the P-Labels, if a new tag-name gets added to the existing document.

Contributions of this paper are,

- Proposing a storage scheme which uses interval encoding as the node identification scheme and strong DataGuide approach to assign path labels.

- Introducing two forms of metadata *Element-Map* and *Path-Map*, which guide the query evaluation and are useful in reducing the number of joins.
- Introducing a query evaluation strategy which uses string matching techniques. The proposed query evaluation technique does not need joins to evaluate linear path expressions. To evaluate twig queries, joins are required at branching points.
- Experimental evaluation on standard benchmark data sets is done to show that the proposed technique performs better than the other path-ID based approaches, namely BLAS, MQEB and XRel. We have considered only these three existing path based systems because these systems outperform join approaches and other path based approaches.

The rest of the paper is organized as follows. Section 2 provides required background material. Proposed storage scheme and query evaluation technique for both linear path expressions and twig queries are explained in Section 3. Implementation details and results of the extensive experimental evaluation are shown in Section 5. We conclude in Section 6.

2   Background

2.1   Interval Encoding

In interval encoding scheme [14], each node is assigned a tuple $(start, end)$. The value of $start(end)$ for an element e can be generated by counting the number of tags from the beginning of the document to the start(end) tag of e. We can leave some gaps while assigning end value to handle updates. Using the interval encoding scheme, finding all the tree structured relationships between two nodes is very easy. Here, tree structured relationships could be ancestor-descendant, parent-child, preceding-following or sibling relationships.

2.2   DataGuide

DataGuide [12] describes every unique label path of the source document exactly once, regardless of the number of times it appears in the source document. In the DataGuide, if each object is reachable by a unique label path then it is considered as a *strong* DataGuide. Strong DataGuide induces a one-to-one correspondence between source paths and DataGuide nodes. An example XML tree and its corresponding Strong DataGuide are shown in Figure 1 and Figure 2 respectively. From the figure it is clear that a new node is created whenever we encounter a new path.

3   Proposed System: PSMQ

The storage of elements is based on the source paths of the elements. Each element is assigned a tuple $(start, end)$, and stored in an appropriate *element list*,

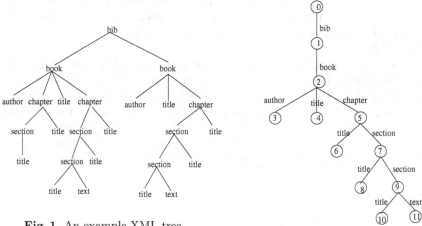

Fig. 1. An example XML tree

Fig. 2. Strong DataGuide

where an *element list* is the list of all elements with the same source path, where
source path of a node n is the root-to-node label path of n. Unlike the other
path-ID based algorithms, we do not store *pid* value for each element along with
start and *end* values. The *number* of the element list in which a particular element e is present, acts as path-ID of e. Note that we may have many different
element lists corresponding to an element *name e*, if *e-nodes* are reachable from
many different paths. Each node in the strong DataGuide of Figure 2 corresponds to an element list and the node number corresponds to distinct path
label in the document. Storing the elements in this way assures that, each path
will have only one element list corresponding to it. As we shall see later, this is
helpful in reducing the number of elements scanned and the disk I/O performed
while evaluating the query. We also find that unnecessary elements(which do
not contribute to the result) will not be considered while evaluating simple path
expressions(path expressions with only parent-child axis) and complex path ex-
pressions(path expressions with mixture of ancestor-descendant and parent-child
axes).

To access the value information efficiently in PSMQ, all values are stored in
a B^+-tree called Value B^+-tree. We use a hash function h(value) to hash the
value. We use the pair (hash value, path label) as the key and *start* and *end*
values as the data for the B^+-tree. We can also store the value without hashing
but this will increase the size of the B^+-tree.

Two forms of metadata is maintained in order to guide the query evaluation.
These two forms help in getting the relevant paths while evaluating the query.

1. **Element-Map:**
   As we can have different element lists corresponding to a tag-name, this
   metadata provides the necessary mapping of tag-names to element lists.
   Given a tag-name t, this metadata helps in finding the set of element list

numbers corresponding to the tag t. The `Element-Map` for the example tree will be: author-3, bib-1, book-2, chapter-5, section-7,9, text-11 and title-4,6,8,10. This information will be sorted on tag-name.

2. **Path-Map:**
   Another form of metadata is also maintained which helps in finding the source path if we know the path label. Each tuple in this metadata contains path label[1] (or path-ID) and the source path corresponding to it. This information is sorted in the order of path labels. Path-Map for the example XML tree will be like *1 - /bib, 2 - /bib/book, , 3 -bib/book/author* and so on. From the Figure 2 it is clear that the example XML document contains 11 distinct paths so `Path-Map` will also have 11 entries.

4   Query Evaluation

We model XML path query evaluation problem as a string matching problem. Here we assume the last element in the path query as the output node. If any other element is the output node then the query is treated as a twig query with one branch. We use combination of both bottom-up and top-down approaches for query evaluation.

Given a query, we consider the element name of the last location step in the query and get all element list numbers corresponding to this element name from the Element-Map. (If the element of the last location step is a wildcard, then all possible element names need to be considered.) These element list numbers are denoted by set S. Some of the elements in these element lists will contribute to the final result. Then we consider the source path corresponding to each member of the set S and try to string match the query to the retrieved paths. If a path satisfies the query then we store it in set P and corresponding element list number in set Res. To match the query with paths, string matching is used. At the end of query matching process we will retain only the element list numbers and their corresponding source paths in sets Res and P respectively. Finally, elements from the element list numbers in set Res are merged to produce the final result.

The query evaluation process for the query $a_0q_1a_1q_2a_2 \ldots a_{n-1}q_n$, where $a_0, a_1 \ldots a_{n-1}$ are either '/' or '//' and $q_0, q_1 \ldots q_n$ are the tag-names, is as follows: First we split the query at each ancestor descendant step and consider each segment as one string to be matched. The query after splitting is $Q_1, Q_2, \ldots, Q_k$. We proceed to match these segments one after the other in the chosen path. First we match Q_1 and in the subsequent part of the path, we match Q_2 and so on. When we match Q_i, we ensure that the last tag name in Q_i is matched to a complete tag name, rather than a prefix of it. For instance, "book" can not be matched to "books".

The process is illustrated with the help of an example query *bib/book//section/title*. This query retrieves titles of all sections in the books in bibliography. First, all element list numbers corresponding to the tag-name *title* are retrieved from

---
[1] Note that path label and element list number are same in our system.

the Element-Map. Now set $S = \{4, 6, 8, 10\}$. We retrieve paths corresponding to these element lists from Path-Map and check whether they match the query using string matching. For all the paths, first *bib/book* is matched and then *section/title* is matched. We find that only the paths corresponding to element lists 8 and 10 match the query. Hence, elements in these element lists are merged to produce the final result.

If the query has value predicate and if we got path label t as the result after evaluating the path expression without considering the predicate, then we need to retrieve only the elements satisfying the value predicate in element list t. We use $h(value)$ and t as the key for the Value B$^+$-tree to retrieve only the elements with the given value. Using this Value B$^+$-tree we can evaluate only the queries with equality predicates. To extend this to evaluate inequality predicates we need to build one more B$^+$-tree which uses *start* value as the key and the leaf value as the data.

To evaluate twig queries, we split the query at branching point and evaluate each branch separately and join the results. Consider an example twig query shown in Figure 3. This query is split as *bib//chapter* till the branching point and the two branching paths are *bib//chapter/section/section* and *bib//chapter/title*. First, we evaluate till the branching point i.e. *bib//chapter* and store this result in a temporary element list res_1. Let us say the path which satisfies this part of the query is *bib/book/chapter*. Now we evaluate the first branching path *bib//chapter/section/section*. When we evaluate branching paths we substitute *bib/book/chapter* for *bib//chapter* and do the matching process as we know the result till the branching point. The result of the first branching path is stored in a temporary list called as res_2. Now we join res_1 and res_2 elements as $res_2/ancestor :: res_1$, which gives ancestors of res_2 present in the set res_1. Join result is stored in res_1. Now second branching path *bib//chapter/title* is evaluated and the result is stored in res_3. We then perform join $res_1/descendants :: res_3$, which gives the final result. Many of the

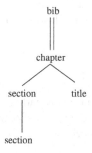

Fig. 3. Query: bib//chapter[section/section]/title

well known structural join algorithms [14,11] give pairs of nodes that join as the output but in our context, pairs are not required as the join output. Hence, we have used staircase algorithm [15] which gives only one set as the output.

4.1   Comparisons with BLAS and MQEB

The proposed system PSMQ has advantages when compared to the storage system of BLAS [17] and MQEB [5].

- The pre-processing overhead is less in PSMQ as it needs only one parsing, whereas, existing systems parse the document twice. The BLAS system needs two parses as the path labelling process requires to know the height of the data tree and the number of distinct element names. These are determined in the first parse.
- PSMQ does not suffer from the problem of running out of integer values for generating path labels. The number of digits in P-Label for different datasets is shown in Table 1. Existing systems might cross the available range of values while handling the datasets like TREEBANK which are deep. TREEBANK

Table 1. Space usage for different datasets

Dataset	Size	B⁺-tree	EM	PM	pathCount	TS	BLAS	LP
NASA	23MB	11MB	988B	4.6KB	94	16.4MB	30MB	17digits
SWISSPROT	109MB	62MB	1.2KB	3.4KB	116	97M	226MB	12digits
DBLP	128MB	98MB	939B	2.4KB	98	138MB	195MB	10digits
TREEBANK	83MB	62MB	3.4MB	17MB	338747	2.4GB	N/A	90digits

dataset needs 90-digit P-Label which none of the data types support. In this case, BLAS and MQEB fail to assign P-Labels. As we follow strong DataGuide approach for assigning path labels we can handle any kind of documents.

- If any new tag is added, existing systems need to reassign the P-Labels for all the nodes again. In our system if new tag is added then we need to just add entries in the metadata and create one element list for the new element.
- When compared to BLAS number of joins in evaluating complex and twig queries is reduced in our system. However number of joins in our system and MQEB is same.

4.2   Comparisons with XRel

- The XRel [10] system has the overhead of converting XML document into relational tables and also the overhead of converting XPath queries into SQL. PSMQ does not have this overhead.
- XRel needs one join for evaluating non-branching path expressions, two joins for non-branching path expressions with value predicates and three joins for each branching point in a twig query. We do not need joins to evaluate non-branching path expressions even in case of value predicates also. Our system PSMQ needs two joins at each branching point in a twig query.

5 Implementation Details

5.1 Offline Processing

Offline processing involves parsing the XML document, building two forms of metadata and creating Value B$^+$tree. SAX [1] parser which is written in Java, is used for parsing the XML document. Parsing phase assigns a tuple (*start,end*) to each element. If an element has value, then the value information is stored in a different file along with the element's *start* and *end* values. After we finish parsing, we construct Value B$^+$tree from this file. If the element to be added exists in one of the already seen paths then it is simply added to the proper element list based on its source path. If a new path comes, then a new element list is created and *Path-Map* is updated accordingly. We do not need extra parsing to build the metadata, it is built while parsing the document.

In the Table 1, columns EM(Element-Map) and PM(Path-Map) show the space occupied by two forms of metadata. The pathCount column shows the number of distinct paths in each of the datasets. The column B$^+$tree shows the size of the Value B$^+$tree. For query evaluation only the NASA and SWISSPROT datasets are used. However to check the metadata size, other datasets TREE-BANK and DBLP are also used. All the datasets are taken from [2]. We see that metadata size is small and it can be fit in the main memory easily. The columns TS and BLAS show the total storage, including metadata and Value B$^+$-tree, taken by our system and BLAS respectively. Last column shows the maximum number of digits needed for BLAS P-Labels. In case of TREEBANK dataset BLAS fails to assign P-Labels as it needs 90 digit number.

5.2 Experimental Setup

Experiments are conducted on a machine with 2.66GHz Intel Celeron processor having 512MB RAM. We have compared our system with BLAS [17], MQEB [5] and XRel [10]. We have used a machine running Fedora core 3 and the other machine with same configuration running Windows XP. For comparing our system with XRel, we have used both Windows and Linux machines. For comparing with BLAS and MQEB we have used Linux machine. String class provided by GNU C^{++} have been used to perform string matching functions. OS files are used to store element lists and the meta data, namely the Path-Map and the Element-Map and Berkeley DB [3] B$^+$-trees are used to create Value B$^+$-tree.

5.3 Performance Evaluation

Comparison with BLAS and MQEB: The example queries are shown in Table 2. Performance results for the example queries are shown in Tables 3 and 4 respectively. In these tables, columns PSMQ, BLAS and MQEB show the time taken in milliseconds for query evaluation in our system, BLAS and MQEB respectively.

Table 2. Queries for NASA and SWISSPROT(SP) datasets along with number of joins

Sl.No	Query	Dataset	BLAS	PSMQ
Q1	//dataset//astroObjects/astroObject/name	NASA	1	0
Q2	/datasets//textFile/name='adc.doc'	NASA	1	0
Q3	/datasets/dataset/identifier	NASA	0	0
Q4	//dataset[//reference/source//year]//tableHead//tableLink/title	NASA	3	2
Q5	/datasets//source//other//author[/lastName='Jackson']/initial	NASA	5	2
Q6	root/Entry/Ref/MedlineID	SP	0	0
Q7	root//Ref/Author='Baumeister H'	SP	1	0
Q8	root[//Features/CARBOHYD/Descr='POTENTIAL']//FLYBASE	SP	2	2
Q9	root/Entry[/Features/CONFLICT]/MENDEL	SP	2	2
Q10	root//Features/METAL/Descr	SP	1	0

Table 3. Query evaluation time in ms for NASA(23MB) dataset

Query	PSMQ	BLAS	MQEB
Q1	9	25	21
Q2	8	8	8
Q3	9	29	31
Q4	67	128	110
Q5	11	30	16

Table 4. Query evaluation time in ms for SWISSPROT(109MB) dataset

Query	PSMQ	BLAS	MQEB
Q6	21	250	200
Q7	8	8	8
Q8	22	23	22
Q9	21	35	33
Q10	11	248	200

Before evaluating the query, BLAS and MQEB systems calculate P-Labels of the given query. In the above comparison, the P-Label calculation time is not taken into consideration. From the Tables 3 and 4, it is clear that the evaluation of simple and complex path queries is efficient in our system. The precomputed P-Labels reduces the query evaluation time. If P-Label calculation time is also taken into account, then our system performs better in all cases. The size of the index structure is almost double for SWISSPROT when compared to our system as shown in Table 1. So the time taken to traverse the index structure will also be high which is clear from the results of queries Q6 and Q10 in Table 4.

Comparison with XRel: We have implemented PSMQ and XRel on a machine running Windows XP, Oracle 9i(with JDBC). We followed the algorithm for query translation proposed in XRel to manually convert the XPath query to SQL. These SQL queries are run on the Oracle database having NASA dataset tables. Table 5 shows the query evaluation time of XRel and PSMQ. The time shown in Table 5 does not include query translation time needed by XRel. Even then it is clear that PSMQ is performing significantly better than XRel. We repeated the experiments on a Linux system(Oracle 9i with JDBC) also. We have not experimented with larger datasets as the results with NASA(23MB) dataset are conclusive of the fact that PSMQ performs much better than XRel.

Table 5. Query Evaluation time in ms for NASA dataset

Query	Windows		Linux	
	PSMQ	XRel	PSMQ	XRel
/datasets/dataset/title	16	266	9	103
/datasets/dataset/tableHead/fields/field/definition/footnote/para	109	312	11	115
//dataset//astroObjects/astroObject/position	31	78	10	1064
/datasets/dataset[/title]/altname	125	812875	249	4441509
/datasets//textFile[/name]/description	78	844	93	690147
/datasets/dataset[//journal/title]/history/ingest	171	272235	183	1468061
/datasets//source//other//author[/lastName]/initial	78	844	66	670694
//dataset//other[/title]/date	46	843	23	494355
//dataset/history//revision[/date]/para	62	843	70	163896

6 Conclusions

In this paper, a storage system which is a combination of interval encoding and path based storage has been proposed. Unlike other path ID based techniques, our system can parse any large document and can assign path labels. We use strong DataGuide to assign path labels to distinct paths in the XML document. A novel system to evaluate XPath expressions using string matching techniques has been given. Proposed query evaluation technique does not need joins to evaluate non-branching path expressions. To evaluate twig queries, joins are required at branching points. We have built a Value B$^+$-tree to efficiently evaluate value predicates with equality condition. This can be easily extended to handle value predicates having inequality condition.

References

1. http://sax.sourceforge.net/
2. http://www.cs.washington.edu/research/xmldatasets
3. http://sleepycat.com/
4. Berglund, A., Boag, S., Chamberlin, D., Simon, J., Fernandez, M.F., Kay, M., Robie, J.: XML Path Language (XPath) 2.0. Technical report, W3C Working Draft (2001), Available at http://www/w3/org/TR/XPath20/
5. Rajesh, A., Sreenivasa Kumar, P.: MQEB: Metadata-based Query Evaluation of Bi-labeled XML data. In: COMAD, pp. 53–60 (2005b)
6. Cooper, B.F., Sample, N., Franklin, M.J., Hjaltason, G.R., Shadmon, M.: A Fast Index for Semistructured Data. In: VLDB, pp. 341–350 (2001)
7. Chung, C.-W., Min, J.-K., Shim, K.: APEX: an adaptive path index for XML data. In: SIGMOD Conference, pp. 121–132 (2002)
8. Zhang, C., Naughton, J.F., DeWitt, D.J., Luo, Q., Lohman, G.M.: On Supporting Containment Queries in Relational Database Management Systems. In: SIGMOD Conference, pp. 425–436 (2001)
9. Chamberlin, D., Robie, J., Florescu, D., Simeon, J., Stefanescu, M.: XQuery: A Query Language for XML. Technical report, W3C Working Draft (February 2001), Available at http://www/w3/org/TR/xquery/

10. Yoshikawa, M., Amagasa, T., Shimura, T., Uemura, S.: XRel: a path-based approach to storage and retrieval of XML documents using relational databases. ACM Trans. Internet Techn. 1(1), 110–141 (2001)
11. Bruno, N., Koudas, N., Srivastava, D.: Holistic twig joins: optimal XML pattern matching. In: SIGMOD '02: Proceedings of the 2002 ACM SIGMOD international conference on Management of data, New York, NY, USA, pp. 310–321. ACM Press, New York (2002)
12. Goldman, R., Widom, J.: DataGuides: Enabling Query Formulation and Optimization in Semistructured Databases. In: Jarke, M., Carey, M.J., Dittrich, K.R., Lochovsky, F.H., Loucopoulos, P., Jeusfeld, M.A. (eds.) VLDB'97, Proceedings of 23rd International Conference on Very Large DataBases, pp. 436–445. Morgan Kaufmann, Washington (1997)
13. Abiteboul, S., Quass, D., McHugh, J., Widom, J., Wiener, J.L.: The Lorel Query Language for Semistructured Data. Int. J. on Digital Libraries 1(1), 68–88 (1997)
14. Al-Khalifa, S., Jagadish, H.V., Patel, J.M., Wu, Y., Koudas, N., Srivastava, D.: Structural Joins: A Primitive for Efficient XML Query Pattern Matching. In: ICDE '02: Proceedings of the 18th International Conference on Data Engineering (ICDE'02), Washington, DC, USA, pp. 141–152. IEEE Computer Society, Washington (2002)
15. Grust, T., van Keulen, M., Teubner, J.: Staircase Join: Teach a Relational DBMS to Watch its (Axis) Steps. In: VLDB, pp. 524–525 (2003)
16. Cheng, J., Yu, G., Wang, G., Yu, J.X.: PathGuide: An Efficient Clustering Based Indexing Method for XML Path Expressions. In: DASFAA, pp. 257–64 (2003)
17. Chen, Y., Davidson, S.B., Zheng, Y.: BLAS: an efficient XPath processing system. In: SIGMOD '04: Proceedings of the 2004 ACM SIGMOD international conference on Management of data, New York, NY, USA, pp. 47–58. ACM Press, New York (2004)

Parameterized XPath Views

Timo Böhme and Erhard Rahm

Database Group
University of Leipzig
{boehme,rahm}@informatik.uni-leipzig.de

Abstract. We present a new approach for accelerating the execution of XPath expressions using parameterized materialized XPath views (PXV). While the approach is generic we show how it can be utilized in an XML extension for relational database systems. Furthermore we discuss an algorithm for automatically determining the best PXV candidates to materialize based on a given workload. We evaluate our approach and show the superiority of our cost based algorithm for determining PXV candidates over frequent pattern based algorithms.

1 Introduction

With XML as the lingua franca for data exchange and an increasingly popular storage format for structured data there is a growing demand for natively storing and querying of XML. Consequently native XML database systems evolve and relational database systems have been augmented with XML support. Query optimization is a main challenge for these systems due to the high flexibility and ordered structure of XML and the complexity of its query languages.

XPath is a crucial component of XML query languages such as XQuery or XSLT and thus has been an essential part for improving query performance. Work on this topic ranges from indexing techniques [15, 21, 22], structural join algorithms [3, 12], containment, equivalence and intersection of XPath expressions [10, 13] to cardinality estimation [20, 25]. Despite the large amount of work on XPath processing, running complex queries on large XML data sets is still a challenge. Moreover, several of the proposed algorithms are not applicable in certain environments like implementations using a relational database system (RDBS) back-end for storing the XML tree structure.

It was shown that caching techniques [4, 14] and materialized views [1, 18, 23] could be used to address these performance problems. However we found that the proposed solutions were not flexible enough to adapt to specific workloads. We therefore propose to enhance the materialized view approach in two directions. First, we parameterize the view definition in order to use materialized views for queries with different comparison values. Second, our views contain extra information to efficiently use them as a replacement for query fragments which do not start at the query root.

With the enhanced flexibility of our views a manual selection of the most profitable views to materialize for a given workload, database and space constraint is not feasible. We therefore developed a method to automate this important decision

R. Cooper and J. Kennedy (Eds.): BNCOD 2007, LNCS 4587, pp. 125–137, 2007.
© Springer-Verlag Berlin Heidelberg 2007

process and show how this can be implemented in an XML extension for RDBS called XMLRDB.

The rest of the paper is organized as follows. Next we discuss related work. Section 0 details our enhancements to materialized views called PXV. The integration of PXVs in XMLRDB is described in Section 4. In Section 5 we present our method for automatically determining the most valuable view candidates to materialize. Section 6 evaluates experimentally the performance gains obtained by employing PXVs. Finally Section 7 concludes the paper.

2 Related Work

Grust et al. proposed efficient implementations for XPath [7] and XQuery [8] based on a RDBS with a generic storage of XML data. The most efficient variant utilized a specific numbering scheme as well as a special join operator. A general problem of RDBS usage is that they need many expensive join operations for complex XPath expressions (see Section 0). This also holds for the related work on XQuery-to-SQL translation. The optimizations proposed in the present paper can complement these previous approaches.

A general framework for materialized XPath views is described in [1]. The views may contain XML fragments, typed data values, references to nodes in the actual data and full paths. The paper covers the XPath query rewriting process. Our work differs from this paper in the following points. We enhanced the view concept by parameterizing comparison values and added information for simplified view application. Furthermore we propose an algorithm to automatically determine valuable views to materialize.

[14] creates materialized views on the fly for query caching. The sampled work-load is parameterized on comparison values. Each view stores its data as an XML fragment. Only the information which parameter values were used to build the frag-ment are kept. Therefore if comparison predicates are used in a query which should be answered by a view, the view must be pruned by a compensation query. Since the view only contains the result of its defining query q_v it is only possible to restrict on predicates of the last step in q_v because the corresponding node is the root node of the stored XML fragment.

Materialized XML views are used to improve performance of an XML interface of a RDBS in [18]. Instead of translating each query to SQL and transforming the relational result to XML it caches frequently accessed data as materialized XML views. This approach differs greatly from ours, as it is based on relational data whereas we depend on XML node based storage.

Query rewriting using views has been extensively discussed for RDBS [9]. Later this problem was studied for semistructured data [6, 17] and recently it was examined for the XML domain with the specialities of the XML data model and XML query languages. [11, 23] focus on subsets of XPath for polynomial time algorithms. [16] covers query rewriting using XQuery based views. In our approach we focus on a query rewriting to find an identical match (cf. Fig. 1) of the view definition within the query which can be achieved in $O(\#_{steps}(q) \cdot \#_{steps}(q_v))$ time complexity.

Finding frequent XML query patterns as candidates for caching or materialization is targeted in [24]. The proposed algorithm FastXMiner finds frequent query patterns of a set of XPath queries. Its limitations however are that it does not support predicates and that the root of a query pattern has to be the root of a query. So it cannot find frequent patterns starting either at the second or a later step of an XPath query or within predicates. FastXMiner as well as other work on mining frequent query patterns from trees [5] consider only workload data but do not rank the patterns according to real or estimated query costs. [14] considers only complete XPath queries from a given workload as view candidates. For each query a template is created by parameterizing all constants. Queries with the same template and templates which contain each other are grouped together.

3 Parameterized XPath Views

We first define some terms to be used in the sequel. A *node* is short for XML node and describes an XML element, attribute or another XML node type. It is part of an XML document stored in the database and is the smallest unit which can be accessed. A *node reference* is a link pointing to a node within the database. Typically a node reference will be a value which uniquely identifies a node. Modelling an XML document as a tree of nodes $t_d\langle V_d, E_d, r_d\rangle$ with V_d the set of nodes, E_d the edges between the nodes and $r_d \in V_d$ the document element, we can define an *XML fragment* as a subtree $t_f\langle V_f, E_f, r_f\rangle$ with $r_f \in V_d$ and $V_f \subseteq V_d$ the descendant nodes of r_f and $E_f \subseteq E_d$ the edges between nodes of V_f.

We will first describe materialized XPath views as found in the literature. Afterwards we discuss two limitations of them and our solution. Materialized XPath views contain precomputed query results and can thus be used to quickly answer queries without the need to query the actual data. A materialized view v can be described by $v\langle q_v, R_v\rangle$ with q_v being the query the view represents, and R_v the query result. A view v can be used to answer query q if the result of q can be obtained by executing a so-called compensation query c on R_v that is $q = c \circ q_v$. Following [1] R_v may contain XML fragments, typed data values, node references or a combination thereof. If it contains XML fragments the compensation query has to be based on the fragment data since only the result nodes and their descendants can be accessed. When only typed data values are stored in the view no compensation (besides restricting the value range) is possible. Storing node references in R_v represents the most flexible variant for compensation and postprocessing the results. Here R_v can be seen as the set of context nodes to run a further XPath expression on.

Examining this standard view concept we found two deficiencies which limit the envisioned flexible applicability of views. To overcome these limitations we propose two enhancements which will be described in the following: support for parameterized comparison values and support for inner query fragments.

3.1 Parameterized Views

The standard definition of view queries assumes fixed specification of XPath expressions. This makes it difficult to efficiently support queries with comparison predicates like */world/country[@name='Germany']/history/entry*. For such a query we would like to utilize a view of history entries of all countries. It would be possible to define a view */world/country/history/entry* which contains node references and rewrite the query to use a compensation *ancestor::country[@name='Germany']*. However this postprocessing, especially for queries with more complex predicates, largely reduces the utility of the materialized view.

To overcome this problem we propose the use of an enhanced view definition supporting parameterized view queries. The main focus is on equality expressions since they occur very frequently. For example, in our workloads we observe common patterns of queries which only differ in a constant value like in

$$/world/country[@name='Germany']/history/entry$$

and   */world/country[@name='France']/history/entry.*

To generalize a view we allow constants within predicates containing only an equality expression to be replaced by a parameter. So in our example we would define the view query as */world/country[@name=$1]/history/entry*.

The materialized view contains for each result node reference all parameter assignments yielding this node. Since the number of possible assignments per node could become quite large the constants to be replaced by parameters should be selected carefully.

Parameterizing of constants in view definition queries was also proposed in [14]. Unlike our approach the parameters can only take values from a fixed set taken from the workload. Furthermore the parameter assignments are only used when materializing the view. Query rewritings cannot use the parameters to restrict the view result.

3.2 Support for Inner Query Fragments

The standard views are primarily tuned for queries which exhibit a similar query prefix as the view query. Otherwise the compensation operations, if possible, would be quite costly. To extend the applicability of materialized views we also want to utilize a materialization of "inner" query fragments which occur after a certain query prefix[1]. This extension is motivated by the observation that different complex queries often use the same inner fragments for different query prefixes. Hence optimizing the execution of such fragments by materialized views is likely to be very effective as it can reduce the number of query steps to be processed. Such a step reduction will improve query performance especially in systems with a relational backend like ours (cf. Section 0) where each step results in an extra join operation.

Example Consider the following two queries
    /world/country/history/entry[@year=1990]/text()
    //town[@name='Leipzig']/../history/entry[@year=1990]/author

Both share the inner fragment *history/entry[@year=1990]* which could be materialized as *//history/entry[@year=1990]*. Using this view would need a possibly costly

---

[1] We define as an XPath query fragment each continuous sequence of steps from the query. Even steps within a predicate can make up a query fragment.

compensation check for each view entry for both queries. [1] proposes to remedy this problem by storing full paths[2] in the view with each node reference, so that no data has to be accessed for the prefix check. However this will not work in cases like query two since the full path can only be used to test for ancestor element nodes.

To support materialization of inner fragments views where the definition starts with '//' are extended by storing the references of the starting nodes, i.e. the nodes identified by the first step after "//". To restrict the number of possible starting node references the first step should have a name test. In the above example with the view definition *//history/entry[@year=1990]*, all *history* elements within the stored XML document are starting nodes. The materialized view not only contains references to the result nodes, i.e. *entry* elements which have *history* elements as parent and a *year* attribute with value '1990' but also a reference to the *history* parent for each of these *entry* result references. Depending on the view definition a result node may have several starting nodes.

$$q \quad = /A_1/../A_t/b_1[p_{1,1}]..[p_{1,n}][p_{1,n+1}]..[p_{1,m}]/B_2/../B_p/b_q[p_{q,1}]..[p_{q,r}][p_{q,r+1}]..[p_{q,s}]/C_1/../C_u$$

$$q_v \quad = //b_1[p_{1,1}]..[p_{1,n}]/B_2/../B_p/b_q[p_{q,1}]..[p_{q,r}]$$

$$q_{rw} = /A_1/../A_t/b_1[p_{1,n+1}]..[p_{1,m}]/v_{q_v}[p_{q,r+1}]..[p_{q,s}]/C_1/../C_u.$$

Fig. 1. XPath query rewriting using PXV with q – source query, q_v – query defining view, q_{rw} – rewritten query using view v_{q_v}

The query *//town[@name='Leipzig']/../history/entry[@year=1990]/author* can now be answered using the materialized view. Its result nodes are selected by the constraint that starting nodes must be contained in the set defined by *//town[@name='Leipzig']/../history*. So we can now treat the view as a special XPath step which replaces a fragment within an XPath query. It takes the context nodes from the previous step, generates the intersection with its starting node references and produces a new set of context nodes from its result node references.

We can define this process more formally as shown in Fig. 1. A_x, B_y, C_z are complete steps comprised of axis, node test and predicates and b_1, b_q are complete steps without predicates. It is depicted that a query fragment q_f can be replaced by a view v if q_f and q_v have identical steps whereas q_f may have further predicates in its first and last step. Steps are identical if they either exactly match or the step from the view definition contains a parameter whereas the other step has a constant. Furthermore the sequence of predicates may be different between two identical steps if no positional predicates are involved.

The application of our view concept which we call PXV (parameterized XPath views) is described in the next two sections. First we show its implementation in an XML extension for RDBS. This is followed by a proposal to automatically determine a reasonable set of PXVs based on a given workload.

---

[2] A *full path* is the sequence of element nodes from the document element to the actual view result.

4 Implementation of PXV

We have implemented PXVs in an XML database system named XMLRDB. We developed this system as an XML extension for RDBS to evaluate schema-independent and document-centric XML processing. XMLRDB stores XML documents generically in a RDBS and translates XPath expressions into SQL. This translation leads to complex SQL statements with a join operation for each XPath step and subexpression. However, this results in performance problems since even relational optimizers of commercial DBMS reach their limit with queries containing many join operations (>10). Hence reducing the number of joins is key to good query performance. Since most proposed XPath processing algorithms depend on fast navigations within the XML tree they are not an option for this kind of system where each navigational step has to be translated and executed as an SQL query. Path oriented index structures are of limited use as well for XPath expressions with predicates. Hence we mainly rely on PXVs to materialize hot spots in our query workload and thus reduce the number of joins. We first briefly introduce XMLRDB and discuss PXV implementation later on.

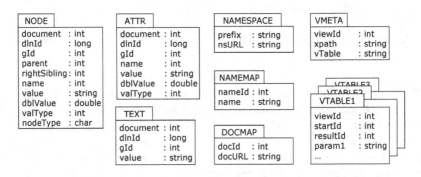

Fig. 2. Relational schema of XMLRDB with PXV tables

4.1 XMLRDB

With XMLRDB we want to evaluate how existing relational database systems without vendor specific XML extensions can be used for XML data processing. We therefore developed an XML layer which transforms XML documents and queries into their relational counterparts and vice versa. The XPath query transformation module employs multiple stages for query optimization like XPath transformation or query rewriting using XML index and views which are managed by the XML layer. We use a generic structure oriented mapping to transform the XML tree structure into predefined relations (see Fig. 2). This kind of mapping was best suited to meet the goals: (1) independence of application-specific XML schemas, (2) support for all kinds of XML documents especially document-centric ones and (3) efficient insert, update and query operations using XML interfaces. In order to support efficient query operations we use an improved version of the node labelling scheme DLN introduced in [2]. It supports efficient evaluation of XPath axes and allows for fast document reconstruction and insert operations.

```
SELECT DISTINCT x3.docId, x3.dlnId
FROM node x1, attr a1, node x2, node x3
WHERE   x1.name='country' AND
            a1.name='name' AND
            a1.gid=x1.gid AND
            a1.value='Germany' AND
            x2.name='history' AND
            x2.parent=x1.gid AND
            x3.name='entry' AND
            x3.parent=x2.gid
ORDER BY x3.doc,x3.dlnId
```

```
INSERT INTO vtable1
SELECT DISTINCT x1.gid, a1.value, x3.gid
FROM node x1, attr a1, node x2, node x3
WHERE   x1.name='country' AND
            a1.name='name' AND
            a1.gid=x1.gid AND
            x2.name='history' AND
            x2.parent=x1.gid AND
            x3.name='entry' AND
            x3.parent=x2.gid
```

Fig. 3. Generated SQL for *//country[@name= 'Germany']/history/entry*

Fig. 4. Generated SQL to materialize *//country [@name=$p1]/history/entry*

4.2   Integration of PXVs in XMLRDB

Making XMLRDB PXV-aware we had to implement a PXV management component and to enhance the XML query processor. The management component stores the materialized views and their metadata within the relational database and uses them during query translation. Table *vmeta* contains the view id, the parameterized XPath view definition and the materialization table names. While it is possible to materialize views with the same number of parameters within the same table it is not advisable. The reason is that views will have different ratios of starting nodes and result nodes. Thus the sampling algorithms of the relational optimizers to gather statistical data typically yield a wrong picture of the distribution of a specific view.

When a view has to be materialized by the management component it can reuse the standard XPath-to-SQL transformation component (XtoS) with only small changes. For an XPath expression, XtoS creates a single SQL query with join operations for each step, even for nested predicates. To generate the view data we only have to specify additional returning node ids from the first step and parameter values. This is illustrated in Fig. 3 and Fig. 4. Fig. 3 shows the generated SQL for a standard XPath query returning node references using the DLN labeling scheme. For enhanced readability we provide real element and attribute names instead of ids here. Fig. 4 shows how the same query is translated for view materialization with the constant value replaced by a parameter. It was generated by the same XtoS component changing only the select clause to return database-wide unique node ids for starting node, result node and value assignments for the parameters. Storing further attributes like DLN id or node value of the result nodes within the view can additionally reduce the number of joins in queries using this view.

We extended the XMLRDB query optimizer to utilize PXVs for rewriting XPath queries. For a given query we first try to apply usable PXVs before considering XMLRDB-maintained indices[3]. Normally the algorithms for finding suitable views for query rewriting exhibit a high complexity [1, 23]. With the PXV concept of replacing query fragments and the parameterization of the views we can greatly simplify the search for relevant views to exact matches since the compensation is given by the remaining part of the original query.

The query rewriting algorithm for PXVs works as follows. Take the first PXV from the list of available views and try to find a query rewriting according to Fig. 1. If it was successful this can be repeated for the remaining fragment of the query. Now repeat these steps for each remaining PXV using the rewritten or, in case no replacement was possible, the unchanged query. So with each iteration more fragments may get replaced by PXVs. Potentially a query can have several different rewritings depending on the order query fragments are replaced by PXVs. In order to ensure that our algorithm finds a good rewriting the list of available views is ordered according to the complexity of the view definition (e.g. number of steps, with steps in predicates counted as well). Thus replacing a small fragment of a query will not prevent replacing a more rewarding, larger one. Generally the view definitions should not overlap to a great extent[4]. The proposed algorithm for automatically generating PXVs (cf. Section 5) respects this property. Alternatively the view list could be sorted according to potential savings of using the views determined during view creation (cf. Section 5.2).

PXV support also required extending the XPath-to-SQL transformation component. Whenever it encounters a special view step, which was inserted during the query rewriting phase, it inserts an equijoin with the table containing the materialized view using the starting node reference attribute. The parameter values given in the view step are added as selection predicates. The result node reference attribute is used to add further steps. Fig. 5 shows the SQL generated for the query

/world/country[@name='Germany']/history/entry/@year

which was rewritten using view

//country[@name=$p1]/history/entry.

The view contains not only the global id for the result nodes but document id and DLN id as well. So we save an additional join with the *node* table. Compared to the SQL expression resulting from the original query we reduced the number of joins from 6 to 4.

```
SELECT DISTINCT a1.value
FROM    node x1, node x2, vtable1 v1, attr a1
WHERE  x1.name='world' AND x1.parent IS NULL AND
        x2.name='country' AND x2.parent=x1.gid AND
        v1.startId=x2.gid AND v1.p1='Germany' AND
        a1.name='year' AND a1.gid=v1.resId
ORDER BY v1.resDoc,v1.resDlnId
```

Fig. 5. Generated SQL for */world/country/view::v1[@p1= 'Germany']/@year*

---

[3] According to [1] most of these index structures can also be seen as a kind of materialized views.

[4] Two view definitions q_{v1} and q_{v2} overlap if they share at least one common XPath step.

5   Automated PXV Creation

While PXVs can be manually created it is a challenging task to find a nearly optimal set of PXVs for a given workload over a database and a maximum space constraint. Therefore we have developed a PXV wizard which suggests a ranked list of PXVs for a given database and workload. Given a constraint on the maximum storage space for materialized views the wizard automatically determines the most promising PXVs for improving query performance.

There exist some previous work on mining frequent query patterns in tree-like structures [5, 24]. However these algorithms consider only the workload data but not the processing costs of the individual patterns. Hence good materialization candidates with high savings on accumulated query time may be missed when their pattern is less frequent than other patterns. Furthermore most of these algorithms are applicable only for a subset of XPath. We therefore implemented our own algorithm which uses a cost estimation to find rewarding view candidates. We will first describe the general idea and discuss later on how we can obtain a good cost estimation in XMLRDB.

5.1   General Approach

The formal notation of the following description is shown in Fig. 6. We assume the workload to be optimized consists of unique queries which may be weighted according to their execution frequency. For each query we generate successively all possible fragments. Since view definitions should exhibit some complexity in order to be relevant simple fragments are filtered out. Per query we now determine the cost saving potential $sav_{f/q}$ for each fragment if it would be materialized. This involves using a cost model and depends on the implementation. We will show this for XMLRDB in the next section.

We use a hash table *frags* to maintain the parameterized query fragments (cf. Section 3) together with their parameter values, query ids and potential savings multiplied by the query weights. If a fragment already exists in *frags* only the query id and potential saving multiplied by the query weight are added. Furthermore it is recorded if parameter values differ. After all queries and their fragments have been processed we check each parameter if only the same values were assigned to it. In this case and if the corresponding fragment was contained in at least two queries the parameter is replaced back by the constant value. Thus we only keep the required parameters. Now a list

```
FOREACH q ∈ workload {
    F ← fragments(q)
    F ← removeSimpleFrag(F)
    FOREACH f ∈ F {
        s ← getSaving(f, q) * weight(q)
        if contains(frags, f)
            e ← getEntry(frags, f)
            addQuery(e, q, s)
        else addEntry(frags, f, q, s)
} }
adjustParameters(frags)
filterMinSupport(frags)
rankedFrag ← descSort(frags)
FOREACH e ∈ rankedFrags {
    FOREACH q ∈ e {
        FOREACH e_r ∈ rankedFrag\e {
            removeQuery(e_r, q)
            if queryCount(e_r) = 0
                removeEntry(rankedFrag, e_r)
    } }
    descSort(rankedFrag)
}
```

Fig. 6. Algorithm to create view candidate list

rankedFrag with all entries from *frags* sorted by their potential savings in descending order is built.

To obtain a practically reasonable ranking we need to adjust the potential savings in *rankedFrag*. At the current stage we may have several top-ranked fragments of the same costly query. However since they typically will overlap it makes little sense to materialize all of them. We rather assume heuristically that only one view will be used for query rewriting. Thus we adjust the potential saving with the following algorithm. From the top entry in *rankedFrag* each query id is checked whether it occurs in the other list entries. For each entry containing such a query id this id is removed and the potential savings are reduced according to the share the query had. After all entries are processed *rankedFrag* is sorted again and the algorithm starts over with the next entry. In the end, the top listed entries are the best candidates for materialization under the assumption that in most cases only one view will be used for query rewriting.

The algorithm described so far has the possible limitation that the fragments of the top view candidates may be helpful for only a single query. Thus materializing such a candidate could benefit only a relatively small number of queries. To circumvent this we additionally require that the support of a query fragment *f*, *supp(f)*, should exceed a threshold *minSupp* [5]. Here, *supp(f)* is simply the number of workload queries containing *f* divided by the absolute number of workload queries ($0 < supp(f) \leq 1$). The *minSupp* filter restriction has to be applied to *rankedFrag* before the potential savings are adjusted.

5.2 Determining Savings in XMLRDB

In the previous section we argued that the potential saving of a materialized fragment for a query depends on the implementation and its cost model. We will now discuss the approach we use in XMLRDB. From a series of experiments we learned that a system independent, general relational cost model does not work because different relational databases may produce highly varying query plans.

Since an external cost model was not an option as explained before, we decided to utilize the *explain* facility of the relational database system. We only had to provide realistic queries to receive suitable cost estimations. Temporarily materializing all query fragments as views was not an option because of the large fragment number. Therefore we materialized dummy views with different cardinality and different ratios between the number of start nodes and result nodes. To calculate the potential saving $sav_{f/q}$ for a materialized fragment *f* and a query *q* we replace *f* by a corresponding dummy view v_d. The decision which dummy view will be used is based on a cardinality estimation component. This component maintains statistical data about the stored XML documents like child count per element type, minimum and maximum height within the document tree etc. For the fragment to be replaced we can now retrieve the estimated input and output cardinality and choose an appropriate dummy view. The query *q* as well as the rewritten query q_{rw} are translated to SQL. Using the explain facility we can calculate the potential saving as $sav_{f/q}=explain(toSQL(q)) - explain(toSQL(q_{rw}))$.

6 Evaluation

We evaluated the introduced PXV concept with our prototype XMLRDB in comparison with the standard configuration which only uses relational index structures but no special XML access structures. Furthermore we wanted to assess the quality of our automated PXV creation algorithm. We were especially interested in the benefit we can gain from using the cost based approach in comparison to a simple frequent pattern matching approach like [24].

Our test environment consists of a computer with 1 GB of main memory and a 2.4 GHz Pentium IV processor. We used the data set from XMark benchmark [19] with a scaling factor of 1 resulting in a raw XML document size of ca. 110 MB. It contains 2,8 million text and element nodes and 380,000 XML attributes. In order to create a reasonable workload we first translated the XMark set of queries which is formulated in XQuery into XPath as far as possible. Additional, more complex queries were generated by an XPath creation tool. It traverses the document and generates queries with multiple and recursive predicates as well as value comparisons. The complete workload consists of 50 queries with a maximum of 14 steps and a mean of 7 steps.

Fig. 7 and Fig. 8 show the execution times for the whole workload. The given values only contain the query execution time without materialization of the results. First (*NoPXV*) we run all workload queries without using PXVs. For the next run (*PXV_cost*) we run our automated PXV creation algorithm (took 6 minutes) and materialized the first 10 view candidates resulting in approx. 200,000 tuples in view tables which were created in 113 seconds. We choose the first 10 candidates because the potential savings of the following candidates were two orders of magnitude lower. Two additional runs were conducted to evaluate a purely frequency-based view selection. For these runs we ignored the cost estimations and sorted the view candidates according to their frequency in the workload queries. Thus we modelled a pure frequent pattern based approach. For *PXV_Pattern_10* we materialized the top 10 view candidates as we did it for the cost based variant. Since the number of tuples materialized were only a third in comparison to *PXV_cost* we materialized further view candidates until we reached the same number. *PXV_Pattern_14* denotes this configuration utilizing 14 materialized views.

Fig. 7 shows that the overall execution time improved by an order of magnitude using our proposed PXV concept. The pattern based candidate selection approach is 5 times slower. Note that adding more materialized views does not need to improve query time. Looking at the ignored saving values from the candidates we could see an estimated negative impact. Fig. 8 shows mean and maximum execution time of single queries within the workload. Here again we can see that the PXVs selected by our proposed algorithm can decrease the maximum execution time by an order of magnitude while the PXVs selected by the pattern based approach have no real impact on maximum execution time. The rewriting of the workload queries took typically less than a millisecond and is thus negligible compared to the query execution time.

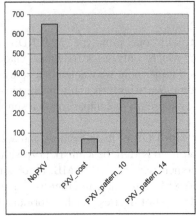
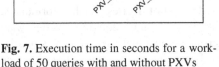
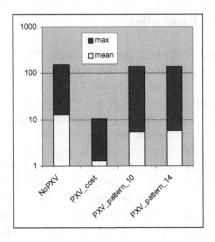

Fig. 7. Execution time in seconds for a workload of 50 queries with and without PXVs

Fig. 8. Maximum and mean execution time in seconds for a workload of 50 queries with and without PXVs

7 Conclusion

We have introduced parameterized XPath views, PXVs, as a new concept for utilizing materialized views for efficient XML query processing. With its parameterization it enables to utilize a view for a broader range of similar queries. The additional information of starting node references stored within the view simplifies the adoption in queries without a costly calculation of compensations. We further showed how PXVs can be implemented in an XML database system like our XMLRDB prototype. Creating a rewarding set of materialized views is a complex task which is hardly feasible to do manually. Therefore we discussed an algorithm for automating it. Unlike other approaches which only take workload data into account for finding common query patterns we base our solution on a cost model and utilize the idea of materialized dummy views. With our evaluation we could verify that the PXV concept can be used to improve execution time of complex XPath queries considerably. Furthermore we showed that our cost based algorithm to automatically create PXVs achieves far better results than a pure workload pattern based approach.

Further work may address the view update problem and study the applicability of proposed solutions for the PXV concept.

References

[1] Balmin, A., Özcan, F., Beyer, K.S., Cochrane, R.J., Pirahesh, H.: A Framework for Using Materialized XPath Views in XML Query Processing. In: Proc. 30th VLDB Conf 2004 (2004)
[2] Böhme, T., Rahm, E.: Supporting Efficient Streaming and Insertion of XML Data in RDBMS. In: Proc. 3rd Int. Workshop Data Integration over the Web (DIWeb) 2004 (2004)

[3] Chen, S., Li, H.-G., Tatemura, J., Hsiung, W.-P., Agrawal, D., Candan, K.S.: Twig2Stack: Bottom-up Processing of Generalized-Tree-Pattern Queries over XML Documents. In: Proc. 32nd VLDB Conf., 2006 (2006)

[4] Chen, L., Rundensteiner, E.A.: ACE-XQ: A Cache-aware XQuery Answering System. In: Proc. 5th Int. Workshop on the Web and Databases (WebDB) (2002)

[5] Feng, J., Qian, Q., Wang, J., Zhou, L.: Exploit sequencing to accelerate hot XML query pattern mining. In: Proc. ACM Symposium on Applied Computing (SAC) (2006)

[6] Grahne, G., Thomo, A.: Query Containment and Rewriting Using Views for Regular Path Queries under Constraints. In: Proc. 22nd ACM Symposium on PODS (2003)

[7] Grust, T., van Keulen, M., Teubner, J.: Accelerating XPath evaluation in any RDBMS. ACM Trans. Database Syst. 29, 91–131 (2004)

[8] Grust, T., Sakr, S., Teubner, J.: XQuery on SQL Hosts. In: Proc. 30th VLDB Conf., 2004 (2004)

[9] Halevy, A.Y.: Answering Queries Using Views: A Survey. VLDB Journal, 10(4) (2001)

[10] Hammerschmidt, B.C., Kempa, M., Linnemann, V.: On the Intersection of XPath Expressions. In: Proc. 9th Int. Database Eng. and App. Symposium (IDEAS) (2005)

[11] Lakshmanan, L.V.S., Wang, H., Zhao, Z.: Answering Tree Pattern Queries Using Views. In: Proc. 32nd VLDB Conf., 2006 (2006)

[12] Mathis, C., Härder, T.: Hash-Based Structural Join Algorithms. In: Proc. 2nd Int. Workshop on Database Techn. for Handling XML Inform. on the Web (DataX) (2006)

[13] Miklau, G., Suciu, D.: Containment and Equivalence for a Fragment of XPath. ACM Journal 51(1) (2004)

[14] Mandhani, B., Suciu, D.: Query caching and view selection for xml databases. In: Proc. 31st VLDB Conf., 2005 (2005)

[15] O'Connor, M., Bellahsene, Z., Roantree, M.: An Extended Preorder Index for Optimising XPath Expressions. In: Bressan, S., Ceri, S., Hunt, E., Ives, Z.G., Bellahsène, Z., Rys, M., Unland, R. (eds.) XSym 2005. LNCS, vol. 3671, Springer, Heidelberg (2005)

[16] Onose, N., Deutsch, A., Papakonstantinou, Y., Curtmola, E.: Rewriting Nested XML Queries Using Nested Views. In: Proc.ACM SIGMOD Int. Conf. Mgmt. of Data. 2006 (2006)

[17] Papakonstantinou, Y., Vassalos, V.: Query Rewriting for Semistructured Data. In: Proc. ACM SIGMOD Conf., 1999 (1999)

[18] Shah, A., Chirkova, R.: Improving Query Performance Using Materialized XML Views: A Learning-Based Approach. In: Jeusfeld, M.A., Pastor, Ó. (eds.) Conceptual Modeling for Novel Application Domains. LNCS, vol. 2814, Springer, Heidelberg (2003)

[19] Schmidt, A., Waas, F., Kersten, M.L., Carey, M.J., Manolescu, I., Busse, R.: XMark: A Benchmark for XML Data Management. In: Proc. 28th VLDB Conf., 2002 (2002)

[20] Wang, W., Jiang, H., Lu, H., Yu, J.X.: Bloom Histogram: Path Selectivity Estimation for XML Data with Updates. In: Proc. 30th VLDB Conf., 2004 (2004)

[21] Wang, H., Park, S., Fan, W., Yu, P.S.: ViST: a dynamic index method for querying XML data by tree structures. In: Proc. ACM SIGMOD Conf., 2003 (2003)

[22] Wang, W., Wang, H., Lu, H., Jiang, H., Lin, X., Li, J.: Efficient Processing of XML Path Queries Using the Disk-based F&B Index. In: Proc. 31st VLDB Conf., 2005 (2005)

[23] Xu, W., Özsoyoglu, Z.M.: Rewriting XPath Queries Using Materialized Views. In: Proc. 31st VLDB Conf., 2005 (2005)

[24] Yang, L.H., Lee, M.L., Hsu, W.: Efficient Mining of XML Query Patterns for Caching. In: Proc. 29th VLDB Conf., 2003 (2003)

[25] Zhang, N., Özsu, T., Aboulnaga, A., Ilyas, I.: XSeed: Accurate and Fast Cardinality Estimation for XPath Queries. In: Proc. 22nd Int. Conf. on Data Engin (ICDE) (2006)

Specifying and Optimising XML Views

Mark Roantree, Colm Noonan, and John Murphy

Interoperable Systems Group, Dublin City University, Ireland
{mark,cnoonan,jmurphy}@computing.dcu.ie

Abstract. Many of today's middleware solutions employ XML to resolve heterogeneities and to create an interoperable layer between sources and systems. However, XML performs poorly when queried in its native format, and local and global views are not supported by current XML products. In this paper, we support the concept of data everywhere by providing a view mechanism for XML together with a highly-optimised query processing strategy.

1 Introduction

In today's computing environment, it is often the case that database information supports a more globally connected computing infrastructure and is accessed through a variety of network architectures. This distribution or multi-sourced data requires an interoperable infrastructure, while the representation of data has changed through the emergence of XML to describe both stored and transmitted data. Subsequently, many of the solutions proposed for the necessary integration in the ubiquitous computing environment involve XML. The impact of this approach is the construction of large XML stores and often there is a need to query XML databases. The work presented in this paper supports the ubiquitous computing environment by ensuring that this canonical representation (XML) of data can be efficiently processed regardless of potentially complex structures. In this paper, we provide a metamodel to support the definition and manipulation of XML views together with a supporting optimisation strategy.

In this paper, we present a view mechanism for XML databases supported by an XML metamodel to describe both the database and view constructs. This metadata is then exploited to provide a powerful query optimisation engine to materialise views. For a more complete version of both metamodel and metadata structures, please refer to [8]. The paper is structured as follows: in §2, we provide some background, concepts and terminology used in our approach; in §3, we describe our view definitions and operators; a brief overview of the query optimisation method is presented in §4; in §5, we describe the results of our experiments while in §6 we discuss similar approaches; before concluding in §7.

2 System Terminology

We refer to the XML data tree as the *database*; the schema tree as the *schema*; and later in the paper, we describe a higher level of abstraction: the *meta-schema*.

R. Cooper and J. Kennedy (Eds.): BNCOD 2007, LNCS 4587, pp. 138–146, 2007.

XML *schemas* are tree structures containing paths and nodes, with the *root node* at the top of the tree. A tree-path that begins at the root node, continuing to some *context* node is called a *FullPath* in our model. A tree-path that begins at the root node and continues to some *leaf* node is called a *LeafPath*. This distinction is necessary because a FullPath may not be unique in an XML schema, whereas the LeafPath is unique.

Property 1. *A Schema S contains a set of FullPaths S = {$P_1,P_1,P_2,..,P_n$}.*

The schema is divided into levels with the root at the topmost level (level 0). Each node has 0 or more child nodes, with child nodes also having 0 or more children (with the level incrementing). As the term sub-tree is rather abstract, we use the term *Family* to refer to a context node and all its descendants.

Property 2. *A Family F is a sub-tree of a Schema S.*

Furthermore, every node within the Family F represents a sub-family f of F.

Property 3. *Where node n is a member of family F, f(n) is contained in F.*

Thus, the *Family* for the root is the entire database, with all other nodes representing sub-families.

Property 4. *Each Node N at level(x) is the context node for a Family F of connected nodes at levels $(x+1),(x+2),...(x+n)$.*

The term *Twig* is used to refer to a Family with some members missing (a pruned Family). This is useful where a Family is very large and one wishes to reduce the size of the Family sub-tree (perhaps for querying performance reasons).

Property 5. *A Twig T is a Family F with 0 or more sub-families removed.*

An XML *View* is a set of Twigs. XML databases are instances of XML schemas. Specifically, they have one or more instances of the FullPath construct, and by extension contain Families and Twigs.

3   View Definitions

In this section, we describe the specification, storage and processing of views. If we follow traditional database theory, then a view is stored query. The XPath language maintains closure by ensuring that the output of a query on an XML document is another XML document. Thus, a View is a new (virtual) XML document comprising some elements of the base document. Furthermore, we provide flexibility in specifying the new document by allowing heterogeneous sub-trees (referred to as Twigs) form part of the new document.

3.1   Specifying Views

A View is a set of families, each with zero or more sub-families removed (clipped). Where a View contains a single Twig (a clipped family), it is referred to as a *Homogeneous View*, and where the View contains multiple Twigs, it is a *Heterogeneous View*. Thus a View comprises a `Name` and one or more `Twig Descriptions`.

As the Twig component is the core of the View definition, we will concentrate on how a Twig is defined. Note that a twig may be a family with zero sub-families removed, in which case the twig is equivalent to the family it is derived from.

A Twig is formed using a `clip` operation (which is a type of expression defined here). The `clip` operation specifies a Twig node and a set of clip nodes. The Twig node identifies a context node and the clip node represents a sub-family which will be removed from context node family.

Definition 1. *Twig*
A Twig T is derived from a family F with zero or more sub-families removed. T is derived from F (T(F)), and we use T where the origin of T is obvious. T may be equivalent to F (zero families removed) in which case T ≡ F. We say that a proper twig T is derived from a family F with at least one sub-family removed.

The `clip` operation comprises a Twig node (XPath expression) and zero or more clip operations (set of XPath expressions representing nodes to be removed) to respectively identify a *context* node for the Twig and the nodes to be clipped. Once defined, each sub-family represented by the clip nodes is eliminated from the Twig.

Definition 2. *Clip*
{XPath} Twig T ::= (clip(ContextNode [,LeafPath]))*

Whereas a Family can be defined in a single XPath expression, a Twig may comprise *a set of* XPath expressions. We can now define the View construct in terms of Twig expressions.

Definition 3. *View*
{XPath} View V ::= { Twig expr}+

3.2   Sample View

Using the DBLP database, assume that we wish to create a new XML document containing information from all proceedings and in the case of articles, only those from 1998. Structurally, we require all journal data, and only one sub-tree from proceedings (normally defined as `/dblp/inproceedings[title/i/sub]`).

We begin by defining the Families in *Example 1*, using an XPath expression in each case. XPath provides a very efficient means of expressing a Family as by default, the location path (XPath expression) returns the context node and all descendants. In this case, there is no need for a `LeafPath` as context nodes are unique across the database.

Example 1. Family1 = Family(//dblp/article[year = '1998'])
Family2 = Family(//dblp/inproceedings)

In the first case, the predicate `[year = '1998']` makes the expression slightly longer but the Twig derived from this Family requires no clipping. In the second case, there is no predicate but we must clip 4 nodes to form the second Twig. Furthermore, it is necessary to provide the LeafPath as all four context nodes are ambiguous.

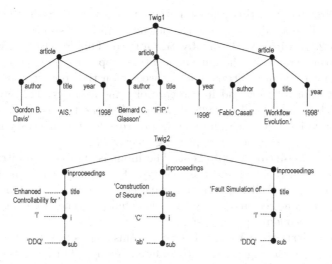

Fig. 1. Sample View comprising 2 Twigs

Example 2. Twig1 = Family1()
Twig2 = Family2(clip(//dblp/inproceedings/cite, //dblp/inproceedings/cite),
(clip(//dblp/inproceedings/cite, //dblp/inproceedings/cite/label),
(clip(//dblp/inproceedings/title, //dblp/inproceedings/title/sup),
(clip(//dblp/inproceedings/title, //dblp/inproceedings/title/sup/i))

Note that this example was designed to illustrate the `Twig` and `clip` functions.
For this particular example, the easier option is to specify a smaller Family
(`//dblp/inproceedings[title/i/sub]`) and thus, no clip operations are required. However, this would not be possible should there be less than 4 clips
required. The view definition is illustrated in *Example 3*.

Example 3. View1 = (Twig1, Twig2)

4   View Optimisation

This section describes our strategy for materialising views by evaluating location
steps along each axis relative to a given set of context nodes. In brief, the strategy
comprises five processes that prune the search space using query structure, axis
properties and preorder encoding logic. Briefly, each XPath expression can be
divided into a series of location steps separated by slashes (/). The role of each
location step is to retrieve a set of nodes based on the context node and this
node set provides the input to the next location step.

- Process 1: **Context Prune by Axis**. This step prunes the current set of
  context nodes using Axis logic. For example, if the location step includes
  the `child` axis, then context nodes without children are pruned. The initial

input (first pass) to this process is the entire set of nodes in the tree. The input to all remaining passes is the output from Process 5 below.

- Process 2: **Arbitrary Prune by Structure**. This Process prunes the set of arbitrary nodes for the current location step. Firstly, it is necessary to generate the set of arbitrary nodes based upon the context node set. This will differ for all axes and in the case of some axes (eg. following) may be very large as it will include all nodes *after* the first context node. Our index provides a starting and ending preorder for the arbitrary node path and thus, provides a very fast pruning mechanism.
- Process 3: **Arbitrary Axis Test**. The input is the set of arbitrary nodes generated by Process 2 and the axis type for the location step. While the node set contains all required arbitrary nodes, it may also contain nodes that are not allowed under a given axis definition. Therefore the *axis filter* provides a secondary pruning step.
- Process 4: **Structure Filter**. The role of this step is to prune the arbitrary node set by removing nodes with different names. This step is ignored in wildcard cases eg. return all children of the given node.
- Process 5: **Predicate Filter**. The filter reduces the set of arbitrary nodes if the location step has a predicate.

In related work, we developed a strategy for each of the XPath axes and used the DBLP database to execute real queries in each case. Our indexing strategy provides a preorder value and level ranking for each node with the full preorder set for the DPLP database being {0,1,2,...,3736375,3736376} (just short of 4 million nodes). We describe the processing for one of the views (View 9 in the experiment set) now.

4.1   Preceding Axis View

The Preceding axis returns nodes that occur *before* the context node, providing they are *not ancestors* of the context node. Suppose one wanted to view all book chapters (*incollection*) by the author Amit Sheth that preceded a specified publication by Mark Roantree. This may happen if one wanted to examine those works by Sheth that may have contributed to the paper published by Mark Roantree. A preceding query can be used in this case.

Example 4 (Retrieve book chapters by Sheth before articles by Roantree).
/descendant::article[author='Mark Roantree']/preceding::incollection[author='Amit P. Sheth']

To explain the strategy we move directly to location step 2. The input to this step (set of nodes generated by the first location step) is the node set {3676350,3678812,3686988,3687576}.

- **Process 1: Context Prune by Axis.** For a preceding axis, this process reduces context node set to a single context node (the last context node). The set of context nodes becomes {3687576}.

- **Process 2: Arbitrary Prune by Structure.** The set of arbitrary nodes will always return all nodes *prior* to the context node. The arbitrary node's fullpath is then used to reduce this set by providing starting and ending preorder values for the set. Note that ancestors are still in the node set at this point. For example 4, the set of arbitrary nodes is 2399330,..,2419224. The cardinality of this set at this point is 19,895 nodes.
- **Process 3: Arbitrary Axis Test.** This process filters the set of arbitrary nodes by removing all namespace and attribute nodes as they are not allowed for this axis type. Additionally, it is used to eliminate all nodes that are ancestors of the (single) context node. This process results in a more compact arbitrary node set i.e. {2399330,2399332,..,2419224} (15,562 nodes).
- **Process 4: Structure Filter.** This process filters the set of arbitrary nodes to remove all nodes whose node name does not match 'incollection' and this provides a dramatic reduction to {2399330,2399339,..,2419214,2419224} (1,009 nodes).
- **Process 5: Predicate Filter.** The *predicate filter* is used to select only book chapters for 'Amit Sheth', resulting in the arbitrary node set: {2406333,2407129,2407542,2413654,2416555}. For example 4, this set forms the final view result as all the location steps have been evaluated (5 nodes).

5   Details of Experiments

Experiments were run using a 3.2GHz Pentium IV machine with 1GB of RAM on a Windows XP operating system. Our View Processor was deployed using

Table 1. DBLP Views

	View Query	Match	eXist	ESR	Comp.
V1	//inproceedings[author = 'Jim Gray'] [year = '1990']/@key	6	1,666	300	5.53
V2	//www[./editor]/url	5	194	49	3.96
V3	//book/author[text() = 'C. J. Date']	13	411	39	10.54
V4	//inproceedings[title/text() = 'Semantic Analysis Patterns']/author	2	13,443	344	39.08
V5	//article[./month = 'August'][./year = '1994']	12	350	59	5.93
V6	//inproceedings[year = '1998'][title]/author	40,226	7,885	1,506	5.24
V7	//proceedings[publisher = 'Springer'][title]	2,109	526	125	4.21
V8	/dblp/article/title	111,609	6,542	3,081	2.12
V9	/descendant::article[author = 'Mark Roantree'] /preceding::incollection[author = 'Amit P. Sheth']	5	n/a	35,135	n/a
V10	/dblp/article[year = '1991']/@key	4,189	3004	227	13.23
V11	//mastersthesis[./author][./year]	5	366	33	11.09
V12	//proceedings[./isbn][./url]	2,708	456	159	2.87
V13	//inproceedings[url]/title	212,270	12,839	6,312	2.03
V14	//article[number]/author	213,539	12,490	6,263	1.99

an Oracle 10G database, running on a Windows XP professional platform, with a 3.0GHz Pentium IV processor and 1GB memory. The eXist database runs on a machine with an identical specification to that of the Oracle 10G server to ensure parity. However, we altered the default JVM settings of the eXist server from -Xmx128MB to -Xmx768MB in order to maximise eXist's efficiency. All experiments were executed using the DBLP dataset [9].

Table 1 illustrates our 14 sample views, together with: the number of instance matches in the DBLP database; eXist responses times; the Extended Schema Repository (ESR) response times; and the comparison between both systems. Views were mainly generated from queries used by other authors and each view is evaluated 11 times for both query engines (the first, cold run is ignored) with times recorded in milliseconds and warm cache results averaged. The Comparison divides the times of the eXist output by those of our optimisation engine, indicating that a value of 1 represents an equal score; any figure less than 1 represents a slower run for our approach; and figures greater than 1 represents an improvement using our approach. For this series of experiments, all views are homogeneous with Twigs unclipped as eXist does not have the facility to return heterogeneous result sets or drop nodes.

Query evaluation commences for a specific location step, by limiting the search space of the target database we achieved superior results over eXist. The eXist query processor on the other hand, fails to limit the search space as it queries nodes that cannot form part of the query result. For example, view V14 selects all `author` elements and that are children of `article` elements that have a child named `number`. The eXist query processor selects all `article`, `number`, `author` elements then joins these lists using their path join algorithm. The Fullpath index allows us to only select `number` and `author` elements that are children of a `article` node, thus dramatically reducing the search space and the size of our joins.

The ESR performs best for queries with highly selective predicates i.e. queries that query a small portion of the target database i.e. V1, V3, V4, V5, V7 and V10. For low selectivity queries our results were less promising as these queries potentially require a join between two large lists of nodes and currently we are using standard relational join mechanisms. View V9 is relatively slow because the preceding axis initially has a large search space (see process 2) and secondly, we must check that all 1,009 nodes identified by process 4 support the predicate. However, the eXist database is unable to process this view.

6   Related Research

In [1] they argue that XML view technology should leverage object database view technology and they strongly emphasise that distributed aspects should be addressed in a declarative fashion (replication, change notification). In their discussion of XML views, consideration is given to relational technology and on Object Database Views based on experience with the O2 Object Database developed at INRIA. They identify a range of important issues including: extensions to standard database view technology for XML; object database views as a foundation for XML views; the exchange of structured data in XML as per relational and ODMG modes; and the control of updates. Our metamodel approach provides the foundation for all of these properties, with a particular focus on applying traditional database foundations to the *management* of semistructured data. In [2], they consider XML Views to be fragments of the database; a list of typed data values; node references; fullpaths; or any combination of the four. While they do not focus on optimisation of views, they utilise stored view results to optimise subsequent queries. There is considerable evidence presented to demonstrate that a major improvement in query performance is achieved, however unlike our approach, they provide no mechanism for defining views.

One of the earliest efforts at building schema repositories for semi-structured sources was in [3] where the authors introduced the concept of a DataGuide. In relation to our work, a DataGuide could be regarded as a form of materialised view. They are used by query processing strategies to limit or prune the search space of the target database. However, DataGuides do not provide any information about the parent-child relationship between database nodes and unlike our approach, they cannot be used for axis navigation along an arbitrary node.

7   Conclusions

In this paper, we introduce our XML Views for the first time, providing a clear understanding of how a Twig is formed, and how this concept is used to comprise a View. The metamodel for views [8] supports our query optimisation for view processing. Our experiments demonstrate that we compare favourably against eXist, one of the market leaders. Although we can also query views, we have no optimisation of this process. As a consequence, our current focus is the optimisation of view queries using metadata mappings to XPath location steps.

References

1. Abiteboul, S.: On Views and XML. SIGMOD Record 28(4), 30–38 (1999)
2. Balmin, A., Ozcan, F., Beyer, K., Cochrane, R., Pirahesh, H.: A Framework for using Materialized XPath Views in XML Query Processing. In: Proceedings of 30th Conference on Very Large Databases, pp. 60–71. Morgan Kaufmann, Washington (2004)
3. Goldman, R., Widom, J.: DataGuides: Enabling Query Formulation and Optimisation in Semisztructured Databases. In: Proceedings of the 23rd VLDB Conference, pp. 436–445. Morgan Kaufmann, Washington (1997)
4. Kaushik, R., Shenoy, P., Bohannon, P., Gudes, E.: Exploiting Local Similarity for Indexing Paths in Graph-Structured Data. In: Proceedings of ICDE, 2002 (2002)
5. Meier, W.: eXist: An Open Source Native XML Database. In: Chaudhri, A.B., Jeckle, M., Rahm, E., Unland, R. (eds.) Web, Web-Services, and Database Systems. LNCS, vol. 2593, pp. 169–183. Springer, Heidelberg (2003)
6. Qun, C., Lim, A., Ong, K.: D(k)-Index: An Adaptive Structural Summary for Graph-Structured Data. In: Proceedings of the 29th VLDB Conference, Morgan Kaufmann, Washington (2003)

7. Roantree, M., Noonan, C.: A Metamodel Approach to XML Query Optimisation (Submitted for publication) (March 2007)
8. Roantree M., Noonan C., Murphy J.: Metadata For Optimising XML Views. Technical Report ISG-06-04, Dublin City University (December 2006) at: URL http://www.computing.dcu.ie/~isg/technicalReport.html
9. Suciu D., Miklau, G.: University of Washington's XML Repository (2002) at: URL http://www.cs.washington.edu/research/xmldatasets/

Isolating Order Semantics in Order-Sensitive XQuery-to-SQL Translation

Song Wang, Ling Wang, and Elke A. Rundensteiner

Worcester Polytechnic Institute, Worcester, MA 01609, USA
{songwang|lingw|rundenst}@cs.wpi.edu

Abstract. Order is essential for XML query processing. Efficient XML processing with order consideration over relational storage is non-trivial, especially for complex nested XQuery expressions. The order semantics may impede efficient query rewriting for nested query blocks. We propose a general order-sensitive XQuery processing approach involving three steps. First an algorithm is proposed for inferencing about and then isolating the order semantics in XQuery expressions specified over virtual XML views. This turns an *ordered* XQuery plan into an *unordered* one decorated with minimized *order context annotations*. Then without loss of semantics, logical optimization via XQuery rewriting can be easily applied to this transformed query plan. As last step, the translation of the optimized logical plan into SQL now correctly incorporates the order context annotations to assure the original order semantics. Our experiments illustrate the performance gains achievable by our order handling strategy.

1 Introduction

Since XQuery semantics are order sensitive, order awareness has been identified as critical for XQuery processors. Order-sensitive XML query processing has been studied for native XQuery engines, such as TIMBER [10], Natix [6] and Rainbow [1,20]. There has also been considerable work on extending relational query engines to process XQueries over XML documents. See [5] for a survey.

Several aspects of supporting order-sensitive XQuery processing over relational storage have been successfully tackled in the literature. XML document order encoding strategies during XML loading, such as Dewey order [15], ORD-PATH [9], and preorder ranks [3], have been proposed. The order-sensitive XPath to SQL translation has been studied for these different order encodings [3,9,15]. However, the order semantics in general impede efficient query rewriting for nested query plan blocks. We thus propose a general order-sensitive XQuery processing approach which overcomes this problem. Our solution does not rely on any specific relational order-encoding.

Our work relates to recent work on the order processing and duplication removal of matched pattern trees for the native XQuery engine Timber [10,11]. The authors propose to use hybrid collections of matched pattern trees to capture the order semantics of XQuery expressions. Although the proposed techniques are sufficient for native XQuery processing, their adoption to an XQuery engine with relational storage faces new challenges, as shown below.

R. Cooper and J. Kennedy (Eds.): BNCOD 2007, LNCS 4587, pp. 147–159, 2007.
© Springer-Verlag Berlin Heidelberg 2007

Motivation Example 1: XML nodes matched by XQuery expressions can be heterogeneous, due to the wildcard "*" navigation step in XPath expressions or the *union* operations in the *For* and *Let* clauses. In Figure 1(a), four XML nodes ($b0$ to $b3$) match the given XPath expression for b. The intermediate result of the translated SQL thus contains four tuples[1]. We observe that every XML node in the matched pattern is represented in a column in the result table shown at the bottom of the figure. No simple sorting on any individual column can achieve the ordering of the *order by* clause, no matter what order encoding is used. Instead, we have to build an extra ordering column to record the order information corresponding to the runtime execution.

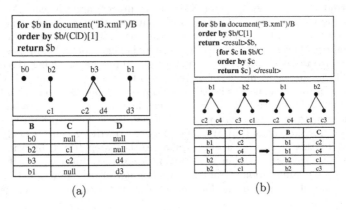

(a)   (b)

Fig. 1. Motivation Examples: (a) XQuery with Heterogeneous Matched XML Nodes; (b) Sorting in Nested XQuery Expressions

Motivation Example 2: We may need to group and sort the results of the translated SQL queries to achieve correct semantics of nested XQuery expressions. Adding simple sortings into the SQL may not be adequate. As shown in Figure 1(b), the XQuery expressions first sort the "b" bindings by the first "C" child, and then all "C" children of each "b" binding. The XML nodes and corresponding tuples on left show the orderings for the outer XQuery expression, while the right ones show the effect of the inner XQuery expression. Obviously we cannot achieve the correct ordering by a simple translated SQL *order by* clause.

The ordering problems shown above are unique to XQuery processing on relational XML views where order can only appear at the top-level of an SQL query. The naive approach to guarantee the correct order processing in the SQL translation is to build an extra order column for each level of the result construction. Such columns are used to capture the runtime order semantics in each of the intermediate results. Those columns can be combined and treated as Dewey order of the result XML. Then a sort at the top-level SQL query can achieve the correct ordering of the tuples. The OLAP amendment *row_number()* with *partition by* and optional *order by* clauses in SQL99 can be used to achieve this [17].

---

[1] For ease of illustration, b_i, c_i and d_i are used for both the XML nodes and the atomized values.

However, such operations tend to be expensive. In fact in many cases they may be redundant, since ordering at all levels of the nesting may not be required.

Our approach tackles the above open problem. We propose a general framework to process XQuery expressions on virtual XML views of relational databases. Our approach first isolates the order semantics in the combined query composed of the user XQuery and the XML view query. Then by identifying and reasoning about essential order information, we minimize the usage of the expensive *row_number()* functions. As result we produce a succinct SQL translation of order-sensitive XQuery expressions. Correctness of the translated SQL is achieved by "attaching" back the order semantics identified as "essential".

Contributions. Our contributions include: (1) We propose a general framework for processing order-sensitive XQuery over virtual XML views defined on relational databases. (2) We introduce order propagation techniques for the XQuery algebra [20] to support order isolation in the XQuery plan. (3) We discuss the strategies for SQL translation with ordered semantics. (4) We implement the order propagation and isolation approach in the Rainbow XQuery Engine [20]. (5) We report experimental studies illustrating the tradeoff among different SQL translation strategies.

Outline. The rest of this paper is organized as follows. Section 2 reviews related work, while Section 3 shows preliminaries. Section 4 enhances the XAT algebra with order context annotations. Section 5 describes order propagation and order isolation for order-sensitive XQueries. Different SQL generation strategies are presented in Section 6. Section 7 provides our experimental study and Section 8 concludes this paper.

2   Related Work

XQuery-to-SQL translation can be broadly classified into two scenarios: *XML Publishing* and *XML Storage* [5]. Since the relational data model is unordered, XML Publishing of relational data need not consider order semantics [2,12]. For XML storage of existing XML data, various order encoding methods have been proposed in [15,17].

Order inference has been used for relational query optimization in [13, 19, 14, 8, 7] to reason about the physical tuple order of intermediate results during execution. We now use similar ideas for the new purpose of logical order inference in virtual XML views focusing in addition on the hierarchical XML data.

In [4], removing unnecessary duplication elimination and sorting operations in Galax is discussed for processing complex XPath expressions with backwards axes. This is orthogonal to our problem. However the approach is complimentary and could fit into our framework for the purpose of syntax level normalization.

[11] addresses order-sensitive XQuery processing in a pattern tree based native XQuery engine. Instead different optimization opportunities exist for order-sensitive XQuery processing over relational XML views, as illustrated by the motivation examples in Section 1.

3   Preliminaries

3.1   The XQuery Subset

In this paper, we deploy a subset of the XQuery language [16], including nested *FLWOR* expressions and order-sensitive functions (e.g., the position function). With syntax rewriting, such XQuery subset covers a large set of XQuery expressions used in practice. Formal definition of the XQuery subset is in [22].

3.2   A Running Example of Order-Sensitive XQuery Processing

Given a relational database, a view query defines an XML view over the relational database bridged through the *default XML view* [12]. We assume that the relational constraints are:

```
PLAY(IID,NAME): Primary Key(IID), Unique(NAME)
MPLAY(IID,PID,NAME): Primary Key(IID), Unique(NAME)
SONG(IID,PID,NAME): Primary Key(IID), Unique(NAME)
```

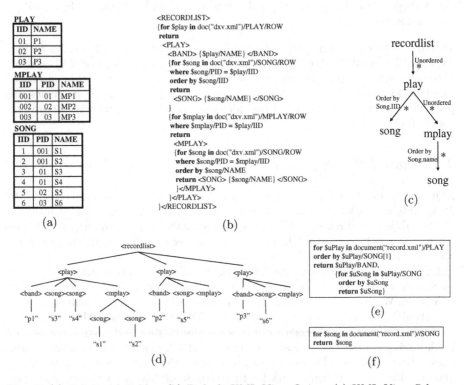

Fig. 2. (a) Relational Tables; (b) Default XML View Query; (c) XML View Schema with Order Information; (d) Order-sensitive XML View; (e) Q1: XQuery with Nested Orderings; (f) Q2: XQuery with Heterogeneous Matched Patterns

Figure 2(b) shows the default XML view query, containing explicit *order by* clauses. Such an XML view is ordered. Figure 2(c) shows the simplified schema tree (with "BAND" omitted) of this view, highlighting the order semantics. Edges are marked as "Unordered" whenever the view query does not impose any *order by* clauses there. We call such an XML view "partially ordered". Figure 2(d) shows one "possible" view result. That is, the order among the play elements can be different from that in Figure 2(d).

Order-sensitive user XQueries can be launched over the default XML view. Figure 2(e) shows a user query using position function and nested orderings. Figure 2(f) shows another user query with a complex XPath containing "//". Since the XPath expression matches multiple paths in the XML view, this complicates the order of the retrieved SONG elements. We will use these two XQueries to show our approach of order-sensitive SQL translation.

3.3 The XQuery Algebra: XAT

Our approach uses the XAT algebra [20] as internal representation of the view query, user query and their composition. A complete discussion of the XAT algebra is in [22]. The intermediate results of an XAT operator is a sequence of tuples, named *XATTable*. An XAT operator is denoted as $op_{in}^{out}(R)$, where *op* is the operator symbol, *in* represents input parameters, *out* newly produced output column and R the input XATTable(s). Figure 3 shows the composition of the decorrelated XAT trees capturing the user query $Q1$ and the view query.

The XAT algebra inherits operators from the relational algebra, extended with order semantics (see Section 4.1). For example, the **GroupBy** operator

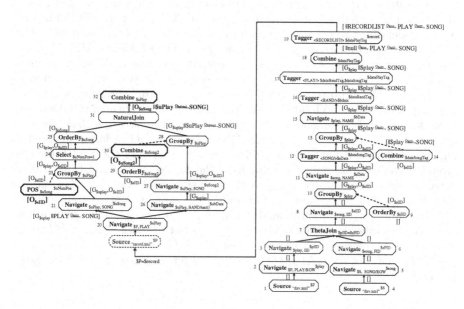

Fig. 3. Composed XAT of View Query and User Query $Q1$

is generated during XAT decorrelation of nested XQuery expressions [18]. The GroupBy operator groups the tuples of the input XATTable by certain column(s), and then performs the embedded functions on each group of tuples. For example, the $GroupBy_{\$uPlay}$ embedded with $POS_{\$uSong}$ (Nodes 22 and 23 in Figure 3) will change the input: $< (p_1, s_3), (p_1, s_4), (p_2, s_5) >$ into output: $< (p_1, s_3, 1), (p_1, s_4, 2), (p_2, s_5, 1) >$. The XAT algebra also introduces new operators to represent XQuery semantics, such as Navigate, Tagger, Combine and POS. The **Navigate** operator extracts destination XML nodes from each entry of XML fragments according to a given XPath expression. Assume the input column $\$uPlay$ of Node 21 in Figure 3 includes two plays p_1 and p_2, which have songs s_3, s_4 and s_5 respectively; the output of the Navigate operator is a sequence of tuples: $< (p_1, s_3), (p_1, s_4), (p_2, s_5) >$. The **Tagger** operator constructs new XML elements by applying a tagging pattern to each tuple in the input XATTable. A tagging pattern (e.g., $<SONG/>$ $\$sData$ in Node 12 of Figure 3) is a template for the XML fragment. The **Combine** operator projects out certain columns from the input XATTable and merges the contents of the remaining columns into one tuple. The **POS** operator captures the semantics of the *position()* function. It assigns a row number to each input tuple.

4   Enhancing XAT with Order Context

4.1   Order Context for XATTable

The *order context* in [13, 19] represents the tuple order of flat relational tables. We extend the *order context* to represent tuple order and XML fragment order in XAT tables. This extension is essential because: (i) hierarchical XML views are defined with multiple level sortings; and (ii) XML view queries define only partial orders in XML views. Figure 2(c) shows a partial order example which captures the order information in a schema graph. The PLAY and MPLAY nodes are not ordered, while SONG nodes are ordered according to different columns.

The order context of an XATTable is composed of two parts, denoted as $[TupleOrder \| XMLOrder]$. *TupleOrder* captures the tuple ordering and grouping properties of an XATTable, while the *XMLOrder* captures the document order for an XML fragment. Both parts can be optional. *TupleOrder* is a sequence of order properties: P_i. Each P_i can be either an ordering denoted as $O_{\$c}$ or a grouping denoted as $G_{\$c}$, where $\$c$ is a column of the XATTable (the grouping could be on multiple columns). The tuples in the XATTable are ordered (or grouped) first according to P_1, with ties broken by P_2, and so on. For each P_i, $O_{\$c}$ implies $G_{\$c}$, but not vice versa. The semantics of grouping on multiple columns $G_{\$c_i, \$c_j}$ are not equal to $G_{\$c_i}$ followed by $G_{\$c_j}$. The order context $[G_{\$c_i}, G_{\$c_j}]$ implies the order context $[G_{\$c_i, \$c_j}]$, but not vice versa. *XMLOrder* is attached to the schema tree of the associated XML fragments. For example, the *XMLOrder* of the XATTable after the Tagger operator (Node 19) is shown in Figure 4[2].

---

[2] For ease of illustration, the XAT tree and order contexts shown in Figure 4 include only part of the XML view query.

Fig. 4. The *XMLOrder* in the output XATTable of Node 19

4.2   Functional Dependencies and Keys

We use the functional dependencies of the base relational tables to propagate the order context through the XAT tree. The constraints of an XATTable can be determined utilizing rules similar to those in [13,19]. We omit the details here due to space limitation. We use the constraints for the following purposes:

- Minimize the order context by removing redundant orderings (groupings).
- Retrieve trivial orderings and groupings if needed during order propagation. "Trivial" [13] implies that it can be omitted. For example, a key constraint implies a trivial grouping on the key column(s).
- Check the compatibility of order contexts.

5   Order Propagation and Isolation

The identification and isolation of the order semantics of the XAT tree is accomplished in two traversals. First the bottom-up traversal (complete order propagation) computes the order contexts of all intermediate XATTables. Second the top-down traversal (selective order isolation) identifies the operators that indeed require the order context to produce correct results, i.e., the essential ones.

5.1   Order Context Propagation

The order contexts of XATTables originate from explicit sorting in the XML view query. They then are propagated through the operators in the XAT tree to form the ordered XML view and the ordered user XQuery result. We call the procedure of determining the order contexts of the XATTables *Order Propagation*. Figure 3 illustrates the propagation of the order context through the composed XAT tree. The order context is associated with each XATTable and attached to edges between operators. During the propagation, the *XMLOrder* part of the input order context will always be carried on to the output, except when the corresponding XML fragments are navigated into or are projected out. The propagation of *TupleOrder* of the XATTable depends not only on the operator semantics but also the constraints in the XATTable.

Select, Project and Tagger. The *TupleOrder* in the output XATTable of most unary operators, such as Select, Project and Tagger, inherits the *TupleOrder* of the input XATTable. If one column in the *TupleOrder* of the input XATTable is projected out, it is also removed from the output order context.

Join. Suppose OC_L and OC_R denote the order contexts of the left and right input XATTables of a Join operator. Then the *TupleOrder* of the output order context inherits the *TupleOrder* in OC_L. The *TupleOrder* of OC_R is attached to the output order context if the *TupleOrder* of the OC_L is not empty. Otherwise, the *TupleOrder* of OC_R is discarded.

Here all ordering and grouping properties in the left input XATTable, even if trivial, need to be included in OC_L for the empty test and order propagation. For example, suppose the left input XATTable has a unique identifier (c_1, c_2) (i.e. key constraint), then G_{c_1, c_2} is trivial since all groups consist of only one tuple. But it is no longer trivial in the Join output since a 1 to m joining between the left and right input tuples may exist.

OrderBy. An OrderBy operator sorting on $c_1, c_2, \ldots$ will generate a new order context $[O_{c_1}, O_{c_2}, \ldots]$. The propagation of the order context associated with its input XATTable through the OrderBy operator is determined by the compatibility of the order contexts. For example, $[G_{c_1}, G_{c_2}]$ is not compatible with the explicit sorting on c_2. Thus the explicit sorting overwrites the output order context as $[O_{c_2}]$ only. But $[G_{c_1}, G_{c_2}]$ is compatible with ordering on (c_1) or on (c_1, c_2, c_3) with the output order context then being set to $[O_{c_1}, G_{c_2}]$ and $[O_{c_1}, O_{c_2}, O_{c_3}]$ respectively. In Figure 3 the OrderBy operator (Node 25) sorts by $\$uSong$. The input order context $[G_{\$play}]$ is compatible with this sorting, since $G_{\$play}$ is implied by $O_{\$uSong}$ due to the selection (Node 24).

GroupBy. Similar with OrderBy, the propagation of *TupleOrder* through the GroupBy is also determined by the compatibility between the input order context and the generated order context. For example, if the input tuples have been sorted on column $\$c_1$ and the grouping is done on column $\$c_2$, where $\$c_2$ is a key column, then the output order context of the GroupBy operator is $[O_{\$c_1}]$, with $G_{\$c_2}$ being a trivial grouping. For example in Figure 3 the generated order context $G_{\$uPlay}$ of the GroupBy operator (Node 23) is compatible with the input order context $[G_{\$uPlay}, O_{\$sIID}]$, since $\$uPlay$ is a key.

Navigate. The Navigate operator passes the *TupleOrder* of its input order context to its output order context. If the input *TupleOrder* including the trivial groupings (if any) is not empty, the extracted order from the XML fragment will be attached to the end of the input *TupleOrder*. Otherwise the output *TupleOrder* is empty. Different permutations of the same set of Navigates may result in different order contexts. For example, consider two Navigate operators $\$a/b$ and $\$a/c$. If we perform $\$a/b$ before $\$a/c$, then the final order context will be $[O_{\$a}, O_{\$b}, O_{\$c}]$. If we perform the two Navigates in the opposite order, then the output tuple order will be $[O_{\$a}, O_{\$c}, O_{\$b}]$. This illustrates the limitation of handling order using query plan rewriting. Our effort of order isolation in Section 5.2 is thus necessary. The output order context of the Navigate operator includes the $XMLOrder$ extracted from its input order context. For example in Figure 3 the Navigate operator (Node 21) extracts the $XMLOrder$: $(PLAY \xrightarrow{O_{\$sIID}} SONG)$ from the XML fragment. The output order context is $[G_{\$uPlay}, O_{\$sIID}]$.

Combine. The Combine operator forms the *XMLOrder* in the output order context. In case that Combine is embedded in a GroupBy operator, the formed *XMLOrder* will use the grouping column(s) as the relative column(s). If Combine is not in a GroupBy operator, *null* will be used for the relative column. For example, in Figure 3, the Combine operator (Node 13) forms:

$$\$play \xrightarrow{O_{\$sIID}} SONG.$$

5.2   Isolating Ordered Semantics in XAT Tree

In the query plan of the user XQuery, if the semantics of an operator are defined based on the tuple order of its input XATTable, we classify this operator as an **order essential operator**. The order context associated with the input XATTable is called an **essential order context**.

In a top-down traversal of the XAT tree representing the user XQuery, we now identify all order-essential operators and bind them with their input order context for possible relocation in future rewriting steps. This denotes the *Order Isolation* phase. In Figure 3, the Combine operator (Node 30), which originates from the user XQuery, is an order-essential operator, since all tuples must be sorted correctly before being "packed" into a collection in the result XML. All operators capturing order sensitive functions are also order-essential operators, e.g., the POS operator (Node 22). An XAT tree, with all OrderBy operators removed and essential order contexts attached to the associated operators, is called an **Order Annotated XAT Tree**.

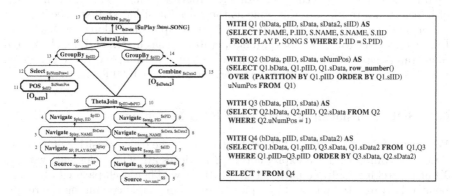

Fig. 5. Optimized XAT Tree   **Fig. 6.** SQL Translation for Q_1

Intuitively the order-essential operators determine the only positions in the query tree where the order context has to be enforced. By enforcing the essential order contexts, the ordered semantics of XQuery are captured. The XAT tree can be optimized now ignoring all OrderBy operators during the subsequent rewriting phase. After applying order-insensitive XQuery rewriting rules, the correct order semantics is restored by inserting explicit sorts below each order essential operator. The optimized annotated XAT tree is shown in Figure 5.

Details of the XAT rewriting are beyond the scope of this paper and can be found in [21].

6   Order-Aware SQL Translation

XML-to-SQL translation based on XML algebra usually assumes some XML middle-ware above the relational engine. For this a simple middle-ware having limited processor and memory resources is commonly desired [12]. We follow the same trend here and limit the computation in the middle-ware to be achievable in a *single* pass over the SQL results. Many operators of the XAT algebra can be achieved in the middle-ware, such as Tagger, Combine, Select, Position and their combinations. The OrderBy and GroupBy operators can clearly not be evaluated by such one-pass middle-ware, unless the input has been sorted by the SQL engine correspondingly.

6.1   SQL Translation for Incompatible Result Orderings

In Figure 5, we can see that the ordering of the left and right branches of the query plan are incompatible with each other. That is, the left branch requires the intermediate result being sorted first on $pIID$ then on $sIID$, while the right branch requires first on $pIID$ then on $sData2$. For such cases, an additional order column, which can be the $sData2$ column after the selection, must be used for the top-level sorting in SQL. The ordering compatibility checking rules of intermediate results are the same as the rules for order context checking.

The SQL generation is conducted in a bottom up fashion along the XAT tree. Each time we try to include the parent operator in the current SQL block. Nested SQL statements will be generated otherwise. For the example Q_1, the generated SQL is shown in Figure 6. We use the *with* clause in SQL99 for clarity.

6.2   SQL Translation for Multiple Path Matching

We use the example XQuery $Q2$ for illustration of the order-sensitive SQL translation for complex XPath expressions. $Q2$ retrieves all SONG elements with an XPath matching multiple paths in the XML view. Then each path can be independently translated into an SQL query. Instead of simply combining the results of the SQL queries, order-sensitive query translation needs to sort the XML elements from different paths correctly according to the ordered semantics of the XML view. The ordered semantics of the XML view include the following three categories of parent-child orders in the schema tree:

- **Sorting Order:** If the child node N_c is sorted under the parent node N_p, we call the parent-child order sorting order, denoted as $S(N_p, N_c) = \$col$, with col as the sorting column(s).
- **Grouping Order:** If the child node N_c is grouped under the parent node N_p, we call the parent-child order grouping order, denoted as $G(N_p, N_c) = \$col$, with col as the grouping column(s).

– **Edge Order:** The order among the sibling nodes N_c below a parent node N_p in the schema tree is called the edge order, denoted as $E(N_p, N_c) = i$, $i \in \mathbb{N}$, which means N_c is the ith child of N_p.

In the XML schema tree in Figure 2(c), sorting order is: $S(PLAY, SONG) = \$sIID$; grouping order is $G(PLAY, MPLAY) = \$mplay$; and edge order is $E(PLAY, SONG) = 1$. These orders determine the ordering of the XML elements retrieved by the XPath expressions. In $Q2$ there are two paths in the XML view schema matching the XPath expression: "//SONG". We can construct a new order column for the SONG elements using concatenation of the parent-child orders along the path in a root-to-leaf direction. In case that both edge order and sorting order (or grouping order) exist for a parent-child pair, the edge order is concatenated prior to the sorting order. Sorting by the constructed order column after the union operations can achieve the correct ordering of the SONG elements. We show the translated SQL for $Q2$ in Figure 7(a)[3].

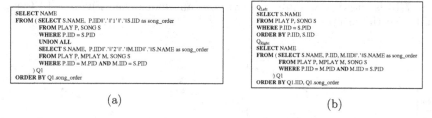

(a)   (b)

Fig. 7. Translated SQL for Merging Multiple Matched Paths

Alternative Computation Separation Strategies

The union operator can be achieved using sorted merge on common columns in the middle-ware by one scan of the pre-sorted result sets. More precisely, one union operator is attached above every parent node that has multiple children (matching paths) in the XML view schema tree. Thus according to different allocations of the union operations in or out of the relational engine, alternative computation pushdown strategies are achievable. Figure 7(b) shows one alternative SQL translation. Q_{Left} and Q_{Right} provide the two sorted inputs for the sorted merge union in the middle-ware.

The SQL is generated as follows: 1) separate the schema tree into upper part and lower part, all the union operators of the upper part are done in the middle-ware; 2) for each path, the parent-child orders below the lowest union operator done in the middle-ware are used to construct the new order column using concatenations; 3) sort by the parent-child orders top-down along each path and the order column constructed (if any).

Pushing more union operators into the relational engine will have a smaller number of SQL queries but suffer from sorting on order columns constructed at runtime. Performing sorted merge union operators in the middle-ware will require a large number of cheap SQL queries, since the sorting can be done

---

[3] We assume that the length of the strings for the IIDs are the same for one table.

utilizing indices. This results in a performance tradeoff. The search space for identifying optimal strategies is linear in the number of possible union operators.

7   Experimental Study

We have implemented the order-sensitive XQuery processing over XML views in the RainbowCore [20] system. We have conducted the performance comparisons among the different order-sensitive SQL translation strategies (Section 6). The experiments are done on a Linux machine with two P3 1GHz CPUs and 1GB memory running Oracle 9.

We compare the performance of the computation separation strategies for the union operators attached to the schema tree formed by multiple matching paths. We compare the execution costs based on the two SQL translations depicted in Figure 7(a) and 7(b). The dataset used includes 1000 to 10000 PLAYs having on average 50 SONGs and 10 MPLAYs per PLAY. Each MPLAY has on average 50 SONGs. The performance comparison of SQL translation in Figure 7(a) versus Figure 7(b) is shown in Figure 8(a) (without any index) and Figure 8(b) (with an index on the primary key).

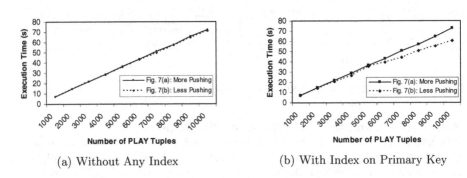

(a) Without Any Index   (b) With Index on Primary Key

Fig. 8. Cost Comparison of SQL Translation for Multiple Matching Paths

When no index is used, the two strategies perform similarly. When an index is present, pushing less union operators into the relational engine outperforms the alternative. The performance difference is increasing with the growth in the size of the relational tables. This experiment demonstrates that pushing less union operators into the relational engine is better than other strategies when indices are deployed.

8   Conclusions

The order semantics of XQuery are crucial for many application domains. We propose a generic approach for inference and isolation of the order semantics in virtual XML views. Our approach turns the order-sensitive XQuery plans into unordered plans by utilizing order context annotations. Alternatives for

SQL translation with order context are also discussed. Performance differences among them are illustrated through an experimental study.

References

1. El-Sayed, M., Dimitrova, K., Rundensteiner, E.A.: Efficiently Supporting Order in XML Query Processing. In: WIDM, pp. 147–154 (2003)
2. Fernandez, M.F., Morishima, A., Suciu, D., et al.: Publishing Relational Data in XML: the SilkRoute Approach. IEEE Data Eng. Bulletin 24(2), 12–19 (2001)
3. Grust, T., van Keulen, M., Teubner, J.: Staircase join: Teach a relational dbms to watch its (axis) steps. In: VLDB, pp. 524–525 (2003)
4. Hidders, J., Michiels, P.: Avoiding Unnecessary Ordering Operations in XPath. In: DBPL, pp. 54–70 (2003)
5. Krishnamurthy, R., Kaushik, R., Naughton, J.F.: XML-SQL Query Translation Literature: The State of the Art and Open Problems. In: Xsym, pp. 1–18 (2003)
6. May, N., Helmer, S., Moerkotte, G.: Nested queries and quantifiers in an ordered context. In: ICDE, pp. 239–250 (2004)
7. Neumann, T., Moerkotte, G.: A combined framework for grouping and order optimization. In: VLDB, pp. 960–971 (2004)
8. Neumann, T., Moerkotte, G.: An efficient framework for order optimization. In: ICDE, p. 461 (2004)
9. O'Neil, P., O'Neil, E., Pal, S., Cseri, I., Schaller, G., Westbury, N.: ORDPATHs: insert-friendly XML node labels. In: SIGMOD, pp. 903–908 (2004)
10. Paparizos, S., Al-Khalifa, S., Chapman, A., Jagadish, H.V., et al.: TIMBER: A Native System for Querying XML. In: SIGMOD, p. 672 (2003)
11. Paparizos, S., Jagadish, H.V.: Pattern tree algebras: sets or sequences? In: VLDB, pp. 349–360 (2005)
12. Shanmugasundaram, J., Kiernan, J., Shekita, E.J., Fan, C., Funderburk, J.: Querying XML Views of Relational Data. In: VLDB, pp. 261–270 (2001)
13. Simmen, D.E., Shekita, E.J., Malkemus, T.: Fundamental Techniques for Order Optimization. In: SIGMOD, pp. 57–67 (1996)
14. Slivinskas, G., Jensen, C.S., Snodgrass, R.T.: Bringing order to query optimization. SIGMOD Record 31(2), 5–14 (2002)
15. Tatarinov, I., Viglas, S., Beyer, K.S., et al.: Storing and querying ordered XML using a relational database system. In: SIGMOD, pp. 204–215 (2002)
16. W3C. XQuery 1.0: An XML Query Language. http://www.w3.org/TR/xquery/
17. Wang, L., Wang, S., Rundensteiner, E.: Order-sensitive XML Query Processing over Relational Sources: An Algebraic Approach. In: IDEAS, pp. 175–184 (2005)
18. Wang, S., Rundensteiner, E.A., Mani, M.: Optimization of Nested XQuery Expressions with Orderby Clauses. In: ICDE Workshops:XSDM, p. 1277 (2005)
19. Wang, X., Cherniack, M.: Avoiding Sorting and Groupin In Processing Queries. In: VLDB, pp. 826–837 (2003)
20. Zhang, X., K.D., et al.: Rainbow: Multi-XQuery Optimization Using Materialized XML Views. In: SIGMOD, pp. 671 (2003)
21. Zhang, X., Pielech, B., Rundensteiner, E.A.: Honey, I Shrunk the XQuery! — An XML Algebra Optimization Approach. In: WIDM, pp. 15–22 (2002)
22. Zhang, X., Rundensteiner, E.A.: XAT: XML Algebra for the Rainbow System. Technical Report WPI-CS-TR-02-24, Worcester Polytechnic Institute (July 2002)

Representation and Management of Evolving Features in OS MasterMap ITN Data

Alex Lohfink, Tom Carnduff, Nathan Thomas, and Mark Ware

Faculty of Advanced Technology, Dept. of Computing and Mathematical Sciences, University of Glamorgan, Pontypridd

1 Background

At the heart of any geographic information system (GIS) is a database system. Data representing geographic entities and spatial features are stored in these GIS and manipulated and visualised according to the user's input. The rapid emergence of GIS has demanded the evolution of database systems to support these spatial data, and to provide powerful analysis operations and functions to assist in decision support, projections, predictions, and simulations in a wide variety of problem domains. The research reported on in this paper investigates a specific area of interest in geospatial database systems, that of the management and representation of evolving features. Features in a GIS group together entities or areas that are of particular interest from a specific viewpoint, such as counties, population, or in this case, roads.

(This project is funded by an EPSRC CASE award and is carried out in collaboration with the Ordnance Survey (OS), and as such will utilise Oracle Spatial and OS MasterMap Integrated Transport Network (subsequently referred to as ITN) data).

2 Project Aims

The aims of the research are as follows:

- to apply object versioning techniques to ITN data within an object-relational data model
- to extend the Oracle Spatial data type to implement spatiotemporal data
- to devise and implement a spatiotemporal data model for ITN data
- to enable the retrieval and manipulation of spatiotemporal ITN features

3 ITN Data

The ITN layer provides a topologically structured representation of the UK's driveable roads. Each road link is supplied with a unique topographic identifier, or TOID, that can be shared with other users across different applications and systems. ITN data is continually updated, capturing real-world change as part

R. Cooper and J. Kennedy (Eds.): BNCOD 2007, LNCS 4587, pp. 160–163, 2007.

of the national geographic database. The data is increasingly used in commercial markets by organisations requiring a variety of information regarding Great Britain's road network. The data supports applications for routing, tracking, scheduling and fleet management and informs traffic analysis and accessibility studies.

4   Object Versioning

The versioning of objects in database systems [7, 4] has been developed within the design engineering environment in CAD systems to represent the evolution of complex design artifacts (composite objects)[6]. Here versions can be defined both at the component level and at the composite object level. The proliferation of configurations of composite objects in CAD versioning has led to the development of versioning models that represent a configuration as a generic object, containing no specific versions of its components. The generic object stores references to its components' types, and specific versions are resolved at run-time by a process called Dynamic Reference Resolution (DRR)[6, 3, 2, 5]. DRR thus minimises version percolation, (where an update to a component triggers cascading updates in the configurations) and allows the free combination of components to create new configurations.

4.1   The Structure of ITN Data

The basic unit of the road feature is the roadlink. Roadlink objects are comprised of a polyline geometry with a roadnode object at each end. A road feature is an aggregate of roadlink objects (see Figure 1). The road feature does not contain the road's geometry, only a reference to its constituent roadlink objects. A roadlink's nodes are marked as 'start' and 'end' to maintain topology.

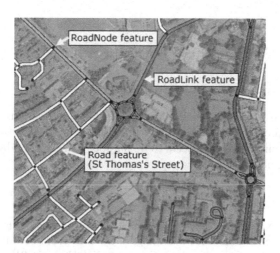

Fig. 1. Road features are comprised of links and nodes

5   The Static Feature Histories Model

Although road features can be regarded as composite objects, their structure represents a single configuration in the system, and this negates the benefits of DRR. The Static Feature Histories model (see Figure 2)is therefore based on the following features

- the road feature is discreetised as a user defined type (UDT)
- aggregation of links is achieved through static references, not DRR
- version descriptors [2] record version information, and are stored as a history attribute of a Road Feature History object
- invariant attributes are stored in the generic object [1]

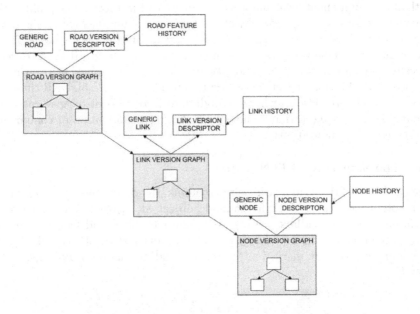

Fig. 2. The Static Feature Histories model 'hard-wires' version references

6   Current Progress and Future Work

The Static Feature Histories model has been implemented in Oracle, and work is now focusing on entering and manipulating data using JDBC strongly typed interfaces, which allow Oracle objects to be mapped to corresponding Java classes, thus preserving object-orientation.

References

[1] Ahmed, R., Navathe, S.B.: Version management of composite objects in cad databases. In: SIGMOD '91: Proceedings of the 1991 ACM SIGMOD international conference on Management of data, New York, NY, USA, pp. 218–227. ACM Press, New York (1991)

[2] Chou, H.-T., Kim, W.: Versions and change notification in an object-oriented database system. In: DAC '88: Proceedings of the 25th ACM/IEEE conference on Design automation, Los Alamitos, CA, USA, pp. 275–281. IEEE Computer Society Press, Los Alamitos (1988)

[3] Dittrich, K.R., Lorie, R.A.: Version support for engineering database systems. IEEE Transactions on Software Engineering 14(4), 429–437 (1988)

[4] Golendziner, L.G., dos Santos, C.S.: Versions and configurations in object-oriented database systems: A uniform treatment. In: Proceddings of the 7th International Conference on Management of Data, pp. 18–37 (1995)

[5] Goonetillake, J.: The Management of Evolving Constraints and Integrity Validation in a Computerised Engineering Design System. Phd, University of Wales Institute, Cardiff (2004)

[6] Katz, R.H.: Toward a unified framework for version modeling in engineering databases. ACM Computing Surveys (CSUR) 22(4), 375–409 (1990)

[7] Sciore, E.: Versioning and configuration management in an object-oriented data model. The VLDB Journal 3(1), 77–106 (1994)

Hopfilter: An Agent for Filtering Web Pages Based on the Hopfield Artificial Neural Network Model

Juan Manuel Adán-Coello[1], Carlos Miguel Tobar[1], Ricardo Luís de Freitas[1], and Armando Marin[2]

[1] PUC-Campinas, Rod. Cx. P. 317, CEP 13012-970, Campinas, SP, Brazil
{juan, tobar, rfreitas}@puc-campinas.edu.br
[2] Senac Ribeirão-Preto, Ribeirão Preto, SP, Brazil
amarin@sp.senac.br

Abstract. With the expansion of the Internet, the amount of information available is continuously reaching higher growth rates. This fact leads to the necessity of developing new advanced tools to collect and filter information that meets users' preferences. This paper presents an agent that uses automatic indexing, concept space generation, and a Hopfield artificial neural network to filter web pages according to users' interests. The experiments that were conducted to evaluate the agent show that it has very satisfactory precision and coverage rates.

1 Introduction

With the expansion of the Web, users face increasing difficulties to fulfill their information needs. The unstructured nature of the data stored in the Web and its dynamic nature contribute to this scenario, which requires users to check frequently for new documents of interest. This situation has motivated the development of personal software agents for continuous information gathering and filtering.

Information needs change from user to user. Therefore, information filtering systems have to be personalized, playing the real role of personal assistants. Such personalized information filtering system has to satisfy three requirements:

1. Specialization: the system selects only documents relevant to the user;
2. Adaptation: information filtering is an iterative process that is performed for long periods of time, during which user's interests change;
3. Exploration: the system should be able to explore new domains, in order to find new information potentially interesting to the user.

A number of different models have been implemented for information retrieval and filtering. Typically, these implementations consist of three main components: document representation, user's interest representation, and algorithms used to match user's interests to documents representations [1] [2].

This paper presents and evaluates the architecture of Hopfilter, a personal agent that mines Web information sources and retrieves documents according to user's

R. Cooper and J. Kennedy (Eds.): BNCOD 2007, LNCS 4587, pp. 164–167, 2007.

interests. It is organized as follows. In section 2 the structure of the Hopfiter agent is presented. Section 3 presents the results of some experiments conducted to evaluate the agent. Section 4 closes the paper with some final remarks.

2 The Architecture of Hopfilter

The filtering agent is composed by User interface (UI), Web interface (WI), Document Preprocessing (DPP), Automatic indexing (AI), Generation of the Space of Concepts (GSC), Artificial Neural Net (ANN). The UI and WI modules interface with the user and with the Web, as the names suggest, and are not the focus of this paper.

The filtering agent can operate in two modes: "concept space generation" and "document filtering". During the concept space generation mode, the DPP, AI, and GSC modules are used. The document filtering mode involves the DPP, AI, and ANN modules. During the document filtering mode, a concept space (CS) for the considered domain must be available. Each mode of operation is briefly described below together with each module.

2.1 Automatic Indexing

When a document is indexed, the result is a list of terms or indexes that represents the document content. AI consists of three operations: stopword removal, work stemming, and term formation.

Removing stopwords. After identifying the words in the input document, using the DPP module, the words that are not relevant for characterizing the document content are removed. To assist this process it is used a dictionary with some 46,000 entries, which can be manually marked by the user as stopwords. All input document words not found in the dictionary are kept in a table for posterior analysis. They can be included in the dictionary if desired.

Word stemming. This step purpose is to reduce the number of cognate words to be indexed. The implemented algorithm is adapted from the Lancaster Stemming Algorithm [3] for the Portuguese language, which only removes words suffixes.

Term formation. A term can be formed by one, two or three adjacent words. For each term, it is computed a term frequency, *tf*, that represents the number of times the term appears in the document. When the agent operates in the concept space generation mode, it is also calculated the document frequency for the term, *df*, that represents the number of documents, in the collection, where the term appears.

2.2 Generation of a Concept Space

The objective of the GSC module is to calculate asymmetric coefficients of similarity for each pair of terms, generating a matrix containing the terms and the respective coefficients, or relationship degrees. This matrix, also called similarity matrix, represents the concept space.

Asymmetric coefficients represent the relationship between two terms better than symmetric coefficients since the probability of co-occurrence of terms i and j can be different from the probability of co-occurrence of j and i, in the same document.

Term selection. Usually, the amount of terms generated by the AI module is very high. To reduce the time needed to compute the coefficients of similarity, only the most important terms should be considered. Term selection is based on the term importance in a document collection.

Computing the asymmetric coefficients of similarity. The asymmetric coefficients of similarity for each pair of terms are calculated by the asymmetric clustering function described in [4].

The result of this step is a similarity matrix that represents the concept space and can be represented by a neural network, where terms represent neurons and the coefficients of similarity the weights of the links that connect the neurons.

2.3 Hopfield Neural Network

The Hopfilter agent is used to filter documents by means of a Hopfield neural network [5] that represents the ideas discussed before. Initially the document to be filtered is submitted to the DPP and AI modules, in order to be represented by a set of terms. These terms will define the elements of an input vector **x** to the net, for a concept space. Each element is 1 if the correspondent term of the concept space is present in the document to be filtered and 0 otherwise.

Initialization of the net. At the beginning, each neuron of the net (representing a given term) will assume its corresponding value in vector **x**.

Activation and iteration. Network activation and iteration are done by a transfer function. The implemented artificial neural network executes the neuron update concurrently.

Convergence. The previous step is repeated until no significant output alterations are detected in the neurons between consecutive iterations.

When the net converges, the number or active neurons is counted. The higher the number of active neurons, the higher the relevance of the document, according to the concept space stored in the memory of the net.

3 Experimental Evaluation

Hopfilter was evaluated using documents related to the Brazilian Tax Legislation A collection of 59 documents was read and selected by an expert user, after verifying the relevance of each document. The concept space was constructed using 22 documents, dealing with the subject "income tax". For the filtering experiment, 37 documents were chosen randomly, of which only 17 were relevant for the chosen subject.

To measure the agent effectiveness in filtering documents, the *precision* and *recall* metrics [6] were employed. A perfect retrieval mechanism will have precision and recall rates equal to 1.0.

We verified that four parameters are decisive to produce satisfactory results: the number of neurons in the net, the energy, E, the bias, θ_I, and the curvature, θ_0. We got good results with the following values: 25 neurons, $\theta_0 = 0.01$; $\theta_I = 0.7$ and $E = 0.025$. With these parameters, we got precision and recall rates of 83.33% and 88.23%, respectively. A good performance if compared with a similar system, an information dissemination agent using genetic algorithm and user feedback that was evaluated using a documents collection on the same domain, reaching a precision of 86%, associated with a recall of 30%; and a recall of 45%, associated with a precision of 69% [6].

4   Concluding Remarks

The textual nature of Web pages presents semantic characteristics that make it very difficult to construct mechanisms for automatic information retrieval, filtering and extraction.

The use of concept spaces seems to be an interesting option to represent document content. However, the selection of terms to compose the concept space is a decisive factor for a good performance of this technique.

During the experimental evaluation of Hopfilter, briefly described in this paper, we verified that the use of terms that are very common in the considered domain can substantially reduce the filtering precision rate. Thus, the process of identifying stopwords must be refined to guarantee that are generated terms with high-level of descriptive power. The use of ontologies is also an approach to be explored to face the difficulties presented by synonymy and polysemy.

References

1. Salton, G., McGill, M.J.: The SMART and SIRE Experimental Retrieval Systems. In: Readings in Information Retrieval, pp. 381–399. Morgan Kaufmann Publishers, San Francisco (1997)
2. Yan, T.W., Garcia-Molina, H.: The SIFT Information Dissemination System. ACM Transactions on Database Systems 24(4), 529–565 (1999)
3. Paice, C.D.: Another Stemer. SIGIR Forum 24(3), 56–61 (1990)
4. Chen, H., Hsu, P., Orwig, R., Hoopes, I., Nunamaker, J.F.: Automatic Concept Classification of Text from Electronic Meetings. C ACM 37(10), 56–73 (1994)
5. Hopfield, J.J.: Neural Network and Physical Systems with Collective Computational Abilities. In: Proceedings of the National Academy of Science, USA, 1982, 79(4), pp. 2554–2558 (1982)
6. Rijsbergen, C.J.: Information Retrieval. Butterworths, London (1979)
7. Vallim, M.S., Adán Coello, J.M.: An Agent for Web Information Dissemination Based on a Genetic Algorithm. In: Proceedings of the IEEE International Conference on Systems, Man and Cybernetics (October 5-8, 2003)

A New Approach to Connecting Information Systems in Healthcare

Alysia Skilton[1], W.A. Gray[1], Omnia Allam[1], and Dave Morrey[2]

[1] Department of Computer Science, Cardiff University, Cardiff, CF24 3AA, UK
[2] Clinical Information Unit, Velindre NHS Trust, Cardiff, CF14 2TL, UK

1 Introduction

A novel approach to managing the information needed by healthcare practitioners working collaboratively to care for a patient is described. Traditionally, healthcare information systems have been disease focused, containing patient data related only to a specific function or concern, such as laboratory results or a particular disease. As healthcare is moving toward a collaborative, patient-centric approach which involves care teams comprising a range of health professionals with different needs, skills and working practices, they require up to date, reliable access to more comprehensive patient data; Data which is currently spread through databases at several treatment centres including hospitals, GP's surgeries and palliative care centres. Additionally, this information must be accessible without disrupting the current systems and services provided by each institution from these systems. A new approach to data sharing based on Virtual Organisations (VO) with a Service Oriented Architecture (SOA) which will allow patient-relevant data to be accessed from the diverse sources available is presented. Preliminary requirements and challenges that such an approach will need to meet are presented, and the approach is compared with existing approaches to illustrate its applicability to this domain. Finally, results and future work are covered.

2 Background

Traditionally, healthcare information systems have been organised around departments and services (such as oncology or laboratory test requests and reporting)[1]. While this served the needs of a healthcare professional working in isolation, the move towards a collaborative approach has led to the creation of multidisciplinary care teams (MDTs) working at different organisations [2, 3]. Each MDT will be different, and the composition of the MDT (people and roles) may change over time as treatment progresses. Similarly, the information requirements of the team will vary with stages of treatment and be specific to the patient. The information required by a member will be unique and will vary with time. An MDT approach results in increased communication needs between team members [4], which current systems cannot readily support [5]. Thus, information provision must change to meet these new requirements without affecting current working practices too radically.

R. Cooper and J. Kennedy (Eds.): BNCOD 2007, LNCS 4587, pp. 168–171, 2007.

3   Challenges

The move towards a MDT approach introduces several information challenges [6]:

- The secure handling of highly sensitive personal data;
- The location of a particular piece of data cannot be pre-determined.
- Handling any number of information systems, practitioners and patients, where each patient has a distinctive care pathway (no one data model can be expected to serve all practitioners' needs);
- Provision of data from heterogeneous databases in a secure environment;
- Provision of required information in the right time without disrupting existing services provision (current systems should remain autonomous).
- The need for a flexible approach accommodating the dynamic nature of health services;
- The need to access historical as well as recent patient data; and
- The need to access external data sources e.g. information about adverse drug reactions.

4   Virtual Organisation Approach

A Service Oriented VO (SOVO) approach is proposed to meet these challenges. This approach supports local autonomy through a modified federation of databases. Identified data is supplied to the VO through a wrapper. Each legacy system has an individualised wrapper, allowing data structures to be adjusted within the wrapper. This means that the VO does not require an enrolled system to conform to a particular data model.

This consists of an access management database, a software component, and constituent databases. The management database records care teams, practitioners, patients, and their relationships. The software component accesses both the management and constituent databases and presents an appropriate view of that data to each user. Constituent databases consist of existing healthcare databases currently in use at care facilities, which have been enrolled in the system.

An individual VO is created for each MDT, which allows limited access to the databases associated with the team's members. Specifically, the system only allows team members to access data about their patients, and can further limit access depending on the individual's information needs, so providing additional security to a patient's data.

Information required by each team member depends on his/her role, hence, developing a 'universal' internal data model to meet everyone's needs is not appropriate. Also, forcing all data into a common data model ignores the diversity of current systems. Hence, our architecture uses several distinct internal data models, which reflect the information system being accessed and the role of the team member. That is, each view will have its own data model, and each system contributes to the views differently. In order to achieve this goal, information requirements need to be determined for each team role, and interfaces designed accordingly. Also, since the system must be able to support the differing viewpoints of practitioners[1] and patients' right to limit access to their data, additional 'limits' are included in the access management system. In this way, access can be defined on a patient by patient and member by member basis.

The approach is flexible and extensible, and does not restrict team management aspects (i.e. teams may be of any size and consist of any combination of members from any participating site who may join or leave a team at any time).

The VO approach provides additional benefits, for example:

- It extends the systems currently used at healthcare sites, and does not interfere with the normal operation of nor require significant changes to these systems;
- By accessing these regularly updated systems, care team members can access the most up to date patient information;
- Members of staff not assigned to MDTs can continue to work with the existing systems, so will not require additional training, which reduces training costs; and
- As databases are enrolled in the system, incremental implementation is supported.

5 Future Work

An embryonic prototype has been developed incorporating three 'sample' health information systems [7]. However, this work is still in its early stages. This section highlights some of the most pressing areas for further study.

Since the trend towards collaborative working in healthcare is recent and continuing, requirements specification is still emerging and will likely evolve over time. A full definition of the requirements and expected usage should be the next step to development so that the system can be tailored to the specific needs of its users.

Determining how permissions will be assigned to users is also critical. The original prototype assigned access rights by user role. However, this may not be adequate. The access management system must evolve to allow for permissions and views to be defined individually and adjusted over time as treatment progresses.

Finally, the incorporation of additional, external medical databases must be considered (e.g. databases listing medication interactions, etc.). These databases will cause an additional level of heterogeneity in that they will not store patient data at all. However, they will provide care team members with patient specific information relevant to their patient's treatment, and so should be considered within the VO system.

6 Critical Analysis and Conclusions

Communication and coordination among healthcare providers is an increasingly important issue in modern medicine. The proposed use of a SOVO approach to combine heterogeneous legacy systems in the healthcare industry facilitates communication among multidisciplinary care team members in their work of treating patients.

---

[1] For example, some practitioners may wish to receive automatic notification that lab results have been returned, while others would consider this 'information overload'.

By accessing the existing, regularly updated systems, the SOVO approach does not suffer from the update and data duplication issues of a data warehousing approach, while the lack of a centralised data store provides increased security as it is handled by the local databases. The use of wrappers to access data in the diverse databases offers the benefits of a traditional federated approach (such as supporting local autonomy of constituent databases) without requiring a common data model. However, there are still many challenges that will need to be addressed including implementation of access privileges and the ability to evolve as provision of care changes over time.

Overall, the proposed SOVO approach has been shown to hold promise in its ability to combine existing autonomous, heterogeneous systems without requiring re-design of those systems. It has the added benefit of providing full access to essential data contained within those systems while simultaneously limiting access on an individual basis. These benefits make it particularly well suited for the healthcare domain.

The implementation of a prototype system allowed investigation into some of the challenges confronting development of a full scale system. It also demonstrated that a system of this type can be created. While the research is still in its early stages, it provides a starting point for further exploration into the design of a full scale system.

References

1. Informing Healthcare. Informing Healthcare (2006). [cited 2006 10/11/2006] http://www.wales.nhs.uk/IHC/
2. Department of Health. The New NHS (1997). [cited 10/01/2007] Available from: http://www.archive.official-documents.co.uk/document/doh/newnhs/forward.htm
3. White Paper: Quality Care and Clinical Excellence; NHS Wales, W. Office (ed.) (1998)
4. Allam, O., et al.: Benefits from accessing the cancer patient pathway in Wales. In: Healthcare Computing 2004 (2004)
5. Griffith, S.M., Kalra, D., et al.: A Portable Communicative Architecture for Electronic Healthcare Records: the Good European Healthcare Record Project. MEDINFO 1, 223–226 (1995)
6. Allam, O.: A Holistic Analysis Approach to Facilitating Communication Between GPs and Cancer Care Teams. In: Computer Science. 2006, Cardiff University: Cardiff (2006)
7. Skilton, A.: The Design and Implementation of a Virtual Organisation to Support Healthcare Teams. In: Computer Science, Cardiff University: Cardiff (2006)

XML Query Result Size Estimation for Small Bandwidth Devices

Stefan Böttcher, Sebastian Obermeier, and Thomas Wycisk

University of Paderborn
Fürstenallee 11
33102 Paderborn, Germany
{stb,so,thwycisk}@upb.de

Abstract. Whenever mobile ad-hoc networks are used as a large data storage, a huge number of queries requesting the same information again and again can slow down the network and drain battery power. In this paper, we introduce an example application, the query classes that are required to be supported, and show up two possible caching methods. The two caching methods are based on the concept of query shipping and data shipping, respectively. Since our caching strategies can be used simultaneously, the decision for doing data shipping depends among other aspects on the overhead of transferred data. We explain why an XML Query Result Size Estimator can assist the application in the question of which mechanism should be used for a certain query, and point to other related estimation techniques.

1 Introduction

Today, ad-hoc networks are researched and used in different contexts for different purposes. Whenever database functionality is needed, the property that ad-hoc networks consist of multiple devices offers new possibilities in terms of interpreting the whole network as a distributed database. This gives each mobile device the possibility to own a local data store, where gathered data can be collected and offered to other devices. In addition, devices may search and query other data stores for certain data. However, besides the limited bandwidth of mobile ad-hoc networks, the limited battery power of devices causes the problem that frequently requested data may have a high effect on up-time of the ad-hoc network. In such a case, caching is considered as a good means to save bandwidth and energy. However, the success of caching depends among other issues on the used caching method. We investigate two possible caching strategies and show why a *Query Result Size Estimator* that gives estimations on the query result size is helpful for setting up a query that reduces the amount of transferred data.

The remainder of the paper is organized as follows. We introduce our application scenario and the supported query classes in Section 1.1. Furthermore, in Section 2, we describe the alternative querying technologies query shipping and data shipping, and explain why the query result size is important in order to decide between these querying technologies. Then, we list the requirements to a query size estimator (Section 3) and compare these requirements with existing estimators (Section 4). Finally, Section 5 concludes the paper.

R. Cooper and J. Kennedy (Eds.): BNCOD 2007, LNCS 4587, pp. 172–175, 2007.
© Springer-Verlag Berlin Heidelberg 2007

1.1   Example Application Scenario

We focus on the following mobile auction application, where the mobile devices form a mobile ad-hoc network on a flea market. Each participant of the flea market may offer, buy, and search articles with his mobile device. Articles are either services or goods. Since the articles can contain details like descriptions, pictures, or videos, we choose the flexible XML format for representation. Whenever users search for items or bid, a multi-hop routing will enable a wide physical area to be covered.

When we look closer at the issued XPath queries in such a scenario, we can see that no arbitrary queries are executed. Instead, the application GUI supports the user when he starts searching for certain items. This means that only a small number of query classes following a few query templates must be supported in the context of this application. We identified the following query classes that are executed in a mobile ad-hoc flea market application:

Q_1: simple path expressions, e.g. searching for product title, current price, description, etc.

Q_2: simple path expressions containing existential filters, e.g. queries searching for items with a picture.

Q_3: queries containing category filters, e.g. filters selecting items of the category music or DVD.

Q_4: queries containing range filters, e.g. filters selecting items of a certain price range.

Q_5: queries containing functions, e.g. a substring function for returning items containing a certain keyword.

2   Query Shipping vs. Data Shipping

Whenever a user U of our mobile auction application issues an XPath query Q_x for a certain data store DS, the following two possibilities exist

Query shipping means the query Q_x is sent to DS via multiple hops. The result is calculated and sent back to U, who can directly display the result.

Data shipping means that the XML document owner splits the document into pairwise disjunct segments $S_1 \ldots S_n$, and informs all clients beforehand about this segmentation schema. When U issues the query Q_x, the client U itself identifies which XML segments are required to answer the query locally by U, and requests these segments. In this case, the network functions as a large file server, since U, and not the database, is responsible for the evaluation of Q_x.

Query shipping has the advantage that transferring a calculated result often involves less data transfer than transferring the data that is necessary to calculate the result locally.

The advantage of data shipping concerns the simple re-use of cached data. A node that routes a request for a certain XML segment must only compare its cached segments with the requested ones. Performing complex logical XPath tests, e.g. [1]), is not necessary for this kind of query processing. Furthermore, a segment S_i may be useful for a variety of different queries, while a concrete query instance that is cached may only help to answer similar queries.

Since both approaches, query shipping and data shipping, can be used concurrently, the decision of which approach should be used depends among other aspects on the estimation of the query result in comparison to the size of the data needed to answer the query.

3   Requirements

Within the scenario outlined in Section 1.1, we can identify the following requirements to a query result size and cardinality estimator. The result size estimator must

- estimate size and cardinality of the nodes returned by a given query
- support the query classes Q_1 to Q_4, explained in Section 1.1
- support filter functions Q_5 that are dynamically invoked during the application execution
- support queries containing a wildcard ($*$) or a descent-or-self axis location step ($//$)
- be based on meta data that is distributable to the mobile clients in order to avoid database access.
- limit meta data size to a predefined constant, e.g. 15kB
- be adaptable to frequent query patterns such that the accuracy increases for frequent queries.

4   Related Work

Existing solutions for estimating the query result size are proposed mainly for two kinds of databases: relational databases and XML databases. However, estimators are mainly used for query optimization, e.g. when the number of intermediate results should be kept small. An example for such optimizers can be found in [2], where histograms are used for relational databases. When we look closer at XML/XPath based estimators, XSKETCH [3, 4] and FXSKETCH [5] are proposals that use the idea of the *Path Tree* and extend it by using id/idref constructs (e.g. XLink) to generate a graph like data structure. The use of this approach is mainly to estimate selectivity of structural joins, e.g. X/Y: i.e. how many child nodes Y has a parent node X, but not to give precise estimation on the result size.

[6], for instance, suggests the use of two data structures, namely *Path Trees* and *Markov Tables*. The concept of *Path Trees* is inspired by methods for estimating selectivity of substring predicates, e.g. [7]. A *Markov Table* contains all sub paths with their frequencies. A similar concept was described in [8] for the *Lore* DBMS. Both data structures allow a selectivity estimation of *simple path expressions*. However, query class Q3 containing category filters is not supported by this approach.

In comparison to all other approaches, our requirement to a size estimator is that is must be able to deal with all query types $Q_1 \ldots Q_5$ introduced in Section 1.1. This means, it is not a requirement to our estimator that it must deal with arbitrary XPath queries, since no user types in arbitrary queries. Our requirement is that the estimator must be adjustable to that set of queries that the concrete underlying mobile ad-hoc flea market application requires.

5   Summary and Conclusion

We introduced a mobile flea market as an example application for mobile networks, and outlined the requirements concerning the supported query classes. Furthermore, we have presented two possible querying strategies for mobile ad-hoc networks, namely query shipping and data shipping, and explained why a requirement for reducing the overall data transfer with data shipping is that the overhead of data shipping can be estimated. Therefore, we have pointed out our demands on a query result size estimator, and have compared these demands with existing solutions. However, we have seen that current approaches do not take the concrete underlying application into consideration. Doing so results in the observation that only a limited set of queries following a few query templates are posed by the application, and that no arbitrary queries are generated. Our conclusion is that the need for a query result size estimator that can be tailored to a specific application still exists, and that we plan to focus our research efforts in this direction.

References

1. Mandhani, B., Suciu, D.: Query caching and view selection for xml databases. In: VLDB '05: Proceedings of the 31st international conference on Very large data bases, VLDB Endowment, pp. 469–480 (2005)
2. Ioannidis, Y.E.: The History of Histograms (abridged). In: VLDB 2003, Proceedings of 29th Intl. Conference on Very Large Data Bases, September 9-12, Berlin, Germany, pp. 19–30 (2003)
3. Polyzotis, N., Garofalakis, M.: Statistical Synopses for Graph-Structured XML Databases. In: SIGMOD '02: Proceedings of the 2002 ACM SIGMOD international conference on Management of data, pp. 358–369. ACM Press, New York (2002)
4. Polyzotis, N., Garofalakis, M.N.: Structure and Value Synopses for XML Data Graphs. In: VLDB '02: Proceedings of 28th Intl. Conference on Very Large Data Bases, pp. 466–477 (2002)
5. Drukh, N., Polyzotis, N., Garofalakis, M.N., Matias, Y.: Fractional XSketch Synopses for XML Databases. In: Bellahsène, Z., Milo, T., Rys, M., Suciu, D., Unland, R. (eds.) XSym 2004. LNCS, vol. 3186, pp. 189–203. Springer, Heidelberg (2004)
6. Aboulnaga, A., Alameldeen, A.R., Naughton, J.F.: Estimating the Selectivity of XML Path Expressions for Internet Scale Applications. In: VLDB '01: Proceedings of the 27th International Conference on Very Large Data Bases, pp. 591–600. Morgan Kaufmann, San Francisco (2001)
7. Jagadish, H.V., Ng, R.T., Srivastava, D.: Substring Selectivity Estimation. In: PODS '99: Proceedings of the eighteenth ACM SIGMOD-SIGACT-SIGART symposium on Principles of database systems, pp. 249–260. ACM Press, New York (1999)
8. McHugh, J., Widom, J.: Query Optimization for XML. In: Atkinson, M.P., Orlowska, M.E., Valduriez, P., Zdonik, S.B., Brodie, M.L. (eds.) VLDB'99, Proceedings of 25th International Conference on Very Large Data Bases, September 7-10, 1999, Edinburgh, Scotland, UK, pp. 315–326. Morgan Kaufmann, San Francisco (1999)

An Efficient Sheet Partition Technique for Very Large Relational Tables in OLAP

Sung-Hyun Shin[1], Hun-Young Choi[2], Jinho Kim[2], Yang-Sae Moon[2], and Sang-Wook Kim[1]

[1] College of Information & Communications, Hanyang University, Korea
[2] Department of Computer Science, Kangwon National University, Korea
{shshin, hychoi, jhkim, ysmoon}@kangwon.ac.kr, wook@hanyang.ac.kr

1   Introduction

Spreadsheets such as Microsoft Excel are OLAP (On-Line Analytical Processing) [2] applications to easily analyze complex multidimensional data. In general, spreadsheets provide grid-like graphical interfaces together with various chart tools [4,5]. However, previous work on OLAP spreadsheets adopts a naive approach that directly retrieves, transmits, and presents all the resulting data at once. Thus, it is difficult to use the previous work for very large relational tables with millions of rows or columns due to the communication and space overhead.

In this paper we propose an efficient spreadsheet-based interface to incrementally browse the query result on very large relational tables. The proposed interface exploits the *sheet partition technique* that selectively browses small parts of the resulting table. Our sheet partition technique first divides a large resulting table into many small-sized sheets, called *partitions*, and then browses the partitions one by one according to the user's request. More precisely, the technique works as follows: (1) the client, i.e., the user requests a query with a specific column (or row); (2) the server stores the query result on the given column (or row) as the temporary data; (3) the server provides an initial partition, which are constructed by using the initial column (or row) range of temporary data; and (4) the client repeatedly interacts with the server to browse more partitions. Since the sheet partition technique enables us to use a few small-sized partitions instead of a single large-sized sheet, we can reduce the communication and space overhead. Also, we can easily analyze large relational tables by exploiting the concept of *divide and conquer* in spreadsheet applications.

2   The Proposed Sheet Partition Technique

There have been many efforts to provide spreadsheet-like views for easy analysis on multidimensional data. In [5], Witkowski et al. defined spreadsheet-typed tables in relational databases by extending standard SQL statements. In [6], Witkowski et al. also proposed an Excel-based analysis method to exploit various powerful Excel functions in handling the original relational data. These works, however, do not consider very large relational tables with millions of rows or

R. Cooper and J. Kennedy (Eds.): BNCOD 2007, LNCS 4587, pp. 176–179, 2007.
© Springer-Verlag Berlin Heidelberg 2007

columns [1] in presenting the tables as the spreadsheets. Therefore, in this paper we focus on the spreadsheet interface for the large relational tables.

The *sheet partition technique* enables us to analyze a few small-sized sheet partitioned from a single large-sized sheet. Figure 1 shows an overall working framework for our sheet partition technique. In Step (1) a user indicates column-based or row-based partitions by providing a specific column or row together with a query. In Step (2), the server evaluates the query and stores the result as temporary data. In Step (3), the server provides an initial partition to the user as the form of a spreadsheet. Finally, in Steps (4) and (5) the client repeatedly interacts with the server to get more partitioned sheets for the user's additional request. Likewise, by using the sheet partition technique, we do not need to handle a large-sized table at once, but we can incrementally process the table with a few small-sized partitions that are selected by the continuous user interactions.

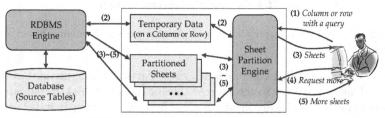

* **(2)**: *Build the temporary data based on the given column or row*

Fig. 1. An overall query processing framework using the sheet partition technique

We first explain the *column-based* sheet partition. This method uses a user-specified column to partition a large table into small sheets, and provides a few selected sheets as the resulting views. Figure 2 shows an algorithm *StoreAColumn* that retrieves the distinct values of the user-specified column and stores them in a temporary array, which will be used to construct the partitions based on the column values. In Line 1, we first declare a temporary array *ColValues*[1..*count*] to store the values of the given column. Here, *count* is the total number of distinct values of the column. In Line 2, we then declare *Cursor* as the **select** statement that retrieves values of the specific column. Since the column may have duplicate values, we explicitly specify the quantifier **distinct**. In Lines 3 to 6, we finally store the resulting values obtained by *Cursur* in *ColValues*[]. Eventually, the array *ColValues*[] contains the distinct values of the given column.

Figure 3 shows an algorithm *ColumnBasedSheet* that retrieves tuples whose column values in the user-specified range. We note that the algorithm uses the array *ColValues*[] obtained by *StoreAColumn* in Figure 2. The inputs to the algorithm are *from* and *to* of a sheet (Line 1). Using them as indexes of *ColValues*[] we select the tuples from the table (Line 2). We then store the tuples in **result** (Line 3), and return them as the partitioned sheet (Line 5). Therefore, using *ColumnBasedSheet* we can interactively and repeatedly access the partitioned sheets by changing the input range (i.e., *from* and *to*).

Algorithm *StoreAColumn*(**Table** *table,* **Column** *column*)
1   **declare string** *ColValues*[1..*count*];
2   **cursor** *Cursor* **is select distinct** *column* **from** *table* **order by** *column*;
3   **open** *Cursor*; *i* := 1;
4   **while** *Cursor* **is** not null
5   fetch *Cursor* into *ColValues*[*i*++];
6   **close** *Cursor*;

Fig. 2. An algorithm *StoreAColumn* for retrieving distinct values of the given column

Algorithm *ColumnBasedSheet*(**int** *from,* **int** *to*)
1   **for** *i* := *from* **to** *to*
2   select * from [*table name*] where [*column name*] = *ColValues*[*i*];
3   store the selected tuples into **result**;
4   **end-of-for**
5   return **result** as the current column-based sheet;

Fig. 3. An algorithm *ColumnBasedSheet* for constructing a column-based sheet

We now briefly explain the *row-based* sheet partition. The method inserts an additional index attribute to the source table (or the join table) to generate serial numbers to be accessed. We consider five methods of assigning an index attribute to the table: (1) adding an index attribute to the source table, (2) creating a duplicated table containing an index attribute, (3) creating a virtual source table using a cursor, (4) creating a join table using primary keys of source tables, and (5) creating a virtual join table using two or more cursors. These row-based methods are more complex than the column-based ones due to using an index. We omit the details on the row-based sheet partition algorithms due to space limitation. We are now trying to find an optimal strategy by implementing all the five methods.

3   Implementation of the Sheet Partition Technique

The hardware platform is an Intel Pentium IV PC. The software platform is Microsoft Windows XP and Microsoft SQL Server 2005 DBMS [3]. As the experimental data, we use a fact table **sales_fact_1988** of **FoodMart** 2000 provided in SQL Server 2005.

Figure 4 shows an example of screen captures obtained by the sheet partition technique. Figure 4(a) shows a screen capture caused by the column-based sheet partition. The sheet in Figure 4(a) is obtained from a value 'Apple' with respect to the column 'fruit.' Figure 4(b) shows a screen capture caused by the row-based sheet partition. The sheet in Figure 4(b) is obtained by dividing a large source table into small sheets, each of which contains ten tuples.

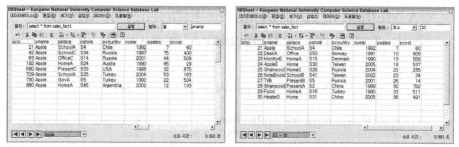

(a) Column-based sheet partition   (b) Row-based sheet partition

Fig. 4. An example of screen captures for the partitioned sheets

4   Conclusions

Spreadsheets are widely used in OLAP for efficient and easy analysis on complex data. In this paper we have proposed the sheet partition technique that divides a large-sized table into small-sized sheets and incrementally browses only a few selected sheets. Our sheet partition technique employs the column-based or row-based methods. The column-based method partitions a large table based on ranges of the given column, and the row-based method does based on serial numbers of an index attribute. We have designed and implemented the partition algorithms to confirm practical effectiveness of our technique. We are now performing various experiments to find an optimal strategy for the row-based partition method.

Acknowledgements

This work was supported by the Ministry of Science and Technology (MOST)/ Korea Science and Engineering Foundation (KOSEF) through the Advanced Information Technology Research Center (AITrc).

References

1. Agrawal, R., et al.: Storage and Querying of E-Commerce Data. In: Proc. the 27th Int'l Conf. on Very Large Data Base, Roma, Italy, pp. 149–158 (September 2001)
2. Chaudhuri, S., Dayal, U.: An Overview of Data Warehousing and OLAP Technology. SIGMOD Record 26(1), 65–74 (1997)
3. Microsoft SQL Server (2005) http://www.microsoft.com/sql/
4. Raman, V., et al.: Scalable Spreadsheets for Interactive Data Analysis. In: Proc. ACM SIGMOD Workshop on DMKD, Philadelphia (May 1999)
5. Witkowski, A. et al.: Spreadsheets in RDBMS for OLAP. In: Proc. Int'l Conf. on Management of Data, ACM SIGMOD, San Diego, California, pp. 52–63 (June 2003)
6. Witkowski, A., et al.: Query By Excel. In: Proc. the 31st Int'l Conf. on Very Large Data Bases, Trondheim, Norway, pp. 1204–1215 (September 2005)

A Method of Improving the Efficiency of Mining Sub-structures in Molecular Structure Databases

Haibo Li[1], Yuanzhen Wang[1], and Kevin Lü[2]

[1] Department of Computing Science, Huazhong University of Science and Technology,
Wuhan 430074, China
`lihaibo.wh@gmail.com`
[2] BBS, Room76, Tin Building, Brunel University, Uxbridge, UK UB8 3PH

Abstract. One problem exists in current substructure mining algorithms is that when the sizes of molecular structure databases increase, the costs in terms of both time and space increase to a level that normal PCs are not powerful enough to perform substructure data mining tasks. After examining a number of well known molecular structure databases, we found that there exist a large number of common loop substructures within molecular structure databases, and repeatedly mining these same substructures costs the system resources significantly. In this paper, we introduce a new method: (1) to treat these common loop substructures as some kinds of "atom" structures; (2) to maintain the links of the new "atom" structures with the rest of the molecular structures, and to reorganize the original molecular structures. Therefore we avoid repeat many same operations during mining process and produce less redundant results. We tested the method using four real molecular structure databases: AID2DA'99/CA, AID2DA'99/CM, AID2DA'99 and NCI'99. The results indicated that (1) the speed of substructure mining has been improved due to the reorganization; (2) the number of patterns obtained by mining has been reduced with less redundant information.

1 Introduction

There have been several efficient substructure mining algorithms by now, such as AGM [1], FSG [2], gSpan [5] and Gaston [4] etc. But as the size of the molecular structure database increasing, the costs in terms of both time and space are increasing so greatly that these algorithms can process no longer. For example, on normal PCs, all of the above algorithms can process the Predictive Toxicology database (PTE), which contains 340 molecular structures. But for the database consisted of 422 confirmed active compounds from AIDS antiviral screen database, only FSG, gSpan and Gaston can do mining. When aiming at the whole AIDS antiviral screen database, which contains 42689 compounds, only gSpan and Gaston can accomplish mining. Finally, for the whole NCI database which contains all 250,251 compounds, none of the above four algorithms can process substructure mining on PCs, excepting Gaston running on SMP servers.

R. Cooper and J. Kennedy (Eds.): BNCOD 2007, LNCS 4587, pp. 180–184, 2007.

To solve this problem, we need to reduce redundant information obtained in mining progress besides to improve performance of substructure mining algorithm. After examining a number of well known molecular structure databases, we found that there are a large number of common loop substructures in molecular structures. We can reduce redundant information greatly in molecular structure databases. If we didn't break these loops, we can avoid perform many same operations during mining process.

The specific method introduced in this paper is: (1) we regard most common loops in molecular structures as some kinds of "atom" structure; (2) we consider common edges and vertexes between loops in condensed cyclic structures as some kinds of "bond" edges. Finally, we maintain the vertexes and edges which are not in any loops. According to these rules, we reorganize molecular structure databases to new ones.

After the reorganization, the number of candidate substructures generated during mining will be decreased, and most of these candidate substructures are tree structures and will spend less time to do graph isomorphism testing. The efficiency of mining will be improved greatly. Finally, we won't get many redundant frequent substructures in the mining result. The performance testing proves the conclusion.

The remaining of this paper is arranged as following. Section 2 takes some statistics and analysis on loops in chemistry molecular structure databases to confirm the regenerating method is feasible. Section 3 introduces the algorithm of reorganizing molecular structures based on atomizing of loops. In section 4, we give the performance testing result on various databases. And section 5 draws a conclusion.

2 Statistics on Loops in Molecular Structure Database

In this paper, we'll mine substructures in four molecular structure databases: AID2DA'99/CA, AID2DA'99/CI, AID2DA'99 and NCI'99 [4]. The sizes of these databases are list in Table 1. The loops' shapes are list in Table 2 to Table 5.

Table 1. Molecular structure databases to be mined

Database	Number of compounds
AID2DA'99/CA	422
AID2DA'99/CM	1081
AID2DA'99	42689
NCI	250251

Table 2. Loops in AID2DA'99/CA

Loops	Freq.	Cumulative Freq.
6-edge loops	76.3%	76.3%
5-edge loops	21.3%	97.6%
7-edge loops	1.2%	98.8%
3-edge loops	0.7%	99.5%
4-edge loops	0.06%	99.56

Table 3. Loops in AID2DA'99/CM

Loops	Freq.	Cumulative Freq.
6-edge loops	74.9%	74.9%
5-edge loops	22.6%	97.5%
7-edge loops	1.2%	98.7%
4-edge loops	0.5%	99.2%
3-edge loops	0.2%	99.4%

As shown by statistics, unlabeled loops in molecular structure databases are mainly 6-edges loops and 5-loops, which sum up more than 90% of total loops. In labeled loops, almost 50% are benzene ring. If we change these loops into "atoms", we can avoid most loops and independent cycles in databases and reduce redundant information of molecular structure databases greatly.

Table 4. Loops in AID2DA'99

Loops	Freq.	Cumulative Freq.
6-edge loops	73.3%	73.3%
5-edge loops	22.3%	95.6%
7-edge loops	1.5%	97.1%
3-edge loops	1.2%	98.3%
4-edge loops	0.7%	99.0%

Table 5. Loops in NCI'99

Loops	Freq.	Cumulative Freq.
6-edge loops	77.0%	77.0%
5-edge loops	19.1%	96.1%
3-edge loops	1.8%	97.9%
7-edge loops	0.8%	98.7%
4-edge loops	0.6%	99.3%

3 Reorganizing Molecular Structure Databases

According to the above statistics, we only change 6-edge loops and 5-edge loops into "atom" structures.

If we avoid break these loop structures, we'll not only reduce the complexity of mining, but also obtain a concise mining result.

For example, in the molecular structure t as , if we are according to the regular substructure mining rules, we may get pattern substructures such as $C-C$, $C=C$, $C-C=C$, $C-C=C$, etc. In fact, these molecular fragments are greatly different from the original molecular structure t and can't well represent the structural features of t. Contrastively, if we regard the benzene ring in t as a "atom" structure, then the pattern

substructures only are , N, and . Molecular fragment in this result are related with t closely, and the mining result is concise with no redundancy.

Given a labeled graph of a molecular structure g, we can divide its vertexes of g into two sets V_H and V_H', where V_H includes all vertexes in any loops of G, and V_H' contains the remaining vertexes. In the same way, the edges of g will be divided into E_H containing edges in loops of g, and E_H' containing edges not in any loops of g. For any elements in V_H, V_H', they will be put into the new graph. For an edge e from E_H', if a vertex of e is in V_H', then this vertex will be maintained with no changes; otherwise, if the vertex is in a loop h_i of g, we need change the vertex into the new "loop atom" corresponding to h_i. The algorithm 1 describes the framework of the reorganizing procedure on a molecular structure. The function *Search_loops* accomplished the task of finding out all loops and the types of these "loop atoms".

Algorithm 1 Generate_new_graph(*g, newg*)
Input: a molecular structure graph *g*.
Output: the new structure graph *newg*.
1: Search_loops(*g, loops, loop_types*);
2: divide the vertexes of *g* into set V_H and set V_H';
3: **for each** h_i in *loops* **do**
4:    change h_i into new loop atom vh_i;
5:    put vh_i into *newg*;
6: **for** each two loops h_i and h_j in *loops*
7:    **if** there is common element between h_i and h_j **then**
8:       get the "loop atom bonds" eh_i between vh_i and vh_j;
9:       put eh_i into *newg*;
10: **for** each vertex v_i in V_H'
11:    put v_i into *newg*;
12: **for** each edge e_i in E_H'
13:    check vertexes of e_i, and put e_i into *newg*;

4 Performance Test

We do our performance testing on a 1.6 GHz Pentium-4 PC with 512MB main memory, running WinXP.

We use four real molecular structure databases AID2DA'99/CA, AID2DA'99/CM, AID2DA'99 and NCI'99 to do performance testing. We reorganize these four databases into four new structure databases: new AID2DA'99/CA, new AID2DA'99/CM, new AID2DA'99 and NCI'99. Then we use the Gaston algorithm to do substructure mining in every database. The contrast results are shown in Fig. 1 and Table 6.

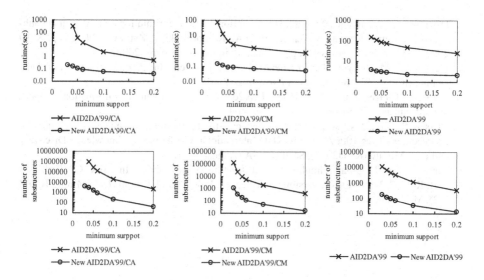

Fig. 1. Result of substructure mining in various database

From the testing result, we found that after reorganizing in every regular molecular structure databases, the speed of the substructure mining has been improved and the number of patterns obtained by mining has been reduced significantly. The mining in the regular NCI'99 can't be processed on the testing PCs, but the new NCI'99 can accomplish the task.

Table 6. The mining result in new_NCI'99 database

Mininum Support	Runtime(s)	Number of frequent substructure
40%	125	14
30%	285	34
20%	639	77

5 Conclusion

In this paper, we introduce a method to consider the most frequent 6-edge loops and 5-edge loops in molecular structures as new kinds of "atoms", and reorganizing the regular molecular structure database on this point. This method can improves the efficiency of the substructure mining greatly by avoiding expensive repeat mining operation in cyclic structures and obtain a concise mining result with less redundant pattern substructures. By performance testing in different databases, we prove this improvement.

References

1. Inokuchi, A., Washio, T., Motoda, H.: An apriori-based algorithm for mining frequent substructures from graph data. In: Zighed, A.D.A., Komorowski, J., Żytkow, J.M. (eds.) PKDD 2000. LNCS (LNAI), vol. 1910, pp. 13–23. Springer, Heidelberg (2000)
2. Kuramochi, M., Karypis, G.: Frequent subgraph discovery. In: Proc. 2001 Int. Conf. Data Mining (ICDM '01), San Jose, CA (November 2001)
3. National Cancer Institute (NCI). Dtp/2d and 3d structural information (1999), http://cactus.nci.nih.gov/ncidb2/download.html
4. Nijssen, S., Kok, J.N.: A quickstart in frequent structure mining can make a difference. In: Proceedings of the 10th ACM SIGKDD International Conference on knowledge Discovery and Data Mining (KDD2004), Seattle, USA (August 2004)
5. Yan, X., Han, J.: gSpan: Graph-based substructure pattern mining. In UIUC-CS Tech. Report: R-2002-2296, A short version published. In: Proc. 2002 Int. Conf. Data Mining(ICDM '02), Maebashi, Japan (2002)

XFLab: A Technique of Query Processing over XML Fragment Stream*

Sangwook Lee, Jin Kim, and Hyunchul Kang

School of Computer Science and Engineering, Chung-Ang University
Seoul, 156-756, Korea
{swlee,jkim}@dblab.cse.cau.ac.kr, hckang@cau.ac.kr

Abstract. We investigate XML query processing in a portable/handheld client device with limited memory in ubiquitous computing environment. Because of memory limitation in the client, the source XML data possibly of large volume is fragmented in the server and streamed in fragments over which query processing is done in the client. The state-of-the-art techniques employ the *hole-filler model* in fragmenting XML data and processing queries over XML fragment stream. In this paper, we propose a new technique where an *XML labeling scheme* is employed instead of the hole-filler model. Through preliminary experiments, we show that our technique outperforms the state-of-the-art techniques both in memory usage and in query processing time.

1 Introduction

In ubiquitous computing environment, there could be a number of heterogeneous portable/handheld client devices deployed. Those include cellular phones, PDAs, and smart cards to name just a few. Despite the rapid advancement of memory technology, it is still usual that memory capacity of such devices is very limited. As such, naïve practice would be that the client sends its query to the server when its source data is of large volume, and the server processes it and ships the result. Such a conventional client-server computing is obviously not scalable.

In this paper, we investigate XML query processing in a client device with limited memory. The source XML data against which the client queries are to be processed could be in large volume. Thus, the whole of it could not be downloaded to the client. Besides, in ubiquitous computing environments, the server data is usually transmitted over a wireless network with limited bandwidth. As such, it is infeasible to transmit a large XML data in its entirety. Rather, it is partitioned into manageable fragments, and they are transmitted as a stream. Their arrival at a client may not be in proper order, and yet the stream query processing over them should return the correct result.

The first proposed system with such capability is XFrag [3]. It employs the *hole-filler model* [1,2] in fragmenting XML data and *pipelined* query processing over XML fragment stream. The hole-filler model is simple and clean in representing

---

* This work was supported by the Basic Research Program of the Korea Science & Engineering Foundation (grant No. R01-2006-000-10609-0).

R. Cooper and J. Kennedy (Eds.): BNCOD 2007, LNCS 4587, pp. 185–189, 2007.

XML fragmentation. Each XML fragment could contain *holes*, which are supposed to be filled with other XML fragments possibly with other holes. For each hole and its corresponding *filler*, a value is assigned. It is called a hole ID (for the hole) or a filler ID (for the filler). The main inefficiency inherent in the hole-filler model is two-fold: (1) The space overhead for the hole/filler IDs along with accompanying XML tagging created in XML fragmentation process could be very huge considering the typical structure of XML documents on the Web [4]. (2) Given two XML fragments that are an ancestor and a descendant with each other, such a structural relationship could not be identified until all the fragments connecting the two are fully streamed in. Because of this, the processing of the widely used descendant axis (//) of XPath would suffer. Due to these limitations, the amount of memory required for query processing over XML fragment stream at the client would increase.

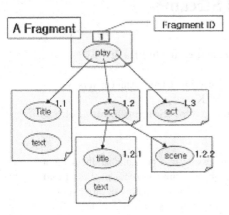

Fig. 1. Example of XML Fragmentation with Labeling

XFPro [5] has improved the query processing pipeline of XFrag. However, it is still based on the hole-filler model, and its improvement is focused on query processing time.

In this paper, we report our on-going efforts for the development of a new technique called *XFLab* where an *XML labeling scheme* replaces the hole-filler model to improve memory efficiency. Section 2 summarizes the salient features of XFLab. Section 3 presents preliminary performance results.

2   XFLab

The XML labeling (or numbering) schemes were devised to represent structural relationship (e.g., parent-child, ancestor-descendant, etc.) among the nodes of XML data modeled as a tree, and to exploit them in query processing. There were many proposed in the literature and most recent and advanced ones include ORDPATH [6] and QED [7]. When an XML document modeled as a tree is fragmented, it could also be represented as a tree, which we call an *XML fragment tree*. Thus, its fragments could be labeled as the nodes of the original XML tree are. Figure 1 shows an example of an XML fragment tree and its labeling with Dewey order encoding.

With our XML fragment labeling, we do not need holes or fillers. Thus, there are no hole/filler IDs. Only the *fragment ID*s (i.e., the labels assigned to fragments) will do. For an XML fragment, there would be only 1 fragment ID needed in our scheme while with the hole-filler model as many hole IDs as the number of holes in a fragment are needed. For a typical structure of XML documents [4], there would be a number of holes in a fragment. As such, our XML fragment labeling considerably reduces the space overhead incurred because of fragmentation. Besides, given any pair of XML fragments of an XML document, their structural relationship can be easily decided only with their labels without accessing other relevant fragments. Thus, it could support efficient processing of the descendant axis (//) of XPath.

The core modules of XFLab consist of two server components, *DTD Analyzer* and *Fragment Generator*, and one client component, *Pipelined Query Processor*. The DTD Analyzer takes the DTD of the source XML documents and generates the *tag structure* and the *fragmentation schema*. The former represents the structural information of the XML document. It is required in query processing over the fragment stream in a client. The latter specifies how the source XML document is to be fragmented and labeled. The main requirement in this process is to guarantee that the original XML document could be reconstructed as it was given its fragments and fragment IDs (though such reconstruction is not really needed in query processing). Since there could be many element instances of the same tag name in an XML document, the labeled fragmentation should not yield any ambiguity in query processing over the fragment stream (and thus in document reconstruction). Finally, the Pipelined Query Processor in the client is an XPath processor derived from an XPath expression. It takes the XML fragment stream, evaluating the XPath expression without reconstructing the whole XML document out of its fragment stream. There are some implementation challenges dealt with for the Pipelined Query Processor because fragment IDs are used instead of the simpler hole/filler IDs.

3 Implementation and Performance Evaluation

We have implemented both XFrag and our proposed XFLab in Java using J2SE Development Kit 5.0 Update 6 on Windows XP Professional. The performance experiments were conducted in a system with 2.6 GHz CPU and 1GB memory. The source XML document against which the client queries are processed is *auction.xml* generated by xmlgen of XMark benchmark [8]. Its original size is 22.8MB, and the total size of XML fragments in XFrag is 30.4MB whereas that in XFLab is 27.0MB. The queries used in the experiments are the same ones used in the evaluation of XFrag in [3]. They are the following three XPath queries:

Query 1: doc("auction.xml")/site/open_auctions//increase
Query 2: doc("auction.xml")/site/open_auctions/open_auction[initial>"10"]/bidder
Query 3: doc("auction.xml")/site/open_auctions/open_auction/bidder[increase>"200"]

Figure 2 through Figure 4 show the experimental results that were the average of 30 measurements for each query. The x-axis denotes the time marked in the course of query processing in the client while the y-axis denotes the total memory usage in the client at those particular moments. For all queries, XFLab outperformed XFrag both in memory usage and in query processing time. As for the memory usage, it was measured using the EclipseProfiler plugin [9]. When the *maximum* amounts of memory used during the entire course of query processing by XFrag and by XFLab are compared, the improvement is 24% (Query 1), 48% (Query 2), and 32% (Query 3). As for the query processing time, the time it took in the client was measured. The

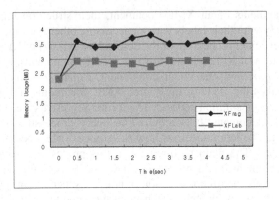

Fig. 2. Experimental Result (Query 1)

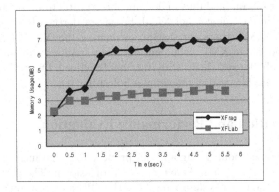

Fig. 3. Experimental Result (Query 2)

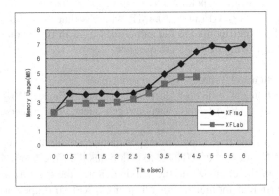

Fig. 4. Experimental Result (Query 3)

curves of XFLab in the graphs are terminated earlier than those of XFrag, which means that query processing by XFLab takes shorter than that by XFrag. The improvement is 20% (Query 1), 8% (Query 2), and 25% (Query 3).

References

1. Bose, S., et al,: A Query Algebra for Fragmented XML Stream Data. In: Proc. DBPL (2003)
2. Fegaras, L., et al.: Query Processing of Streamed XML Data. In: Proc. CIKM, pp. 126–133 (2002)
3. Bose, S., Fegaras, L.: XFrag: A Query Processing Framework for Fragmented XML Data. In: Proc. Web and Databases (2005)
4. Mignet, L., et al.: The XML Web: a First Study. In: Proc. WWW (2003)
5. Huo, H., et al.: Efficient Query Processing for Streamed XML Fragments. In: Lee, M.L., Tan, K.-L., Wuwongse, V. (eds.) DASFAA 2006. LNCS, vol. 3882, Springer, Heidelberg (2006)
6. O'Neil, P., et al.: ORDPATHs: Insert-Friendly XML Node Labels. In: Proc. SIGMOD (2004)
7. Li, C., Ling, T.: QED: A Novel Quaternary Encoding to Completely Avoid Re-labeling in XML Updates. In: Proc. CIKM (2005)
8. Schmidt, A., et al.: XMark: A Benchmark for XML Data Management. In: Proc. VLDB. pp. 974–985 (2002)
9. http://eclipsecolorer.sourceforge.net/index_profiler.html

Knowledge Discovery from Semantically Heterogeneous Aggregate Databases Using Model-Based Clustering

Shuai Zhang, Sally McClean, and Bryan Scotney

School of Computing and Information Engineering, University of Ulster, Coleraine,
Northern Ireland, UK
{zhang-s1,si.mcclean,bw.scotney}@ulster.ac.uk

Abstract. When distributed databases are developed independently, they may be semantically heterogeneous with respect to data granularity, scheme information and the embedded semantics. However, most traditional distributed knowledge discovery (DKD) methods assume that the distributed databases derive from a single virtual global table, where they share the same semantics and data structures. This data heterogeneity and the underlying semantics bring a considerable challenge for DKD. In this paper, we propose a model-based clustering method for aggregate databases, where the heterogeneous schema structure is due to the heterogeneous classification schema. The underlying semantics can be captured by different clusters. The clustering is carried out via a mixture model, where each component of the mixture corresponds to a different virtual global table. An advantage of our approach is that the algorithm resolves the heterogeneity as part of the clustering process without previously having to homogenise the heterogeneous local schema to a shared schema. Evaluation of the algorithm is carried out using both real and synthetic data. Scalability of the algorithm is tested against the number of databases to be clustered; the number of clusters; and the size of the databases. The relationship between performance and complexity is also evaluated. Our experiments show that this approach has good potential for scalable integration of semantically heterogeneous databases.

Keywords: Model-based clustering, Semantically heterogeneous databases, EM algorithm.

1 Introduction

In fast developing distributed open environments, e.g., the Semantic Web [1], for the same problem domain, distributed databases may be developed independently by different organisations using various ontologies. These databases can be semantically heterogeneous, arising from the use of different terminologies, granularities of data, schemas (conceptualisation) at which objects and their properties are described, and embedded heterogeneous context information [2]. This heterogeneity brings a considerable challenge for distributed knowledge discovery on those databases, for organisations that have common application interests and are willing to cooperate with each other. Most DKD methods in the literature assume that the distributed data are somehow partitioned either horizontally or vertically from a single virtual global table,

R. Cooper and J. Kennedy (Eds.): BNCOD 2007, LNCS 4587, pp. 190–202, 2007.

where all the data have the same statistical distribution, and share the same semantics. However, this assumption does not hold in most practical applications [3]. Distributed data sources contain various underlying semantics due to different backgrounds, environment and purposes when they were developed. A single global view (table) is not sufficient to describe all the distributed data; instead, two or more integrated virtual global tables are needed to capture different data distributions and semantics.

In this paper, we are concerned with heterogeneous databases where the heterogeneity is caused by different classification schemes. Such data are often summarised in Data Warehouses. The summaries may be obtained by pre-processing native databases to provide materialised aggregate views of the information held in very large databases. The objective of our work is to capture different underlying characteristics of these distributed databases, while resolving heterogeneity issues efficiently. We propose a model-based clustering method on the distributed heterogeneous aggregate counts data that are obtained by data summaries. A mixture model is constructed where the databases that are in the same cluster share the same semantics and can be integrated to one virtual global table; and they are different from databases in other clusters that correspond to different virtual global tables. Our approach carries out the integration as part of the clustering process, and the heterogeneity is resolved without previously having to homogenise the heterogeneous local schema to a shared schema. In this way, all the data information available is used for carrying out the clustering, which should lead to better results than methods that are based on data homogenisation. New knowledge can be discovered from the generated global tables, and latent information in the databases is made explicit. The clusters represent different signature profiles of the distributed databases based on proportions (probabilities) of particular values of attributes. For example, for supermarket shopping data from distributed chain-stores, each cluster contains local stores that have similar customer shopping patterns. Each cluster of stores may be of course geographically distributed. The learned clusters contain useful commercial information. When it is required to classify a new instance, only the relevant cluster information is needed instead of the whole data for all the stores. In general, the learned clusters can be used for the construction of Bayesian Belief Networks; alternatively association rules of interest can be extracted [5].

The proposed algorithm evaluation is carried out on both real and synthetic data. Scalability is tested against the number of datasets and the size of the dataset. A clustering complexity measure is designed, and the relationship between the performance (accuracy, computation time) and complexity is evaluated.

The rest of the paper is organised as follows: the data model is briefly introduced, followed by an introduction to the principles of model-based clustering. Clustering of homogeneous data is discussed initially. We then describe our proposed model-based clustering method for heterogeneous data, with an illustrative example. Finally we present algorithm evaluation and conclusions.

2 Terminology and Data Models

Definition 1: An ontology is defined as the Cartesian-product of a number of attributes $A_1,...,A_n$, along with their corresponding schema. The attributes we are concerned with are categorical attributes.

Definition 2: Each attribute A has its domain D, where the classes of the domain are given by classes $\{c_1,... c_m\}$. These classes form a partition of the set of base values of domain D. This partition is called a classification scheme.

Definition 3: Two ontologies are defined to be semantically equivalent if there is a mapping between their respective schemas. Mappings between the schema values are represented in the form of correspondence matrices.

In Example 1 we illustrate the concepts of heterogeneous datasets, classification schemes of the attributes, local ontologies, and mappings to a global ontology. In Table 1, the cardinalities represent the numbers of people in different categories of 'Job' attribute, for three different datasets, each with their own ontology. The corresponding ontology mappings are presented in Figure 1.

Example 1:
Attribute: A=Job; *Domain*: D={Full-time, Part-time, Retired, Unwaged}.

Table 1. Heterogeneous datasets with different classification schemes for attribute "Job"

Job \ Data	Working		NotWorking		Total
	Full-time	Part-time	Retired	Unwaged	
Dataset D_1	200		40	20	260
Dataset D_2	70	60	110		240
Dataset D_3	150	60	25	10	245

The classification schema for attribute "Job" in the three Datasets are as follows:

D_1={Working, Retired, Unwaged}, where Working = {Full-time, Part-time}.
D_2={Full-time, Part-time, NotWorking}, NotWorking = {Retired, Unwaged}.
D_3={Full-time, Part-time, Retired, Unwaged}.

The local ontologies together with the mappings to the global ontology are:

Fig. 1. Ontology mappings for Table 1

Dataset D_1 D_3 contain quite a high proportion of people 'Working', while in Dataset D_2, there a much greater proportion of 'NotWorking' people who are either 'Retired' or 'Unwaged'. Dataset D_1 D_3 share the same characteristics and thus can be grouped to one cluster, while they are different from Dataset D_3 so it should be in another cluster.

3 Principles of Model-Based Clustering

A probability is a quantitative description of the likelihood of occurrence of a particular event. The probability distribution of a random variable is a list of probabilities associated with each of its possible values. From a statistical standpoint, data is a random sample from an unknown population represented by probability distribution. Data analysis is performed to identify the population by a corresponding probability distribution that is most likely to have generated the data. Maximum likelihood estimation is a popular statistical method used to reveal parameters of the underlying probability distribution. Model-based clustering is a principled way of clustering based on statistical models. Data are seen to be from several different underlying probability distributions. The approach constructs a mixture model where each component corresponds to a cluster with its probability distribution. Data class labels are the 'incomplete' information to be discovered. The model for the composite of the clusters is formulated by maximising the mixture model likelihood using the EM (expectation-maximisation) algorithm [6]. EM is a general effective approach to maximum likelihood estimation in the presence of incomplete data. Its results provide a measure of uncertainty about the associated class labels of datasets. Compared with our previous work in [7], the method uses parameterisation as the basis for a class of models, and thus it can accommodate data with widely varying characteristics [8].

Given data $\mathbf{y}$ with n independent observations $y_1,...,y_n$, the likelihood of a mixture model with G components is defined as $L_{MIX}(\theta_1,...,\theta_G; \tau_1,...,\tau_G| y) = \prod_{r=1}^{n}\sum_{k=1}^{G}\tau_k f_k(y_r| \theta_k)$

where f_k and θ_k are the probability density function and parameters of the kth cluster; τ_k is the probability that a randomly selected datum is in the kth cluster. The 'complete data' $x_r =(y_r , z_r)$ can be viewed as consisting of n observations recoverable from (y_r , z_r), where y_r is the observed data, $z_r =(z_{r1},..., z_{rG})$ is unobserved portion of data indicating the conditional probability of the observation r belonging to cluster k.

Assuming that z_r is independent and identically distributed according to the probability distribution function f_k drawn from G clusters with probabilities $\tau_1,...,\tau_G$. Probability mass function of an observation y_r is then $\prod_{k=1}^{G} f_k(y_r| \theta_k)^{z_{rk}}$ given z_r, the complete-data x_r log-likelihood is $ll(\theta_k,\tau_k,z_{rk}| x) = \sum_{r=1}^{n}\sum_{k=1}^{G} z_{rk} \log[\tau_k f_k(y_r|\theta_k)]$.

The EM algorithm alternates between E-step and M-step. Given the observed data and the current estimated parameters, 'E-step' computes the conditional expectations (membership) for all datasets $\hat{z}_{rk} \leftarrow \dfrac{\hat{\tau}_k f_k(y_r|\hat{\theta}_k)}{\sum_{c=1}^{G}\hat{\tau}_c f_c(y_r|\hat{\theta}_c)}$; in 'M step', parameters τ_k , θ_k are computed the of the kth component that maximise the log-likelihood with the just updated z_{rk} values. Iteration terminates when the likelihood converges.

4 Model-Based Clustering on Homogeneous Data

We start with a discussion of clustering homogeneous datasets that share the same ontology. This is a special case of heterogeneous databases, where local ontologies are the same as global ontology. For aggregate counts data, the probability density function is defined as $P(X_1 = x_1, ..., X_m = x_m) = p_1^{x_1} ... p_m^{x_m}$ where $p_1, ..., p_m$ is the probability distribution for attribute values $(X_1, ..., X_m)$, x_i is the cardinality of attribute value X_i. In Example 1, denote $p_1, ..., p_4$ as the probability distribution for the attribute 'JOB', the probability of dataset D_3 with global ontology is thus $p_1^{150} p_2^{60} p_3^{25} p_4^{10}$.

For a clustering problem with G clusters, the probability distribution for m attribute values in cluster k is denoted as $\pi_{k1}, ..., \pi_{km}$, where π_{ki} is the probability for attribute value X_i. The complete-data log-likelihood of mixture model is given by Equation 1.

$$ll(\pi_{ki}, \tau_k, z_{rk} \mid x) = \sum_{r=1}^{n} \sum_{k=1}^{G} z_{rk} \log[\tau_k \prod_{i=1}^{m} \pi_{ki}^{n_{ri}}] \tag{1}$$

where n_{ri} is the aggregate count for value X_i in dataset r.

For homogeneous case, the 'unobserved' (incomplete) data are just the class labels.

In the E-step, z_{rk} is updated by: $\hat{z}_{rk} \leftarrow \dfrac{\hat{\tau}_k (\hat{\pi}_{k1}^{n_{r1}} ... \hat{\pi}_{km}^{n_{rm}})}{\sum_{c=1}^{G} \hat{\tau}_c (\hat{\pi}_{c1}^{n_{r1}} ... \hat{\pi}_{ck}^{n_{rm}})}$.

In the M-step, parameters τ_k π_{ki} are estimated (Equation 2) with updated z_{rk} values.

$$\hat{\tau}_k \leftarrow \frac{n_k}{n} \text{ where } n_k \leftarrow \sum_{r=1}^{n} \hat{z}_{rk} ; \ \hat{\pi}_{ki} \leftarrow \frac{\sum_{r=1}^{n} \hat{z}_{rk} n_{ri}}{\sum_{r=1}^{m} \hat{z}_{rk} (\sum_{i=1}^{m} n_{ri})} \tag{2}$$

These estimates are quite intuitive; in each iteration we update the cluster membership probabilities, followed by calculating the cluster descriptors. The stopping criteria is that the relative improvement of the log-likelihood which is less than $10^{(-7)}$.

5 Model-Based Clustering on Semantically Heterogeneous Data

In an environment with distributed databases, heterogeneity is a very common issue that needs to be overcome. Data integration has been used to solve heterogeneity issues with ontology mappings provided ab initio using correspondence matrices [9]. In clustering of heterogeneous data, except the unobserved class labels, the 'incomplete' information also arise from data at coarser granularity that do not hold completely detailed information on the global ontology level. The EM algorithm is an intuitive approach to the integration of aggregates to resolve the data heterogeneity issue. This gives the opportunity to carry out data integration while solving heterogeneity issues simultaneously in clustering without having to carry out homogenisation beforehand.

5.1 EM for Model-Based Clustering on Semantically Heterogeneous Databases

For the EM algorithm, in the E-step the equation for updating of cluster membership probabilities $\hat{z}_{rk}$ is given in Equation 3 (left); g_r is the number of partitions in dataset r; s is the index for g_r, $s = 1,...,g_r$. q_{isr} is the representation of the mapping from a local ontology to the shared global. For dataset r, q_{isr} is 1 if there is mapping from category i of the ontology used by dataset r, to the category s in the global ontology.

In the M step, τ_k remains the same as in Equation 2. The calculation of $\pi_{ki}^{(n)}$ is modified in order to deal with heterogeneity issue. For the coarser category in the ontology, the algorithm apportions its cardinalities to values of finer categories in global ontology according to their mappings, based on the probability distribution from the previous iteration $\pi_{ki}^{(n-1)}$. It is shown in Equation 3 (right).

$$\hat{z}_{rk} \leftarrow \frac{\hat{\tau}_k \prod_{s=1}^{g_r} (\sum_{u=1}^{m} \hat{\pi}_{ku} q_{usr})^{n_{rs}}}{\sum_{j=1}^{G} \hat{\tau}_j \prod_{s=1}^{g_r} (\sum_{u=1}^{m} \hat{\pi}_{ju} q_{usr})^{n_{rs}}} \; ; \; \hat{\pi}_{ki}^{(n)} \leftarrow \frac{\hat{\pi}_{ki}^{(n-1)} \times \sum_{r=1}^{n} \sum_{s=1}^{g_r} (\frac{\hat{z}_{rk} n_{rs} q_{isr}}{\sum_{u=1}^{m} \hat{\pi}_{ku} q_{usr}})}{\sum_{r=1}^{n} \hat{z}_{rk} (\sum_{s=1}^{g_r} n_{rs})} \qquad (3)$$

5.2 Determining the Optimal Number of Clusters by Using BIC

Finding an optimal integration model includes both aspects of model structure (e.g., the number of clusters) and parameters (cluster descriptors). Bayes factors, approximated by the Bayesian Information Criterion (BIC) [10], have been applied successfully to the problem of determining the optimal number of clusters [11]. The BIC considers both the likelihood and the penalisation of the complexity of the data model. The criterion can be maximised with more parsimonious parameterisations and smaller number of groups. It is defined as $BIC = 2\log p(x|M) + const \approx 2ll_M(x,\hat{\theta}) - m_M \log(n)$ where $ll_M(x,\hat{\theta})$ is the ultimate maximised mixture data log-likelihood; m_M is the number of independent parameters to be estimated and n is the number of datasets to be clustered.

In our case, with parameters τ_k π_{ki} having $(G-1)$, $G \times (m-1)$ independent parameters respectively, we obtain $m_M = (G-1) + G \times (m-1)$. The BIC formula for our clustering model on heterogeneous databases can be obtained straightforwardly, and the optimal data model is the one that has the largest BIC value.

5.3 An Example

Here, we illustrate our proposed algorithm on datasets in Example 1. Assume we know there are 2 clusters. τ_1 τ_2 indicate the probabilities of clusters 1 and 2. π_{1i} π_{2i} are the probability distributions over the attribute values i of 'Full-time', 'Part-time', 'Retired' and 'Unwaged' in the two clusters. The probability distributions need to be initialised firstly by a uniform distribution, so $\pi_{ki}^{(0)} = 1/4 \ \forall k = 1, 2 \ \forall i = 1, .., 4$. For easier illustration, we start with dataset D_1 and D_2 belonging to cluster1 with probability 1, and dataset D_3 belong to cluster 2, in the first iteration. Thus we get $z_{11} = z_{21} = z_{32} = 1$. In practical, z_{rk} can be randomly initialised, kmeans or other efficient methods. Then $\tau_1 = 2/3$ and $\tau_2 = 1/3$ can be obtained because there are 2 datasets in cluster1 and 1 in cluster2. Next, we obtain the descriptors of clusters—the probability distribution π_{ki} for different values of 'Job'. We illustrate the calculation using as an example, $\pi_{13}^{(1)}$, which is the probability for attribute value 'Retired' in cluster 1. The total cardinality in cluster 1 is $1 \times 260 + 1 \times 240 + 0 \times 245 = 500$ because datasets D_1 and D_2, belong to cluster 1 with probability 1, and dataset D_3 with probability 0. Now, we need the cardinality for 'Retired' in cluster1. It is clear that in dataset D_1 and D_3, there are 40 and 25 people 'Retired'. However, we don't know the number in dataset D_2 because the value 110 is the cardinality for people both 'Retired' and 'Unwaged'. $(\frac{\pi_{13}^{(0)}}{\pi_{13}^{(0)} + \pi_{14}^{(0)}}) \cdot n_{23}$ is thus taken as the contribution of dataset2 to value 'Retied' in cluster 1. It apportions 85 using probabilities for categories 'Retied' and 'Unwaged' from the last iteration.

Thus $\hat{\pi}_{13}^{(1)} = \dfrac{1 \times 40 + 1 \times \dfrac{0.25}{0.25 + 0.25} \times 110 + 0 \times 25}{500} = 0.19$, $\pi_{ki} = \begin{pmatrix} 0.34 & 0.32 & 0.19 & 0.15 \\ 0.61 & 0.24 & 0.10 & 0.04 \end{pmatrix}$ can be obtained in the same way. After the M step, the log-likelihood is then -303.0937.

In the 2nd iteration, in the "E step", given the datasets and the current parameter values τ_k π_{ki} , we compute the conditional probability z_{rk} . For example, z_{11} is calculated by the probability of dataset D_1 belonging to cluster1 divided by the sum of probabilities of dataset D_1 belonging to cluster 1 (defined as a) and the probability of D_2 belonging to cluster 2 (defined as b). So $a = \frac{2}{3} \times [(\pi_{11} + \pi_{12})^{200} \times \pi_{13}{}^{40} \times \pi_{14}{}^{20}]$ because the cardinality 200 is for combined values 'Full-time' and 'Part-time'; similarly $b = (1/3) \times [(\pi_{21} + \pi_{22})^{200} \times \pi_{23}{}^{40} \times \pi_{24}{}^{20}]$. Thus, $z_{11} = a/(a+b) = 0.3357$ and $z_{12} = 0.6643$. In the same way $z_{21} = 1, z_{12} = 0, z_{31} = 0, z_{32} = 1$

After obtaining z_{rk} , the M-step updates the parameters τ_k and π_{ki} of the kth cluster that maximise model log-likelihood, giving $\tau_1 = \frac{(0.3357 + 1 + 0)}{3} = 0.4452$, $\tau_2 = 0.5548$

and $\pi_{ki} = \begin{pmatrix} 0.32 & 0.28 & 0.23 & 0.17 \\ 0.59 & 0.23 & 0.12 & 0.06 \end{pmatrix}$. The log-likelihood for this iteration is -298.9032.

The iterations continue until the algorithm converges or the stopping criteria are met. For this example, the algorithm took 4 iterations to converge. Datasets D_1 and D_3 belong to the same cluster with probability vector (0.58 0.23 0.13 0.06) for {Full-time, Part-time, Retired, Unwaged}. Dataset D_2 belongs to a different cluster with very different working status distribution pattern (0.3 0.25 0.26 0.19) with almost as many people who do not work as people working.

6 Evaluation

6.1 Experimental Framework

The scalability of our proposed algorithm was tested against (i) the size of the datasets and (ii) the number of datasets. Performance is evaluated for both clustering accuracy and computation time. For this purpose, a collection of synthetic datasets has been generated using Matlab© that are based on the probability distributions designed to represent the clusters, and the required size of the dataset.

A combination of probability distributions, each of which represents a cluster, forms the basis to generate the synthetic data. The dataset size denoted as NoTrials is the total cardinality (aggregate counts) over all attribute categories. Values are generated from a uniform distribution on the unit interval. For a given probability distribution, the cardinality for an attribute category is the number of the generated values falling into the corresponding probability interval. For example, if NoTrials=10, and the probability distribution for categories 'Full-time', 'Part-time', 'Retired' and 'Unwaged' are (0.5 0.3 0.1 0.1) for one cluster, then 4 corresponding probability intervals are [0, 0.5), [0.5, 0.8), [0.8, 0.9), and [0.9, 1] respectively. If 10 values are as {0.95, 0.23, 0.61, 0.48, 0.89, 0.76, 0.45, 0.01, 0.82, 0.44}, then there are 5 values in the probability interval [0, 0.5), and thus 5 is the cardinality for category 'Full-time'. Similarly, 2, 2, 1 are the cardinalities for categories 'Part-time', 'Retired' and 'Unwaged'. A dataset {5, 2, 2, 1} is thus generated for this cluster. Data are generated in this way for a number of datasets (denoted as NoEvents) in each cluster.

For different probability distribution combinations, the level of difficulty to achieve accurate clustering is different. The evaluation is to be carried out for a wide range of clustering complexity from easy to hard. For this purpose, a complexity measure is proposed in the next section. The algorithm scalability is evaluated from the following two aspects, each over clustering problems of a wide range of complexity values:

(1)   Size of the datasets (NoTrials): the number of datasets (NoEvents) remains the same, accuracy and computation time is evaluated against different sizes of datasets, also over different clustering complexity problems.

(2)   the number of datasets (NoEvents): the size of the datasets (NoTrials) is kept constant, and performance is evaluated as the number of datasets is increased.

Clustering accuracy is calculated according to the classes of the synthetic data labelled generated. Computation time is recorded for the algorithm to converge or to meet the stopping criteria.

6.2 Complexity Measure

A complexity measure is designed to evaluate how difficult a clustering problem in terms of achieving accurate clustering. The distance between the clusters has a great impact on the complexity measure. If clusters are distinct from each other, it is an easier problem. However, if any two or more of the clusters are similar, it is difficult for an algorithm to identify and separate them. If $C_1, C_2,...,C_G$ are the G clusters of a clustering problem, the complexity S is defined as $S(C_1, C_2, ..., C_G) = \sum (\frac{1}{D(C_i, C_j)})$ where

$D(C_i, C_j)$ is the distance between any two clusters C_i, C_j and summation is over all combinations of clusters C_i, C_j. Since the probability distributions are the descriptors of clusters, $D(C_i, C_j)$ can be measured by the distance between the distributions. Kullback-Leibler information divergence (KL) is the distance measure between two probability distributions. It has been successfully used in our previous work [5]. Here we use a symmetric KL-based distance $D(C_i, C_j) = D_{KL}(P\|Q) + D_{KL}(Q\|P)$, where P and Q are the probability distributions for clusters C_i and C_j. In Figure 2 are shown the clustering accuracies of our proposed algorithm against the complexity value of probability distributions combination (synthetic data are generated with NoTrial=25, NoEvents=50). The clustering accuracy decreases monotonically as the complexity increases. This shows that the designed complexity formula is an appropriate measure for the clustering problem. Other complexity measure using different distances have been also investigated (e.g., Euclidean, chi-square or log-likelihood ratio), and the performances are found to be either worse than or similar to using the KL distance.

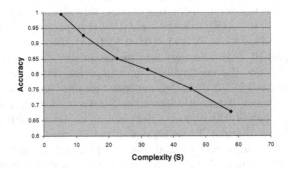

Fig. 2. Accuracy against Complexity measure (S)

6.3 Performance Evaluation

Firstly, we evaluate the performance against the size of the datasets (NoTrials). With NoTrials remaining constant, for any one clustering problem, the sizes of the datasets are the same for all clusters. The relationship between clustering accuracy and size of datasets is evaluated over clustering problems of different complexity values S. From Figure 3, we can observe that the size of the database plays an important role in the clustering process. The cardinalities improve the clarity of the clusters. Also, the bigger size databases speeds up the convergence process (Figure 4).

Figure 5, and 6 describe the algorithm performance as a function of the size of the clustering problem i.e. the number of datasets, when the dataset sizes do not change (NoTrials=200). The evaluation is carried out over clustering problems with different complexity values S. From the results in Figure 5 we observe that, for the same set of probability distribution combinations, if the size of the dataset remains constant, by just increasing the number of datasets in the clustering problem, accuracy cannot be improved very much except in the case of relatively small database sizes of high complexity. However, the computation time (Figure 6) increases. Therefore, for large-scale real problems, the clustering problem can be solved by appropriately scaling it down to a smaller problem to reduce the cost but without affecting the accuracy.

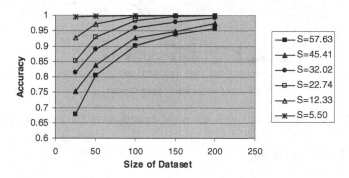

Fig. 3. Accuracy against the size of the dataset, for different complexity values S

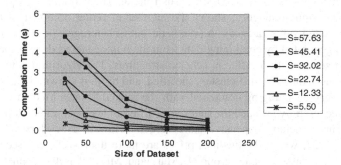

Fig. 4. Computation Time against size of the dataset, for different complexity values S

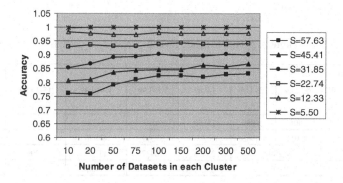

Fig. 5. Accuracy against the number of datasets, for different complexity values S

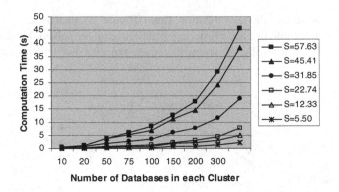

Fig. 6. Computation Time against the number of datasets, for different complexity values S

6.4 Real Data Evaluation

We complete an evaluation with a real-life example of heterogeneous data. The national U.S. "gross rent" database for 2000 is composed of 51 state-specific homogeneous datasets from the U.S. Census Bureau. The cardinality (aggregates) for each attribute value (category) shows the number of renter-occupied housing units within each rental value category. A (synthetic) set of heterogeneous databases (Table 2) was then generated by combining data from the homogeneous dataset for a random selection of states, with 5 different schema structures. The algorithm is tested on the heterogeneous database with 5 clusters specified, and result is shown in Figure 7. These results are very encouraging compared with the ranked "States Median Gross Rent" table. We successfully grouped the states with different levels of units renting prices in the U.S. These include expensive states group {Hawaii, New Jersey, California, Alaska, Nevada}, where the medians prices are more than $700. The second cluster contains less expensive 7 states group of {Maryland, Massachusetts, Connecticut, New York, Colorado, Washington and Virginia}, whose medians are $650-$699. The remaining clusters include the states with ranging from $555-$650, $497-$555, and $400-$496 respectively.

Table 2. A sample heterogeneous Gross Rent database

Gross rent ($100) / State	≤ 2.49	2.5-4.99	5-7.49	7.5-9.99	10-14.99	15-19.99	≥ 20
Wyoming	5906	26685	13150	3076	1124	280	95
Connecticut	32102	63966	152735	97511	47845	16522	
Arizona	12898		26096	18437	11296	2209	381
Delaware	19979		49972		5688	627	922
... ...							

Fig. 7. Clustering US States with Heterogeneous Gross Rent Census Data

7 Conclusion and Future Work

A model-based clustering method has been proposed for distributed heterogeneous aggregate databases with respect to their classification schemes, using the EM algorithm. The method carries out data integration while solving the heterogeneity issues simultaneously in the clustering process without having to carry out homogenisation beforehand. Unlike traditional DKD methods, data are integrated to several different virtual global tables in order to capture different underlying semantics corresponding to different global tables. The evaluation of the algorithm on both real and synthetic data shows encouraging results. The algorithm is scalable to large sizes of datasets and large numbers of datasets. It can be further applied to databases distributed in an open heterogeneous environment like the Semantic Web. The new knowledge discovered from the clustering can assist the construction of Bayesian Belief Networks to help build more efficient prediction models and also to enable association rule mining.

Future work includes employing an appropriate initialisation method for the EM algorithm; speeding up the convergence of the EM algorithm when dealing with large datasets; and more extensive evaluation using real data.

References

1. Berners-Lee, T., Hendler, J., Lassila, O.: The Semantic Web. Scientific American 284(5), 34–43 (2001)
2. Doan, A., Halevy, A.Y.: Semantic Integration Research in the Database Community: A Brief Survey. AI Magazine 26(1), 83–94 (2005)
3. Tsoumakas, G., Angelis, L., Vlahavas, I.: Clustering classifiers for knowledge discovery from physically distributed databases. Data & Knowledge Engi. 49(3), 223–242 (2004)

4. Wirth, R., Borth, M., Hipp, J.: When distribution is part of the semantics: A new problem class for distributed knowledge discovery. In: Proceeding of 5th ECML and PKDD Workshop on Ubiquitous Data Mining for Mobile and Distributed Environments, Freiburg, Germany, pp. 56–64 (2001)
5. McClean, S., Scotney, B., Shapcott, M.: Aggregation of imprecise and uncertain information in databases. IEEE Transactions on Knowledge and Data Engineering 13(6), 902–912 (2001)
6. Dempster, A.P., Laird, N.M., Rubin, D.B.: Maximum Likelihood from Incomplete Data via the EM Algorithm. Journal of the Royal Statistics Society, Series B 39(1), 1–38 (1977)
7. McClean, S.I., et al.: Knowledge discovery by probabilistic clustering of distributed databases. Data & Knowledge Engineering 54(2), 189–210 (2005)
8. Fraley, C.,, Raftery, A.E.: Model-Based Clustering, Discriminant Analysis, and Density Estimation. Journal of the American Statistical Society 97(458), 611–631 (2002)
9. McClean, S.I., Scotney, B.W., Greer, K.: A Scalable Approach to Integrating Heterogeneous Aggregate Views of Distributed Databases. IEEE Transactions on Knowledge and Data Engineering 15(1), 232–235 (2003)
10. Schwarz, G.: Estimating the Dimensions of a Model. The Annals of Statistics 6(2), 461–464 (1978)
11. Dasgupta, A., Raftery, A.E.: Detecting features is spatial point processes with clutter via model-based clustering. Journal of the American Statistical Society 93(441), 294–302 (1998)

Speeding Up Clustering-Based k-Anonymisation Algorithms with Pre-partitioning

Grigorios Loukides and Jianhua Shao

School of Computer Science
Cardiff University
Cardiff CF24 3AA, UK
{G.Loukides,J.Shao}@cs.cf.ac.uk

Abstract. K-anonymisation is a technique for protecting privacy contained within a dataset. Many k-anonymisation algorithms have been proposed, and one class of such algorithms are clustering-based. These algorithms can offer high quality solutions, but are rather inefficient to execute. In this paper, we propose a method that partitions a dataset into groups first and then clusters the data within each group for k-anonymisation. Our experiments show that combining partitioning with clustering can improve the performance of clustering-based k-anonymisation algorithms significantly while maintaining the quality of anonymisations they produce.

1   Introduction

A vast amount of data about individuals is being collected and stored worldwide. Such data can contain private information about individuals, for example, their credit card numbers, shopping preferences and medical records. When the data is released for studies such as lifestyle surveys, business analysis and healthcare research, privacy protection becomes a serious concern. Unfortunately, simply removing unique identifiers (e.g. credit card numbers) from data is not enough, as individuals can still be identified using a combination of non-unique attributes such as age and postcode [1].

K-anonymisation is a technique that has been proposed to address this issue. Assume that we have a table T consisting of m attributes $(a_1, \ldots, a_m)$. Without loss of generality we assume that the first q attributes are *quasi-identifiers* (QIDs) - they contain information that can potentially be used to identify individuals (e.g. age and postcode), and the remaining attributes are *sensitive attributes* (SAs) - they contain sensitive information about individuals (e.g. their shopping preferences or diagnosed diseases). K-anonymising T is to derive a view of T such that each tuple in the view is made identical (through some form of data generalisation) to at least $k - 1$ other tuples with respect to QIDs [1]. It is easy to see that k-anonymised data helps prevent linking sensitive information to individuals, thereby providing privacy protection.

Many k-anonymisation algorithms have been proposed, employing different search strategies and optimality criteria [2,3,4,5,6]. Broadly speaking, they all

R. Cooper and J. Kennedy (Eds.): BNCOD 2007, LNCS 4587, pp. 203–214, 2007.

attempt to maximise data usefulness (by making as little change to a dataset as possible) and privacy protection (by making individual identification as difficult as possible). One class of such algorithms are clustering-based [4,6,5]. They derive k-anonymisations by first grouping data into clusters of at least k tuples using some quality measures, and then anonymising the data in each group separately using some form of data generalisation. These algorithms offer flexibility in k-anonymisation process and produce high quality anonymisations as result, but they can be rather inefficient to execute, making them not useful for large datasets.

In this paper, we propose a method that partitions a dataset before clustering it for k-anonymisation. Our method is based on the following observation: tuples in a cluster typically belong to a small subspace. Thus, instead of searching the whole dataset when clustering data, we can first find a partition of a dataset and then perform the clustering in each subspace separately. Our experiments show that combining partitioning with clustering can improve the performance of clustering-based k-anonymisation algorithms significantly while maintaining the quality of anonymisations they produce.

The paper is organised as follows. Section 2 describes a metric that we use to measure the quality of k-anonymisations. In Section 3 we introduce two representative clustering-based algorithms for illustrating our pre-partitioning approach. Our approach is presented in Section 4 and evaluated in Section 5. Finally, we conclude in Section 6.

2   Usefulness and Protection Measures

A k-anonymisation of a dataset is commonly derived through some form of data generalisation. Such a generalisation process can result in information loss. To see this, consider the generalisation of data in Table 1 to 4-anonymous data in Table 2, for example.

Table 1. Original data

Age	Height	Sal(K)
20	170	20
23	175	21
25	180	22
27	180	25
28	180	60
29	185	61
58	190	62
80	190	65

Table 2. A 4-anonymisation of Table 1

Age	Height	Sal(K)
[20-58]	[170-190]	20
[20-58]	[170-190]	21
[20-58]	[170-190]	60
[20-58]	[170-190]	62
[25-80]	[180-190]	22
[25-80]	[180-190]	25
[25-80]	[180-190]	61
[25-80]	[180-190]	65

Table 3. Another 4-anonymisation of Table 1

Age	Height	Sal(K)
[20-27]	[170-180]	20
[20-27]	[170-180]	21
[20-27]	[170-180]	22
[20-27]	[170-180]	25
[28-80]	[180-190]	60
[28-80]	[180-190]	61
[28-80]	[180-190]	62
[28-80]	[180-190]	65

Suppose that we need to answer query Q1 using Table 2. As the values in *Age* and *Height* are generalised in Table 2, it is obvious that only an approximate answer to Q1 can be obtained. To illustrate how this can be done, consider the 2D space depicted on the left chart of Figure 1 where R represents the area covered by the first group in Table 2 (as no tuples in the second group can satisfy Q1) and Rq represents the area requested by Q1. Comparing R to R_q and assuming a uniform distribution of data in R, we can calculate that the probability of a tuple in Table 2 is in the answer to Q1 is $p = \frac{Rq \cap R}{R} \approx 0.033$ [7]. As we have 4 tuples in the first group of Table 2, the estimated answer to Q1 is $4 \times p = 0.132$. Clearly, this estimation is not accurate, as the correct answer to Q1 using the original data in Table 1 is 2. Now consider another anonymisation of Table 1 as shown in Table 3. The 2D space depicted on the right chart of Figure 1 shows that this time the overlap between R and R_q is much larger. Computing p using the same method again, we obtain a much more accurate approximated answer of $4 \times p \approx 1.429$ for Q1.

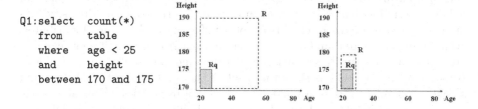

```
Q1:select   count(*)
   from     table
   where    age < 25
   and      height
   between 170 and 175
```

Fig. 1. Estimating answers using generalised data

Intuitively, maximising the overlap between answers to queries using original and anonymised data is desirable, as it can make anonymised data more useful. However, how data might be queried cannot be assumed to be known in general. Therefore, it is plausible that we should try to minimise data ranges in each group w.r.t. QIDs, so that R is kept small, increasing the chance for it to have a large overlap with R_q. In the case of an interval attribute this is quite straightforward to achieve, as ranges can naturally be captured using, for example, the Euclidean distance. In the case of discrete attributes, however, there is no ordering among the values and thus distance is often defined in terms of semantic relationships between different values using a hierarchy [5]. For simplicity of presentation, we assume a flat hierarchy for each discrete QID [3] in this paper . That is, we assume that the distance between any pair of distinct values is the same, and the overall distance of a group of discrete values is the number of distinct values in the group. This then gives us the following definition:

Definition 1 (Attribute diversity). *Assume that a is an attribute, the domain of a is D_a, and $V_a \subseteq D_a$ is a subset of values obtained from a. The attribute diversity of V_a, denoted by $da(V_a)$, is defined as:*

$$da(V_a) = \begin{cases} \frac{max(V_a)-min(V_a)}{max(D_a)-min(D_a)} & \textit{interval values} \\ \frac{|distinct(V_a)|}{|D_a|} & \textit{discrete values} \end{cases}$$

where $max(V_a)$, $min(V_a)$, $max(D_a)$ and $min(D_a)$ denote maximum and minimum values in V_a and D_a respectively, $|distinct(V_a)|$ is the number of unique values in V_a, and $|D_a|$ is the size of domain D_a.

It is easy to see that for a set of QID values, a small attribute diversity score is desirable as it implies that the values are close to each other, hence require less modification in anonymisation. For an SA, however, a large attribute diversity score is preferred. This is because if the values in an SA are not diverse enough, then it will still be possible for one to infer their sensitive information [8].

Having a large attribute diversity score to ensure that values in an SA are sufficiently diverse is in principle similar to the idea of l-diversity [8], which suggests that an SA should have at least l distinct values in each anonymised group. This will then ensure that the actual sensitive information about an individual can only be inferred with a probability no more than $1/l$. However, in l-diversity, SAs are considered to be discrete. This is not satisfactory as for interval attributes, even if there are more than l distinct values in each group, a small range can still give information away. To see this, consider the salary attribute (Sal) of Table 1. If data was anonymised as shown in Table 3 then Sal ranges for the first and second anonymised groups are [20-25] and [60-65] respectively. This allows one to estimate a quite close salary value for an individual. In contrast, if data was anonymised as shown in Table 2, then the larger Sal ranges ([20-62] and [22-65] for the first and second groups respectively) make an accurate estimation more difficult. Our attribute diversity measure can handle interval values in SAs better, as it takes the range of interval values into consideration.

We now extend our diversity measure to datasets that consist of more than one attribute. We measure the diversity of a set of tuples as the sum of attribute diversities over a set of attributes, assuming attribute independence.

Definition 2 (Tuple diversity). *Given a set of tuples $\tau \subseteq T$ over a set of attributes $A = \{a_1, a_2, \ldots, a_m\}$, the tuple diversity of τ w.r.t. A, denoted by $dt(\tau, A)$, is defined as: $dt(\tau, A) = \sum_{i=1}^{m} da(\pi_{a_i}(\tau))$ where $\pi_{a_i}(\tau)$ denotes the projection of τ on attribute a_i.*

This measure has some interesting properties. First, interval and discrete attributes are treated uniformly, therefore datasets with mixed attributes can be handled. Second, it deals with both data usefulness and privacy protection. This is particularly useful as it allows each of these properties to be considered and balanced during k-anonymisation. Third, it allows anonymisers to introduce weights to reflect the importance of some attributes. For example, *Age* may be considered to be more important than *Height* in a particular study and can thus be given more weight in calculating tuple diversity. Finally, it can support semantic relationships that may exist among discrete values by extending Definition 1 to include hierarchies [5,4].

Based on tuple-diversity we define usefulness of anonymised data to be the average tuple diversity of all groups over QIDs, and protection of original data to be the average of the inverse of tuple diversity of all groups measured over the SAs. A small usefulness score implies that tuples are close together with respect to these attributes, therefore incurring little information loss, and a small protection score means that the values of each SA are far apart, therefore exercising more protection.

Definition 3 (Usefulness and Protection). *Assume that a table T is clustered into groups $\{g_1, g_2, \ldots, g_h\}$, such that $|g_i| \geq k, 1 \leq i \leq h$, and tuples of g_i will have the same QID value after anonymisation. The usefulness and protection of T under this clustering are defined as:*

$$usefulness = avg(dt(g_1, q), dt(g_2, q), \ldots, dt(g_h, q))$$

and

$$protection = avg(\frac{1}{dt(g_1, s)}, \frac{1}{dt(g_2, s)}, \ldots, \frac{1}{dt(g_h, s)})$$

where $dt(g_i, q)$ and $dt(g_i, s)$ denote the tuple diversity of group $g_i, 1 \leq i \leq h$, w.r.t. q (the set of QIDs) and s (the set of SAs), respectively.

3 Grouping Data

Forming "good" groups of data is essential to minimising information loss and enhancing data utility in k-anonymisation. Using the metrics proposed in Section 2, the problem of finding an optimal grouping of data for k-anonymisation is formally defined in Definition 4.

Definition 4 (Optimal grouping using tuple diversity). *Given a table T consisting of n tuples and weights w_u and w_p such that $w_u, w_p \in [0, 1]$ and $w_u + w_p = 1$, an optimal grouping of T is a partition $P = \{c_1, \ldots, c_h\}$ such that $|c_i| \geq k, i = 1, \ldots, h, \bigcap_{i=1}^{h} c_i = \emptyset, \bigcup_{i=1}^{h} c_i = T$ and $\frac{\sum_{i=1}^{h}(w_u \times dt(c_i, QID) + w_p \times \frac{1}{dt(c_i, SA)})}{h}$ is minimal.*

So an optimal grouping of a dataset T for k-anonymisation w.r.t. the metrics given in Section 2 is to partition T into groups of at least k tuples such that the average weighted tuple diversity is minimised. w_u and w_p are user-specified weights that allow requirements for data usefulness and privacy protection to be balanced. However, achieving this grouping using clustering is NP-hard [1]. So heuristic methods are required. In this section, we describe two clustering-based algorithms, K-Members [4] and Greedy Clustering [6], whose sketches are given in Figures 2 and 3 respectively.

They both allow interval and discrete attributes to be treated uniformly and perform greedy clustering to derive groups of at least k tuples. However, these

---

[1] It is straightforward to proove this based on [9].

1. $C \leftarrow \emptyset$;
2. randomly choose $r \in T$;
3. **while** $|T| \geq k$ **do**
4.   find $t_i \in T$ s.t. $dt(\{t_i, r\}, QID)$ is maximum;
5. $T \leftarrow T - \{t_i\}$;
6. $c \leftarrow \{t_i\}$;
7.   **while** $|c| < k$ **do**
8.   find $t_j \in T$ s.t. $dt(\{c \cup \{t_j\}\}, QID)$ is minimum;
9. $T \leftarrow T - \{t_j\}$;
10. $c \leftarrow c \cup \{t_j\}$;
11. $r \leftarrow t_j$;
12. $C \leftarrow C \cup c$;
13. **while** $T \neq \emptyset$ **do**
14.   randomly choose $t_i \in T$;
15.   find $c \in C$ s.t. $dt(\{c \cup \{t_i\}\}, QID)$ is minimum;
16. $T \leftarrow T - \{t_i\}$;
17. $c \leftarrow c \cup \{t_i\}$;

Fig. 2. K-Members

1. **while** $T \neq \emptyset$ **do**
2. $c \leftarrow t_i \in T$;
3. $T \leftarrow T - \{t_i\}$;
4.   **while** true **do**
5.   find $t_j \in T$ s.t. $c' \leftarrow c \cup \{t_j\}$ and $w_u \times dt(\{t_i, t_j\}, QID)$ $+ w_p \times \frac{1}{dt(\{t_i, t_j\}, SA)}$ is minimum;
6.   **if** $(w_u \times dt(c', QID)$ $+ w_p \times \frac{1}{dt(c', SA)} > \delta)$; **exit**;
7. $c \leftarrow c'$;
8. $T \leftarrow T - \{t_j\}$;
9.   **if** $|c| \geq k$ k-anonymise(c);
10. **else** reject c;

Fig. 3. Greedy Clustering

two algorithms differ along three main dimensions. First, the objective of K-Members is to maximise usefulness (i.e. setting $w_u = 1$ in Definition 4), while Greedy Clustering attempts to balance between usefulness and protection. Second, they use different heuristics to decide which tuple should be added to a cluster in each step. K-Members adopts a brute-force approach, examining every unclustered tuple and inserting the tuple that results in a minimum increase in tuple-diversity over QIDs (line 8 of Figure 2), while Greedy Clustering inserts the tuple that is nearest to the "seed" tuple of this cluster w.r.t. weighted tuple-diversity over QIDs and SAs (line 5 of Figure 3, where t_j is the seed and w_u and w_p are the respective weights). Third, there is a significant difference between these two algorithms in terms of how a group is deemed to be derived. K-Members uses a size-based criterion, which restricts the maximum size of clusters to $2k - 1$, while Greedy Clustering uses a threshold δ to avoid creating clusters with an unacceptably large tuple diversity.

To illustrate the quality of k-anonymisation produced by K-Members and Greedy Clustering, we compare them to Mondrian [2], a well-known non-clustering based algorithm, using an example. As shown in Figure 5, when applied to T, both clustering-based algorithms achieved better usefulness than Mondrian did (scoring 1.008 and 1.017 compared to 1.117) and Greedy Clustering also achieved better protection (scoring 2 compared to 2.5). However, both K-Members and Greedy Clustering have quadratic time complexity with respect to the size of the dataset [4,6], hence are not scalable to large datasets.

4   Pre-partitioning

Attempts to improving clustering performance in general have been reported in the literature [10,11,5]. Sampling has been used to derive a set of initial clusters and final clusters are produced by assigning the remaining tuples to their closest clusters [11]. McCallum [12] suggested a method that derives large clusters using a similarity measure for categorical attributes first, and then use the main clustering algorithm to cluster the data. Xu et al. [5] used a top-down heuristic, which recursively splits data into two groups by choosing two distant tuples as seeds and assigning all remaining tuples to their closest groups. However, all of these methods have a quadratic complexity to the size of the dataset, hence are not efficient when a large number of small clusters are to be created, as in k-anonymisation. Furthermore, their similarity measures do not capture data usefulness and privacy protection, thus their results are not directly useful to k-anonymisation.

Age	Height	Gender	Disease
20	170	M	HIV
23	175	F	HIV
25	180	M	Obesity
27	180	F	HIV
28	180	F	Cancer
29	185	F	Obesity
58	190	M	Heart Attack
80	190	F	Cancer

Fig. 4. Original data

(a)

20	170	M	HIV
25	180	M	Obesity
80	190	F	Cancer
58	190	M	Heart Attack
23	175	F	HIV
27	180	F	HIV
29	185	F	Obesity
28	180	F	Cancer

(b)

20	170	M	HIV
25	180	M	Obesity
58	190	M	Heart Attack
80	190	F	Cancer
27	180	F	HIV
29	185	F	Obesity
23	175	F	HIV
28	180	F	Cancer

(c)

20	170	M	HIV
23	175	F	HIV
58	190	M	Heart Attack
80	190	F	Cancer
28	180	F	Cancer
29	185	F	Obesity
25	180	M	Obesity
27	180	F	HIV

Fig. 5. Grouping of data in Table 4 using (a) K-Members, (b) Greedy Clustering and (c) Mondrian

In this section, we propose a method that divides the entire space into a number of well-organised subspaces in log-linear time to the size of the dataset [13,2] and maintains the quality of anonymisations that clustering-based algorithms can produce. We use a kd-tree type of strategy to recursively split the data into subspaces. That is, we assume a total order for the values in each QID attribute and split a group of tuples (initially the entire dataset) along the median of a QID attribute that has the largest domain. This process is repeated (i.e. the two resultant subspaces from the split are split again using the same criteria) until all the subspaces are "small" enough w.r.t. a pre-specified size threshold.

Our partitioning strategy can significantly improve the performance of clustering-based methods. This is because, informally, if we assume that the average size of subspaces created by pre-partitioning is s, then the complexity of clustering data within a subspace is $O(s^2)$. Since we have roughly $\frac{n}{s}$ number of subspaces, where n is the size of the dataset, the clustering complexity for the entire dataset becomes $O(\frac{n}{s} \times s^2) = O(n \times s)$. Thus, a significant speed up can be achieved if the subspaces created by pre-partitioning are relatively small.

To maintain the high quality of anonymisations that clustering-based algorithms can produce, it is essential that close tuples are put in the same subspace. We split data along the median of the QID attribute with the largest domain [14,2]. This heuristic can create "compact" subspaces that contain reasonably close tuples, especially when clusters are roughly of equal size [15]. For example, observe the solution produced by K-Members in Figure 6. Table T (the same as the table given in Figure 4) is partitioned, using this heuristic and a size threshold $s = 4$ into two subsets T_1 and T_2. As can be seen, clustering the data using K-Members in T_1 and T_2 separately produced the same 2-anonymisation as the one derived from clustering the whole dataset (compare the result to Figure 5 (a)), but was performed more efficiently.

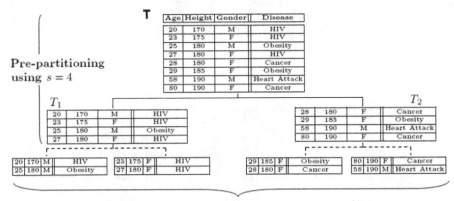

Clustering data in T_1 and T_2 using K-Members

Fig. 6. Pre-partitioning and clustering dataset T in Figure 4

Obviously, selecting the size threshold in pre-partitioning can affect both the efficiency and quality of the subsequent clustering. Using a very small size threshold (e.g. one equal to k) can produce solutions very fast but often degrades the quality of anonymisations. This is because the resultant subspaces offer little room for clustering to optimise grouping. On the other hand, using a large size threshold helps produce anonymisations of high quality, but clustering in these subspaces is not efficient. Our experiments show that partitioning a dataset into relatively small subspaces is often sufficient to allow the high quality of anonymisations to be produced by the subsequent clustering.

Finally, we comment on the effect of pre-partitioning on protection. As discussed in Section 2, a good k-anonymisation also needs to ensure that values in SAs are quite diverse, so that protection is enhanced. The proposed partitioning strategy does not take SAs into consideration, thus the resultant subspaces may compromise protection. For instance, consider the *Disease* value in the third tuple of table T given in Figure 6. If it was 'HIV' instead of 'Obesity', then pre-partitioning would create a subspace that consists of tuples having the same SA value. This does not help protection. However, our partitioning strategy can easily be modified to incorporate protection as well [16]. For instance, avoiding further splitting a subspace when it causes protection to exceed a specified threshold will allow clusters with better protection to be formed. Limited by space we will not discuss such extensions in this paper.

5   Experimental Evaluation

We experimentally evaluated the efficiency and quality of our pre-partitioning approach by applying it to K-Members and Greedy Clustering (configured to treat usefulness and protection equally important, i.e. $w_u = w_p$ in Figure 3). We used the Adults dataset [14] in our experiments, which has become a standard benchmark for k-anonymisation. This dataset is comprised of 8 attributes and 30162 tuples, and we configured it as in [6]. All the algorithms were implemented in Java and ran on a Pentium-D 3GHz machine with 1 GB of RAM under Windows XP.

Efficiency evaluation. First, the performance of K-Members and Greedy Clustering without pre-partitioning was evaluated. We ran the two algorithms with $k = 10$, using random samples with sizes ranging from 500 to 10000. As illustrated in Figure 7, these algorithms are not particularly efficient: K-Members and Greedy Clustering needed more than 18 minutes and 44 seconds to cluster 10000 tuples, respectively.

We then studied the improvement in efficiency that our pre-partitioning method brings to clustering algorithms. We applied our method to the entire Adults dataset (30162 tuples) setting $k = 10$. In this experiment, the number of subspaces created was reduced by half in each execution and varied from 32 ($s = 500$) to 1 ($s = 30162$). Figures 8 and 9 show that the efficiency improvement is significant when pre-partitioning is used. For instance, pre-partitioning reduced the runtime of K-members from 2.5 hours to 5 minutes when $s = 500$.

Quality evaluation. In order to examine how pre-partitioning affects the quality of solutions we performed two sets of experiments. First, we studied the impact of pre-partitioning on the quality of clustering. We partitioned the Adults dataset using various size thresholds and applied K-Members and Greedy Clustering using $k = 10$. We experimented with increasingly larger size thresholds, starting from $s = k = 10$ (this effectively makes clustering redundant and the outcome is the same as that produced by Mondrian) and reducing by half the

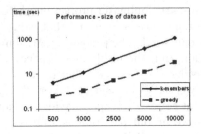
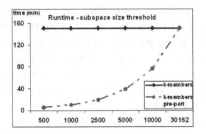

Fig. 7. Run-time of K-Members and Greedy Clustering

Fig. 8. Run-time of K-Members vs. subspace size

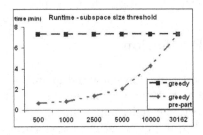

Fig. 9. Run-time of Greedy Clustering vs. subspace size

number of subspaces created in each run. As can be seen from Figures 10, 11 and 12 usefulness and protection measures achieved by combining clustering and partitioning are substantially better than those achieved by using partitioning alone (see Figures 10, 11 and 12 for $s = 10$). This confirms that clustering-based algorithms are able to generate anonymisations of much higher quality compared to those produced by partitioning-based methods.

Furthermore, the scores for usefulness and protection are similar after the number of subspaces reached a certain level, suggesting that the clustering performed by K-Members and Greedy Clustering is not affected by the increase in the subspace size. We have also conducted experiments using synthetic datasets and the results were similar. Due to space limitations we do not report the results here. This means that in practice data can be partitioned into relatively small subspaces, which will not significantly affect the quality of anonymisations produced by the subsequent clustering, but can improve its efficiency substantially.

We also investigated how pre-partitioning affects the quality of clustering when k changes. We applied our method with a fixed size threshold and compared the clustering outcome from K-Members and Greedy Clustering with and without pre-partitioning. For this experiment we ran pre-partitioning with a size-threshold of 1000 creating 16 subspaces. Figure 13 presents the results for K-Members. Observe that the usefulness scores for K-Members with pre-partitioning are very close to those when the clustering was applied to the whole dataset. Again, this validated that the quality of anonymisations produced

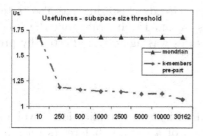

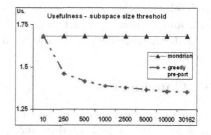

Fig. 10. Usefulness of K-Members with pre-partitioning

Fig. 11. Usefulness of Greedy Clustering with pre-partitioning

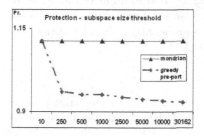

Fig. 12. Protection of Greedy Clustering with pre-partitioning

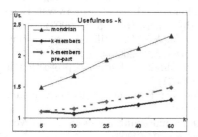

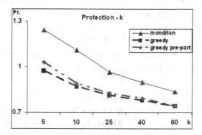

Fig. 13. Usefulness of K-Members with different k's

Fig. 14. Usefulness of Greedy Clustering with different k's

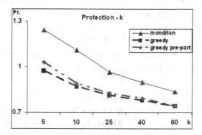

Fig. 15. Protection of Greedy Clustering with different k's

by K-Members w.r.t. usefulness is preserved. Greedy clustering was also tested with and without pre-partitioning. Figures 14 and 15 illustrate that the result w.r.t. both usefulness and protection measures was again not affected by pre-partitioning.

6　Conclusions

As privacy protection is increasingly required by many applications involving personal data, a high quality anonymisation of a dataset before its releasing is important. Although clustering-based k-anonymisation algorithms manage to achieve this goal, they are rather inefficient to execute. In this paper, we proposed a pre-partitioning method to improve the performance of clustering-based algorithms, and we have shown through experiments that combining partitioning with clustering can significantly reduce execution time while maintaining the quality of anonymisations.

References

1. Sweeney, L.: k-anonymity: a model for protecting privacy. International Journal on Uncertainty, Fuzziness and Knowledge-based Systems 10, 557–570 (2002)
2. LeFevre, K., DeWitt, D., Ramakrishnan, R.: Mondrian multidimensional k-anonymity. In: ICDE '06, vol. 25 (2006)
3. Bayardo, R., Agrawal, R.: Data privacy through optimal k-anonymization. In: ICDE '05, pp. 217–228 (2005)
4. Byun, J., Kamra, A., Bertino, E., Li, N.: Efficient k-anonymity using clustering technique. In: Kotagiri, R., Krishna, P.R., Mohania, M., Nantajeewarawat, E. (eds.) DASFAA '07. LNCS, vol. 4443. Springer, Heidelberg (to appear, 2007)
5. Xu, J., Wang, W., Pei, J., Wang, X., Shi, B., Fu, A.W.C.: Utility-based anonymization using local recoding. In: KDD '06, pp. 785–790 (2006)
6. Loukides, G., Shao, J.: Capturing data usefulness and privacy protection in k-anonymisation. In: SAC '07, pp. 370–374 (2007)
7. Thaper, N., Guha, S., Indyk, P., Koudas, N.: Dynamic multidimensional histograms. In: SIGMOD '02, pp. 428–439 (2002)
8. Machanavajjhala, A., Gehrke, J., Kifer, D., Venkitasubramaniam, M.: l-diversity: Privacy beyond k-anonymity. In: ICDE '06, vol. 24 (2006)
9. Aggarwal, G., Kenthapadi, F., Motwani, K., Panigrahy, R., Thomas, D., Zhu, A.: Approximation algorithms for k-anonymity. Journal of Privacy Technology (2005)
10. McCallum, A., Nigam, K., Ungar, L.: Efficient clustering of high-dimensional data sets with application to reference matching. In: KDD '00, pp. 169–178 (2000)
11. Guha, S., Rastogi, R., Shim, K.: Cure: an efficient clustering algorithm for large databases. In: SIGMOD '98, pp. 73–84 (1998)
12. Oliveira, S., Zaiane, O.: Privacy preserving clustering by data transformation. In: Proceedings of the XVIII SBBD, pp. 304–318 (2003)
13. Friedman, J., Bentley, J., Finkel, R.: An algorithm for finding best matches in logarithmic time. ACM Trans. on Mathematical Software 3(3) (1977)
14. Hettich, S., Merz, C.: Uci repository of machine learning databases (1998)
15. Narayan, B., Murthy, C., Pal, S.K.: Maxdiff kd-trees for data condensation. Pattern Recognition Letters 27, 187–200 (2006)
16. Byun, J., Sohn, Y., Bertino, E., Li, N.: Secure anonymization for incremental datasets. In: Secure Data Management '06, pp. 48–63 (2006)

Fine-Grained Access Control for Database Management Systems*

Hong Zhu[1] and Kevin Lü[2]

[1] Huazhong University of Science and Technology, Wuhan, Hubei, 430074, P.R. China
[2] Brunel University, Uxbridge, UK UB8 3PH

Abstract. A practical approach for developing fine-grained access control (FGAC) for database management systems is reported in this paper. We extend SQL language to support security policies. The concept of the *policy type* for databases is proposed. We implement the policy reuse through the use of policy types and policy instances to alleviate the administration workload of maintaining security policies. The policies for rows and columns can be expressed with policy types. Moreover, complicated database integrity constraints can also be expressed by policy types, and no further purpose-built programs are needed to create specific security control policies. We implement the fine-grained access control in a relational database management system DM5 [4]. The performance test results based on TPC-W are also presented.

1 Introduction

With the wide integration of Internet and database technology, the resources in information systems have been shared by more and more users. The first feature of these systems is that the number of users is enormous, but the number of roles for users is relatively small. The second feature is that different users with the same role may access different data sets. When more and more data is stored in database systems, privacy and security become important issues in these systems. The privacy and security concerns mean that Internet-based information systems must provide fine-grained access control for users, and, in many cases, even single user-based access control is needed[1][2][8].

However, the current standard SQL language for access control is coarse grained, in that it grants access to all rows of a table or none at all. It provides access controls on rows on a table by views. The access control by views is suitable for applications with a fixed small number of users. It is not applicable to the cases with a large number of users, such as in the Internet environment. Also, with this method, the administrators have to manage and maintain many views; this aggravates the workload. For a long time, the fine-grained access control has been embedded in application programs according to the requirements of applications. This approach has several disadvantages. The first is that access control has to be checked at every

---

* This paper is supported by 863 hi-tech research and development program of China, granted number: 2006AA01Z430.

R. Cooper and J. Kennedy (Eds.): BNCOD 2007, LNCS 4587, pp. 215–223, 2007.

user-interface. This increases the overall code size. The second is that the access control in the application tier can be bypassed easily. The third is that it is easy for application programmers to create trap-doors with malicious intents, because it is almost impossible to check every line of code in a large application. For the above reasons, fine-grained access control should be enforced for database management systems.

This study focused on the issues of constructing FGAC in database systems. The main contributions of this paper are:

(1) The concept of *policy type* for databases is proposed. We extend SQL statements to support the security policy type. Security policy instances based on the security policy type can be created to express different security policy requirements. Moreover, complicated integrity constraints in database can be expressed by policy types to specify the condition of the policy to take effect.

(2) We implement the FGAC in the relational database management system DM5. The performance evaluations based on TPC-W benchmark have been conducted.

This paper is organized as follows: Section 2 describes the related work. Section 3 presents the detailed extension of SQL statements. Section 4 reports performance tests based on TPC-W and the results. Section 5 presents a summary.

2 Related Work

The first FGAC access control model was proposed by M. Stonebraker in Ingres system [9]. It is implemented by a "query modification" algorithm. But the algorithm does not handle rows and columns symmetrically. The Virtual Private Database (VPD) in ORACLE [11] has provided a PL/SQL procedure function to describe the security policy. Nevertheless, writing policy functions corresponding to business policies requires a large amount of work [6]. Also, it is difficult to write predicates involving cases of cross-ref, joins of tables etc., and no element level security in VPD is presented.

Based on the access control in System R and Ingres, Motro proposed an FGAC model for database based on algebraic manipulation of view definitions [7]. That model has some limitations [8]. The costs of the query optimiser in DBMS are high. The Non-Truman model [8] is based on authorization views and a validity notion of queries. Using an inference mechanism, when a query is submitted from a user, the query is evaluated and rewritten according to the accessible authorization views. However, in the worst case, the algorithm may not be able to infer validity of some unconditionally valid queries.

Recently, work on the policy for preserving privacy has boosted the research of FGAC [1, 3]. Elisa Bertino et al [3] proposed a privacy preserving access control model for relational databases. Actually, the model proposed needs a basis of FGAC in a database system. Nevertheless, they did not describe how to implement the model in a database management system. Agrawal et al [1, 2] proposed a framework for FGAC implementation in a Hippocratic database system. In their work, the DBMS provides column level, row level, and element level access control. However, that model is based on the Hippocratic database system and is limited in purpose.

Ponder policy language [5] is a high level language for security policy description. But they cannot be used to describe the security policy in database management systems. Motivated by the Ponder policy language, we extend the SQL statement to describe security policies for database systems.

3   The Extension of the SQL

In order to illustrate our work in detail, we use the following database application in **Example 1** (Figure 1) to explain our concepts and the extension of SQL language.

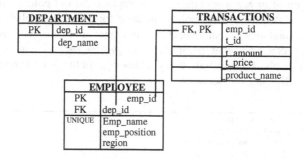

Fig. 1. The relationships of the three tables of the corporation

Example 1. A database with three tables is used to record the daily sale activities of a computer corporation. The *DEPARTMENT* table records the information about all the departments in the corporation, for example, department name (*dep_name*). Every department has a serial number in *dep_id*, which is the primary key (PK) of the table. The *EMPLOYEE* table records staff personal details, such as *emp_id*, *emp_name*, *emp_position*, *region* and the *dep_id*. The *emp_names* are unique to each other to guarantee the employee names are not duplicated in the information system. The *dep_id* indicates the department that the employee belongs to and is a nullable foreign key (FK) of the table. Because some of the employees may not belong to any department, at this time the *dep_id* for the employees would be null. The primary key of the *EMPLOYEE* is *emp_id*. The table *TRANSACTIONS* records the person (*emp_id*) dealing with this transaction, and *t_id*, *t_amount*, *t_price*, and *t_product_name* for transaction serial number, amount, price, and product name of the transaction. The *emp_id* and *t_id* is the primary key and the *emp_id* is the foreign key. Figure 1 shows the relationships among these three tables. The employees of the corporation are located in different regions. They can be in one of three roles: *DIRECTOR, MANAGER,* and *SALESPERSON*. The security policies for these three roles are arranged as follows:

(1) *DIRECTOR* of the corporation can read all the transactions;

(2) *MANAGER* of *department of desktop computer* can read the transactions in *department* of *desktop computer* and *department of printer;* the other *MANAGERs* can only read transactions in their own departments;

(3) *SALESPERSON* can take part in a transaction process only when he/she belongs to a department, and the salesperson can only read his/her own transactions.

3.1   The Statement for the Creation of Policy Type and Its Instance

We extend the SQL language to express the FGAC security policies. Figure 2 shows the statements of policy type creation and their instantiation. The *create policy* statement creates a policy type with at least two parameters, *subject* and *target* to describe information about subjects and objects and they may not appear in policy body. The option of *or replace* is designed to replace the old policy with a new one. The *inst policy* statement creates policy instance for a specific policy type. When a policy type is instantiated, a real subject and an object are bound with the policy type. In addition, we can add other parameters (in *param_list*) to express the security policies more flexibly. We illustrate every component in the policy creation statement in detail in the following sub-sections.

```
The statement of of the policy type creation:
create [or replace] policy policyType(
                        subject  identity ,
                        target   identity ,
                        param_list)
begin
  action  action_list
    begin filter
       filter_list
    end
    [when   constraint_Expression ]
end

The instantiation of the security policy:
inst policy policyName=policyType(subject_expression, target_expression,...)

The symbol [] denotes contents in [ ] can be omitted, the words in boldface are key words.
```

Fig. 2. The SQL statements for creating the security policy type and instance

3.1.1   The Subjects and Objects
The definitions of subjects and objects are described as follows:

```
subject_expression:: = user user_name | role role_name | group group_name
target_expression:: = [database.][schema.]table[(col1, col2, ...) ] |
                      [database.][schema.]view[(col1, col2, ...)]
```

The key words *user, role,* and *group* indicate the subject can be user, role, and users in a group. The *target_expression* specifies a table (or view, or columns in the table) in a database.

3.1.2 Operations List

The operation list is in the *action* clause in the *create policy* statement. It specifies the operations on the objects that the security policy restricts. As shown in the following, '*' denotes all the operations on the specific objects.

```
action_list ::= a_action | a_action, action_list
a_action ::= select | update | insert | delete | *
```

3.1.3 Filters List

A filter specifies the data to be accessed in specific objects. The fine-grained access control is implemented through filters. All of the operations in the operations list have the same list of filters.

```
filter_list ::= filter | filter, filter_list
filter ::= [if condition] filter_body [endif] | [ elseif condition ( filter_body ) | else ( filter_body ) endif]
filter_body ::= boolean_Expression | call function_name
condition ::= boolean_Expression
```

The *booeanl_Expression* consists of two sub-expressions linked by binary operators (<, >, >=, <=, =, in, exist). The sub-expressions can be sub-queries or sub-expressions. The function **call** is the stored procedures existing in databases, which can be created by users or system-stored procedures.

One filter consists of two components. One is the optional condition which describes the restriction condition of the subject. The format is *if* condition clause or *elseif* condition clause. The other is the predicate producer, namely *filter_body*, for creating those predicates to filter the data not to be accessed in the object. When the filter in a policy is evaluated, the optional condition is processed first. If the result of a condition is TRUE, the filter body corresponding to the condition is executed to produce a predicate.

Example 2. The policy type and instance describe the security requirements of the salesperson who can only read his/her own transaction records. In the following policy type, the font of filter is in italic style and the policy type returns a Boolean expression with sub-query because the policy type has no restricted condition for the subjects.

```
create or replace policy RepPol(subject s, target t)
      begin action select
   begin filter
   (emp_id=(select emp_id from employee where emp_name=USER))
   end
      when (select dep_id from employee where emp_name=USER) in (select dep_id from department)
   end;
   inst policy repp1=RepPol(role SALESPERSON, transactions);
   inst  policy rep2 = RepPol(user  ZHU, transaction(t_id, t_amount, t_price));
   inst policy rep3 = RepPol(role SALESPERSON,  employee);
```

USER is a system function which returns the user name of the current sessions. The expression in *When* clause denotes the integrity constraint whereby the salesperson can take part in a transaction process only when he/she belongs to a department.

We can create different policy instances from one policy type. In this example, we can create another instance *rep2* for user *ZHU* on the columns t_id, t_amount, t_price in table *transactions*. Also, we can create the policy instance on another object such as in instance *rep3*. In this way, the policy type is reused.

Example 3. The policy type and instance in the following are for the requirement (2) in **Example 1**.

```
create or replace policy ManPol(subject s, target t)
  begin action select
    begin filter
    if ((select dep_name from department where dep_id in
            (select dep_id from employee where emp_name = USER)) = 'desktop computer')
      (emp_id in (select emp_id from employee where emp_name = USER) and
          emp_id in (select emp_id from department, employee where
              department.dep_id=employee.dep_id and (dep_name='desktop computer' or dep_name='printer')))
    else
      (emp_id in (select emp_id from employee where emp_name = USER) and
          emp_id in (select emp_id from department, employee where department.dep_id = employee.dep_id))
    endif
  end
end;
inst policy manp1=ManPol(role MANAGER, transactions);
```

3.1.4 The Policy Constraint

The policy constraint describes the outer features of the subjects or integrity constraints in databases. The policy constraint is specified in the *When* clause in the policy type creation statement. Only when the policy constraint is evaluated as TRUE, the policy will be executed; otherwise, the policy will not take effect. The grammar in constraint definition is shown as follows.

```
constraint   ident = constraint_Expression or constraint_Expression |
                constraint_Expression and constraint_Expression
```

where "constraint_Expression" is defined as:

```
constraint_Expression ::= const_query | time_constraint | location_constraint
const_query ::= query_expression operator query_expression | scalar_query
operator = in | exist | > | >= | <= | < | and | or
time_constraint ::= Time.operation(actual_param_list)
location_constraint::= IP.operation(actual_param_list)
```

We divide the constraints for the security policy into two types:

(1) The constraint describes integrity constraints in databases. The query expressions can be linked by the operator *and*, *or*. In this case, the results of every query expression are scalar sub-query, namely *scalar_query*, which returns TRUE when the result of the expression is not NULL and otherwise returns FALSE, or a set of values in one column from the query expression which the operator can be in, *exist*. If the *operator* is the one in $\{<, >, >=, <=, =\}$, then the results of the query expressions are values of one column in one row.

(2) The constraints based on accessing time (*time_constraint*) or location (*location_constraint*) of the subject are time constraints or location constraints respectively. The time constraint specifies the time when the policies takes into effect. It includes the operator: *before*, *after* and *between* for specifying time. The location constraint specifies the IP address or IP address scope of the current subject. The operators of IP are *between* and *in*.

If a policy constraint is deleted, the policy constraint in policy type would be NULL in all the instances of the policy type.

4   Experimental Results

We implement the fine-grained access control policy in DM5. Then we use the TPC-W testing tool [12] to test the performance of the DBMS with FGAC. The tool is developed according to the TPC-W benchmark specification [10]. The TPC-W evaluates the throughput of a database with an average number of Web interactions per second (WIPS). We use this tool to test the performance of our system in different number of users connecting to the database. We compare the system performance with or without users who are assigned FGAC policy on table *orders* and *order_line* respectively. The test environment is shown in Table 1.

Table 1. The TPC-W testing environment

	Client	Web server	Database Server
OS	WINDOWS 2000 SERVER	WINDOWS 2000 SERVER	WINDOWS 2000 SERVER
Database	No	No	DM5 with /without FGAC
Testing program	TPCW Testing program	Weblogic	No
CPU	P4 2.6G×3 computer	P4 3G×3 computer	P4 2.0G
Memory	2×512M	2×512M	2×512M

Table 2. The roles and their security policies for testing

Role	Security policy

Manager: MAN	create policy orderman(subject s, target t)
	  begin action select
	  begin filter
	   (o_date = curdate)
	  end
	  end;
	inst policy orderp2= orderman(role man, orders);

Customer: CUST	create policy orderpolicy (subject s, target t)
	  begin action select
	 begin filter
	 (o_c_id = (select c_id from sysdba.customer where c_uname=user))
	  end
	  end;
	inst policy orderp1=orderpolicy(role cust, orders);

	create policy orderins(subject s, target t)
	  begin action insert
	 begin filter
	 (ol_I_ID > 50)
	  end
	 end;
	inst policy orderp3 = orderins(role cust, order_line);

Regional Customer: REGION	create policy orderreg(subject s, target t)
	  begin action insert
	  begin filter
	   if not exists (select 1 from sysdba.address a,sysdba.customer b,sysdba.country c where a.addr_id
	= b.c_addr_id and a.addr_id= c.co_id and b.c_uname=USER and c.co_name = 'United States')
	  then
	   (o_ship_addr_id = (select a.addr_id from sysdba.address a, sysdba.customer b where a.addr_id =
	b.c_addr_id and b.c_uname=USER))
	   end if
	  end
	  end;
	inst policy orderp4 = orderreg(role region, orders);

We create 40 users in the TPC-W testing database, and divide them into three roles: manager (*MAN*), customer (*CUST*), and regional customer (*REGION*). The roles and their policy types and instances are described in Table 2. Then we examined the performance of the system. Figure 3 illustrates the comparison results of the system performance with and without installing our newly introduced FGAC access control policies under different numbers of EBSs. We found that although the FGAC policy indeed affects the performance, the system performance is rational, close to linear and acceptable.

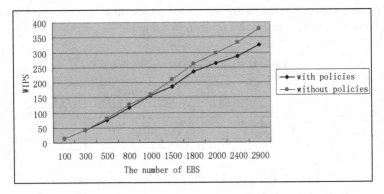

Fig. 3. The TPC-W test results under different EBSs

5 Summary

Providing efficient and effective fine-grained access control policies for database management systems has long been an unresolved issue, however, it is critically important for Internet-based data management systems. Motivated by the Ponder policy language, this study investigated a practical solution for this problem. We extended SQL language to describe the security policies and proposed the concept of the policy type in databases. In comparison with Oracle VPD, our policy has two features. First, we can create one policy type and then create many policy instances of that policy type. This alleviates the administration workload for maintaining policies and reduces errors. Second, we can express complicated database integrity constraint in policy type, and the policy creator does not need to develop a purpose-built program to create or modify security policies. We implemented the FGAC policy in DBMS DM5 and tested the performance by TPC-W testing tools. The test results are very promising. Our FGAC approach is practical, flexible, and easy to implement and use. At present, there are some limitations to our approach, for example, it can only express accessing policy for one object, not for several objects every time. This is one of the areas that we are currently working on.

References

[1] Agrawal, R., Bird, P., Grandison, T., Kiernan, J., Logan, S., Rjaibi, W.: Extending Relational Database Systems to Automatically Enforce Privacy Policies. In: Proceedings of 21st International Conference on Data Engineering (ICDE), pp. 1013–1023 (2005)

[2] Agrawal, R., Kiernan, J., Srikant, R., Xu, Y.: Hippocratic databases. In: Bressan, S., Chaudhri, A.B., Lee, M.L., Yu, J.X., Lacroix, Z. (eds.) CAiSE 2002 and VLDB 2002. LNCS, vol. 2590, pp. 563–574. Springer, Heidelberg (2003)

[3] Elisa, B.: Purpose Based Access Control for Privacy Protection in Database Systems. In: Zhou, L.-z., Ooi, B.-C., Meng, X. (eds.) DASFAA 2005. LNCS, vol. 3453, Springer, Heidelberg (2005)

[4] Database Management System DM5. http://www.dameng.com

[5] Damianou, N.: A Policy Framework for Management of Distributed Systems, Ph.D. thesis, Imperial College of Science, Technology and Medicine of London University (2002)

[6] Santosh, D., Bernard, M., Ashish, S.: Database Access Control for E-Business – A case study. In: Proceedings of 11th International Conference on Management of Data COMAD, pp. 168–175 (2005)

[7] Motro, A.: An access authorization model for relational databases based on algebraic manipulation of view definitions. In: Proceedings of International Conference on Data Engineering, pp. 339–347 (1989)

[8] Shariq, R., Mendelzon Alberto, S., Prasan, R.: Extending Query Rewriting Techniques for Fine-Grained Access Control. In: Proceedings of SIGMOD Conference. pp. 551–562 (2004)

[9] Stonebraker, M., Wong, E.: Access control in a relational database management system by query modification. In: Proceedings of the ACM Annual Conference, pp. 180–186 (1974)

[10] Transaction Processing Performance Council (TPC), TPC BENCHMARK™ W (Web Commerce) Specification Version 1.8. http://www.tpc.org

[11] The Virtual Private Database in Oracle9ir2: An Oracle Technical White Paper, http://otn.oracle.com/deploy/security/oracle9ir2/pdf/vpd9ir2twp.pdf

[12] Hong, Z., Xin, F., Hui, L.Q., Kevin, L.: The Design and Implementation of a Performance Evaluation Tool with TPC-W Benchmark. Journal of Computing and Information Technology-CIT 14. 2, 149–160 (2006)

Extracting Temporal Information from Short Messages

Richard Cooper and Sinclair Manson

Computing Science, University of Glasgow, 17 Lilybank Gardens, Glasgow G12 8QQ
rich@dcs.gla.ac.uk

Abstract. Information Extraction, the process of eliciting data from natural language documents, usually relies on the ability to parse the document and then to detect the meaning of the sentences by exploiting the syntactic structures encountered. In previous papers, we have discussed an application to extract information from short (e-mail and text) messages which takes an alternative approach. The application is lightweight and uses pattern matching rather than parsing, since parsing is not feasible for messages in which both the syntax and the spelling are unreliable. The application works in the context of a high level database schema and identifies sentences which make statements about data describable by this schema. The application matches sentences with templates to identify metadata terms and the data values associated with them. However, the initial prototype could only manage simple, time independent assertions about the data, such as "Jane Austen is the author." This paper describes an extension to the application which can extract temporal data, both time instants and time periods. It also manages time stamps - temporal information which partitions the values of time varying attributes, such as the monarch of a country. In order to achieve this, the original data model has had to be extended with a temporal component and a set of sentence templates has been constructed to recognise statements in this model. The paper describes the temporal model and the extensions to the application, concluding with a worked example.

1   Introduction

Information Extraction (or Text Mining) is the process of eliciting data from natural language documents. An Information Extraction application takes a textual document and attempts to discover domain-relevant information in the text. Most standard approaches assume either that the document is in syntactically sound language or, at least, in the kind of regular structure which typically underpins a formal report. In these situations, the approach almost always taken is to parse the text first and to use the syntactic structure to aid in the detection of information-bearing assertions [1, 2].

As explained in [2], the motivation for this work was to extend a collaboratively developed information system with the ability to gather information sent by correspondents in the form, firstly of electronic mail messages, and later of SMS text messages. In attempting to extract information from the kinds of message sent via electronic mail or SMS, the situation is not so simple. The person sending these messages is interested in brevity not syntax or spelling. As a result, parsing runs into the dual

R. Cooper and J. Kennedy (Eds.): BNCOD 2007, LNCS 4587, pp. 224–234, 2007.

problem of identifying the syntax of the "sentences" and of identifying the syntactic category of the "words" in the message in the first place. Consequently, parsing becomes a much harder, if not impossible task.

Our approach therefore has been to abandon any attempt at a full parse of the message, but rather to try to effect the equivalent of a parse by matching each sentence against a number of a patterns appropriate to the domain [3, 4]. This approach can be considered lightweight in the sense of Kang *et al* [5] who take a similar approach to natural language database querying or template-driven as in the work of Vargas-Vera [6]. As an example of the original system, the data "author = Jane Austen" is extracted from the sentence "The author is Jane Austen" by matching the sentence with the pattern "The author is <authorValue>". The patterns available for a domain are created by instantiating a set of domain independent sentence templates for each component of an information domain schema, a technique which could well be an additional stage following the generation of a schema from an ontology. The pattern above is generated from the template "The <attribute> is <<value>>." for the attribute *author*. The value of the pattern matching approach is that the system can just as easily recognise "Author : Jane Austen" given the template "<attribute> : <<value>>".

Templates are grouped into template types by the information they extract. All templates of a given type capture the same structure of data and result in the same set of updates. This template given above belongs to the template type which captures the value of one attribute of the entity which is currently the focus of attention in the message and results in a update which modifies the current object by setting the attribute value. Setting up the set of sentence templates is a complex and time consuming task, but as the templates are domain independent, once set up they are available for use in a wide range of applications.

The system maintains a context of the most recently mentioned entities in order to disambiguate pronouns and other anaphoric references. The context contains references to the most recently mentioned entities and is updated at the end of each sentence. It also has a sophisticated system of synonyms using WordNet [7], vowel stripping and the user entry of synonyms, so the system can as easily recognise "authr : Jane Austen".

An important aspect of the application is the nature of the data model used. Although any data extracted is likely to end up in a relational or XML database, it would greatly complicate the application to program it against such an implementation model. Instead the schema is described in terms of a high level model in the certainty that data captured in this model can easily be stored in either of these forms later. We start with a basic object model, but enhance it to incorporate various aspects of everyday discourse. For instance, the gender of any entity referred to is important to the understanding of a message. Thus the model has a data type gender, applicable to one attribute of an entity type, its presence indicating that this type of entity can have different genders. Secondly, the notion of key has to be modified and, in fact, has two different flavours in the application. A database key (Dkey) is a unique attribute capable of identifying an object in the database key, while a human detectable key (Hkey) is an attribute used in natural language to identify an object. These need not be the same (although in our example they are), and great care is needed in the application to turn Hkeys into Dkeys resolving ambiguity as we do so.

One aspect of messages which is not specifically catered for is anything that conveys temporal information and, in order to achieve this, we would need to extend our model in a manner analogous to the addition of gender. For many applications, temporal information is of little or no importance, since they deal with time invariant information. Returning to our literary example, for instance, the system handles the sentences "The author is Jane Austen" and "The author was Jane Austen" equally since they match the templates "The <attribute> is <<value>>." and "The <attribute> was <<value>>." and, as these templates are both the same type, they both capture the same information. This is acceptable in this instance since the two sentences are synonymous in common parlance and because book authorship is invariant over time and so past and present are taken to have the same meaning.

Where the information varies over time, the equivalence disappears. For instance, "The Prime Minister is Tony Blair" and "The Prime Minister was Tony Blair." do not have the same meaning. Furthermore, sentences with temporal information have systematic ways of conveying that information – for instance, "Clement Attlee was Prime Minister from 1945 to 1951" explicitly delimits a time period. The way we could capture this information in the previous version of the application would be to define an entity type *PrimeMinister* with attributes name, start date and end date and then the system would cope with "Clement Attlee was a Prime Minister with start date 1945 and end date 1951." which requires an extremely verbose sentence mapping onto a semantically poor information structure.

The work described here puts the extraction of temporal information onto a much firmer footing by extending the data model to include a temporal aspect and by producing a set of sentence templates and template types which can match temporal sentences. The paper proceeds as follows. The next section motivates the work by describing an example domain and is followed by a sentence describing our temporal model. The following section describes how the application had to be extended and then provides a full worked example. The paper concludes with some ideas for furthering the work.

2 Example

2.1 Background

To demonstrate the requirements for this work and to exemplify the complexity involved, we sought a domain which uses time information in a variety of ways. We needed to ensure: that the representation of both time instants and time periods was required; that time periods could be discontinuous; that partitions of time were used; that time was used both as an ordinary attribute and as one which essentially identifies an entity (time stamping); and that the representation of various relationships between time periods would be needed, including ordering and concurrency.

We chose as our information domain the reigns of British monarchs and the terms of office of British Prime Ministers. This domain was chosen because it exhibited a number of features:

1. It contained entities of the same type occupying different time periods – Prime Ministers effectively partition the historical time domain we are using.

2. It contained references to events taking place at single moments of time – the entry into parliament of a Prime Minister.
3. It contained entities that occupied multiple time periods – the terms of office of a particular Prime Minister.
4. It contained entities occupying simultaneous time periods – monarch and PM.

We started by eliciting sentences from correspondents with which they would convey the kinds of information we were looking for. After eliminating sentences which contained extraneous information such as "George V's wife was Queen Mary" and sentences which were insufficiently definite "George reigned before Edward", we were left with a number of sentences including the following:

John Major was prime minister in 1993
George IV from 1820 – 1830
The prime minister in 1947 was Clement Attlee

Some of the messages string together several informative sentences, such as:

George III was king from 1760 to 1820. George II was king before him. Thomas Pelham-Holmes was prime minister when George II was king. William Pitt the Elder and William Pitt the Younger were Prime Minister when George III was king.

2.2 The Schema

The schema to capture this described three entity types as shown in Figure 1 *Country* is an entity with a name, one or more monarchs and a prime minister, both of attributes of *Country* being time varying.. A monarch has a name, a gender and a reign, while a prime minister has a name and gender, a term of office and a date for entry into the parliament. The names are single valued strings and the gender attributes are also single valued and are identified specially in our model for the reasons given previously. The others are time attributes. Each line in the schema describes the name and type of an

Database: Political History Entity Type Attributes								
Name	Name	Type	Gen	Dkey	Hkey	Card	TV	Ttype
Country	name	string	n	y	y	sv	n	n
	monarch	Monarch	y	n	n	mv	c	n
	thePM	PM	y	n	n	mv	u	n
Monarch	name	string	n	y	y	sv	n	n
	reign	time	n	n	n	sv	n	pt
	gender	gender	n	n	n	sv	n	n
PM	name	string	n	y	y	sv	n	n
	term	time	n	n	n	mv	n	pt
	entparl	time	n	n	n	sv	n	i
	gender	gender	n	n	n	sv	n	n

Fig. 1. The Political History Schema

attribute, whether it has gender, whether it is a database key or a human detectable key, whether it is single valued or multi-valued and whether it is time varying and if it is temporal, what kind of time object it is – see Section 3.2 for more on this.

The date of entry into parliament is a time instant attribute (Ttype='i') giving added information about the PM, but semantically differing little from attributes such as name or gender. However, term of office and reign are rather different kinds of attribute. Their value is essential to the entity they are describing in the sense that the entry of a person into the monarch table is only valid for the duration of the reign, and the entry of a person into the PM table is only valid for their term of office. We would therefore say that these two attributes identify their entities as *timestamps* [8]. In both these cases, the timestamps are periods (shown as Ttype='pt'), but there are many examples of timestamps as instants. For instance, the time varying entity, Olympic Champion, is time stamped to a particular year. We speak of the champion of 1960 and so on.

2.3 Extracting Data

The technique which the original system uses to capture data uses sentence templates to identify the sentence structure and then matches placeholders in the template with text strings in the sentence. Contextual information is used to complete the set of data necessary to generate an update. For instance, if the sentence *"John Major was prime minister."* was encountered in a reduced time-independent version of the schema with one time invariant prime minister per country, this would be matched with the template "<<value>> was <attribute>". The object that the attribute belonged to would be found from the context – in this case the country, "United Kingdom" – and the update would effectively be "update Country set PrimeMinister = 'John Major' where name = 'United Kingdom'".

When we add temporal information, we have a much more complex situation. The sentence *"John Major was prime minister in 1993"* must be used to add date information in the following way.

i)   The sentence now matches the template "<<value>> was <attribute> in <atime>", where <atime> refers to a slot for a time instant.

ii) The context is examined to get the country "United Kingdom" as before.

iii) The PM, John Major, is sought and if not found, a new PM object is created and added to the set of PMs for the United Kingdom.

iv) This now needs a time period to use as the term of office. In the sentence, 1993 is matched with <atime> which produces a time instant. This is used to create a new time period whose start date is 1993 at the latest and whose end date is 1993 at the earliest. We would hope for more messages extending the period.

v)   This time period is set as the value of *term-of-office* for this prime minister.

The matching process has to deal with various temporal values which are indicated by different templates. Thus the sentence *"George IV from 1820 – 1830"* creates a time period with different start and end points.

The second sentence of the pair *"George III was king from 1760 to 1820. George II was king before him."* must use the context to identify the meaning of "him", before creating a new monarch object whose reign is a time period ending in 1760 and which is before the time period 1760-1820.

To sum up the extraction process must be able to identify time instants and time period, to be able to define the end points of a period with more or less precision and to be able to capture relationships between the temporal values.

3   The IE Temporal Data Model

3.1   Requirements for the Model

We seek to capture temporal information concerning assertions in the domain. We require the ability to record temporal statements about the instant on which something happened, such as the birth of a person, and about a period during which some property held, such as the duration of a monarch's reign. The sentences we expect to capture include statements about instants, about something beginning, something ending or about the relative occurrence of two events or time periods. For instance, we would like to capture sentences such as "Harold Wilson was Prime Minister before James Callaghan" or "Winston Churchill was Prime Minister at the same time that George VI was king."

There has been a lot of research into appropriate data models for temporal information. We take most of our inspiration from the Interval-Extended Relational Model (IXRM) of Lorentzos [8] and TSQL, the temporal extension to SQL of Navathe and Ahmed [9]. IXRM extends the relational model with domains that record an interval, where that interval may be spatial, temporal or any other value which has a start point and an end point and which lies on a continuum. Using this, IXRM can hold cells whose value is essentially is the whole of an interval from start to finish, e.g. from a start time to an end time. Time instants are recorded as intervals with coincident start and end points. By including time interval and time instant attributes, the database can record the times at which the data in the rest of the tuple is valid – making IXRM an example of a valid time database. Lorentzos also identifies thirteen ways in which two intervals can be related which involve which starts first, which ends first, whether the two overlap and if not, whether their start and end points meet.

TSQL extends SQL with comparison operators for comparing time intervals, the ability to retrieve data according to timestamps, a special temporal ordering feature, the ability to query the data a particular point in time and an extension to GROUP BY to use temporal information to specify the groups.

Whereas, we are not querying the database, we are definitely interested in a data model based on time intervals and are happy to accept that instants are a special case of intervals. The sentences we are extracting data from express very much the same conditions as the queries in TSQL. For instance, a TSQL query might include "WHERE PM1.termOfOffice PRECEDES PM2 termOfOffice", we would be looking to understand "Harold Wilson was prime minister before James Callaghan" and capture it in very much the same form as the TSQL expression.

However, we do have some different requirements. Firstly, the information we will have will be uncertain and, at any moment, incomplete, i.e. we might know the time of an attribute relative to another temporal value, we might only know when a time periods starts, when it ends or we might know some instant or period within it. Secondly, the periods we are trying may be discontinuous. The terms of office of some Prime Ministers – Disraeli, Gladstone and Wilson, for instance, consisted of more than one period separated by gaps. Moreover, such data exhibits the unusual feature that the addition of new information can lead to an overall reduction in data, since a discontinuous period may become continuous by the addition of extra knowledge filling in a gap. Thus Margaret Thatcher was PM from 1979 to 1983 and 1987-1990 is simplified to one period by the addition of the period between 1982, say, and 1988.

3.2 The Data Model

The original data model allows a simple database of entities to be described. A schema consists of a set of entity types and these have attributes. Attributes have either a scalar type or an entity type, and can be single- or multi-valued or unique. Scalar domains include not only numbers, booleans and strings, but gender as well.

The revised model required no change to the entity structure but did require two extra qualifiers for attributes: whether their values were time varying and what kind of time value they were. Each attribute can be either invariant over time, varying with only one value at any one instant, or varying but potentially with multiple values at any one moment. This indicated by the TV column in Figure 1, with 'n' meaning time invariant, 'u' meaning unique at any given point in time, and 'c' meaning potentially having more than one value simultaneously.

There are four possible ways in which an attribute can represent a time value and these are shown in Figure 1 in the *Ttype* column. The four values are:

'i':   It represents an instant which is not used to identify the entity – e.g. date of birth;

'p':   It represents a period, also not used for identification purposes – e.g. time at university;

'it': It represents an instant as a timestamp – e.g. an Olympic championship as mentioned above; or

'pt': It can represent a period as a timestamp – holding any role in an organisation will be an example of this.

To take examples from our domain as shown in Figure 1, the prime minister of a country is a time varying attribute whose values are unique at a given instant. The date of entry into parliament of the PM is an instant time valued attribute, not used to identify the person. The term of office is a period which is used as a timestamp – i.e. it will be usable in querying the database for the value of the Prime Minister attribute of a country at a particular time. There is a relationship here between the two qualifiers – a time varying attribute is either a scalar or an entity of a type which has one timestamp attribute.

3.3 Temporal Operations on the Data

Underlying the schema is a number of classes which represent the various aspects of the temporal information. On identifying temporal information in the message, these are used to create data according to the schema. The main class are:

IETimePeriodSet holds a set of time periods. It has methods which provide definitive information – set the start or end of a time period – and ones which are less precise – indicate that the period is after a particular time or that there is a gap in the time period set.

IETimePeriod objects are the fundamental aspect of the information, since time instants are merely time periods with coincident start and end times. A time period has a start and an end point and methods to compare itself with other time periods in terms of the five basic relationships managed by the system:

CAPS – The time period does not start until the other has ended.

CONCURS – The time period overlaps with the other period to some extent.

PRECEDES – The start point of this period is before the start point of the other.

SUCCEEDS – The end point of the period is after the end point of the other.

NON-CONCURS – Either the period is wholly before or wholly after the other but we don't know which.

IETime represents a single point of time which may not be known precisely. It therefore can store possible minimum and maximum values.

IETimePoint is a precise moment in time, while *IETimeLength* represents a duration.

Using these classes, the data model supports a number of operations:

i)   *setStart*, *setEnd* and *setDuration* specify the detail of a period;
ii) *concur* and *notConcur* indicate if two periods coincide;
iii) *setAfter*, *setBefore* and *setBetween* indicate the temporal relationship between two periods;
iv) *setGap* sets the duration between periods; and
v)   *setTime* sets the value of a simple temoral attribute.

4 The Revised Application

The application required enhancement in a number of areas. Conceptually, the most important areas were the extension of the template structure, the template type structure and the context together with the provision of a module to turn numerical strings into numbers ("one year" is turned into ?/?/1, a temporal value representing an unknown number of days and months and one year). The context was extended with a current time period, permitting the interpretation of clauses such as "at the same time".

The template structure provides a method for determining the structure of the sentences which can be recognised. They are strings containing words which must be in the sentence (constants), placeholders for metadata terms in single angle brackets and placeholders for data values in double angle brackets. Placeholders for meta-data include ones for attributes and human keys. There are also placeholders for the various kinds of pronoun – for instance, <spronoun> matches subject pronouns. This structure only had to be extended with new placeholders for a point in time <atime> and for a length of time <rtime>. For example:

In <<atime1>>, <<value1>> was still <attribute1>.

matches with sentences such as "In 1901, Victoria was still queen." Since Victoria is one of the values of the attribute Monarch, the attribute is time varying and so can use the time value to time stamp the data. The example bellows shows some more complicated templates.

The template structure was more thoroughly extended to include temporal updates. Whereas the original structure of a template type identified the information type that would have been extracted by matching a template of that type (e.g. an attribute and its value), and a set of SQL-like updates, the revised version added a different structure for temporal updates. Essentially the effect of a match is to create SQL-like updates including those to set up a temporal attribute. The added temporal updates add the ability to specify specific or relative information through calls to the IETimePeriodSet methods – such *setStart*, *setDuration* or *setAfter*.

5   A Final Example

To complete the description, we present an example of the application in action, as it processes a message. The message is:

> *Edward VII was king from 1901, one year before Arthur Balfour was prime minister. Arthur Balfour became an MP in 1874. After Arthur Balfour was Henry Campbell-Bannerman and then Herbert Henry Asquith. Herbert Henry Asquith was prime minister before George V was king in 1910. Herbert Henry Asquith was prime minister when George V was king in 1910.*

The first sentence matches the template:

> *<<value1>> was <attribute1> from <atime1>, <rtime1> before <<value2>> was <attribute2>*

This extracts: value1 = 'Edward VII' and attribute1 = 'king'

atime1 = 1901, rtime1 = "one year" which becomes ?/?/1
value 2 = 'Arthur Balfour' and attribute = 'pm'.

This is tied to the template type which includes the following updates:

  i)   Update the current object setting attribute1 = value1 and attribute2=value2. As these are both multi-valued, this amounts to adding them to the set if they are not there and may involve creating new objects with new temporal objects for the temporal attributes (null for instants, null start and end points for periods).
 ii)   Set the start point for the time period attribute of <<value1>> to <atime1>.
iii)   Set the time period attribute for <value1> to precede the time period attribute of <<value2>> by <rtime1>.

The effect of this is to ensure that monarch, Edward VII, and PM, Arthur Balfour, both exist in the sets of monarchs and pms belonging to the United Kingdom. Then the start date for the reign of Edward is set to 1901 and the start date of Balfour's term of office is 1902 by the addition of the one year.

The second sentence matches the template:

<<hkey1>> <attribute1> in <<atime1>>

This extracts: <<Hkey1>> = Arthur Balfour

<attribute1> = "entparl" through the use of the synonym "became an MP"
<atime1> = 1902

The template type here consists of updating <attribute1> of the data object indicated by <Hkey1> to the time found in <atime1> - the effect of this being to set *entparl* to 1874 for Arthur Balfour.

Briefly, sentence three matches "*After <<value1>> was <<value2>> and then <<value3>>*" and this causes the times in office of the three prime ministers to be in sequence. Sentence four matches "*<<value1>> was <attribute1> before <<value2>> was <attribute2> in <<atime1>>*". This ensures that Asquith and George V are in the database, sets a concurrency relationship between their time periods, sets the start point for George's reign and a precedes relationship on Asquith's term of office. The final sentence matches "*<<value1>> was <attribute1> when <<value2>> was <attribute2> in <<atime1>>*". This again confirms the two individuals in the database, sets concurrency between their periods and the date 1910.

6 Conclusions

We have described the extension of a simple information extraction application to cope with temporal information. The application uses pattern matching to identify sentences with templates which describe the structure of the sentence and where extracted data will be found. The original application coped with simple time invariant assertions and the extension allows the extraction of both temporal attributes which are themselves time invariant (such as date of birth) and of time varying data.

We took as our domain information about the monarchs and prime ministers of the United Kingdom, both of which are time varying attributes of the country. To achieve the extension, we had to build a sophisticate data model which captured time instants and (possibly discontinuous) time periods. It had to cope both with creating new objects and new time periods, but also with updates which are rather more complex than for time invariant data. New values did not merely replace old ones, but modified them, perhaps merging two time periods for instance. Relationships had also to be captured which indicated temporal ordering.

The major contribution of the work was the development of the data model. No model of how to handle a mixture of absolute and relative, precise and imprecise temporal data was available at the start of the undertaking. However, this project should be viewed as a good start with a number of improvements necessary.

Firstly, of course, we cannot hope to have captured all of the ways in which English speakers use temporal information in short text messages – we have only 35 templates. This requires a more thorough investigation of messages in practice than has so far been possible. A separate project has attempted to learn sentence templates, but this far from complete. Only a few of the many ways that a date or time may be written in a message have been implemented. This is a more extensive version of the problem that all database systems face when allowing users to enter and display dates and times, typified by the use of TO_CHAR and TO_DATE in Oracle. However, we have demonstrated that complex temporal information can be extracted from natural language in a systematic and extensible fashion.

The technique of extending the data model is itself of interest. Essentially what we have achieved is to capture a domain independent aspect of natural language in a structure which describes the semantics. A separate paper [11] considers this more extensively in the context of other domain independent aspects of language. Starting with the treatment of gender and time, that paper continues with proposals for dealing with negation, uncertainty and inference and this seems to lead to a novel account of semantics in natural language in which syntax plays an unusually minor role.

References

1. Cardie, C.: Empirical Methods in Information Extraction. AI Magazine 18(4), 1–17 (1997)
2. Gaizauskas, R., Wilks, Y.: Information Extraction: Beyond Document Retrieval. the Journal of Documentation 54(1), 1–34 (1998)
3. Cooper, R., Ali, S.: Extracting Data from Short Messages, Natural Language Processing and Information Systems. In: Montoyo, A., Muñoz, R., Métais, E. (eds.) NLDB 2005. LNCS, vol. 3513, pp. 388–391. Springer, Heidelberg (2005)
4. Cooper, R., Ali, S.: Extracting Data from Personal Text Messages, Technical Report, Computing Science, University of Glasgow (2006)
5. Kang, I., Na, S., Lee, J., Yang, G.: Lightweight Natural Language Database Interfaces. Meziane & Métais, 76–88 (2004)
6. Vargas-Vera, M., Dominque, J., Kalfoglou, Y., Motta, E., Buckingham-Schum, S.: Template-driven information extraction for populating ontologies. In: Proceedings of IJCAI'01 Workshop on Ontology Learning, Seattle, WA, USA (2001)
7. Miller, G.: WordNet: A Lexical Database for English. Communications of the ACM 38(11), 39–4 (1995)
8. Lorentzos, N.: The Interval-extended Relational Model and Its Application to Valid-time Databases, in [10], pp. 67–91 (1993)
9. Navathe, S., Ahmed, R.: Temporal Extensions to the Relational Model and SQL, in [10], pp. 92–109 (1993)
10. Tansel, A., Clifford, J., Gadia, S., Jajodia, S., Segev, A., Snodgrass, R.: Temporal Databases Theory, Design And Implementation, Benjamin Cummings, 1992 (1993)
11. Cooper, R.: A Strategy for Using More of the Language in Extracting Information from Short Messages (submitted to NLDB) (2007)

Max-FTP: Mining Maximal Fault-Tolerant Frequent Patterns from Databases

Shariq Bashir and A. Rauf Baig

National University of Computer and Emerging Sciences, Islamabad, Pakistan
shariq.bashir@nu.edu.pk, rauf.baig@nu.edu.pk

Abstract. Mining Fault-Tolerant (FT) Frequent Patterns in real world (dirty) databases is considered to be a fruitful direction for future data mining research. In last couple of years a number of different algorithms have been proposed on the basis of Apriori-FT frequent pattern mining concept. The main limitation of these existing FT frequent pattern mining algorithms is that, they try to find all FT frequent patterns without considering only useful long (maximal) patterns. This not only increases the processing time of mining process but also generates too many redundant short FT frequent patterns that are un-useful. In this paper we present a novel concept of mining only maximal (long) useful FT frequent patterns. For mining such patterns algorithm we introduce a novel depth first search algorithm **Max-FTP** (<u>Max</u>imal <u>F</u>ault-<u>T</u>olerant Frequent <u>P</u>attern Mining), with its various search space pruning and fast frequency counting techniques. Our different extensive experimental result on benchmark datasets show that Max-FTP is very efficient in filtering un-interesting FT patterns and execution as compared to Apriori-FT.

Keywords: Fault Tolerant Frequent Patterns Mining, Maximal Frequent Patterns Mining, Bit-vector Representation, and Association Rules.

1 Introduction

Mining frequent patterns from transactional or relational datasets with support greater than a certain user defined threshold, plays an important role in many data mining applications such as intrusion detection, finding gene expression patterns, web log patterns etc. In recent years, a number of algorithms have been proposed for efficient mining of such frequent patterns, on the basis of Apriori property proposed by Agrawal et al. [1]. These algorithms take a transactional dataset and support threshold *(min_sup)* as an input and output those exact matching frequent patterns which contain support greater than *min_sup*, with assuming that the dataset is very well pre-processed and noise free. However, the real world datasets are dirty and contain missing and noisy values. In such situations, users face difficulties in setting this *min-sup* threshold to obtain their desired results. If *min-sup* is set too large, then there may be a small number of frequent patterns, which does not give any desirable result. If the *min-sup* is set too small, then there may be many redundant short un-useful frequent patterns, which not only take a large processing time for mining but also increase the

R. Cooper and J. Kennedy (Eds.): BNCOD 2007, LNCS 4587, pp. 235–246, 2007.

complexity of filtering un-interesting frequent patterns. In both situations, the ultimate goal of mining interesting frequent patterns is undermined.

For handling such situations, J. Pei at el. in [6] introduced a new application of finding only interesting frequent patterns in a real world dirty datasets, instead of finding exact patterns. This approach is known as fault-tolerant (FT) frequent pattern mining. The problem of mining all FT frequent patterns from a dirty transactional dataset can be considered from the following two conditions [6].

1. Under user defined fault tolerance factor δ, a pattern X with cardinality greater than δ is called a FT frequent pattern, if it appears in at least k number of FT-transactions. A transaction t is called a FT-transaction under fault tolerance factor δ, if it contain at least $|X|$-δ number of items of X. The number k is called the frequency of X which must be greater or equal than the minimum FT support threshold (min_sup^{FT}).

2. Each individual single item i of X must be appeared in at least l number of FT-transaction of X, where l is called the minimum item support threshold under fault tolerance factor δ (item_sup$^{FT}_\delta$).

For example, with min_sup^{FT} = 3 and item_sup$^{FT}_\delta$ = 2, the pattern $\langle A, B, C, D \rangle$ is a FT frequent pattern under fault tolerance factor $\delta = 1$, since 3 out of 4 items are present in FT-transaction T1, T3 and T5 which qualifies min_sup^{FT} threshold and each single item A, B, C and D is present in at least 2 transactions with qualifies item_sup$^{FT}_\delta$ threshold. In [6] they also proposed an Apriori-FT algorithm for finding all type of such patterns. The Apriori-FT was extended from the Apriori approach, in which downward closure property is used for mining FT frequent patterns. Similar to Apriori algorithm, Apriori-FT applies a bottom-up search that enumerates every single FT frequent pattern. This implies that in order to produce a FT frequent pattern of length l, it must produce all 2^l of its subsets, since they too must be frequent FT. This exponential complexity fundamentally restricts Apriori-FT like algorithms in discovering only useful interesting FT frequent patterns in a reasonable time limit. Moreover, mining FT frequent patterns are very complex than mining all frequent patterns, in terms of both search space exploration and frequency counting of candidate patterns. In frequent pattern mining, a candidate pattern X is declared to be frequent, by checking its frequency in only one dataset scan. While in FT frequent pattern mining, a number of dataset scans are needed to declare a candidate FT pattern X as frequent, which depends on the cardinality of pattern X. In addition to frequency counting, most of the search space pruning techniques, such as parent equivalence pruning (PEP) and 2-Itemset Pair of frequent pattern mining can not be applied on mining FT frequent patterns for filtering infrequent FT patterns.

To overcome these limitations, in this paper we have introduced a novel maximal or long FT frequent pattern mining (MFP^{FT}) concept. Similar to maximal frequent pattern mining [3], a pattern X is called a maximal FT frequent pattern, if it has no superset that is also a maximal frequent FT pattern. Mining only MFP^{FT}s has many advantages over mining all FT frequent patterns. Firstly, long patterns are very useful in some very important data mining applications such as biological data from the field of DNA and protein analysis and clustering. Secondly, different search space pruning techniques such as FHUT and HUTMFI (Section 5) can be also applied easily on mining MFP^{FT}s algorithm, which dynamically prune the irrelevant search space during mining process. Thirdly, we know MFP^{FT}s are supersets of all FT frequent patterns; therefore Max-FTP output implicitly and concisely represents all FT frequent patterns. Finally, a single dataset scan can collect all the FT frequent patterns, once we have MFP^{FT}s.

2 Problem Definition

To consider the problem of mining MFP^{FT}s, let us take a sample transactional dataset of Table 1. It consists of 8 transactions with 12 different items. Let us take the $min\_sup^{FT} = 3$ and $item\_sup^{FT}{}_\delta = 2$ with fault tolerance factor $\delta = 1$. Since some of the items contain frequency less than $item\_sup^{FT}{}_\delta = 2$. Therefore, according to subset-superset property of Apriori-FT [6], these items can be safely removed from the dataset transactions and list of single frequent FT patterns, before starting the actual FT mining algorithm. Column 3 of the Table 1 dataset shows the modified representation of actual dataset transactions, which consist of only those items which have frequency greater than $item\_sup^{FT}{}_\delta$.

The search space of FT frequent pattern mining can be considered as a lexicographical order [7], where root node contains an empty pattern, and each lower level k contains all the k-patterns. Figure 1 shows the search space of Table 1 dataset, where

Table 1. A sample transactional dataset with 8 transactions and 12 items

Transaction ID	Items	Frequent Items
T1	A, B, C, I	A, B, C
T2	B, C, E, J, K	B, C, E
T3	A, C, D, L	A, C, D
T4	A, C, E, G	A, C, E
T5	A, B, C	A, B, C
T6	D, E	D, E
T7	D, E	D, E
T8	D, E	D, E

each node is composed of head and tail elements. Head denotes the FT frequent pattern of that node, and tail consists of those items which are possible extensions of new candidate FT patterns. For example node P in Figure 1 contains a head ⟨A, B, C⟩ and tail ⟨D, E⟩, which generates 2 child nodes or candidate FT patterns: node ⟨A, B, C, D⟩ and node ⟨A, B, C, E⟩. This FT frequent pattern mining search space can be traversed using either depth-first-search (DFS) or breadth-first-search (BFS) approach.

The problem of mining FT frequent patterns can be considered as a finding of cut in the search space, where the patterns above the cut are frequent FT and patterns below the cut denote infrequent FT. While the problem of mining MFP^{FT}s is to mine only those frequent FT patterns above the cut, which are not subset of any other frequent FT pattern. For example the node S1 with head ⟨A, B, C, D⟩, node S2 with head ⟨A, B, C, E⟩ and node S3 with head ⟨D, E⟩ in Figure 1 are those patterns which are not subset of any other frequent FT pattern.

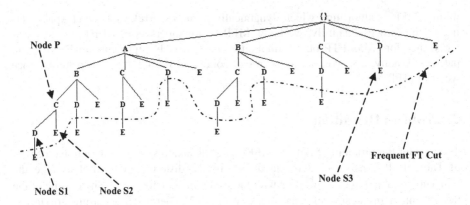

Fig. 1. The FT Search Space of Table 1 dataset with min_sup^{FT} = 3 and item_sup$^{FT}_\delta$ = 2 under fault tolerance factor δ = 1

To decrease the processing time of mining useful FT frequent patterns, different search space pruning techniques can also be applied during MFP^{FT}s mining on the basis of known MFP^{FT}s list. The known MFP^{FT}s list at any node n consists of only those maximal FT patterns which are discovered priori the traversal of n. For example in Table 1 with min_sup^{FT} = 3, item_sup$^{FT}_\delta$ = 2 and fault tolerance factor δ = 2. Once a pattern ⟨A, B, C, D, E⟩ is known to be MFP^{FT}, then using this information the search space consisting of sub trees ⟨A, B, C, E⟩, ⟨A, B, D⟩, ⟨A, B, E⟩, ⟨A, E⟩, ⟨A, D⟩, ⟨A, E⟩, ⟨B⟩, ⟨C⟩, ⟨D⟩ and ⟨E⟩ can be safely pruned away. This is because they are all subsets of known MFP^{FT} ⟨A, B, C, D, E⟩. Where, a pure Apriori-FT like algorithm will have to done extra work and will traverse and generate these many short redundant FT frequent patterns.

3   Related Work

Mining FT frequent patterns in a real world dirty datasets has remained as a central core of attention in last couple of years. The basic concept behind FT frequent pattern mining is to discover more general and interesting patterns instead of finding exact frequent patterns. J. Pei et al. in [6] proposed an Apriori like FT pattern mining algorithm. Apriori-FT uses a complete, bottom up search, with a horizontal layout and prune away infrequent FT patterns using anti-monotone Apriori-FT property heuristic: if any length k FT pattern is not frequent, then all of its length $(k+1)$ supersets will be also infrequent. The major weakness of Apriori is its difficulty in mining long FT patterns. For example, to find a frequent FT pattern of $X = \{1,..., 200\}$ items. Apriori-FT has to generate-and-test all candidate 2^{200} FT patterns.

J. L. Koh et al. in [4] proposed their VB-FT-Mine FT patterns mining algorithm. In their approach, FT appearing vector are designed to represent the distribution of the candidate FT patterns under fault tolerance factor δ using bit-vector representation approach. VB-FT-Mine algorithm applies DFS traversal to generate candidate FT patterns. The major feature of VB-FT-Mine is its fast frequency counting operation.

The algorithm decides quickly that, whether a candidate FT pattern is frequent or infrequent by performing bitwise operations on appearing vectors.

4 Max-FTP: Algorithmic Description

In this section, we describe our maximal frequent FT pattern mining algorithm Max-FTP with its various techniques used for search space pruning and performance improvements. For FT pattern representation at any node, in Max-FTP we use the vertical bit-vector representation approach. The major advantage of using vertical bit-vector approach over any other pattern representation approach is that, it is more efficient in pattern frequency counting. Since the frequency of any candidate FT pattern can be obtained by performing the bitwise-AND operations on head and tail bit-vectors. Therefore, on a processor which supports 32-bits per AND operation, there 32 transactions are checked for support (frequency) counting in only one bitwise-AND operation. This optimizes the candidate FT pattern frequency counting cost with a factor of 1/32. Firstly, we describe a simple DFS traversal algorithm with no pruning. Then, we use this algorithm to motivate the pruning and dynamic reordering of tail items in section 5.

Max_FTP_SimpleDFS (Node n)

1. *for each item X in n.tail*
2.   *m.tail = n.tail $\cup X$*
3.   *m.tail = n.tail $- X$*
4.   *n.tail = n.tail $- X$*
5.   *if (m.head is frequent)*
6.   *Max_FTP_SimpleDFS (m)*
7.   *if (n is a leaf and n.head in not in list (known $MFP^{FT}s$))*
8.   *Add n.head in (known $MFP^{FT}s$)*

Fig. 2. Pseudo code of Max-FTP with simple DFS traversal

4.1 Max-FTP with Simple DFS Traversal

In a simple DFS traversal we generate the candidate FT patterns by following simple lexicographical order [7]. At any node n, the candidate FT patterns or child nodes of n are generated by performing join operation on n's head pattern with each item of n's tail, and checked for frequency counting. If the frequency of candidate FT pattern *{n's head $\cup$ n's tail item}* is less than min_sup^{FT} or the frequency of any single item of pattern *{n's head $\cup$ n's tail item}* is less than item_sup$^{FT}_{\delta}$. Then we can stop by the Apriori-FT principle, since the superset of any infrequent FT pattern will be also infrequent FT. If all of the candidate FT patterns of any node are found to be infrequent, then that node is considered to be a candidate maximal FT frequent pattern. To check whether the current candidate maximal FT pattern X is not subset of any known MFP^{FT}, we must check its maximality in known MFP^{FT}s list. If none of the known MFP^{FT} is superset of this candidate pattern X, then X is considered to be a valid

MFP^{FT} pattern and added in the known MFP^{FT}s list. The set of all patterns in known MFP^{FT}s list denotes the required long or maximal frequent FT patterns. Figure 2 shows the pseudo code of Max-FTP with simple DFS traversal.

4.2 Dataset Representation and Fast Frequency Counting

As introduced earlier, in Max-FTP we use the vertical bit-vectors for FT pattern representation at any node. In contract to tradition bit-vectors representation used in [2], Max-FTP associates more than one bit-vectors at each node for FT pattern representation, depending on the size of fault tolerance factor δ. The first bit-vector at any node n represents FT transactions containing pattern P of node n under fault tolerance factor δ, which is called as bitmap(n). This bit-vector representation is almost similar to pattern representation that was used in [4]. In bitmap(n) there is one bit for each transaction of the dataset. If the pattern P of node n does not contain a FT transaction at position j under fault tolerance factor δ. Then the y bit of bitmap(n) is set to 0, otherwise to 1.

In addition to the representation of FT transactions containing pattern P of any node n under fault tolerance factor δ, we also have to count the number of items of pattern P that are not present at any transaction position j. For example in Figure 1, the pattern $\langle A, B, C, E \rangle$ at node S1 does not contain item $\langle E \rangle$ at transaction position 1 and 5, so the count of missing items must be 1 at these position. In Max-FTP we use the FT bit-vectors FT-bitmap$_1$(n), FT-bitmap$_2$(n), ..., FT-bitmap$_\delta$(n) for this purpose. If at any node n, the pattern P does not contain its $k \leq \delta$ items at transaction position j. Then the bits at position j of exactly k FT bit-vector (FT-bitmap$_1$(n),...., FT-bitmap$_k$(n)) are set to 1, which indicates that exactly the k items of pattern P are not present at this position.

Candidate FT Pattern Frequency Counting. Before considering, how Max-FTP count the frequency of any candidate FT pattern at any node n by performing the bitwise operations on $n'head$ and $n'tail$ item bit-vectors, let us consider the following definition.

Definition 1. Let $n' = n \cup \{x\}$ denotes a candidate FT pattern at node n, where x is the tail item and n is the frequent FT pattern. A transaction T contains FT under fault tolerance factor δ with pattern n', if at least one of the following two properties holds.

  1. T contains FT under fault tolerance factor $(\delta-1)$ with pattern n, or
  2. T contains x and FT under fault tolerant factor (δ) with pattern n'.

Candidate FT pattern frequency counting using bit-vectors. The property 1 of definition 1 can be obtained by performing bitwise-AND operations on bit-vectors bitmap(n) with bitmap(x). While the property 2 of definition 1 can be obtained by performing bitwise-OR operations on bit-vectors bitmap($n \cup x$) with FT-bitmap$_1$(n),...,FT-bitmap$_\delta$(n). The number of ones in the resulting bit-vector, after performing the bitwise-AND and bitwise-OR operations of property 1 and property 2 of definition 1 denotes the frequency of candidate FT pattern $n' = n \cup \{x\}$.

Single Item support checking. The procedure that we describe above calculates only the frequency of FT transactions contain pattern n' under fault tolerance factor δ. If this frequency is greater than min_sup^{FT}, then the frequency of each individual item i of pattern n' can be calculated by performing bitwise-AND operations on bit-vectors bitmap(n') with bitmap(i). While, the number of ones in the resulting bit-vector denotes the frequency of item i in pattern n', which should be greater than item_sup$^{FT}_\delta$, otherwise the pattern is declared as infrequent FT pattern.

5   Improving Max-FTP Performance

The depth-first-search traversal algorithm that we present in section 4.1 is ultimately no better than the Apriori-FT algorithm. Since exactly the same number of candidate FT patterns are generated and checked for frequency counting. Therefore, for gaining performance, in Max-FTP we used two search space pruning techniques name as FHUT (frequent head union tail) and HUTMFP^{FT} (head union tail maximal frequent FT pattern). In addition to the two search space pruning techniques, Max-FTP also reorders the tail items using dynamic reordering heuristic. This heuristic was first used in [3], which keeps the search space as small as possible.

FHUT (Frequent Head Union Tail). In [3], it was observed that the longest pattern that can be mined using DFS traversal is the *head* $\cup$ *{all items of tail}*. If at any node, it has been known that the entire *head* $\cup$ *{all items of tail}* or left most sub tree is found to be frequent. Then a substantial amount of performance can be obtained by pruning rest of the sub tree of *head* $\cup$ *{all items of tail}*. In Max-FTP we track this information at each node by using a boolean flag, which determines whether the left most item of tail is frequent or infrequent FT. If all of the left most childs of any node $n's$ subtee is found to be frequent FT, or in other words the left most path of the node $n's$ subtee is found frequent, then the pruning can be obtained under the concept of FHUT.

HUTMFP^{FT} (Head union Tail Maximal Frequent FT Pattern). Before checking the frequencies of any candidate FT patterns at node n, if it is found that the entire *head* $\cup$ *{all items of tail}* is already a subset of any known MFP^{FT}. Then by following the Apriori-FT property [6], we can safely prune away the entire sub tree of *head* $\cup$ *{all items of tail}*. In Max-FTP we found that a substantial amount of performance can be obtained by using this HUTMFP^{FT} pruning technique.

Dynamic Reordering of Tail Items. If any candidate FT pattern y at any node n is found to be frequent, then according to the Apriori-FT property all the supersets of y will be also infrequent FT and can be safely pruned away. For achieving this look ahead pruning technique, in Max-FTP we calculate the frequency of all the tail items of node n, before traversing any of them. Then by using this tail items frequencies information, Max-FTP reorders the node n tail items and removes all those which are found infrequent FT. Obviously, in one side this creates an additional burden of counting frequencies of node n's tail items by two times. First, at the time of reordering tail items and second, at the time of creating bit vectors of bitmap(n $\cup$ *tail item*)

Max_FTP_withPruning (Node n, FHUT_Flag)

---

1. *HUT = n.head ∪ n.tail*
2. *if (HUT is in list (known (known MFP^{FT}s))*
3. *stop searching and return*

4. *remove infrequent items from n.tail and recorder them by increasing frequency.*
5. *for each item X in n.tail*
6.   *m.tail = n.tail ∪ X*
7.   *m.tail = n.tail − X*
8.   *n.tail = n.tail − X*

9.   *FHUT_Flag = true if X is the left most item of n.tail*
10.   *if (m.head is frequent)*
11.   *Max_FTP_SimpleDFS (m)*

12.   *if (n is a leaf and n.head in not in list (known MFP^{FT}s))*
13.   *Add n.head in (known MFP^{FT}s)*
14.   *if (HUT_Flag and all extensions are frequent)*
15.   *stop exploring this subtree and go back up tree to where FHUT_Flag was changed to True.*

Fig. 3. Pseudo code of Max-FTP with search space pruning techniques

and FT-bitmap$_1$(n ∪ *tail item*), ...,FT-bitmap$_8$(n ∪ *tail item*). However, on the other side most of the infrequent FT nodes are pruned away using this look ahead pruning technique.

In addition to the removing of infrequent items from node n's tail, Max-FTP also arranged the frequent tail items by increasing support. This heuristic was first used by Bayardo in [3], which keeps the search space as small as possible. Figure 3 shows the pseudo of Max-FTP with embedded search space pruning techniques and dynamic reordering heuristic.

6 Candidate Maximal FT Pattern Maximality Checking

In our opinion efficient mining of MFP^{FT}s depend upon two main factors. First, at the search space traversal approach and using different search space pruning techniques. Second, at the maximal candidate FT pattern maximality (superset) checking approach which takes O(known MFP^{FT}s) in worst case. Let list (known MFP^{FT}s) be the currently known maximal FT frequent patterns. To check whether pattern P is subset of any known MFP^{FT} pattern. We must perform a maximal superset checking, which takes O(MFP^{FT}s) in worst case. In Max-FTP for speeding up the cost of superset checking, we used the local maximal frequent pattern (LMFI) superset checking approach with the name (LMFP^{FT}) [5]. LMFP^{FT} is a divide and conquer strategy which contains only those maximal FT frequent patterns at any node n, in which n's head appears as a prefix.

Definition 1. Any MFP^{FT} pattern P can be a superset of $P \cup _{subsets(P)}$ or $P \cup _{freq\_ext(P)}$. The set of $P \cup _{freq\_ext(P)}$ is called the LMFP^{FT} with respect to P, denoted as LMFP$^{FT}_p$. To check whether P is a subset of any existing MFP^{FT}s, we can checked them in only LMFP$^{FT}_p$, which takes O(LMFP$^{FT}_p$) cost which is smaller than O(MFP^{FT}s). If LMFP$^{FT}_p$ is empty, then P will be our new maximal FT pattern, otherwise it is the subset of LMFP$^{FT}_p$.

6.1 Child (LMFP^{FT}) Construction and Representation

Max-FTP used vertical bitmap representation approach for LMFP^{FT} representation. In a vertical bitmap, there is one bit for each item of known maximal frequent FT pattern. This is the same concept as we have described for candidate FT pattern representation in section 4.2. If the pattern P at node n is the subset of any existing known maximal FT pattern at position j, then the bit j of bitmap(LMFP$^{FT}_p$) is set to one; otherwise zero.

The LMFP^{FT} of tail item X at node n with pattern P *(n's head)* can be constructed simply by taking bitwise-AND of bitmap(LMFP$^{FT}_p$) with bitmap(X in the known maximal frequent FT pattern vertical bitmap representation).

bitmap(LMFP$^{FT}_{(P \cup X)}$) = **bitmap**(LMFP$^{FT}_p$) bitwise-AND **bitmap**(X in the known maximal frequent FT vertical bitmap representation).

7 Experiments

We performed 3 experiments to evaluate the performance of Max-FTP. In first experiment we compare the number of FT frequent patterns mine from the two different algorithms Apriori-FT and Max-FTP. The second experiment compares the running time of Max-FTP and Apriori-FTP. Finally, the effectiveness of different components of Max-FTP is evaluated in third experiment. All the source code of Max-FTP and Apriori-FT is written in C language. The experiments are performed on 3.2 GHz processor with main memory of size 512 MB, running windows XP 2005 professional. For experiments, we used the benchmark datasets available at http://fimi.cs.helsinki.fi/data/. These datasets are frequently used in many frequent pattern mining algorithms. Unfortunately, due to lack of space we could not show our experiments that we have performed on all the available datasets, therefore, we select the three best datasets from different sparse, dense and large categories. Table 2 shows the description of our experimental datasets.

Table 2. Datasets use in our experimental results

Dataset	Items	Average Length	Records
BMS-POS	1658	7.5	515,597
Mushroom	119	23	8,124
Kosarak	20,753	8.1	900,000

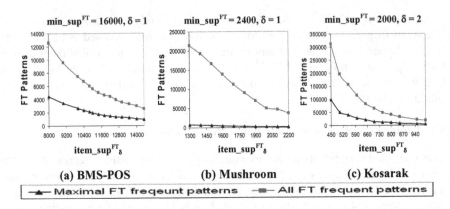

Fig. 4. Number of FT patterns mines using Max-FTP and Apriori-FT algorithms

Experiment 1. Figure 4 shows the number of FT frequent patterns mined by the two algorithms Apriori-FT and Max-FTP with different min_sup^{FT}, item_sup$^{FT}_\delta$ and δ thresholds. As clear from Figure 4, when the values of these thresholds decreases, the gap between number of useful FT frequent patterns mined with maximal and all FT frequent pattern mining algorithms becomes wider. In our experiments we found that as the average transactional length of dataset increases Max-FTP performs more well behaved as compared to Apriori-FT, since it mines only long pattern instead of small redundant patterns.

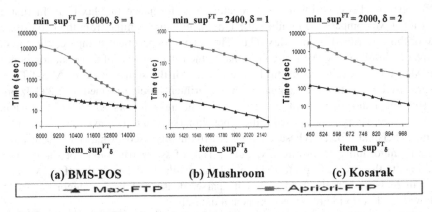

Fig. 5. Exectuion Time of Max-FTP and Apriori-FT on different FT thresholds levels

Experiment 2. In this experiment, we evaluate the performance of execution time of both algorithms with different min_sup^{FT}, item_sup$^{FT}_\delta$ and δ thresholds. As clear from Figure 5, the Max-FTP outperforms the Apriori-FT algorithm on almost all threshold levels, due to its effective search space pruning and frequency counting techniques. The Apriori-FT lacks of these effective search space pruning techniques; therefore, a much large set of candidate FT patterns are generated in order to build the complete set of frequent FT patterns. In experiments we found that on sparse datasets allowing more noise (δ) and smaller item_sup$^{FT}_{\delta}$ threshold in Apriori-FT results millions of frequent FT patterns; but consequently, more candidate FT patterns are explored, and computational cost increases exponentially with respect to the dimensionality of the patterns. While, Max-FTP with a very high rate of δ and small threshold values of min_sup^{FT} and item_sup$^{FT}_{\delta}$ generates only useful interesting maximal frequent FT pattern in a very small amount of processing cost.

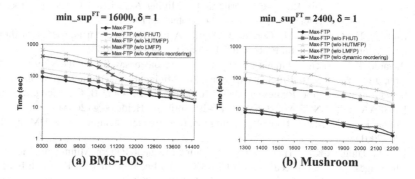

Fig. 6. Performance analysis of Max-FTP components on BMS-POS and Mushroom datasets

Experiment 3. In this experiment, we present a full analysis of each component of Max-FTP algorithm. There are three types of search space pruning techniques used to trim the tree: FHUT, HUTMFP^{FT} and dynamic reordering (of tail items). Moreover, LMFP^{FT} is used for fast maximal superset checking. Figure 6 shows the effects of each component of Max-FTP on Mushroom (dense) and BMS-POS (sparse) datasets. As clear from results, each component yields some saving in running time, but LMFP^{FT} is more effective than other techniques. The effect of FHUT and HUTMFP^{FT} is more encouraging on dense dataset (Mushroom) than sparse (BMS-POS) dataset; due to small number of items and larger average transactional length. The advantage of dynamic reordering is more effective on sparse dataset (BMS-POS) than dense dataset (Mushroom). Since most of the infrequent tail items are pruned earlier at lower level nodes of search space.

8 Conclusion

Mining fault tolerant frequent patterns in a real world dirty datasets is considered to be a fruitful direction for future data mining research. Previous FT frequent patterns mining algorithms such as Apriori-FT, generates not only long (interesting) FT patterns but also their many redundant short subset (un-useful) patterns. This not only increases the processing time of pattern mining process but also increases the size of rules. In this paper, we introduce a new concept of mining only maximal (long) frequent FT patterns. For mining such long patterns, we present a maximal FT pattern mining algorithm called Max-FTP with its various search space pruning techniques and fast frequency counting of candidate maximal FT pattern. Our different results on benchmark datasets show that Max-FTP mines not only a small number of interesting frequent FT patterns as compared to Apriori-FT, but it is also efficient in term of execution due to limited number of candidate FT patterns generation.

References

[1] Agrawal, R., Srikant, R.: Fast Algorithms for Mining Association Rules. In: Proc. Int'l Conf. Very Large Data Bases, pp. 487–499 (September 1994)
[2] Burdick, D., Calimlim, M., Gehrke, J.: Mafia: A maximal frequent itemset algorithm for transactional databases. In: Proc. of ICDE Conf, pp. 443–452 (2001)
[3] Bayardo, R.J.: Efficiently mining long patterns from databases. SIGMOD, 85–93 (1998)
[4] Koh, J.L., Yo, P.: An Efficient Approach for Mining Fault-Tolerant Frequent Patterns based on Bit Vector Representations. In: Zhou, L.-z., Ooi, B.-C., Meng, X. (eds.) DASFAA 2005. LNCS, vol. 3453, pp. 17–20. Springer, Heidelberg (2005)
[5] Gouda, K., Zaki, M.J.: Efficiently mining maximal frequent itemsets. In: ICDM, pp. 163–170 (2001)
[6] Pei, J., Tung, A.K.H., Han, J.: Fault-Tolerant Frequent Pattern Mining: Problems and Challenges. In: The proceedings of ACM-SIGMOD Int. Workshop on Research Issues on Data Mining and Knowledge Discovery (DMKD'01) (2001)
[7] Rymon, R.: Search through Systematic Set Enumeration. In: Proc. Of Third Int'l Conf. On Principles of Knowledge Representation and Reasoning, pp. 539–550 (1992)

A New Approach for Distributed Density Based Clustering on Grid Platform

Nhien-An Le-Khac, Lamine M. Aouad, and M-Tahar Kechadi

School of Computer Science and Informatics,
University College Dublin, Dublin 4, Ireland
{Nhien-An.Le-Khac,Lamine.Aouad,Tahar.Kechadi}@ucd.ie
http://www.csi.ucd.ie/

Abstract. Many distributed data mining *DDM* tasks such as distributed association rules and distributed classification have been proposed and developed in the last few years. However, only a few research concerns distributed clustering for analysing large, heterogeneous and distributed datasets. This is especially true with distributed density-based clustering although the centralised versions of the technique have been widely used fin different real-world applications. In this paper, we present a new approach for distributed density-based clustering. Our approach is based on two main concepts: the extension of local models created by *DBSCAN* at each node of the system and the aggregation of these local models by using tree based topologies to construct global models. The preliminary evaluation shows that our approach is efficient and flexible and it is appropriate with high density datasets and a moderate difference in dataset distributions among the sites.

Keywords: distributed data mining, distributed clustering, density-based, large dataset, tree topology.

1 Introduction

Today a deluge of data are collected from not only science fields but also industry and commerce fields. Massive amounts of data that are being gathered and stored in different sites. In this context, distributed data mining (*DDM*) techniques have become necessary for analyzing these large and multi-dimensional datasets. Actually, in order to tackle large, graphically distributed, high dimensional, multi-owner, and heterogeneous datasets, some projects have just been started such as Knowledge Grid[2], Grid Miner[1] and ADMIRE[12]. The last project is a new *DDM* framework which is being developed in the Department of Computer Science at University College Dublin. ADMIRE is not only a platform based on *P2P-Grid*[5] infrastructure for implementing *DDM* techniques but also it provides new distributed algorithms for exploring very large and distributed datasets. The first step of the development of these algorithms concern distributed clustering techniques that have few of researches by comparison with distributed association rules and distributed classification.

R. Cooper and J. Kennedy (Eds.): BNCOD 2007, LNCS 4587, pp. 247–258, 2007.

There are two major strands of research into distributed clustering: parallel clustering and distributed clustering. In the first strand, researchers developed parallel versions of the centre-based clustering algorithms. The second strand is based on two principal steps: perform partial analysis on local data at individual sites and then generate a global model by aggregating these local results. Although this later strand is more appropriate for Grid platforms where datasets are often geographically distributed and owned by different organisations, there is more research work in the first strand than in the second[9]. This is especially true with distributed clustering approaches based on density. In this context, recent researches[9][10] have proposed a distributed clustering consisted of two steps: local clustering to build local models and global clustering on these models to build a global model. Global clustering could not scale well when huge amounts of data are available in large-scale networks. In this paper, we propose a new approach of distributed density based clustering. This new approach is composed of the local clustering and the hierarchical aggregation of local models to rebuild a global model.

In our approach, the aggregating process is based on a decentralized model and the local clustering is a density-based. Density-based clustering approaches have been widely used in mining large dataset. Moreover, density based clustering algorithms have been recognized to be powerful and capable of discovering arbitrary shapes of clusters as well as dealing with noise and outliers. There are some density based algorithms such as DenClue[6] and DBSCAN[4]. In this paper, DBSCAN is chosen because it is simple and efficient in very large databases. It requires a minimum domain knowledge to determine input parameters and discover clusters with arbitrary shapes[4]. The rest of this paper is organized as follow: Section 2 deals with background and related projects then we will present and discuss our new distributed density based clustering in section 3. Section 4 presents our preliminary evaluations of this approach. Finally, we conclude on Section 5.

2   Related Works

In spite of a large amount of research conducted in distributed clustering such as [11][18][16], there are very few algorithms proposed in distributed density based clustering. Until now, to the best of our knowledge, there are four approaches in this paradigm that were presented in[17][9][10] and [13]. The former deals with a parallel approach of DBSCAN algorithm. This approach is appropriate for shared memory or distributed shared memory systems. The last three approaches include two main steps: local clustering to create local model and processing these local models to rebuild a global model.

In [9], authors used DBSCAN as a local clustering algorithm. They extended primitive elements of this algorithms such as core points, ϵ, Minpts by adding new concepts as specific core points, specific ϵ_{range} to build a local representative at each site. The global model will be rebuilt by executing the DBSCAN algorithm on a set of local representatives with two global values: $Mintps_{global}$ and ϵ_{global}.

$Mintps_{global}$ is a function of two local parameters i.e. $Mintps_{global} = 2 \times Minpts$. ϵ_{global} is tunable by the user and its default value is the maximum value of all ϵ_{range} values of all local representatives. This approach has some advantages: firstly, local clustering can be executed rapidly and independently at each site. Secondly, by using local representatives, it decreases the communication cost by avoiding to send all datasets and therefore the global clustering can be done quickly. However, this approach has two crucial problems: it ignores the local noise and the default value is set to ϵ_{global}. There is no representation of noise in the local representatives. In the global view, local noise from one site can belong to one or many clusters of other sites. Moreover, a set of local noises from all local sites can form one or more new clusters. Furthermore, the use of the high and static value ϵ_{global} led to incorrect cluster merging as shown in [9]. In addition, the location of special core point may also effect the merging process when they are located at the border of cluster.

Although the approach proposed in [10] has also two main steps as in the first approach but the definition of local representatives is different. In [10], a local representative is based on the condensation of datasets via *static and dynamic representation quality*. Moreover, this approach added two metrics for local representatives: *covering radius* and *covering number*. The former value is the maximum distance between a representative and its covered objects with ϵ-radius. The later value is the number of these covered objects. Besides, the number of local representatives at one site that can be tunned by users, global clustering also uses DBSCAN algorithm on local representatives and their special metrics from all sites. This DBSCAN uses *Minpts* in local site and the individual ϵ values for each representative r_i is defined by $\epsilon(r_i) = \epsilon + coveringradius(r_i)$. This approach has same advantages as above. Moreover, it can tackle not only with the problem of noise but also border problem as mentioned above. However, choosing a suitable number of local representatives is difficult task.

A density-based clustering for *P2P* systems was proposed in [13]. The authors also used DBSCAN-based for mining local dataset mapping. This is followed by the execution a hierarchical cluster assembly with cluster expansion and cluster merging process. The advantage of this approach is that it can deal with *P2P* system and investigate density-based clustering. However, this approach is based on the Content Addressable Network (CAN)[15] which may cause a huge communication overhead in large distributed dataset case.

3 Distributed Density Based Clustering

Our new approach is also composed of two important steps: local clustering to create local models and hierarchical agglomeration of local models to build a global model. These two steps use different algorithms as in [9][10]. We have also the pre-processing and post-processing stage. For the convenient, we define firstly the convention of symbols used in the next sections: (i) the letters x, y, z are reserved for local sites e.g. site x, site y; (ii) i, j, k, l: index of elements in a set; (iii) t, u, v: number of elements in a set; (iv) s, c, n: elements; (v) S, C, $CorC$, N, A, L: sets; (vi) ϵ, δ, θ: value or threshold.

3.1 Local Clustering

All sites carry out a clustering process independently from each other to discover local models. The local clustering algorithm chosen in our approach is DBSCAN, because it is strong approach concerning outliers and it can be used for all kinds of metric data space and vector spaces and it is simpler than other density-based algorithms e.g. DenClue[6]. At each site, the local model created consists of a set of representatives. Choosing a set of representative is very important because it will affect the performance of the merging step as well as the accuracy of the global model built. This depends normally on local mining algorithm. In DBSCAN algorithm, core points w.r.t ϵ and *Minpts* play an important role in the determination of different clusters. We can naturally use core points w.r.t ϵ and *Minpts* as representatives. However, the number of core points is not small enough with regard to the number of data points. Using core points is not efficient in the case of large amount of local data. We will use, instead a set of absolute core points S_{cor} w.r.t ϵ and *Minpts* as the first part of our representatives. Let $CorC_i^x \subseteq C_i^x$ (cluster C_i^x in a set of cluster C^x at site x) be a set of the core points belonging to this cluster at site x. The definition of S_{cor} is as follows: $S_{corC_i^x} \subseteq CorC_i^x$ is a set of absolute core object iff $(\forall s_k, s_l \in S_{corC_i^x} : s_k \neq s_l \Rightarrow s_k \notin N_{\epsilon_x}(s_l))$ and $(\forall c \in CorC_i^x, \exists s \in S_{corC_i^x} : c \in N_{\epsilon_x}(s))$ with $N_{\epsilon_x}(p_i)$ of a point p_i is defined as $\forall p \in N_{\epsilon_x}(p_i) : \|p_i - p\| \leq \epsilon_x$.

The distance used is either Euclidian or Manhattan distance. The concept of absolute core point was also proposed in [9] where it is called special core point. In the definition of an absolute core point s, there is at least one core point within the range of s w.r.t ϵ and *Minpts*. So we also add the furthest core point within the range of s w.r.t ϵ and *Minpts* in the first part of our local representative. Briefly, this first part is R^x which includes clusters representative R_i^x containing their set of pair (absolute core point s, its farthest touchable core point c_s):

$$R^x = \{ \bigcup_{i:1..t} R_i^x \mid R_i^x = \bigcup_{j:1..u} \{(s, c_s) \mid s \in S_{corC_i^x}\}\} \tag{1}$$

The Fig. 1a shows an example of absolute core point. Our approach is different from [9] as we do not use an ϵ-range value for each absolute core point. One of the reasons of using this value is to deal with data points in the range of a core point (w.r.t. ϵ and *Minpts*) and this core point is the furthest of an absolute core point (Fig. 1b). However, using this value might lead into the problem of merging clusters that are not similar. It can happen when the absolute core is on the border of its cluster (Fig. 1c). In order to tackle this problem, we do not use this value but adding the furthest core point of an absolute core point in our local representative. The second part of it is the value ϵ_x which is the local ϵ_x value and it can be estimated as discussed in [4]. These local values are different between local sites. Finally, the last part is a set of noise data N^x in this local

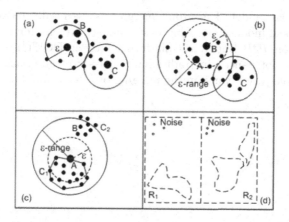

Fig. 1. (a) A & C are Absolute Core points;(b) B is the furthest core point of A;(c) A is on the border of cluster C_1: by using ϵ-range, two clusters C_1, C_2 will be merged ;(d) merging of noise from two local sites R1, R2 might create a new cluster

site. The noise at one local site might belong to a cluster at other sites and moreover the aggregating of noise from all local sites might create one or few new clusters (Fig. 1d). The noise at a local site is defined as data points that is not belong to any cluster in this local site.

$$N^x = \{ \bigcup_{j:1..v} d_j \mid d_j \notin C_i^x : \forall C_i^x \in C^x \} \tag{2}$$

So, our representative of local model is defined as follows:

$$Local Model L^x = \{R^x, \epsilon_x, N^x\} \tag{3}$$

In the next sub-section, we present the merging process of local clusters to obtain global model.

3.2 Hierarchical-Agglomeration of Local Model to Build Global Model Based on Tree Topology

The process of merging local models is based on tree structure (binary or TreeP[3] Fig. 2b). At lowest level (leaf-level), each node of a tree is a physical site where a local model is stored. Nodes at higher levels are virtual sites. At the beginning, local models of a local site are stored at a leave node. These local models are merged by binary tree or by group (Tree-P) into sub-global model at its logical site. For instance, as in Fig. 2a, local models from site X and Y will be merged into a sub-global model at site z. These sub-global models are at their turn merged into other logical node at higher levels until we reach the root. At root, we have a global model. The group merging is essentially based on merging two or more local models. By using tree topology, we can implement not only our approach on *P2P* Data Grid platforms such as DGET[7] but also avoid the problem of bottle-neck in traditional client-server approach. Moreover, in tree-based topology, we can stop the merging process at any level.

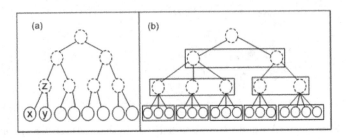

Fig. 2. (a) Binary Tree and (b) Tree-P topology

We assume that the local clustering at all of the sites uses the same value of *Minpts*. Meanwhile, each site x has its own value of epsilon ϵ_x. Normally, the merging process needs a global epsilon. However, finding a suitable global epsilon value ϵ_{global} is a difficult task. The higher ϵ_{global} is the more risk of merging wrong clusters. In [9], authors proposed a tunable ϵ_{global} value depending on ϵ-range values of all local representatives. An ϵ-range value is composed of ϵ value and a distance between an absolute core point at its furthest core point. And all of the local sites use the same ϵ value. In the Grid environment where datasets are produced and processed by a large number of different owners, suppose that they use the same mining algorithm, e.g. DBSCAN it is difficult to have the same parameter e.g. ϵ for all sites. Actually, in our approach, we use different value of epsilon ϵ_x for each local site x and the global ϵ_{aver}. This ϵ_{aver} is determined as shown at the end of this section.

Merging Process. Suppose that at site z, we will merge local models L^x and L^y from two sites x and y to build a new sub-global model L^z. If z is a root site, this sub-global model becomes the global model that should be returned. The term "cluster" used in this section means a set of representatives of that cluster.

Firstly, we find the minimum value of epsilon ϵ from two sites as $\epsilon = \min(\epsilon_x, \epsilon_y)$. We have also to solve with the problem of the difference δ of epsilon value between two sites: $\delta = |\epsilon_x - \epsilon_y|$. If δ is small enough, we could merge directly two clusters, this case is called a direct aggregating. If δ is too large, we can only merge separately representatives of the site for which the epsilon value is the largest. Some of their representatives might be disaggregated and then will be merged with other clusters. This case is called a disaggregating of cluster. We define a threshold of disaggregating θ. If δ is less than θ then we are in the first case, else we are in the second case. Moreover, an ϵ_{aver} is be used instead of ϵ in the second case. We propose a simple method to determine both θ and ϵ_{aver} as shown at the end of this section.

We assume that the local model at site x contains the minimum ϵ value without loss of generality. The merging process has two important steps: cluster extension and cluster merging. In the first step, each cluster from site x will be extended by adding noise data from N^y. A noise $d_i \in N^y$ will be included in the cluster $R_i^x \in R^x$ if:

$$\exists (s, c_s) \in R_i^x : \|d_i - s\| \leq \epsilon \vee \|d_i - c_s\| \leq \epsilon \tag{4}$$

Let A_i^x be a set of noise data from N^y that belongs to the cluster R_i^x. After the first step we have a set A_i^x. We execute the same process with each cluster from site y by adding noise data from N^x if we are in the direct aggregating case and we will also have a set A_i^y.

In the second step, we have two cases that correspond to aggregating-disaggregating cases defined above. In the direct aggregating case, we will merge two clusters R_i^x and R_j^y, if $\forall R_i^x \subseteq R^x, \forall R_j^y \subseteq R^y, \exists (s_k, c_{sk}) \in R_i^x, \exists (s_l, c_{sl}) \in R_j^y$:

$$\|s_k - s_l\| \leq \epsilon \vee \|c_{sk} - s_l\| \leq \epsilon \vee \|s_k - c_{sl}\| \leq \epsilon \vee \|c_{sk} - c_{sl}\| \leq \epsilon \tag{5}$$

The result of this merging will create a new cluster $R_k^z \subseteq R^z$. Meanwhile, in the disaggregating case, we only merge separately each representative (s_l, c_{sl}) of a cluster R_j^y with cluster R_i^x if it satisfies the equation (5) by using of ϵ_{aver} instead of ϵ.

These representatives will be removed from R_j^y and included in the set A_i^x. After two step of merging the new local model L^z is created:

$$L^z = \{R^z, \epsilon_z, N^z\} \tag{6}$$

with:

- $\epsilon_z = \epsilon$ or ϵ_{aver}
- $R^z = \bigcup_{\forall (i,j)} (R_i^x \bigcup R_j^y) \bigcup \bigcup_{\forall i} A_i^x \bigcup \bigcup_{\forall j} A_j^y$, if R_i^x and R_i^y satisfies equation (5) and $N^z = N^x \bigcup N^y$ for aggregating case or
- $R^z = \bigcup_{\forall i} (R_i^x \bigcup A_i^x) \bigcup (\forall (s_l, c_{sl}) \in R_j^y) : (s_l, c_{sl}), R_i^x$ satisfies equation (5) and $N^z = N^x \bigcup N^y$ for disaggregating case.

We use this model to continue the merging process with the local model from another site depending on the topology chosen until we obtain a global model. Moreover, as we mentioned above, we can stop at any level of the tree topology and the sub-global models are returned as the final results.

Determination of disaggregating threshold. We propose a simple method for determining the threshold based on the evaluation of local epsilon values from all sites as shown in the Fig. 3. These values are sorted in ascending order.

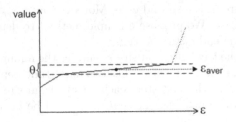

Fig. 3. Determination of θ and ϵ_{aver}

Using the same curve, we can also determine the ϵ_{aver} value as the average of all values of local ϵ in θ range. Note that θ and ϵ_{aver} can be set by users.

4   DDC Algorithm

4.1   Description

This section presents the principal function of our approach: merging process. The input of this *MergingCluster* function is the local model from two sites x and y. Its output is the merging model of them.

Algorithm - MergingCluster
Input: Local model L^x and L^y from site x and site y.
Output: Merging model L^z of this site z.

Step 0: Initialization

$\epsilon := \min (\epsilon_x, \epsilon_y)$;
merge_id := 0;
Determinate θ and ϵ_{aver};

Step 1: Cluster Extension

$\forall n_k \in N^y, \forall R_i^x \subseteq R^x$: If $\exists (s_j, c_{sj}) \in R_i^x$: $\|s_j - n_k\| \leq \epsilon \vee \|c_{sj} - n_k\| \leq \epsilon$ then
    Remove n_k from N^y and then Add n_k in A_i^x
EndIf

If $\delta \leq \theta$ then
    $\forall n_k \in N^x, \forall R_i^y \subseteq R^y$:If $\exists (s_j, c_{sj}) \in R_i^y$: $\|s_j - n_k\| \leq \epsilon \vee \|c_{sj} - n_k\| \leq \epsilon$
    then
        Remove n_k from N^x and then Add n_k in A_i^y
    EndIf
EndIf

Step 2: Cluster Merging
Step 2a: Marking

If $\delta \leq \theta$ then
    $\forall R_i^x \subseteq R^x, \forall R_j^y \subseteq R^y$:
    If $\exists (s_k, c_{sk}) \in R_i^x, \exists (s_l, c_{sl}) \in R_j^y$: $\|s_k - s_l\| \leq \epsilon \vee \|c_{sk} - s_l\| \leq \epsilon \vee \|s_k - c_{sl}\|$
        $\leq \epsilon \vee \|c_{sk} - c_{sl}\| \leq \epsilon$ then
        If $R^y.status =$ Merged then
            $R_i^x.merge\_id := R_j^y.merge\_id$;
        else
            $merge\_id := merge\_id + 1$;
            $R_i^x.merge\_id := merge\_id$;
            $R_j^y.merge\_id := merge\_id$;
            $R_j^y.status :=$ Merged
        EndIf
    EndIf
Else
    $\epsilon := \epsilon_{aver}$;
    $\forall R_i^x \subseteq R^x, \forall R_j^y \subseteq R^y$:
    If $\exists (s_k, c_{sk}) \in R_i^x, \exists (s_l, c_{sl}) \in R_j^y$: $\|s_k - s_l\| \leq \epsilon \vee \|c_{sk} - s_l\| \leq \epsilon \vee \|s_k - c_{sl}\|$
        $\leq \epsilon \vee \|c_{sk} - c_{sl}\| \leq \epsilon$ then
        Remove (s_l, c_{sl}) from R_j^y and then Add (s_l, c_{sl}) in A_i^x
EndIf

Step 2b: Merging

$\epsilon_z := \epsilon$
If $\delta \leq \theta$ then
    $N^z := N^x \bigcup N^y$
    For k:=1 to merge_id do
        $\forall R_i^x \subseteq R^x, R_i^x.merge\_id = k$: $R^z = R^z \bigcup R_i^x \bigcup A_i^x$
        $\forall R_i^y \subseteq R^y, R_i^y.merge\_id = k$: $R^z = R^z \bigcup R_i^y \bigcup A_i^y$
    End For
Else
    $\forall R_i^x \subseteq R^x$: $R^z = R^z \bigcup R_i^x \bigcup A_i^x$
    $\forall R_i^y \subseteq R^y$: $R^z = R^z \bigcup R_j^y$
EndIf
$L^z = \{R^z, \epsilon_z, N^z\}$

4.2 Complexity

We suppose that there is a total of N data points divided equally among m computing nodes. So, each node has n = N/m data points. We also assume that the number of representatives in one node is approximately $\mu\%$ of the total data points of this node. The complexity of our approach is composed of two parts: local mining and global aggregating. The local mining is based on DBSCAN algorithm so its complexity is $O(n \log n)$[4]. The complexity of global aggregating is $(n\mu)^2 \log m$). Briefly, the complexity of our approach is

$O(n \log n + (n\mu)^2 \log m))$. The speedup compared with centralization approach is:

$$S_p = \frac{(m-1)\log N}{(\mu^2 m - 1)\log m}, with(\mu^2 m - 1) \geq 0 \qquad (7)$$

This speed up depends on μ and number m of computing nodes. The more nodes we use and the less number of representatives that we can have, the more speed up that we could gain for the same dataset.

5   Experimental Results

This section presents the preliminary evaluation of our approach. In this simulation, we use datasets from LOCAL project [14]. This datasets includes 322 objects of two dimensions. We firstly execute DBSCAN algorithm on this datasets with ϵ=0.004 and *Minpts*=4 and there are six clusters as shown in Fig. 4. Next, we distribute equally by round robin this datasets in two subsets. Then, we execute separately DBSCAN algorithm on each subset with ϵ=0.005 and *Minpts*=4. The local ϵ value is chosen based on the local distribution of each subset. As shown in Fig. 5, there are 7 clusters for the first subset (Fig. 5 left) and 8 clusters for the second (Fig. 5 right).

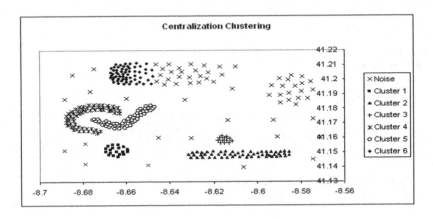

Fig. 4. Centralization Clustering

In the next step, we build the local representatives for each subset of data. Then, we execute the merging process based on the algorithm presented in section 3 and merging result is shown as in Fig. 6. Note that we obtained the same number of clusters as in centralized clustering but some data points of cluster 6 became noise points. The reason is that these points were apparently noise points in local clustering. Moreover we compute the quality of distributed clustering by using the **continuous object quality P** as proposed in [9](page 100). The value of **P** in this simulation is 94.43%. The result shows that our merging process is efficient.

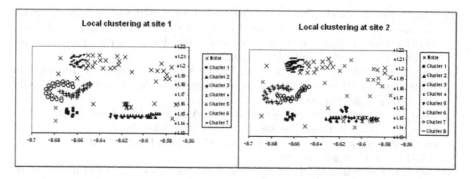

Fig. 5. Local clustering at two sites

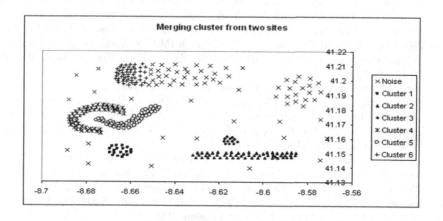

Fig. 6. Global merging

6 Conclusions and Future Works

In this paper we proposed a new approach of distributed density based clustering for *P2P-Grid* environments. This approach will be integrated in ADMIRE framework[12] in the module of distributed data mining techniques on very large and distributed heterogeneous datasets. The motivation of this approach as well as its implementation have been presented. The preliminary evaluation of our approach shows that it is efficient and flexible.

The deployment of this approach on tree topology will be improved and more experiments will be executed on "real" data such as Hurricane Isabel datasets[8].

References

1. Brezany, P., Janciak, I., Woehrer, A., Tjoa, A.: GridMiner: A Framework for Knowledge Discovery on the Grid - from a Vision to Design and Implementation. In: Cracow Grid Workshop. Cracow, pp. 12–15 (December 2004)

2. Cannataro, M., et al.: A data mining toolset for distributed high performance platforms. In: Proc. of the 3rd International Conference on Data Mining Methods and Databases for Engineering, Finance and Others Fields. Southampton, UK, pp. 41–50, September 2002, WIT Press (2002)
3. Edi, E., Kechadi, M-T., McNulty, R.: TreeP: A Self-Reconfigurable Topology for Unstructured P2P Systems. Workshop on State-of-the-Art in Scientific & Parallel Computing, Ume, Sweden (June 18-21, 2006)
4. Ester, M., Kriegel, H.-P., Sander, J., Xu, X.: A Density-Based Algorithm for Discovering clusters in Large Spatial Databases with Noise. In: Proc. 2nd Int. Conf. on Knowledge Discovery and Data Mining (KDD'96), Portland, OR, pp. 226–231. AAAI Press, California (1996)
5. Foster, I., Kesselman, C.: The Grid: Blueprint for a New Computing Infrastructure, pp. 593–620. Morgan Kaufmann, Elsevier Press (2004)
6. Hinneburg, A., Keim, D.A.: An efficient approach to clustering in large multimedia databases with noise. In: Proc. 1998 Int. Conf. Knowledge Discovery and Data Mining (KDD'98), pp. 58–65, New York (1998)
7. Hudzia, B., McDermott, L., Illahi, T.N., Kechadi, M-T.: Entity Based Peer-to-Peer in a Data Grid Environment. In: the 17th IMACS World Congress Scientific Computation, Applied Mathematics and Simulation. Paris, France, July 2005, pp. 11–15 (2005)
8. http://vis.computer.org/vis2004contest/data.html#format
9. Januzaj, E., Kriegel, H-P., Pfeifle, M.: DBDC: Density-Based Distributed Clustering. In: Bertino, E., Christodoulakis, S., Plexousakis, D., Christophides, V., Koubarakis, M., Böhm, K., Ferrari, E. (eds.) EDBT 2004. LNCS, vol. 2992, pp. 88–105. Springer, Heidelberg (2004)
10. Januzaj, E., Kriegel, H-P., Pfeifle, M.: Scalable Density-Based Distributed Clustering. In: Boulicaut, J.-F., Esposito, F., Giannotti, F., Pedreschi, D. (eds.) PKDD 2004. LNCS (LNAI), vol. 3202, pp. 231–244. Springer, Heidelberg (2004)
11. Kargupta, H., Chan, P.: Advances in distributed and Parallel Knowledge Discovery, 1st edn. AAAI Press/The MIT Press, London (2000)
12. Le-Khac, N-A., Kechadi, M-T., Carthy, J.: ADMIRE: framework: Distributed data mining on data grid platforms. In: Proc. 1st Int. Conf. on Software and Data Technologies ICSOFT'06, pp. 67–72 (2006)
13. Li, M., Lee, G., Lee, W-C., Sivasubramaniam, A.: PENS: An algorithm for Density-Based Clustering in Peer-to-Peer Systems. In: Proceedings of the 1st international conference on Scalable information systems, May 30-June 01, 2006, Hong Kong, pp. 39 (2006)
14. LOCAL   Location   contexts   for   location-aware   applications: http://get.dsi.uminho.pt/local/
15. Ratnasamy, S., Francis, P., Handley, M., Karp, R-M., Schenker, S.: A scalable content-addressable network. In: Proc. of ACM SIGCOMM, pp. 161–172 (August 2001)
16. Silva, J-C., Giannella, C., Bhargava, R., Kargupta, H., Klusch, M.: Distributed Data Mining and Agents. International Journal of Engineering Applications of Artificial Intelligence 18(7), 791–807 (2005)
17. Xu, X., Jager, J., Kriegel, H-P.: A Fast Parallel Clustering Algorithm for Large Spatial Databases. Journal of Data. Mining and Knowledge Discovery 3, 263–290 (1999)
18. Zhang, Bin, Hsu, M., Forman, G.: Distributed Data clustering System and Method. United States Patent, Patent No.: US 7,039,638 B2, Date of Patent (May 2, 2006)

Author Index

Lecture Notes in Computer Science

For information about Vols. 1–4480

please contact your bookseller or Springer

Vol. 4526: M. Malek, M. Reitenspieß, A. van Moorsel (Eds.), Service Availability. X, 155 pages. 2007.

Vol. 4525: C. Demetrescu (Ed.), Experimental Algorithms. XIII, 448 pages. 2007.

Vol. 4524: M. Marchiori, J.Z. Pan, C.d.S. Marie (Eds.), Web Reasoning and Rule Systems. XI, 382 pages. 2007.

Vol. 4523: Y.-H. Lee, H.-N. Kim, J. Kim, Y. Park, L.T. Yang, S.W. Kim (Eds.), Embedded Software and Systems. XIX, 829 pages. 2007.

Vol. 4522: B.K. Ersbøll, K.S. Pedersen (Eds.), Image Analysis. XVIII, 989 pages. 2007.

Vol. 4521: J. Katz, M. Yung (Eds.), Applied Cryptography and Network Security. XIII, 498 pages. 2007.

Vol. 4519: E. Franconi, M. Kifer, W. May (Eds.), The Semantic Web: Research and Applications. XVIII, 830 pages. 2007.

Vol. 4517: F. Boavida, E. Monteiro, S. Mascolo, Y. Koucheryavy (Eds.), Wired/Wireless Internet Communications. XIV, 382 pages. 2007.

Vol. 4516: L. Mason, T. Drwiega, J. Yan (Eds.), Managing Traffic Performance in Converged Networks. XXIII, 1191 pages. 2007.

Vol. 4515: M. Naor (Ed.), Advances in Cryptology - EUROCRYPT 2007. XIII, 591 pages. 2007.

Vol. 4514: S.N. Artemov, A. Nerode (Eds.), Logical Foundations of Computer Science. XI, 513 pages. 2007.

Vol. 4513: M. Fischetti, D.P. Williamson (Eds.), Integer Programming and Combinatorial Optimization. IX, 500 pages. 2007.

Vol. 4511: C. Conati, K. McCoy, G. Paliouras (Eds.), User Modeling 2007. XVI, 487 pages. 2007. (Sublibrary LNAI).

Vol. 4510: P. Van Hentenryck, L. Wolsey (Eds.), Integration of AI and OR Techniques in Constraint Programming for Combinatorial Optimization Problems. X, 391 pages. 2007.

Vol. 4509: Z. Kobti, D. Wu (Eds.), Advances in Artificial Intelligence. XII, 552 pages. 2007. (Sublibrary LNAI).

Vol. 4508: M.-Y. Kao, X.-Y. Li (Eds.), Algorithmic Aspects in Information and Management. VIII, 428 pages. 2007.

Vol. 4507: F. Sandoval, A. Prieto, J. Cabestany, M. Graña (Eds.), Computational and Ambient Intelligence. XXVI, 1167 pages. 2007.

Vol. 4506: D. Zeng, I. Gotham, K. Komatsu, C. Lynch, M. Thurmond, D. Madigan, B. Lober, J. Kvach, H. Chen (Eds.), Intelligence and Security Informatics: Biosurveillance. XI, 234 pages. 2007.

Vol. 4505: G. Dong, X. Lin, W. Wang, Y. Yang, J.X. Yu (Eds.), Advances in Data and Web Management. XXII, 896 pages. 2007.

Vol. 4504: J. Huang, R. Kowalczyk, Z. Maamar, D. Martin, I. Müller, S. Stoutenburg, K.P. Sycara (Eds.), Service-Oriented Computing: Agents, Semantics, and Engineering. X, 175 pages. 2007.

Vol. 4501: J. Marques-Silva, K.A. Sakallah (Eds.), Theory and Applications of Satisfiability Testing – SAT 2007. XI, 384 pages. 2007.

Vol. 4500: N. Streitz, A. Kameas, I. Mavrommati (Eds.), The Disappearing Computer. XVIII, 304 pages. 2007.

Vol. 4499: Y.Q. Shi (Ed.), Transactions on Data Hiding and Multimedia Security II. IX, 117 pages. 2007.

Vol. 4498: N. Abdennahder, F. Kordon (Eds.), Reliable Software Technologies – Ada Europe 2007. XII, 247 pages. 2007.

Vol. 4497: S.B. Cooper, B. Löwe, A. Sorbi (Eds.), Computation and Logic in the Real World. XVIII, 826 pages. 2007.

Vol. 4496: N.T. Nguyen, A. Grzech, R.J. Howlett, L.C. Jain (Eds.), Agent and Multi-Agent Systems: Technologies and Applications. XXI, 1046 pages. 2007. (Sublibrary LNAI).

Vol. 4495: J. Krogstie, A. Opdahl, G. Sindre (Eds.), Advanced Information Systems Engineering. XVI, 606 pages. 2007.

Vol. 4494: H. Jin, O.F. Rana, Y. Pan, V.K. Prasanna (Eds.), Algorithms and Architectures for Parallel Processing. XIV, 508 pages. 2007.

Vol. 4493: D. Liu, S. Fei, Z. Hou, H. Zhang, C. Sun (Eds.), Advances in Neural Networks – ISNN 2007, Part III. XXVI, 1215 pages. 2007.

Vol. 4492: D. Liu, S. Fei, Z. Hou, H. Zhang, C. Sun (Eds.), Advances in Neural Networks – ISNN 2007, Part II. XXVII, 1321 pages. 2007.

Vol. 4491: D. Liu, S. Fei, Z.-G. Hou, H. Zhang, C. Sun (Eds.), Advances in Neural Networks – ISNN 2007, Part I. LIV, 1365 pages. 2007.

Vol. 4490: Y. Shi, G.D. van Albada, J. Dongarra, P.M.A. Sloot (Eds.), Computational Science – ICCS 2007, Part IV. XXXVII, 1211 pages. 2007.

Vol. 4489: Y. Shi, G.D. van Albada, J. Dongarra, P.M.A. Sloot (Eds.), Computational Science – ICCS 2007, Part III. XXXVII, 1257 pages. 2007.

Vol. 4488: Y. Shi, G.D. van Albada, J. Dongarra, P.M.A. Sloot (Eds.), Computational Science – ICCS 2007, Part II. XXXV, 1251 pages. 2007.

Vol. 4487: Y. Shi, G.D. van Albada, J. Dongarra, P.M.A. Sloot (Eds.), Computational Science – ICCS 2007, Part I. LXXXI, 1275 pages. 2007.

Vol. 4486: M. Bernardo, J. Hillston (Eds.), Formal Methods for Performance Evaluation. VII, 469 pages. 2007.

Vol. 4485: F. Sgallari, A. Murli, N. Paragios (Eds.), Scale Space and Variational Methods in Computer Vision. XV, 931 pages. 2007.

Vol. 4484: J.-Y. Cai, S.B. Cooper, H. Zhu (Eds.), Theory and Applications of Models of Computation. XIII, 772 pages. 2007.

Vol. 4483: C. Baral, G. Brewka, J. Schlipf (Eds.), Logic Programming and Nonmonotonic Reasoning. IX, 327 pages. 2007. (Sublibrary LNAI).

Vol. 4482: A. An, J. Stefanowski, S. Ramanna, C.J. Butz, W. Pedrycz, G. Wang (Eds.), Rough Sets, Fuzzy Sets, Data Mining and Granular Computing. XIV, 585 pages. 2007. (Sublibrary LNAI).

Vol. 4481: J. Yao, P. Lingras, W.-Z. Wu, M. Szczuka, N.J. Cercone, D. Ślęzak (Eds.), Rough Sets and Knowledge Technology. XIV, 576 pages. 2007. (Sublibrary LNAI).